Active Maths

Ordinary Level – Book 2

2013 onwards

$$m = \frac{y_2 - y_1}{x_2 - x_1}$$

πr^2

$2\pi r$

Michael Keating, Derek Mulvany and James O'Loughlin

Special Advisors:
Oliver Murphy and Colin Townsend

FOLENS

Editor: Priscilla O'Connor, Sarah Reece

Designer: Liz White

Layout: Compuscript

Illustrations: Compuscript, Denis M. Baker, Rory O'Neill

ISBN: 978-1-84741-937-8

© Michael Keating, Derek Mulvany, James O'Loughlin and Colin Townsend, 2011

Folens Publishers, Hibernian Industrial Estate, Greenhills Road, Tallaght, Dublin 24, Ireland

Acknowledgements

The authors would like especially to thank Jim McElroy for his work on the written solutions and his invaluable advice.

The authors and publisher wish to thank the following for permission to reproduce photographs:
Alamy, Corbis, Getty, iStockphoto, Moviestore Collection, Science Photo Library, Sportsfile, Thinkstock.

The authors and publisher wish to thank Bank of Ireland and Bord Gáis Energy for permission to reproduce copyright material.

Contents

Introduction

Active Maths 3 is a comprehensive **two-book series** covering the **complete Leaving Certificate Ordinary Level course**.

- **Book 1** corresponds to **Paper 1** and therefore contains **Strands 3 (Number), 4 (Algebra) and 5 (Functions old syllabus)**.

- **Book 2** corresponds to **Paper 2** and therefore contains **Strands 1 (Statistics and Probability) and 2 (Geometry and Trigonometry) plus the Strand 3 topic Length, Area and Volume.**

Teachers and students will find that they have the new syllabus fully covered.

- A separate **free Activity Book** provides a wealth of activities designed to develop students' understanding of each topic in a hands-on way. The textbooks are linked throughout with the Activity Book to introduce topics and emphasise key Learning Outcomes.

Active Maths 3 is packed with student-friendly features:

- Prepares students for the new style of exam question with comprehensive **graded exercises** on each topic and **end-of-chapter revision exercises** include Project Maths-type exam questions based on all material that has been released by the NCCA and SEC.

- **Learning Outcomes** from the new syllabus are stated at the beginning of each chapter.

- Each chapter includes a **You Should Remember** section so that students can check they are fully prepared before starting the chapter.

- A list of **Key Words** at the start of each chapter helps students to consolidate learning. On first occurrence in each chapter, key words are set apart in **Definition boxes** to reinforce the importance of understanding their meaning.

- Clear and concise **Worked Examples** show students how to set out their answers, including step-by-step instructions with excellent diagrams to explain constructions.

- Essential formulae are set apart in **Formula boxes**.

- **Answers** to exercises are given at the end of each book.

  Additional **teacher resources, including digital activities** and **fully worked-out solutions** for the textbooks, will be available online at www.folensonline.ie.

Active Maths 3 allows teachers to meet the challenge of the new syllabus for Leaving Certificate Ordinary Level, and encourages students to discover for themselves that mathematics can be enjoyable and relevant to everyday life.

> Note: Constructions in Book 2 are numbered according to the NCCA syllabus for Project Maths Ordinary Level.

chapter 1

Statistics I

Learning Outcomes

In this chapter you will learn about statistics in today's world, including:

- ➲ How to find, collect and organise data
- ➲ How to generate data from other sources
- ➲ How to work with different types of data
- ➲ Populations and samples
- ➲ How to select a sample
- ➲ Representativeness and biased samples
- ➲ How to use stem-and-leaf plots and histograms to display data
- ➲ Distribution of data, including concepts of symmetry and skewness
- ➲ Scatter plots and correlation

Nowadays, numbers appear all around us. Making sense of numbers is the purpose of statistics. Open a newspaper or watch TV, and you will come across **statistics** in news reports, sports reports, advertisements and documentaries.

> The word **statistics** comes from the Latin word *status*, (meaning 'state').

Statistics play a very important part in understanding the world in which we live. When we turn on our TVs, browse the Internet or open a newspaper, we encounter numbers, charts, tables, graphs and other statistical results.

YOU SHOULD REMEMBER...

- How to construct a bar chart

- How to construct a pie chart

KEY WORDS

- Numerical data
- Categorical data
- Primary data
- Secondary data
- Population
- Sample
- Survey

- Designed experiment
- Questionnaire
- Stem-and-leaf diagram
- Scatter graph
- Correlation
- Histogram

1.1 STATISTICS IN TODAY'S WORLD

Statistics are used in many different areas. Here are just a few examples:

- Weather reports
- Stock market reports
- Football league tables
- Music charts
- Summaries of road traffic deaths
- Elections

This list is not exhaustive. Can you think of any other areas in which statistics are used?

Statistics can be either **descriptive** or **inferential**.

- Statisticians are often faced with large amounts of data that must be summarised and presented to the public in a way that people can understand. Bar charts, pie charts and averages are some of the methods statisticians use to summarise and present data. We call such statistics **descriptive statistics**.

ACTIVITIES 1.1, 1.2, 1.3, 1.4

- Before an election is held, statisticians try to predict the outcome of the election. They do this by asking a small number of people how they will vote in the upcoming election. They then try to predict the outcome from the responses of this group. When statisticians are trying to make predictions or forecasts based on responses from a small group, they are doing **inferential statistics**.

1.2 STATISTICAL INVESTIGATIONS

Statistical investigations are an integral part of the work of many professionals. Economists, scientists and engineers use statistical investigations to solve numerous problems. Research students use statistical investigations to prove many of their theories. Newspapers often conduct statistical investigations to gauge the public mood on various issues. In lots of ways, modern societies are dependant on the information provided by statistical investigations.

A large part of any statistical investigation is the production of **data**.

We collect data by asking questions, taking measurements, observing what is happening or doing experiments. The characteristic we record is called a **variable**.

> Any unordered list is called **data**. When this list is ordered in some way, it becomes **information**.

A statistical investigation on the heights of students in your class will produce data in the form of measurements. In this case, height is the variable being measured.

Types of Data

> When we study one variable at a time, the data we work with is called **univariate** data.

All data is either **categorical** data or **numerical** data.

Categorical Data

Questions that **cannot be** answered with **numbers** provide categorical data. The following are examples of such questions:

- What films have you seen in the last year?
- What colour are your eyes?
- What is your favourite soccer team?
- What colour is your phone?
- What grade did you get in Junior Certificate maths?

There are two types of categorical data, **ordinal** and **nominal**:

Ordinal categorical data **can be ordered** in some way.

Examples include exam results (A, B, C, D, E, F, NG), stress levels (low, medium, high) and social class (lower, middle, upper).

Nominal categorical data **cannot be ordered**.

Examples include hair colour, phone type and favourite band.

> **Ordinal** categorical data **can be ordered** in some way.
>
> **Nominal** categorical data **cannot be ordered**.

Numerical Data

Questions that **can be** answered with **numbers** provide numerical data:

- How many people in the EU are employed in agriculture?
- How many Irish people emigrated in 2009?
- How many houses were built in Ireland in 2006?
- What was the the temperature in Dubai at midday on 5 June 1998?

There are two types of numerical data, **continuous** and **discrete**:

The greatest annual total rainfall recorded in this country was at Ballaghbeema Gap, Co. Kerry. The year was 1960, and the amount of rainfall recorded for the year was 3964.9 mm. Of course, this measurement could have been 3964.89764 mm, but Met Éireann give rainfall measurements corrected to one decimal place. Rainfall measurements are an example of **continuous numerical data**, as rainfall measurements for a particular region can be any one of an infinite number of values within a given range.

Numbers or measurements that can only have certain values, for example shoe size and family size, are called **discrete numerical data**. Your family size must be a number such as 3, 4, 5, etc. It cannot be 3.5.

- If numerical data can have any value inside some range, then the data is **continuous numerical data**.
- If numerical data can only have a fixed number of values, then it is **discrete numerical data**.

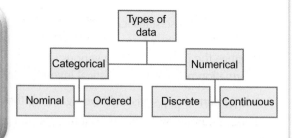

Worked Example 1.1

Which of the following are continuous numerical data and which are discrete numerical data?

(i) The number of aeroplanes flying out of Shannon every day

(ii) The heights of basketball players

(iii) The number of times each county has won the Sam Maguire

(iv) The magnitude of an earthquake

(v) The time taken by each student in your class to run 100 metres

Solution

(i) The number of aeroplanes flying out of Shannon every day is **discrete** numerical data. This data can only have certain values, i.e. 0 and the positive whole numbers.

(ii) The heights of basketball players is **continuous** numerical data. Heights can be any one of an infinite number of values within a given range.

(iii) The number of times each county has won the Sam Maguire is **discrete** numerical data. Again, the answer could be 0 or some positive whole number.

(iv) The magnitude of an earthquake is **continuous** numerical data, as the amount of energy released by an earthquake can have any value within a given range.

(v) The times taken by students to run 100 metres is **continuous** numerical data. Times can take on any value within a given range.

ACTIVITIES 1.5, 1.6

Populations and Samples

Suppose that you wish to do a study on the TV viewing habits of students in your school. You realise that it is impractical to interview everybody, so instead you decide to interview 80 out of the 1,000 students in the school. In this case, the group of all 1,000 students is called the **population**.

The **population** is the entire group that is being studied.

The group of 80 students is called a **sample**. It is very important that a sample is representative of the population. For example, the sample of 80 students mentioned above would not be representative of the whole school if they were all First Year students.

A **sample** is a group that is selected from the population.

Choosing a Simple Random Sample with Excel

When choosing a sample, it is useful to be able to choose a random set of whole numbers between two given numbers. For example, to choose a sample of size 80 from a population of 1,000, first assign each student a different number from 1 to 1,000. Then generate 80 random numbers between 1 and 1,000. Most spreadsheet applications will do this for you. Finally, match the random number with the student number to create your sample.

> Note that it may be necessary to generate more than the required random sample number in case of repetition (some random number appearing more than once).

 Worked Example 1.2

Generate 80 random numbers between 1 and 1,000 using Excel.

Solution

Excel 2007

(i) Move the cursor to cell A1.

(ii) Type the formula =RANDBETWEEN (1,1000) and press RETURN.

(iii) Highlight cells A1 to A80.

(iv) Now use Excel's FILL DOWN command.

or

Excel 2003

(i) Move the cursor to cell A1.

(ii) Type the formula =RAND() and press RETURN.

(iii) Highlight cells A1 to A80.

(iv) Now use Excel's FILL DOWN command.

(v) Move the cursor to cell B1.

(vi) Type the formula =INT(A1*1000)+1 and press RETURN.

(vii) Highlight cells B1 to B80.

(viii) Now use Excel's FILL DOWN command.

(ix) You should now see 80 numbers randomly selected from the numbers 1–1,000.

A	B
0.60023	600
0.69713	697
0.70354	703
0.26089	260
0.95556	955
0.6224	622
0.3761	376
0.6456	645
0.34983	349
0.16506	165
0.5339	533
0.32716	327
0.9099	909
0.0782	78
0.15234	152
0.78169	781
0.77952	779
0.27432	274
0.79897	798
0.85012	850
0.34045	340
0.18671	186
0.3798	379
0.3146	314
0.11969	119
0.70209	702
0.93735	937
0.58333	583
0.07516	75
0.81083	810
0.77456	774
0.01765	17
0.6964	696
0.09878	98

> If you wanted to generate 10 random numbers between 1 and 30, you would highlight and fill down 10 cells at steps (iii) and (iv), and you would type =INT(A1*30)+1 at step (vi).

- RAND() generates a number between 0 and 1.
- Multiplying this by 1,000 yields a number between 0 and 1,000.
- The INT function removes the decimal parts of the number, leaving only the integer part, e.g. INT(314.867) = 314. So this produces a whole number between 0 and 999.
- Adding 1 to this creates a random whole number between 1 and 1,000, as desired.

ACTIVITY 1.7

Reliability of Data

When choosing a sample from a population, it is important to ensure that:

■ The sample is large enough. For large populations, i.e. populations greater than 100,000, a sample size of at least 400 should be selected. Many statisticians would choose a sample size of 1,000 from such a population. For smaller populations, the sample size as a proportion of the population needs to be quite large. In fact, for populations as small as 2,000, statisticians would still pick a sample size of 400.

■ The sample is a random selection from the population.

■ Everybody has an equal chance of being selected.

■ The response rate is as high as possible.

If sample data is not collected in an appropriate way, then the data may be completely useless.

Bias in Sampling

Samples that are not representative are called **biased samples**. If there is a tendency for a particular group in a population to be omitted from a sample, then the sample is biased. To minimise bias, samples should be randomly selected.

Primary and Secondary Data

Primary data is collected by or for the person who is going to use it. Therefore, the person collecting the data must organise a study to collect the data. There are different types of studies for which primary data is collected. We will look at two of them:

■ Observational studies

■ Designed experiments

In an **observational study**, the researcher collects the information of interest but does not influence events. A study into the TV viewing habits of teenagers, in which data is collected by means of a questionnaire, is an example of an observational study.

In a **designed experiment**, the researcher sets up an experiment and investigates the effects of the experiment, e.g. a pharmaceutical company testing the effects of a drug. In this case the drug is called an **explanatory variable**, and the effect of the drug is called a **response variable**.

Very often, it is not possible to collect data from everybody. In such cases, a sample is chosen and data is collected from the sample. This is known as a **sample survey**.

Secondary data is **not** collected by the person who is going to use it. Sources for secondary data include *The Guinness Book of Records*, the Census of Population or Internet-based sources such CensusAtSchools. If you are using data from a secondary source, there are some important questions you should ask before you believe the results:

■ Who carried out the survey?

■ How was the sample chosen?

■ What was the population?

■ What size was the sample?

■ What was the response rate?

Steps in a Statistical Investigation

All statistical investigations begin with a question.
Here are the steps in a statistical investigation:

- Pose a question.
- Collect data.
- Present the data.
- Analyse the data.
- Interpret the results.

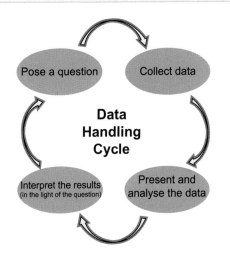

Pose a question | Collect data

Data Handling Cycle

Interpret the results (in the light of the question) | Present and analyse the data

1.3 COLLECTING DATA

Statistical data can be collected in different ways. The most common way of collecting data is by **survey**.
There are several ways to carry out a survey:

- Face-to-face interview
- Telephone interview
- Questionnaire that is sent out by post
- Questionnaire that is available online
- Observation

Here are the advantages and disadvantages of each type of survey:

Survey	Advantages	Disadvantages
Face-to-face interview	■ Questions can be explained to the interviewee.	■ Not random. ■ Expensive to carry out.
Telephone interview	■ It is possible to select sample from almost the entire adult population. ■ Questions can be explained to the interviewee.	■ Expensive in comparison to postal and online surveys.
Postal questionnaire	■ Inexpensive.	■ People do not always reply to postal surveys and those who reply may not be representative of the whole population.
Online questionnaire	■ Very low cost. ■ Anonymity of respondents ensures more honest answers to sensitive questions.	■ Not representative of the whole population. Only those who go online and do online surveys are represented.
Observation	■ Low cost. ■ Easy to administer.	■ Not suitable for many surveys. ■ Questions cannot be explained.

Designing a Questionnaire

A **questionnaire** is an important method of collecting data.

In the next activity, you will get a chance to design a questionnaire. Here are some important points to note when designing questionnaires:

> A questionnaire is a set of questions designed to obtain data from a population.

Questionnaires should:

- Be useful and relevant to the survey you are undertaking.
- Use clear and simple language.
- Be as brief as possible.
- Begin with simple questions to encourage people to complete the questionnaire.
- Accommodate all possible answers.
- Be clear where answers should be recorded.
- Have no leading questions, which give a clue as to how you would like the person to respond. For example, 'Manchester United are losing a lot of games this season. Do you think their manager should resign?'
- **Not** ask for a response to more than one topic. For example, 'Do you think the government spends too much money on sport and should be voted out of office in the next election?'

Worked Example 1.3

John wants to gather information on people's interest in music. Here is the questionnaire he designed.

---

1. What is your favourite type of music?

    (i) Dance   ☐

    (ii) Rap   ☐

    (iii) Rock   ☐

2. How far would you travel to see your favourite band play?

    (i) Less than 1 km   ☐

    (ii) 5–10 km   ☐

    (iii) More than 20 km   ☐

3. Do you play a musical instrument, or would you like to be able to play an instrument?

    (i) Yes   ☐

    (ii) No   ☐

(a) What is wrong with these questions?

(b) Design better questions for John to use.

Solution

Question 1

(a) The question does not allow for all possible tastes in music. While it may not be possible to include all types of music, it is possible to cater for everybody if an 'Other' alternative is included.

(b)

---

1. What is your favourite type of music?

    (i) Dance   ☐

    (ii) Rap   ☐

    (iii) Rock   ☐

    (iv) Other   ☐

Question 2

(a) There are gaps between 1 km and 5 km and also between 10 km and 20 km.

(b)

> **2.** How far would you travel to see your favourite band play?
>
> (i) Less than 1 km ☐
>
> (ii) 1–10 km ☐
>
> (iii) Greater than 10 km but less than 20 km ☐
>
> (iv) 20 km or more ☐

Question 3

(a) This question needs to be split into two questions.

(b)

> **3.** Do you play a musical instrument?
>
> (i) Yes ☐
>
> (ii) No ☐
>
> **4.** If you answered No to Question 3, then would you like to be able to play a musical instrument?
>
> (i) Yes ☐
>
> (ii) No ☐

ACTIVITIES 1.9, 1.10

1.4 FREQUENCY TABLES

When data is collected, it is often convenient to display it in a frequency table. Frequency tables show you how frequently each piece of data occurs. It is good practice to include a tally row in your table. Tallies are marks to help you keep track of counts. The marks are bunched in groups of five.

Worked Example 1.4

A class sits a mathematics test. Their marks out of 10 are as follows:

7	8	9	7	9	10
8	8	6	9	7	5
9	6	4	8	6	9
7	8	9	7	9	10
9	7	5	9	8	8

(i) Sort the data into a frequency table. Include a tally column in your table.

(ii) How many students sat the test?

(iii) What percentage of students scored 9 or better?

ACTIVITIES 1.11, 1.12

Solution

(i)

Mark	4	5	6	7	8	9	10
Tally	I	II	III	ⅢⅡ I	ⅢⅡ II	ⅢⅡ IIII	II
Frequency	1	2	3	6	7	9	2

(ii) $1 + 2 + 3 + 6 + 7 + 9 + 2$

$= 30$ students

(iii) The number of students who scored 9 or 10 marks is $9 + 2 = 11$.

$\therefore$ Percentage $= \dfrac{11}{30} \times \dfrac{100}{1} = 36\dfrac{2}{3}\%$

Exercise 1.1

1. What is categorical data?
   Give four examples of categorical data.

2. What are the two types of categorical data?
   Explain each one, giving a relevant example.

3. What is numerical data? Give four examples.

4. What are the two types of numerical data?
   Explain each one, giving a relevant example.

5. Explain the terms 'population' and 'sample'.

6. List two sources of secondary data.

7. Formulate two questions that can be answered
   with numerical data.

8. Formulate two questions that can be answered
   with categorical data.

9. Write a brief note on each of the following,
   giving an appropriate example in each case:

   (i) Observational studies

   (ii) Designed experiments

   (iii) Sample surveys

10. Explain the terms 'explanatory variable' and
    'response variable'.

11. Alan would like to predict the winning time
    for the men's 100-m final in the next Olympic
    Games. He gathers data from past editions of
    The Guinness Book of Records. Explain why
    the data collected by Alan is secondary data.

12. What questions should you ask about a
    secondary source to determine whether the
    data is reliable?

13. Use Excel to generate seven random numbers
    between 1 and 100.

14. Shauna rolls a die 50 times. Her scores are
    listed below.

5	3	3	3	5	1	2	5	1	5
1	3	3	6	4	6	1	2	1	1
1	6	5	6	3	4	2	2	5	2
4	6	5	1	2	6	1	1	6	2
2	6	2	5	2	3	4	4	6	6

(i) Sort the data in a frequency table that
   includes a tally row.

Outcome	1	2	3	4	5	6
Tally						
Frequency						

(ii) How many times did Shauna roll a 6?

(iii) How many times did Shauna roll a 1?

(iv) What percentage of the rolls were 4's?

15. Below is some data selected at random from
    the CensusAtSchools database. The data gives
    the different modes of transport a group of
    students uses to go to school.

Walk	Bus	Walk	Walk	Walk
Bus	Walk	Car	Car	Bus
Walk	Bus	Car	Walk	Walk
Car	Rail	Bus	Walk	Rail

(i) Sort the data into a frequency table.

(ii) What is the most popular mode of
    transport?

(iii) What is the least popular mode of
    transport?

(iv) What type of data has been selected?

16. A survey is made of the number of goals
    scored in a series of soccer matches. The
    findings are as follows:

2	0	1	2	2	1	3
1	1	4	0	1	3	4
0	2	0	4	2	0	4
3	1	2	4	2	2	0
1	1	2	1	2	2	0

(i) Sort the data into a frequency table.

(ii) What type of data is given?

(iii) How many soccer matches were played?

(iv) How many scoreless draws were there?

(v) What is the maximum number of games
   that could have been drawn?

(vi) What is the minimum number of games
    that could have been drawn?

17. John takes three coins from his pocket and flips the three coins together. He repeats this experiment 25 times and records his results as follows:

TTT	TTH	HTT	THT	HHH
HTH	THH	HHT	HHH	HTT
TTH	HHT	TTT	THH	HHH
THT	HTH	HTH	HTH	THH
THT	TTH	HHT	HTH	HTT

(i) Describe the type of data used in this question.

(ii) Copy and complete the frequency table.

Result	3 Heads	2 Heads	1 Head	0 Head
Tally				
Frequency				

(iii) What percentage of the throws revealed one head only?

1.5 GRAPHING DATA

In this section, we look at important methods of graphing sets of data. Data that is graphed is always easier to analyse and interpret. In your Junior Certificate maths course, you learned how to graph data using bar charts and pie charts. You will still need to construct bar charts and pie charts to display discrete data. Another way to display discrete data is to construct a stem-and-leaf diagram.

Florence Nightingale (1820–1910), regarded by many as the founder of the nursing profession, compiled massive amounts of data in an attempt to convince the British Parliament to invest in supplying nursing and medical care to soldiers in the field. Included in her presentation was the first 'pie chart'.

Stem-and-Leaf Diagrams

Stem-and-leaf diagrams represent data in a similar way to bar charts. A stem-and-leaf diagram represents data by separating each value into two parts: the stem and the leaf (the final digit). This allows you to show the distribution in the same way as a bar chart.

It is important to arrange the data in ascending order when drawing the stem-and-leaf diagram. All diagrams should have a key.

Worked Example 1.5

Here is a stem-and-leaf diagram showing the marks obtained by 30 boys in a maths test.

Stem	Leaf
0	7, 9
1	3, 4
2	9
3	5
4	3, 4, 4, 7, 9
5	2, 2, 3, 5, 7, 7, 8
6	1, 2, 5, 8, 9
7	3, 4, 5, 9
8	4, 7
9	1 Key: 3|5 = 35

Using the stem-and-leaf diagram, answer the following questions.

(i) What is the lowest mark?

(ii) What is the highest mark?

(iii) How many students scored higher than 80?

(iv) If 40 is the pass mark, what percentage of the group failed the test?

This tells us that the stem denotes tens and the leaves denote units.

Solution

(i) 7 is the lowest mark.

(ii) 91 is the highest mark.

(iii) Three students scored higher than 80, scoring 84, 87 and 91.

(iv) Six students scored less than 40 marks. Percentage that failed:
$$\frac{6}{30} \times 100 = \frac{1}{5} \times 100 = 20\%$$

Worked Example 1.6

Twenty people from the audience of a TV programme are randomly selected and each person is asked his/her age. Their ages are as follows:

15	14	25	23	33
45	13	51	62	48
19	57	47	56	44
11	38	46	21	16

(i) Represent the data on a stem-and-leaf diagram.

(ii) How many people in their fifties are in the audience?

Solution

(i) **Step 1** Begin by writing out the stems:

Stem
1
2
3
4
5
6

Step 2 Write each leaf on the proper stem:

Stem	Leaf
1	5, 4, 3, 9, 1, 6
2	5, 3, 1
3	3, 8
4	5, 8, 7, 4, 6
5	1, 7, 6
6	2

Step 3 Arrange the leaves in ascending order and write the key:

Stem	Leaf	
1	1, 3, 4, 5, 6, 9	
2	1, 3, 5	
3	3, 8	
4	4, 5, 6, 7, 8	
5	1, 6, 7	
6	2	Key: $1|4 = 14$

(ii) Reading from the stem-and-leaf diagram, we see that there are three people in their fifties in the audience. Their ages are 51, 56 and 57.

Back-to-Back Stem-and-Leaf Diagrams

A back-to-back stem-and-leaf diagram is a useful way of comparing data from two different groups. The leaves on each side are ordered out from the common stem in ascending order.

Worked Example 1.7

Here is a back-to-back stem-and-leaf diagram showing the marks obtained by 30 girls and 30 boys in a physics test. The girls' marks are on the left-hand side of the diagram.

Leaf (Girls)	Stem	Leaf (Boys)
6	0	9
9, 7, 2	1	3, 4, 5
	2	9
6, 6	3	5, 7
8, 6, 6, 6, 4, 2, 2	4	3, 4, 4, 9
9, 8, 6, 4	5	2, 2, 3, 5, 7, 7
8, 2	6	1, 2, 5, 8, 8, 9
9, 6, 5, 4	7	3, 4, 5, 9
5, 2, 0	8	4, 7
9, 8, 4, 3	9	1

Key: 2|6| = 62

Key: |3|5 = 35

(i) How many girls scored more than 80?

(ii) How many boys scored more than 80?

(iii) If 50 is the pass mark, did more boys than girls pass the test?

Solution

(i) Six girls scored more than 80. Their scores are 82, 85, 93, 94, 98 and 99.

(ii) Three boys scored more than 80. Their scores are 84, 87 and 91.

(iii) Yes –19 boys passed and 17 girls passed.

 ACTIVITIES 1.13, 1.14, 1.15

Line Plots

A line plot is used to display discrete numerical data and also categorical data. Line plots are very effective for showing the distribution of data. A line plot uses symbols – usually x's or dots – to represent the frequency of a piece of data.

Worked Example 1.8

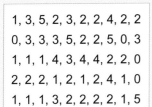

A PE teacher carried out a survey into the participation of teenagers in sport. He selected a sample of 50 students in his school and asked them the question: 'How many sports do you play?' The data he collected is given in the table below:

1, 3, 5, 2, 3, 2, 2, 4, 2, 2
0, 3, 3, 3, 5, 2, 2, 5, 0, 3
1, 1, 1, 4, 3, 4, 4, 2, 2, 0
2, 2, 2, 1, 2, 1, 2, 4, 1, 0
1, 1, 1, 3, 2, 2, 2, 2, 1, 5

Display the data on a line plot.

Solution

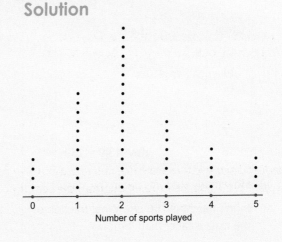

Number of sports played

Exercise 1.2

1. Here are the marks obtained by 20 students in an English test:

30	86	90	52	62
57	69	86	55	40
54	61	70	76	62
77	45	86	60	48

(i) Copy and complete the stem-and-leaf diagram:

Stem	Leaf
3	0
4	
5	
6	
7	0, 6, 7
8	
9	Key:

(ii) What percentage of students achieved a mark higher than 50?

2. John measures the heights (in centimetres) of all students in his class. Here are his results:

160	155	166	154	150
158	170	175	156	153
140	168	170	149	145
157	160	165	180	181
165	153	139	183	160

(i) Copy and complete the stem-and-leaf diagram.

Stem	Leaf
13	9
14	
15	
16	
17	
18	Key: 13|9 = 139

(ii) How many students are in the class?

(iii) John's height is 166 cm. What fraction of the class is taller than him?

3. A group of students are asked to choose a number between 50 and 100. Here are the results:

72	77	60	72	51	62
75	60	63	77	67	72
79	63	82	93	89	97
60	73	83	99	69	72
67	83	76	51	55	90

(i) Represent the data on a stem-and-leaf diagram. Make sure to include a key.

(ii) What was the most popular choice?

4. A class has to elect two representatives to the student council. An election is held and the results are as follows:

Student	Rachel	Alan	Tom	Tanya	Joe
Votes	7	4	5	9	6

(i) Draw a line plot to illustrate the data.

(ii) Which students were elected?

5. Fifteen plants are randomly selected and their heights (in centimetres) are measured.

49	27	44	37	43
32	40	46	45	32
38	27	40	37	45

(i) Show the results on a stem-and-leaf diagram. Include a key.

(ii) What was the smallest height recorded?

(iii) What was the tallest plant in the sample?

(iv) What fraction of the sample had heights greater than 43 cm?

6. John randomly selects 20 students from his school. He asks the 20 students to take an Internet IQ test. Here are the results:

109	100	111	127	114
103	116	120	128	132
94	88	129	108	127
110	109	104	119	133

(i) Show the results on a stem-and-leaf diagram.

(ii) If 100 is the average IQ score for the whole population, then how many students scored higher than average?

(iii) How many students scored lower than 100?

7. The stem-and-leaf diagram shows the number of CDs owned by a group of 12 students. The diagram contains three different errors. Describe each error.

2	1, 2, 2
3	2, 4
4	1, 4, 3
5	1, 5
6	8

8. The table below shows the modes of transport used by a group of students to travel to school:

Mode of transport	Walk	Bus	Cycle	Car	Train
No. of students	6	15	5	2	1

(i) How many students are there in the group?

(ii) What is the most popular mode of transport?

(iii) Represent the data on a bar chart.

(iv) Represent the data on a line plot.

(v) State one difference and one similarity between the line plot and the bar chart.

9. The following back-to-back stem-and-leaf diagram compares the pulse rates of 25 people before and after a 5-km run.

Before run		After run
7, 5, 2	5	
8, 6, 4, 2, 1, 1, 0	6	
8, 8, 8, 8, 6, 5, 3, 3, 1	7	
3, 2, 1	8	0, 2, 5
8, 5	9	8, 6
9	10	0, 0, 1, 5, 6, 6, 8, 9
	11	1, 2, 2, 6, 9
	12	7, 8, 8
	13	0, 1, 7
	14	2 Key: 11|1 = 111 beats/min

(i) How many people had pulse rates of 100 or more beats per minute after the run?

(ii) How many people had pulse rates of 100 or more beats per minute before the run?

(iii) What conclusions can you draw from the stem-and-leaf diagram?

10. The following table shows the heights (in centimetres) of a group of men and a group of women.

Men	179, 183, 181, 186, 185, 175, 191, 171, 174, 176, 179, 184, 159, 160, 166, 170, 178, 175, 170, 161, 168, 174, 183
Women	157, 155, 148, 171, 151, 157, 167, 162, 174, 166, 165, 149, 169, 178, 158, 154, 153, 152, 155, 150, 161, 158, 163

(i) Copy and complete the back-to-back stem-and-leaf diagram to compare their heights:

Men		Women
	14	
	15	
	16	
	17	
	18	
	19	

(ii) What conclusion can be drawn from this diagram?

11. Tom has randomly selected two groups of 20 students from his school. The first group consists of people who play at least one sport. The second group is made up of people who do not play any sport. Each individual in both groups is given the same puzzle to complete. Here are the times (to the nearest minute) taken to complete the puzzle.

Group 1

10	10	18	9	15	30	13	19	38	7
28	25	12	32	23	10	12	21	18	15

Group 2

24	12	24	19	18	17	26	33	15	10
25	13	34	9	17	20	16	30	22	30

(i) Draw a back-to-back stem-and-leaf diagram for the data.

(ii) What was the fastest time?

(iii) What was the slowest time?

(iv) From which groups did the fastest and slowest times come?

12. In a class of 20 students, five are girls and 15 are boys.

(i) Draw a pie chart to represent this data.

(ii) What percentage of the class consists of boys?

(iii) Draw a bar chart to represent the data.

(iv) You are asked to find the approximate fraction of the class that is female by referring to one of the charts you have drawn. Which chart would you select? Explain your choice.

13. The air we breathe is made up of 78% nitrogen, 21% oxygen and 1% other gases. Draw a pie chart to represent this information.

14. Here is some random data from the CensusAtSchools site. All lengths are measured in centimetres.

Gender	Height	Foot length	Gender	Height	Foot length
Male	167	25	Female	135	20
Female	151	22	Male	164	31
Female	171	31	Male	158	24
Male	151	24	Male	147	24
Female	158	24	Female	160	32
Male	158	24	Female	156	24
Male	170	24	Female	171	31
Female	149	21	Male	118	23
Male	154	24	Female	154	23
Female	150	22	Male	148	22

(i) Use an appropriate diagram to compare the heights of males and females in the group.

(ii) Use an appropriate diagram to compare the foot lengths of males and females in the group.

Histograms

If you wish to graph height, foot length or arm span, then you could use a histogram. Histograms are used to represent continuous data.

Histograms are similar to bar charts. In a bar chart, the height of the bar represents the frequency. In a histogram, the area of the bar represents the frequency. However, in our course we will deal only with histograms in which the bars have a width of 1. Therefore, the **area** of the bar will have the same value as the **height** of the bar.

Worked Example 1.9

The following frequency table shows the times, in minutes, spent by a group of women in a boutique. Draw a histogram of the distribution.

Time	0–10	10–20	20–30	30–40	40–50
Number	1	4	8	7	9

Note: 10–20 means 10 or more but less than 20, and so on.

Solution

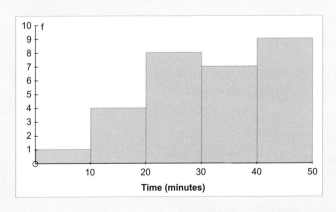

ACTIVITY 1.16

1.6 DISTRIBUTION OF DATA

Here are the times (in minutes) taken by a group of 14 students to complete a maths problem.

1	1.5	2	2.5	3	4	4.5
5.5	5.7	6	7	7.5	8.5	9.5

While it may not be obvious from the list, many of the times are between 4 minutes and 6 minutes. Also, few people had very low times or very high times. A histogram shows this distribution very well.

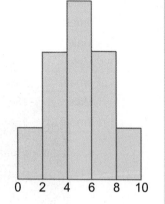

> We call this distribution a **symmetric distribution**.

In a symmetric distribution, the left half of the histogram is roughly a miror image of its right half.

Here are the times (in minutes) taken by another group of 21 students to complete the same maths problem.

1.5	2	2.4	3.8	4	4.2	4.5
5.7	5.8	6.1	6.3	6.4	7	7.2
8.2	8.3	8.5	8.8	9	9.2	9.5

In this distribution, many students took a relatively long time to complete the problem. Here is the histogram for this distribution, which tails off towards the lower numbers on the left.

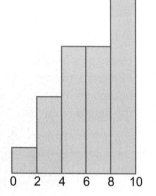

> We call this a **negatively skewed distribution**. It is also referred to as a **skewed left distribution**.

The following are the times of another group of 25 students who also took the maths problem.

0.9	1.1	1.2	1.3	1.3	1.6	1.6	1.9	2	2
3.1	3.2	3.6	3.9	4.1	4.5	5.1	5.8	5.8	6
7.1	7.5	7.9	8	9					

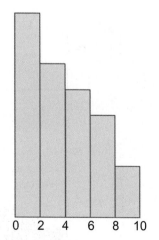

In this distribution, many students solved the problem in a short time. Here is the histogram for this distribution, which tails off towards the higher numbers on the right.

> We call this a **positively skewed distribution**. It is also referred to as a **skewed right distribution**.

Exercise 1.3

1. For each of the following distributions, identify whether the distributions are skewed left, skewed right or symmetric.

(i)

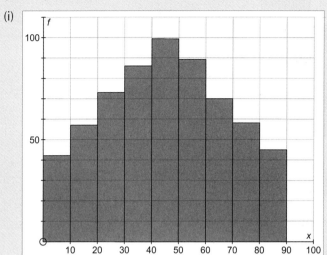

(ii)

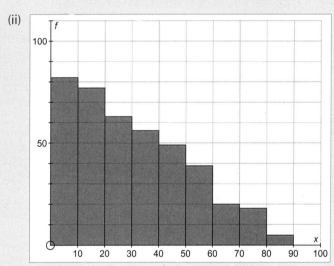

(iii)

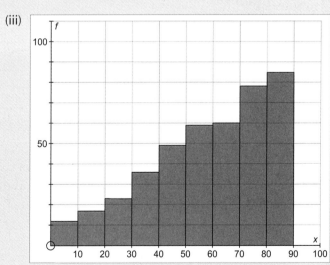

(iv)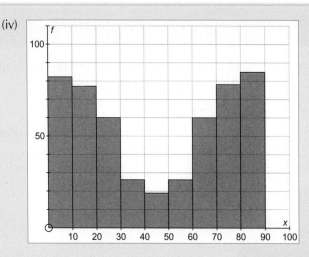

2. Display the following datasets on a stem-and-leaf plot and then identify whether the distributions are skewed left, skewed right or symmetric.

(i) {12, 21, 34, 41, 52, 13, 22, 35, 41, 52, 14, 22, 36, 42, 54, 15, 23, 37, 43, 54, 15, 24, 44, 55, 16, 16, 55, 56}

(ii) {31, 42, 56, 63, 71, 32, 43, 58, 62, 33, 43, 58, 61, 34, 44, 58, 36, 45, 37, 37, 38}

(iii) {19, 28, 29, 33, 34, 35, 36, 42, 43, 44, 44, 45, 45, 52, 52, 52, 53, 55, 57, 59, 59}

(iv) {42, 53, 61, 77, 82, 83, 78, 62, 54, 43, 55, 62, 79, 79, 63, 68, 69}

3. The histogram shows the distances, in kilometres, that some students have to travel to school.

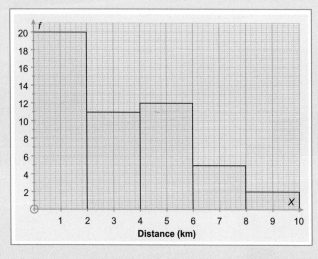

(i) Complete the following table:

Distance (km)	0–2	2–4	4–6	6–8	8–10
Number					

(ii) Is this distribution symmetric, positively skewed or negatively skewed?

4. The ages (in years) of a group of people at a party were recorded. The results are shown in the table below:

Age	15–20	20–25	25–30	30–35	35–40
Frequency	4	8	16	12	4

Note: 15–20 means 15 or more but less than 20.

Draw a histogram to represent the data.

5. The time, in minutes, taken by each member of a group of students to solve a problem is represented in the histogram below.

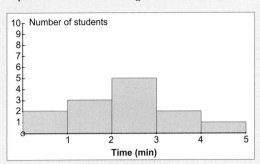

Copy and complete the following table:

Time (min)	0–1	1–2	2–3	3–4	4–5
Number					

(i) What is the total number of students in the group?

(ii) How many students solved the problem in less than 3 minutes?

(iii) What percentage of students solved it in less than a minute? (Give your answer correct to two decimal places.)

6. The number of hours' sleep taken by 50 people on a certain night was tabled as follows:

Time (hours)	0–3	3–6	6–9	9–12
Number	4	11	20	15

Note: 0–3 means 0 or more but less than 3, and so on.

(i) Draw a histogram that will represent the data.

(ii) What is the highest possible number of people who had more than 8 hours' sleep?

(iii) What is the lowest possible number who had more than 8 hours' sleep?

7. Twenty students are asked how many minutes they watched television on a particular day. The following frequency distribution summarises their replies:

Time (min)	0–20	20–40	40–60	60–80	80–100
Freq.	2	6	5	3	4

Note: 0–20 means 0 or more but less than 20, and so on.

(i) Draw a histogram to represent the data.

(ii) What percentage spent less than 20 minutes watching television?

8. The stem-and-leaf diagram shows the time (in seconds) it took contestants to answer a general knowledge question. All contestants answered in less than 7 seconds.

2	1, 2, 2
3	2, 4, 8, 9
4	1, 3, 4, 6, 7
5	1, 5
6	8 Key: 5|1 = 5.1 sec

(i) Describe the distribution (symmetric, left-skewed or right-skewed).

(ii) Copy and complete the table.

Time (sec)	2–3	3–4	4–5	5–6	6–7
Number		4			

(iii) Draw a histogram to represent the data.

9. Identify the following types of distribution (skewed left, symmetric or skewed right).

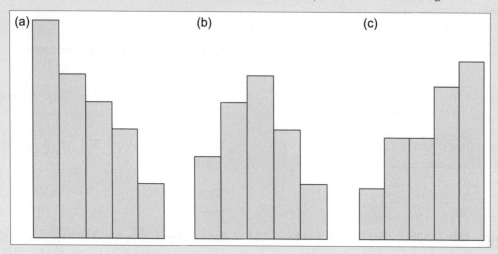

(a) (b) (c)

10. The following frequency distribution shows the lengths, in millimetres, of a sample of insects taken from a field.

Length	0–10	10–20	20–30	30–40	40–50
Number	2	8	11	10	4

Note: 0–10 means 0 or more but less than 10, and so on.

(i) Draw a histogram for this data.

(ii) Describe the distribution (symmetric, left-skewed or right-skewed).

11. The frequency distribution below shows the weights, in kilograms, of 25 baskets of fruit:

Weight (kg)	1–2	2–3	3–4	4–5
Number	10	8	4	3

Note: 1–2 means 1 or more but less than 2, and so on.

(i) Draw a histogram for this data.

(ii) Describe the distribution.

12. The amount of rain, in millimetres, was recorded for 60 days. The results are shown in the frequency table below:

Rain	0–4	4–8	8–12	12–16	16–20	20–24	24–28	28–32	32–36
No. of days	40	7	6	3	2	1	0	0	1

Note: 0–4 means 0 or more but less than 4, and so on.

(i) Represent the data on a histogram.

(ii) Describe the shape of the distribution.

1.7 SCATTER GRAPHS AND CORRELATION

Scatter graphs are used to investigate relationships between two sets of data.

If the points on a scatter graph are close to a straight line, then we say there is a strong **correlation** between the two sets of data.

Suppose you measure the arm span and height of all students in your class. For each height measurement there is a corresponding arm span measurement, so the data can be **paired**. The following tables show the height and arm span of a group of randomly selected students. All measurements are in centimetres.

Data that can be paired is known as paired data or bivariate data.

Height	160	170	165	159	161	163	165	166
Arm span	159	168	162	161	162	164	164	164

Height	166	167	167	169	170	171	171	177
Arm span	165	166	167	171	169	169	170	175

Each height measurement and corresponding arm span measurement form a couple. The following are the couples for the data above:

(160,159), (170,168), (165,162), (159,161), (161,162), (163,164), (165,164), (166,164), (166,165), (167,166), (167,167), (169,171), (170,169), (171,169), (171,170), (177,175)

Here is the scatter graph for the data:

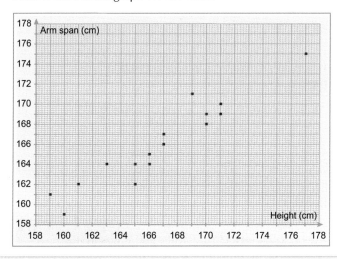

You can see from the graph shown that for this data the points lie reasonably close to a straight line. This means that there is a relationship between arm span and height. We can say that, **in general**, the greater the height, the greater the arm span.

Worked Example 1.10

The table below gives the marks obtained by 10 students taking a maths test and a physics test. Both tests are marked out of 50.

Maths mark	40	43	28	49	34	31	32	40	38	39
Physics mark	43	46	32	47	39	36	38	45	43	42

(i) Draw a scatter graph for the data.

(ii) Is there a correlation between the two sets?

Solution

(i)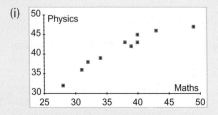

(ii) The points are reasonably close to a straight line, so we can say that a correlation exists between the sets. We cannot say that a student who scores highly in maths will definitely score highly in physics. We can only conclude that, in general, the better you are at maths, the more likely you are to do well in physics.

The Correlation Coefficient

The **correlation coefficient**, r, is a number in the following range: $-1 \leqslant r \leqslant 1$.

- If r is close to 1, then there is a strong **positive correlation** between two sets of data.

- If r is close to -1, then there is a strong **negative correlation** between the two sets.

- If r is close to 0, then there is **no correlation** between the two sets.

> The **correlation coefficient** is a measure of the strength of the relationship between two sets of data. It has a value between -1 and 1.

Types of Correlation

It is important that you state both the **direction** (positive or negative) and the **strength** of a correlation when asked for the type of correlation.

(i) Strong positive correlation

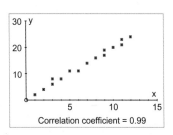

Correlation coefficient = 0.99

(iii) Weak positive correlation

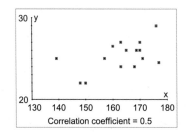

Correlation coefficient = 0.5

(v) No correlation

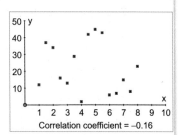

Correlation coefficient = -0.16

(ii) Strong negative correlation

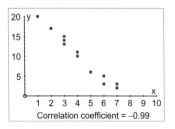

Correlation coefficient = -0.99

(iv) Weak negative correlation

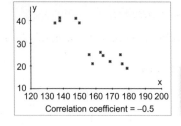

Correlation coefficient = -0.5

> Note: For our course, we will not be asked to evaluate r.

Worked Example 1.11

At the end of a marathon, eight athletes are randomly selected. All of the athletes are asked to give their age and their time (in minutes) for the race. The results are given in the table below:

Age	33	33	31	26	26	25	30	29
Time	132.6	132.1	133.1	134.0	134.1	134.6	133	133.5

(i)   Draw a scatter graph of the data.

(ii) What is the type of correlation between the two sets of data?

(iii) Describe the correlation between age and time.

(iv) Explain why the correlation described in part (iii) will not apply for athletes in the 54–64 age bracket.

Solution

(i)

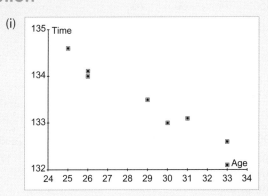

(ii) Strong negative correlation

(iii) As age increases, the times, in general, decrease.

(iv) In the 54–64 age bracket one would expect marathon times to increase as athletes got older. In the 24–34 age bracket, times improve as the athletes get older, as marathon athletes generally achieve their best times in their early thirties. Therefore, it is important that we are careful when making predictions that are outside the range of the sample data.

Exercise 1.4

1. Four scatter graphs are shown.

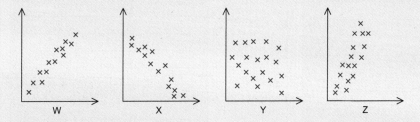

(i)   Identify the graphs with positive correlation.

(ii) Which graph has negative correlation?

(iii) Which graph has the correlation coefficient which is closest to zero?

2. Four scatter graphs are shown below.

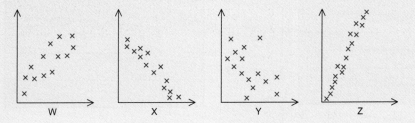

(i) Identify the graph with the strongest positive correlation.

(ii) Identify the graph with the weakest negative correlation.

(iii) Which set has the strongest correlation?

3. The heights (in centimetres) and ages (in years) of 10 girls are tabled as follows:

Age	8	9	9	10	11	12	12	13	14	15
Height	145	139	140	142	147	154	153	158	160	162

(i) Using suitable scales, plot the scatter diagram for these results.

(ii) Describe the correlation between age and height.

4. The marks obtained by eight candidates in two tests – maths and science – are as follows:

Maths	48	87	56	90	59	82	62	78
Science	50	82	58	80	65	70	80	76

(i) Plot the marks on a scatter diagram.

(ii) How are scores in maths tests correlated with scores in science tests?

5. A car dealer has eight vehicles for sale. The year of manufacture and the price, in euro, of the vehicles is tabled below:

Year	2000	2001	2002	2003	2004	2005	2006	2007	2008
Price (€)	2,650	2,995	4,950	6,950	7,800	13,500	11,750	14,600	17,690

(i) Using suitable scales, plot a scatter diagram for these results.

(ii) Describe the correlation in the context of the question.

6. For each of the following diagrams, describe the correlation.

(i)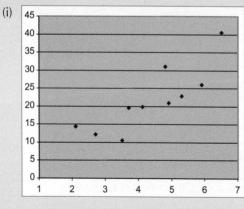

(ii)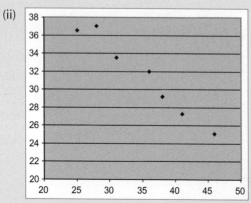

(iii)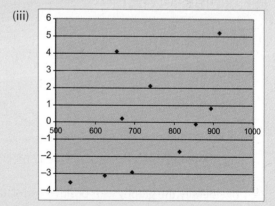

(iv)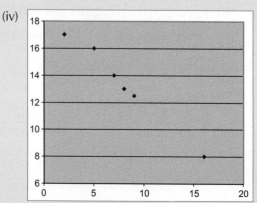

(v)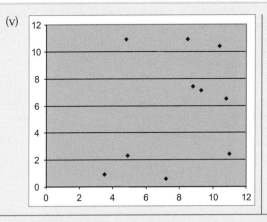

(vi)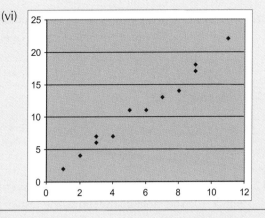

7. The table below shows the marks obtained by a group of students in a maths test, and the number of hours' sleep the students had on the night before the test.

Hours slept	9	8	6	8	5	8	9	5	7	8
Mark	85	89	70	87	71	84	90	63	80	70

(i) Using suitable scales, plot the results on a scatter diagram.

(ii) Describe the type of correlation in the context of the question.

(iii) Explain why the results and number of hours slept on the night before the test may not correlate in the same way for students who get over 12 hours' sleep and students who get between 5 and 9 hours' sleep.

8. The heights and foot lengths, in centimetres, of nine students were recorded and tabulated as follows:

Height (cm)	139	140	142	143	147	154	158	160	162
Foot length (cm)	22.6	22.2	22.3	22.1	22.7	23.4	23.7	23.9	23.8

(i) Using suitable scales, plot the data.

(ii) Describe the correlation, with reference to the information given.

9. The heights (in centimetres) and weights (in kilograms) of eight adults were as follows:

Height (cm)	157	181	203	214	197	178	162	210
Weight (kg)	59	84	81	100	92	77	61	105

(i) Plot the results on a scatter graph.

(ii) Describe the correlation, in the context of the question.

10. The scatter plot shows the fuel consumption (in litres/100 km) of seven petrol engines:

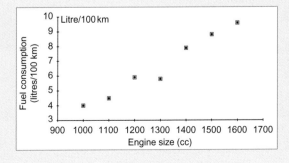

(i) What is the fuel consumption of the 1400 cc engine?

(ii) What size engine has a fuel consumption rate of 4 litres/100 km?

(iii) Describe the correlation, with reference to the information given.

11. The following table shows the age and annual income of a sample of eight employees from a large company. The incomes are in thousands of euro.

Age	36	25	44	48	32	50	33	40
Income	36	29	53	55	34	62	38	46

   (i) Draw a scatter diagram of the data.

  (ii) Explain the correlation between age and income.

12. At a job interview, eight candidates are given tests on numeracy and IT skills. The tests are marked out of 10. The table below shows the results of the tests:

Numeracy	6	9	10	4	3	5	9	5
IT	7	8	9	2	1	5	6	4

   (i) Draw a scatter diagram of the data.

  (ii) Explain the correlation between numeracy and IT skills.

13. The petal width and petal length of a random sample of 150 irises are plotted on the scatter graph below. Three different classes of iris are included in the sample.

All measurements are in centimetres.

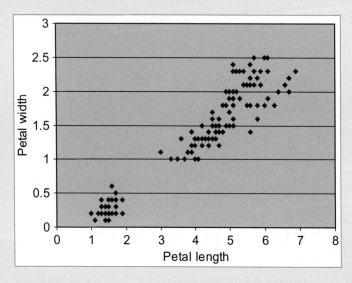

   (i) Describe the correlation between petal length and petal width.

  (ii) How many irises in the sample had a petal width of 2.5 cm?

 (iii) How many irises in the sample had a petal length of 2.5 cm?

 (iv) Estimate from the graph the longest petal length in the sample.

  (v) Select the correct value of the correlation coefficient from this list:
−0.2, 0.96, 0.5, 0.1, −0.8.

      Justify your selection.

1. A random sample of 90 workers revealed that the car was the most popular mode of transport for getting to work. The results of the survey are given in the table below:

Mode	Car	Bus	Bike	Walk
Number	40	20	15	15

   (i) Represent the data using a pie chart.

   (ii) Is this data categorical data or numerical data? Explain.

   (iii) What percentage of the group walked to work?

2. A teacher decides to investigate the connection between progress at school and the number of hours of TV watched per week. He collects data from 10 randomly selected students. The data includes the number of hours of TV watched by each student and his/her mean mark across all subjects in a recent end-of-term test.

TV hours	21	4	9	11	12	7	13	5	25	14
Mean mark	47	76	70	55	65	68	50	70	40	55

   (i) Represent the data on a scatter graph.

   (ii) Using your graph, estimate the correlation coefficient.

   (iii) Describe the correlation between number of hours of TV watched and the mean mark obtained.

   (iv) Explain the term 'bivariate data'.

3. The following data was downloaded from the CensusAtSchools database:

   Right-handed   Right-handed   Right-handed   Right-handed   Right-handed

   Ambidextrous   Right-handed   Left-handed   Right-handed   Right-handed

   (i) Show the data on a frequency table.

   (ii) Represent the information on a pie chart.

   (iii) You would like to collect this data from your class. What question should you pose?

   (iv) Using your question from (iii), collect the data from your class.

   (v) Represent the information on a pie chart.

   (vi) Find the percentage of students that are right-handed in the CensusAtSchools sample.

   (vii) Find the percentage of students in your class that are right-handed.

4. The marks, out of 5, in a maths quiz for a class of 20 pupils are as follows:

4	2	3	5	4
1	1	2	3	5
4	3	1	5	3
3	1	3	5	3

   (i) Show the data on a frequency table.

   (ii) Represent the data on a line plot.

   (iii) If 2 is the mark needed to pass the test, then how many students failed the test?

   (iv) What percentage of students passed the test?

   (v) Represent the data on a pie chart.

   (vi) If you wanted to find the number of students who got a mark of 3, would you consult the line plot or the pie chart? Why?

5. A company has been asked to design and market a magazine for teenagers. Explain what primary data sources and secondary data sources the company might use in its research.

6. In 'The Effects of Temperature on Marathon Runners' Performance' by David Martin and John Buoncristiani (*Chance* magazine), high temperatures and times (in minutes) were given for women who won the New York City marathon in recent years. The results are shown in the table below.

Temp. (°F)	55	61	49	62	70	73	51	57
Time (min)	145.28	148.72	148.30	148.10	147.62	146.40	144.67	147.53

(i) Represent the data on a scatter graph.

(ii) Using your graph, describe and estimate the correlation coefficient.

(iii) Does it appear that winning times are affected by temperature? Explain your answer.

7. A sample of young people were asked how many songs were on their iPods. Here are the results:

401	412	422	430	424
425	440	412	402	472
426	457	458	438	472
464	402	409	482	467

(i) How many people were surveyed?

(ii) Represent the data on a stem-and-leaf diagram.

(iii) What percentage of those surveyed had fewer than 450 songs?

(iv) You decide to carry out a similar survey in your school. Outline the method you would use to select a sample.

8. John asked a group of friends to write down a number greater than 0 and less than 50. Here are his results:

41	15	25	26	36
32	14	12	23	36
11	16	13	15	33
46	33	31	11	22

(i) How many friends did John survey?

(ii) Use a stem-and-leaf diagram to represent the data.

(iii) Describe the distribution.

9. Comment on the reliability of the following ways of finding a sample. Suggest a more reliable method where necessary.

(i) Find out how many people have computers in their home by interviewing people outside a computer shop.

(ii) Find out whether the potatoes are cooked by testing one with a fork.

(iii) Find out the most popular make of car by counting 100 cars in a five-star hotel car park.

(iv) You decide to do a survey on the amount of pocket money received by students in your school. You use your phone and ring 15 of your friends. All respond to the survey.

10. The manager of a company relies on travelling salespersons to sell the company's products. She wishes to investigate the relationship between sales and the amount of time spent with customers. She collects data from 10 salespersons. This data includes the sales for the month and the time (in hours) spent with customers. The results are given in the table below.

Time (hours)	3.1	4.5	3.8	5.2	6.0	4.1	5.5	5.2	5.0	7.0
Sales	1,648	2,000	1,800	2,440	2,860	2,000	2,440	2,400	2,280	3,200

(i) Represent the data on a scatter graph.

(ii) Using your graph, describe the correlation estimate the correlation coefficient.

(iii) Describe the correlation between sales and times spent with customers.

11. The ages of all the teachers in a school are as follows:

21, 21, 22, 23, 23, 25, 27, 28, 30, 31 32, 34, 34, 35, 37, 38, 39, 40, 40, 41, 42, 42,
43, 44, 44, 44, 45, 46, 46, 47, 49, 49, 50, 50, 50, 54, 55, 57, 57, 58, 59, 59, 60, 60,
63, 63, 64

(i) Represent the data on a stem-and-leaf plot.

(ii) Copy and complete the frequency table below:

Age	20–30	30–40	40–50	50–60	60–70
Frequency					

Note: 20–30 means more than 20 but less than 30, and so on.

(iii) Construct a histogram to represent the data.

(iv) Describe the distribution.

(v) In your opinion, which graph best represents the data? Explain.

12. Using Excel, generate 30 random numbers between 1 and 100, and then complete the frequency table below.

x	0–10	11–20	21–30	31–40	41–50	51–60	61–70	71–80	81–90	91–100
f										

(i) Construct a bar chart from the data in the table.

(ii) Describe the distribution.

(iii) Did you expect this distribution? Explain.

13. A random sample of 500 households in Dublin is selected and several questions are asked of the householders. Which of the following statements is **not** correct?

(a) Total household income is ordinal categorical data.

(b) The number of persons in the household is discrete data.

(c) Socioeconomic status is coded as 1 = low income, 2 = middle income and 3 = high income, and is nominal categorical data.

(d) The primary language used at home is nominal categorical data.

Now correct the incorrect statements.

14. The ages of participants in a triathlon competition are given in the tables below:

Males	Females
22, 41, 52, 15, 43, 36, 31, 31, 32, 28, 17, 22, 22, 28, 36, 34, 34, 48, 29, 29, 27, 26, 28, 31, 34, 32, 48, 36, 16, 29, 38, 16, 24, 22, 24, 21, 29, 28, 36, 37, 31, 32, 34, 38, 39, 31, 35, 36, 39, 30	32, 31, 38, 17, 19, 36, 37, 16, 35, 32, 21, 22, 41, 42, 43, 50, 51, 28, 29, 32, 31, 32, 48, 19, 42, 26, 36, 37, 39, 41, 42, 48, 31, 40, 31, 35, 32, 43, 47, 36, 36, 38, 31, 22, 19, 39, 11, 32, 61, 59

(i) Copy and complete the back-to-back stem-and-leaf diagram:

Males		Females
	1	
5	1	6
1	2	
6	2	
0	3	
6, 6, 5	3	5, 5, 6, 6, 6, 6
	4	
	4	
	5	
	5	
	6	

(ii) State one difference and one similarity between the distributions of the two samples.

chapter 2

Counting and Combinations

Learning Outcomes

In this chapter you will learn to:

- List all possible outcomes of an experiment using:
  - Systematic listing
  - Two-way tables
  - Tree diagrams
- Apply the Fundamental Principle of Counting
- Count the arrangements of n distinct objects ($n!$)
- Count the number of ways of selecting r objects from n distinct objects $\binom{n}{r}$

2.1 OUTCOMES

In mathematics and in everyday life it is important to be able to list all the possible outcomes that can occur in real-life situations or in experiments.

Worked Example 2.1

For lunch a student has a choice of two types of bread (a bread roll or sliced bread) and two fillings (ham or chicken).

What are the possible lunch choices that the student could have?

Solution

We can list the choices, or outcomes, that the student has:

- Ham roll
- Ham sandwich
- Chicken roll
- Chicken sandwich

> The list of all possible outcomes is referred to as the **sample space**.

When listing all the outcomes (the **sample space**), three main methods can be used:

- **Systematic listing**

  > **Systematic listing** involves writing down all the possible outcomes.

- **Two-way tables**

  > **Two-way tables** are used to write down all the possible outcomes when there are two sets of options.

- **Tree diagrams**

  > The branches of **tree diagrams** are used to show all the possible outcomes when the outcome involves two or more steps.

2.2 LISTING OUTCOMES

Systematic Listing

This method involves writing down all the possible outcomes. Here are two examples.

 Worked Example 2.2

A die is thrown. List all the possible outcomes. _____ of rolling one die are:

Solution

This is a normal six-sided die.

ling one

 Worked Example

A coin is flipped once. What are all ___

Solution

The possible outcomes are either ___

 ACTIVITIES 2.1,

Two-way Tables

Systematic listing can be difficult and can take a long time _____ comes in the sample space. Two-way tables are a much more convenient way of showing num___ possible outcomes. Here is an example. It is used when there are **two** sets of options.

 Worked Example 2.4

Harry has a choice of three types of bread (pitta, rye or white) and four fillings (beef, chicken, ham or turkey). How many different sandwiches can Harry order?

Solution

We put the outcomes of Harry's choice of fillings on the side of the table and the outcomes of his choice of bread on the top of the table. It is much easier to use letters to represent each of Harry's choices.

We then look at the intersection of beef and pitta in the table. In this box we fill in beef and pitta (BP). The outcome in the blue box is that Harry has chosen a beef pitta sandwich.

		Bread		
		Pitta (P)	Rye (R)	White (W)
Fillings	Beef (B)	BP		
	Chicken (C)			
	Ham (H)			
	Turkey (T)			

Intersection of beef and pitta

We then fill in the rest of the table.

		Bread		
		Pitta (P)	Rye (R)	White (W)
Fillings	Beef (B)	BP	BR	BW
	Chicken (C)	CP	CR	CW
	Ham (H)	HP	HR	HW
	Turkey (T)	TP	TR	TW

It is now a simple matter of using the table to list all the outcomes. With an example like this, it would be more common to ask how many different choices Harry could have. It is clear from the table that there are $4 \times 3 = 12$ choices.

 **ACTIVITIES 2.6, 2.7**

Tree Diagrams

A tree diagram is another method of listing outcomes. Its name comes from the fact that, when completed, the diagram looks like the branches of a tree.

> The tree diagram method is useful when listing the outcomes of **two or more events**.

 Worked Example 2.5

A coin is flipped twice. Use a tree diagram to show all the outcomes.

Solution

Head is written as H, and tail is written as T.

Head   Tail

```
1st Flip    2nd Flip    Outcome
                H         HH
       H
                T         HT
                H         TH
       T
                T         TT
```

The list of outcomes is {HH, HT, TH, TT}.

Worked Example 2.6

A motorist drives through two sets of traffic lights. List all the possible colours of traffic lights that she could encounter.

Solution

At the first set of traffic lights, the outcomes (red, amber and green) can be drawn on the tree diagram as follows:

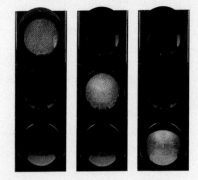

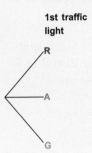

1st traffic light

R

A

G

At the second set of traffic lights, the driver could meet the following outcomes:

1st traffic light	2nd traffic light
R	R, A, G
A	R, A, G
G	R, A, G

If we follow each branch, we can fill in all the outcomes.

1st traffic light	2nd traffic light	Outcomes
R	R	RR
	A	RA
	G	RG
A	R	AR
	A	AA
	G	AG
G	R	GR
	A	GA
	G	GG

ACTIVITIES 2.8, 2.9

We can then list all the outcomes (nine in total):

Red, Red	**RR**	Red, Amber	**RA**	Red, Green	**RG**
Amber, Red	**AR**	Amber, Amber	**AA**	Amber, Green	**AG**
Green, Red	**GR**	Green, Amber	**GA**	Green, Green	**GG**

Exercise 2.1

In the following questions, use the most appropriate method unless stated otherwise.

Methods	Systematic listing	Two-way tables	Tree diagrams

1. A spinner with 10 equal sectors numbered 20 to 29 is spun once. What are all the possible outcomes?

2. In a restaurant there are four choices for the main course (steak, burger, fish, pasta) and three choices for dessert (jelly, fruit or cake).
   List all the different two-course meals you can eat at this restaurant.

COUNTING AND COMBINATIONS

3. John throws a six-sided die and flips a coin. List all the possible outcomes. How many outcomes are possible?

4. Customers at a fast-food restaurant can choose a medium or large meal size, and they can choose chicken, a hamburger or a vegetarian option for their meal. Show all the possible combinations of meals and sizes.

5. In a certain deck of cards there are two types of cards: numbered and pictured. Each card can also be a Heart, a Club, a Spade or a Diamond. Use a tree diagram to show all the possible outcomes when a single card is picked at random.

6. A spinner lettered A, B, C and D is spun. Another spinner numbered 1 to 5 is then spun. Copy the two-way table below to list all the outcomes:

		Second spinner				
		1	2	3	4	5
First spinner	A					
	B					
	C			C3		
	D					

(i) How many different outcomes are there?

(ii) How many outcomes have an odd number?

7. An athlete participates in a cross-country event. She has to run from A to B and then from B to C. There are two paths that lead from A to B and three paths that lead from B to C. Show, using a tree diagram, all the different paths she can take to complete the course.

8. A bag contains a number of red, yellow and orange balls. Two balls are taken from the bag. What are the possible outcomes?

9. A fair spinner numbered from 1 to 3 is spun, and another spinner numbered 10 and 11 is spun. The scores from each spin are added together.

(i) Draw a two-way table to show all the outcomes.

(ii) How many of these outcomes add up to an even number?

10. A café has a choice of five possible drinks (tea, coffee, water, latte, cappuccino). Caroline buys a drink for herself and a friend. List all the possible different drinks she could have ordered for herself and her friend.

11. A family has three children. Use a tree diagram to show all the different combinations of boys and girls possible.

12. Two dice are thrown. A score is obtained by subtracting the lower number from the higher number (this is done to ensure that there are no negative numbers). Complete the table below to show all the outcomes. (Some have been filled in for you.)

		Second die					
		1	2	3	4	5	6
First die	1		2 – 1 = 1				
	2					6 – 2 = 4	
	3						
	4						
	5						
	6	6 – 1 = 5					

(i) What is the most common outcome?

(ii) What is the least common outcome?

(iii) How many outcomes total to an odd number?

Gambling with dice was a very popular game among the Romans. It became so popular that the authorities tried to have it banned!

2.3 THE FUNDAMENTAL PRINCIPLE OF COUNTING

The Fundamental Principle of Counting is a quick and easy way to determine the number of outcomes of two or more events.

 ## Worked Example 2.7

A normal die is rolled and a spinner numbered 1, 2, 3 is spun. How many different outcomes are possible?

Solution

The **number of outcomes** for the first event – the die being rolled – is 6: {1, 2, 3, 4, 5, 6}.

The **number of outcomes** for the second event – the spinner being spun – is 3: {1, 2, 3}.

The total possible number of outcomes is:

Event	Die roll		Spinner	
Number of outcomes	6	×	3	= 18

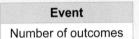

FORMULA

Fundamental Principle of Counting

If one event has m possible outcomes and a second event has n possible outcomes, then the total number of possible outcomes is $m \times n$.

Remember that it is the **number of outcomes** that we multiply each time.

 ## Worked Example 2.8

A dress comes in three sizes and seven colours. How many different types of dress are possible?

Solution

- The number of outcomes for the dress size is 3.
- The number of outcomes for the dress colour is 7.

The total number of dresses possible is:

Event	Dress size		Dress colour	
Number of outcomes	3	×	7	= 21

COUNTING AND COMBINATIONS

Worked Example 2.9

A spinner numbered 1, 3, 5, 7 and 9 is spun twice, and a coin is flipped once. How many different outcomes are possible?

Solution

■ The number of outcomes for the first event is 5: {1, 3, 5, 7, 9}.

■ The number of outcomes for the second event is 5: {1, 3, 5, 7, 9}.

■ The number of outcomes for the third event is 2: {Head, Tail}.

The total possible number of outcomes is:

Event	1st Spin		2nd Spin		Coin flip	
Number of outcomes	5	×	5	×	2	= 50

 ## Worked Example 2.10

A customer wishes to place an order in a pizzeria and is given the following choices for a meal.

Starter	Pizza	Drink	Dessert
Potato wedges	Margherita	Cola	Ice-cream
Garlic bread	Ham & pineapple	Juice	Apple tart
Chicken wings	Pepperoni	Water	
Ciabatta			

If the customer chooses a starter, pizza, drink and dessert, how many different meals can be ordered?

Solution

Event	Starter		Pizza		Drink		Dessert	
Number of outcomes	4	×	3	×	3	×	2	= 72

 ACTIVITIES 2.10, 2.11

 ## Exercise 2.2

1. A furniture shop has five different types of sofa in four different colours. How many different sofas can a customer order?

2. A cinema has 10 films showing. Each film can be viewed in standard format or in 3D. How many choices of film are there?

3. Andrea is choosing a new pair of shoes. The shoes come in sizes 5, 5½, 6, 6½ and 7. They also come in five different colours and three different styles. How many different choices of shoes are possible?

4. A boy is preparing to go out to a disco. He has five different tee-shirts and two pairs of jeans. Ignoring the rest of his clothes, find how many different ways he can dress.

5. In a restaurant, there are four choices for the starter, six choices for the main course and five choices for dessert. How many possible three-course meals are there?

6. A girl has 10 tops, three skirts and five pairs of shoes. If we ignore the rest of her clothes, in how many different ways can she dress for the evening?

7. A town decides to introduce registration plates for bicycles. Each registration plate has a single letter followed by a single digit (for example, J7, L8, Z0, etc.). How many different registration plates are possible?

8. In Archimedes' Academy, all First Year students have to choose from the following lists:

   ■ One of {Business, Music, German or Spanish}

   ■ One of {Technology, Computers or Art}

   Oliver is a First Year student at Archimedes' Academy. He has to choose two subjects. How many different pairs of subjects can he choose?

9. How many outcomes are there if a card is drawn from a pack of 52 cards, a coin is flipped and a six-sided die is rolled? Name one possible outcome.

10. A six-sided die is rolled five times. How many outcomes are possible? Name one possible outcome.

11. A coin is flipped 10 times. How many possible outcomes are there?

12. A photographer arrives at a co-educational school. He wants to take a photo for a newspaper. The Principal asks four boys (Alan, Bert, Con and Darren) and three girls (Eve, Fiona and Gina) to meet the photographer. The photographer decides that he wants a picture with just one boy and one girl. How many photos are possible with this restriction?

13. Eight people are in a race. How many ways can gold, silver and bronze medals be awarded if there are no dead heats?

14. An ID badge is made up of four letters. How many different ID badges are possible if no letter can be used more than once?

   Example:

   BRSV

15. A code is made up of two letters of the English alphabet followed by three digits. Find the total number of codes possible when:

   (i) No letter may be used more than once.

   (ii) No digit may be used more than once.

   (iii) No letter or digit may be used more than once.

2.4 ARRANGEMENTS

When using the Fundamental Principle of Counting we often multiply a list of numbers in descending order: for example, $5 \times 4 \times 3 \times 2 \times 1$. In mathematics, a shorter way of writing this list is to use the factorial symbol, which is the exclamation mark. So $5 \times 4 \times 3 \times 2 \times 1$ is written as 5! (pronounced '5 factorial').

FORMULA

The factorial $n!$ is defined for a positive integer n as $n! = n(n-1)(n-2) \dots 3.2.1$

Worked Example 2.11

Calculate 10! (This is pronounced '10 factorial'.)

Solution

$10! = 10 \times 9 \times 8 \times 7 \times 6 \times 5 \times 4 \times 3 \times 2 \times 1 = 3,628,800$

We can use the factorial button $\boxed{n!}$ or $\boxed{x!}$ on the calculator. Press 10 followed by $n!$, which should give you an answer of 3,628,800.

2

Factorials can be useful when we are using the Fundamental Principle of Counting and outcomes have to be arranged in a particular order or position.

Worked Example 2.12

Find how many ways the letters of the word LEAVING can be arranged in each of the following cases:

> Note: No letter may be used more than once.

(i) If there are no restrictions

(ii) If the arrangements must begin with a V

(iii) If the arrangements must **not** begin with a V

(iv) If the arrangements must begin and end with a vowel

Solution

(i) If there are no restrictions

- We note that there are seven letters in the word LEAVING.
- For the first letter of the arrangement, we have a choice of seven letters.
- For the second letter of the arrangement, we now have a choice of six letters, as one letter has already been used. This continues until we come to our last letter, where there is only one choice left.

Letter	1st		2nd		3rd		4th		5th		6th		7th	
Number of choices	7	×	6	×	5	×	4	×	3	×	2	×	1	= 7! = 5,040

(ii) If the arrangements must begin with a V

- The first letter must be a V (there is only one V, so there is only one choice).
- This means that we now have six letters to choose from for our second letter, and so on.

Letter	1st		2nd		3rd		4th		5th		6th		7th	
Number of choices	1	×	6	×	5	×	4	×	3	×	2	×	1	= 1 × 6! = 720

(iii) If the arrangements must **not** begin with a V

- There are a total of 5,040 different ways to arrange the seven letters of the word LEAVING, and 720 of these arrangements start with the letter V.
- The rest of the arrangements must not start with the letter V. The number of arrangements that do not start with the letter V is:

$$5040 - 720 = 4320$$

(iv) If the arrangements must begin and end with a vowel

- The **first letter** must be a vowel. There are only three vowels (A, E, I), so there are three choices.
- The **last letter** must also be a vowel. As we have already picked one vowel for the first letter, we now have two choices left.
- Then the arrangements must be filled with the remaining five letters.

Letter	1st		2nd		3rd		4th		5th		6th		7th	
Number of choices	3	×	5	×	4	×	3	×	2	×	1	×	2	= 720

Note that because the question asked for the arrangement to begin and end with a vowel, those are the choices that we filled in first.

In general, we first fill in the choices that have restrictions placed on them.

Worked Example 2.13

How many four-digit numbers can be made using the digits 4, 6, 7 and 8?

(i) If there are no restrictions

(ii) If the number must be even

(iii) If the number must be odd

(iv) If the number must be greater than 7,000

Note: No digit may be used more than once.

Solution

(i) If there are no restrictions

- We are looking at four-digit numbers.

- For our first digit we have four numbers to choose from. It is important to realise that we fill in our number of choices, not the actual number.

- For our second digit we have three numbers to choose from, and so on.

Digit	1st		2nd		3rd		4th	
Number of choices	4	×	3	×	2	×	1	= 4! = 24

(ii) If the number must be even

- Even numbers are determined by their last digit being even (e.g. 4,876).

- The last digit must be even; therefore there are three choices for this last digit (4, 6 or 8).

- Once this choice has been filled in, we can return to the first digit. For the first digit we now have three numbers to choose from (one number has already been used for the last digit).

Digit	1st		2nd		3rd		4th	
Number of choices	3	×	2	×	1	×	3	= 18

(iii) If the number must be odd

- A total of 24 different four-digit numbers can be made from the digits 4, 6, 7 and 8. Of these four-digit numbers, 18 are even.

- Therefore, the remaining numbers must be odd: 24 − 18 = 6.

(iv) If the arrangements must be greater than 7,000

- If the number is greater than 7,000, then its first digit must be a 7 or an 8. For the first digit, we therefore have two choices.

- For the next digit, we have three choices (one number has already been used), and so on.

Digit	1st		2nd		3rd		4th	
Number of choices	2	×	3	×	2	×	1	= 12

Astragalomancy is the use of dice in fortune-telling and has been practised since ancient times. The term 'astragalomancy' comes from the Greek word *astragalos*, which refers to the knucklebone or vertebra of a sheep or goat. The earliest dice were made from small animal bones of this kind.

ACTIVITIES 2.12, 2.13, 2.14

COUNTING AND COMBINATIONS

1. Investigate if:

   (i) 4! + 5! = 9!   (ii) 3! × 4! = 12!

2. (i)   List all the three-digit numbers that can be made from the digits 6, 7 and 8, if no digit can be repeated.

   (ii) How many of these numbers are even?

   (iii) How many are odd?

3. (i)   List all the ways of arranging the letters of the word MATH.

   (ii) How many ways are there of arranging the letters of the word MATHS?

4. (i)   In how many ways can the letters of the word SET be arranged?

   (ii) How many of these arrangements begin with T?

   (iii) How many do not begin with T?

5. (i)   In how many ways can the letters of the word MODAL be arranged?

   (ii) How many of these arrangements begin with L?

   (iii) How many do not begin with L?

   (iv) How many end with M?

6. (i)   In how many ways can the letters of the word MEDIAN be arranged?

   (ii) How many of these arrangements begin with D?

   (iii) How many begin with a vowel?

7. Six greyhounds (A, B, C, D, E and F) enter a race. A special betting slip must be filled out in which you must predict which greyhound will come first, which second and which third. In how many different ways can the betting slip be filled?

Placement	Greyhound
1st	
2nd	
3rd	

8. Every PIN for an ATM machine consists of four digits. The first digit is never zero. How many different PINs are there if digits may be repeated?

9. Every member of a computer club is given an access code, which consists of two different letters (e.g. RP, LH, KZ, ZK, but not KK or XX). If each member has a different code, how many members can the club have?

10. Seven horses (A, B, C, D, E, F and G) take part in a race. (Assume no dead heats.)

    (i)   In how many different orders can they finish the race?

    (ii) If A wins, how many orders are possible?

    (iii) If A wins and B comes last, how many different orders are possible?

11. Karen has seven exercises to do: Maths, French, Irish, CSPE, English, History and Geography. Find the number of different orders in which she can do the exercises:

    (i)   If there are no restrictions

    (ii) If she must start with maths

    (iii) If she must **not** start with maths

    (iv) If she must start with a language

    (v)   If she must **not** start with a language

12. How many three-digit numbers can be made using any of the digits 2, 3, 4 and 5:

    (i)   If repetitions are not allowed (e.g. 233 and 555 are **not** allowed)

    (ii) If repetitions are allowed

    If repetitions are not allowed, how many of these numbers are:

    (iii) Odd   (iv) Even

13. (i)   How many four-digit numbers can be made using the four digits 1, 3, 5 and 7:

       (a) If repetitions are not allowed (e.g. 7,333 and 5,155 are **not** allowed)

       (b) If repetitions are allowed

    (ii) How many different numbers between 3,000 and 9,000 can be made using only the digits 1, 3, 5 and 7, if no digit may be repeated?

14. In how many ways can the letters of the word TRIANGLE be arranged:

    (i)   If there are no restrictions

    (ii) If the arrangements must begin with N

(iii) If they must begin with a vowel

(iv) If the three vowels must come at the start

15. In how many ways can the letters of the word FACETIOUS be arranged:

    (i) If there are no restrictions

    (ii) If the arrangements must end with T

    (iii) If they must begin with a vowel

    (iv) If the five vowels must come at the start

    (v) If the four consonants must come at the start

16. Three girls (Aoife, Betty and Carol) and two boys (Darren and Eoin) are to line up for a photograph. How many different ways are there of arranging them in a straight line:

    (i) If they may line up in any order

    (ii) If they must be girl–boy–girl–boy–girl

17. Eleven students (six boys and five girls) are to line up in a straight line for a uniform inspection. In how many different ways can they be arranged:

    (i) If they can line up in any order

(ii) If the five girls must be at the start, followed by the six boys

(iii) If no students of the same gender may be next to one another

18. In how many different ways can the letters of the word PIGLET be arranged:

    (i) If there are no restrictions

    (ii) If the arrangements must begin with a vowel

    (iii) If the arrangement must begin with a vowel and end with T

    (iv) If the two vowels must be together at the start

    (v) If the two vowels must be together

    (vi) If the two vowels must be apart

19. In how many different ways can the letters of the word BARKING be arranged:

    (i) If there are no restrictions

    (ii) If the letters A and R must be beside each other at the start

    (iii) If the letters A and R must be beside each other

2.5 COMBINATIONS

Combinations are a way of selecting items from a group when **the order of selection does not matter**. An example would be the variations of ingredients in a sandwich. The sandwich could contain meat, cheese and tomato, **or** tomato, cheese and meat, **or** any other combination of these three fillings; the order in which we list the fillings does not matter.

Worked Example 2.14

In how many ways can two numbers be chosen from the numbers 1 to 5?

Solution

In this example, we just want to pick two numbers; the order in which we pick them does not matter. This means that 2, 1 counts as the same outcome as 1, 2.

If we list the possible outcomes, we find that there are 10 different ways in which two numbers can be chosen from the numbers 1–5.

1, 2	1, 3	1, 4	1, 5
2, 3	2, 4	2, 5	
3, 4	3, 5		
4, 5			

We can write $\binom{5}{2} = 10$.

This means that there are 10 ways of choosing two numbers out of five possible numbers.

If we are asked to select or choose a number of objects from a group of objects, we are using **combinations**.

Worked Example 2.15

Seven people are on a panel, and a team of three is chosen from this panel. How many different choices are there?

Solution

If Colm, Sharon and Emmet are picked, the order in which they are picked does not matter. The team of Colm, Emmet and Sharon is the same team as Emmet, Sharon and Colm.

Trying to list all the possible choices could take a long time, so we can use the following formula as a shortcut:

FORMULA

$$\binom{n}{r} = {}^nC_r = \frac{n!}{r!(n-r)!}$$

Formulae and Tables, page 20

$\binom{n}{r}$　　(pronounced 'n C r')

We can do this formula on the calculator by using the button nCr.

- n is the total number of objects or items to choose from.
- r is the number of objects or items we have to choose.

In this case, it would be $\binom{7}{3} = 35$.

On the calculator, we would press:

Without the calculator, the $\binom{n}{r}$ formula can be evaluated in the following way:

7　nCr　3　=

$$\binom{7}{3} = \frac{7!}{3! \times 4!} = \frac{7 \times 6 \times 5 \times 4 \times 3 \times 2 \times 1}{3 \times 2 \times 1 \times 4 \times 3 \times 2 \times 1} = \frac{7 \times 6 \times 5 \times 4 \times 3 \times 2 \times 1}{3 \times 2 \times 1 \times 4 \times 3 \times 2 \times 1} = \frac{7 \times 6 \times 5}{3 \times 2 \times 1} = \frac{210}{6} = 35$$

Worked Example 2.16

Evaluate $\binom{10}{2}$.

Solution

$\binom{10}{2}$ is the number of ways of choosing two items out of 10 items.

$\binom{10}{2}$ could also be written as ${}^{10}C_2$ (pronounced '10 C 2').

$$\binom{10}{2} = \frac{10!}{2! \times 8!} = \frac{10 \times 9 \times 8 \times 7 \times 6 \times 5 \times 4 \times 3 \times 2 \times 1}{2 \times 1 \times 8 \times 7 \times 6 \times 5 \times 4 \times 3 \times 2 \times 1}$$

$$= \frac{10 \times 9 \times 8 \times 7 \times 6 \times 5 \times 4 \times 3 \times 2 \times 1}{2 \times 1 \times 8 \times 7 \times 6 \times 5 \times 4 \times 3 \times 2 \times 1} = \frac{10 \times 9}{2 \times 1} = \frac{90}{2} = 45$$

However, we can usually write:

$${}^{10}C_2 = \frac{10 \times 9}{2 \times 1} = \frac{90}{2} = 45$$

COUNTING AND COMBINATIONS

Here is an easy way to use the formula $\binom{n}{r}$:

$$\binom{n}{r} = \frac{\text{First } r \text{ numbers in the countdown}}{\text{Last } r \text{ numbers in the countdown}}$$

For example, $\binom{7}{3} = \frac{7 \times 6 \times 5}{3 \times 2 \times 1}$ ⟵ First three numbers in countdown
⟵ Last three numbers in countdown

Worked Example 2.17

Find $^{100}C_3$.

Solution

The countdown from 100 is: 100, 99, 98, 97, 96 ... 4, 3, 2, 1.

$$^{100}C_3 = \frac{\text{First three numbers in the countdown}}{\text{Last three numbers in the countdown}} = \frac{100 \times 99 \times 98}{3 \times 2 \times 1} = \frac{970{,}200}{6} = 161{,}700$$

Some Rules for Combinations

An important rule we must remember is the **twin rule**:

For example: $\binom{20}{17} = \binom{20}{3}$ $(20 - 17 = 3)$

Again: $^{100}C_{99} = {}^{100}C_1$ $(100 - 99 = 1)$

This rule can be written as:

FORMULA

$$\binom{n}{r} = \binom{n}{n-r}$$

Another rule is that $\binom{n}{n} = 1$.

If we have five people in a panel and we must choose a team of five players, there is only one team we can make.

$\therefore \binom{5}{5} = 1$.

Using the twin rule, we get $\binom{5}{5} = \binom{5}{0}$, which are both equal to 1.

This rule can be written as:

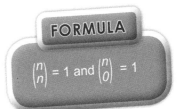

FORMULA

$$\binom{n}{n} = 1 \text{ and } \binom{n}{0} = 1$$

Worked Example 2.18

Evaluate:

    (i) $\binom{12}{3}$ (ii) $\binom{50}{48}$ (iii) $10\binom{9}{2}$

Solution

    (i) $\binom{12}{3} = \frac{12 \times 11 \times 10}{3 \times 2 \times 1} = \frac{1320}{6} = 220$ (ii) $\binom{50}{48} = \binom{50}{2} = \frac{50 \times 49}{2 \times 1} = \frac{2450}{2} = 1225$

    (iii) $10\binom{9}{2} = 10 \times \binom{9}{2} = 10 \times \frac{9 \times 8}{2 \times 1} = 10 \times \frac{72}{2} = 10 \times 36 = 360$

Exercise 2.4

Evaluate each of the following:

1. (i) $\binom{5}{2}$ (ii) $\binom{8}{3}$ (iii) $\binom{15}{4}$ (iv) $\binom{30}{2}$

2. (i) $\binom{20}{10}$ (ii) $\binom{50}{5}$ (iii) $\binom{100}{4}$ (iv) $\binom{6}{5}$

3. (i) $\binom{16}{2}$ (ii) $\binom{10}{3}$ (iii) $\binom{14}{4}$ (iv) $\binom{12}{1}$

4. (i) $^{10}C_7$ (ii) $^{13}C_{13}$ (iii) $^{19}C_{18}$ (iv) $^{1000}C_0$

5. (i) $\binom{11}{0} + \binom{11}{1}$ (ii) $\binom{9}{6} \times \binom{10}{6}$ (iii) $\binom{14}{10} \div \binom{14}{11}$ (iv) $5\binom{6}{1} + 2\binom{6}{2} \times 2\binom{6}{3}$

6. Verify the following, showing as much work as possible:

   (i) $\binom{5}{2} + \binom{5}{3} = \binom{6}{3}$

   (ii) $\binom{9}{3} - \binom{8}{3} = \binom{8}{2}$

   (iii) $\binom{14}{5} + \binom{14}{8} = \binom{15}{6}$

   (iv) $\binom{11}{1} + \binom{11}{2} = \binom{12}{2}$

7. Investigate if $\binom{5}{2} + \binom{5}{3} = \binom{10}{5}$.

8. (i) If $\binom{12}{x} = \binom{12}{4}$, write down the value of x, if $x \neq 4$. Verify your answer.

   (ii) If $\binom{19}{x} = \binom{19}{14}$, write down the value of x, if $x \neq 14$. Verify your answer.

   (iii) If $\binom{22}{10} = \binom{22}{x}$, write down the value of x, if $x \neq 10$. Verify your answer.

9. (i) If $\binom{n}{2} = 28$, find the value of n, for $n \in N$.

   (ii) If $\binom{n}{2} = 15$, find the value of n, for $n \in N$.

2.6 PROBLEMS INVOLVING COMBINATIONS

Combinations can be used to solve problems involving real-life situations where order is not important.

 Worked Example 2.19

There are 20 students in a class. The history teacher wants to pick four students to represent the class in the school quiz. How many ways are there to pick the team of four?

Solution

- $n = 20$, the total number of students in the class.
- $r = 4$, the number of students that we have to choose.

The total number of teams is $\binom{20}{4} = 4{,}845$.

Worked Example 2.20

There are eight people in a club. A committee of six people must be chosen. How many committees can be formed if:

    (i)   Any person can be on the committee

   (ii)   A certain person must be on the committee

  (iii)   A certain person cannot be on the committee

Solution

    (i)   Any person can be on the committee

$n = 8, r = 6$

$$\binom{8}{6} = 28$$

   (ii)   A certain person must be on the committee

- $n = 7$; as a person has already been picked, we have a total of seven people to choose from.

- $r = 5$; as a person is already on the committee, we now have to choose only five people.

$$\binom{7}{5} = 21$$

  (iii)   A certain person cannot be on the committee

- $n = 7$; as one person cannot be picked, we have a total of seven people to choose from.

- $r = 6$; we must still pick a committee of six people.

$$\binom{7}{6} = 7$$

Another way to attempt part (iii) is:

- There are 28 possible committees in total, and we know from part (ii) that there are 21 possible committees if one person is included.

- So, $28 - 21 = 7$ gives us the number of committees possible if one person is **not** included.

AND/OR Combinations

Sometimes problems involving combinations will make you choose from different groups. We can spot these problems, as they use the words **AND** and **OR**.

When shopping, if you were told that you had to buy a drink AND a bar, you would have only one choice:

> In mathematics, the word AND generally means 'to multiply', while the word OR generally means 'to add'.

If however you were told that you could buy a drink OR a bar you would have two choices.

> AND ⇒ Multiply
>
> OR ⇒ Add

Worked Example 2.21

There are seven women and five men in a table-tennis club. A team of four must be chosen. How many different teams can be chosen if:

    (i)   Any person can be on the team

   (ii)   There must be two women and two men on the team

  (iii)   There must be more women than men on the team

COUNTING AND COMBINATIONS

Solution

(i) The total number of people in the club = 7 + 5 = 12. Any person can be on the team.

We can choose from any of the 12 people to make up the team of four.

$n = 12, r = 4$ $\qquad \binom{12}{4} = 495$

(ii) There must be two women and two men on the team.

We must choose two women from seven, **and** we must choose two men from five.

2 Women	AND	2 Men		
$\binom{7}{2}$	×	$\binom{5}{2}$	= 21 × 10	= 210

(iii) There must be more women than men on the team.

We could choose three women from seven and one man from five, **or** four women from seven and no men from five.

3 W	AND	1 M	OR	4 W	AND	0 M
$\binom{7}{3}$	×	$\binom{5}{1}$	+	$\binom{7}{4}$	×	$\binom{5}{0}$
35	×	5	+	35	×	1
175			+	35		

ACTIVITIES 2.15, 2.16

175 + 35 = 210 different teams.

Exercise 2.5

1. In how many ways can you select 15 people from a group of 22 people?

2. A shop sells 20 different magazines. If a customer wants to buy two magazines, how many choices can she make?

3. A sandwich offers three different fillings from a choice of 15. How many different sandwiches are possible?

4. How many different committees can be formed if four people must be chosen from a panel of 14?

5. A lottery card has 45 numbers on it. You have to choose six of these. How many ways are there of choosing these six numbers?

6. Thirty students audition for a school play. How many different ways can 15 students be picked for the play:

(i) If there are no restrictions

(ii) If five of the students must be in the play

7. Thirteen people all shake hands with one another. How many handshakes take place?

8. Ray wants to make a playlist for his MP3 player. He has a choice of 50 songs, from which he chooses eight. How many playlists could he create:

(i) If there are no restrictions

(ii) If four particular songs must be on the playlist

(iii) If one particular song must **not** be on the playlist

9. A lottery card has 45 numbers on it. You have to choose six of these. How many ways are there of choosing if you have already decided on three of the numbers?

10. A committee of four people is to be formed from a panel of nine people. How many different committees of four people can be formed if:

(i) Anyone from the panel can be selected for the committee

(ii) Two particular people from the panel must be selected for the committee

(iii) One person withdraws from the panel

11. A pizza can have two different toppings from a choice of 10. How many different pizzas are possible if:

    (i)   Any topping can be used

    (ii) A certain topping must be used

    (iii) Five toppings may **not** be used

12. Seventeen people enter a chess competition in which each player plays everybody else once. How many chess matches take place?

13. There are seven members in a club: Alan, Bob, Carl, Denise, Elaine, Fiona and Greg. The president has to choose three of them to represent the club at a convention.

    (i)   How many different choices are there?

    (ii) How many choices are there if Greg must be chosen?

    (iii) How many choices are there if Greg must **not** be chosen?

    (iv) How many choices are there if both Alan and Bob must be included?

14. Ten points are marked on a circle as shown.

    (i)   How many chords can be formed by joining any two of these two points?

    (ii) How many triangles can be formed that have these points as vertices?

15. Twenty-two teams play in a league in which every team plays every other team twice. How many games take place?

16. A committee of four junior and five senior students is to be formed from a group of 20 junior and seven senior students. How many committees are possible?

17. How many teams can be chosen from 10 men and 15 women if a team must consist of three men and two women?

18. A clothes shop has 20 dresses and five hats. How many different ways are there to choose five dresses and two hats?

19. A student must choose two subjects from Block A, one from Block B and two from Block C.

Block A	Block B	Block C
Biology	French	English
Physics	German	Maths
Chemistry	Spanish	Irish

How many different selections are possible?

20. How many three-person committees can be chosen from a panel of five men and seven women if a committee consists of:

    (i)   Anyone from the panel

    (ii) Three men

    (iii) More women than men

21. There are 10 women and six men in a bridge club. Three members have to be chosen for a committee.

    (i)   How many different committees can be chosen?

    (ii) How many different committees can be chosen if they must contain two women and one man?

    (iii) How many different committees can be chosen if they must contain more women then men?

22. A squad consists of a group of 10 senior and 15 junior members. In how many different ways can a team of five players be selected:

    (i)   If there are no restrictions

    (ii) If the selection must contain exactly three senior players

    (iii) If the selection must contain at least two senior and at least two junior members

    (iv) If the selection must contain one specific senior and one specific junior member

1. An electrical store has numerous televisions for sale. A television can have a large, medium or small screen size, and it can have a plasma or LCD screen.

   (i) Show all possible different types of televisions using a two-way table.

   (ii) Find the number of different types of televisions a customer can purchase.

2. A factory produces a range of shirts. They can be: short-sleeved or long-sleeved; black, white or blue; and medium or large size.

   Use a tree diagram to show all the different types of shirts that this factory produces.

3. A restaurant menu offers four different starters and seven different main courses. A customer chooses a starter and main course for a meal.

   How many different types of meals can be ordered? Show clearly how you arrived at your answer.

4. There are three horses in a race: A, B and C.

   (i) Use a tree diagram to show the different orders in which they can finish the race.

   (ii) Use another method to show the different orders in which they can finish the race.

   (iii) Which method did you prefer? Explain why you preferred this method.

   (iv) If B comes first, how many different orders are possible?

   (v) If B comes first and A last, how many different orders are possible?

5. A team of six players is to be chosen from a panel of 10 players.

   (i) In how many ways can the six players be chosen if all players can be picked?

   (ii) The 10 players include just one goalkeeper. In how many ways can the team of six be chosen if every team must include the goalkeeper?

6. The letters of the word POWERS are arranged in as many different ways as possible.

   (i) In how many ways can this be done?

   (ii) How many of these arrangements begin with a vowel?

   (iii) How many of these arrangements begin with a vowel and end with a vowel?

7. There are five girls and seven boys in a table-tennis club. Two members have to be chosen for a committee.

   (i) How many different committees can be chosen?

   (ii) How many of these committees consist of one girl and one boy?

   (iii) How many of these committees consist of all girls?

   (iv) How many of these committees consist of at least one girl?

8. The five letters A, B, C, D and E are arranged in a row.

   (i) In how many ways can this be done?

   (ii) How many of these arrangements begin with B?

   (iii) How many arrangements begin with a vowel?

   (iv) How many arrangements begin with a consonant?

9. (i) How many ways are there of arranging the letters of the word WINTER?

   (ii) How many arrangements begin with a vowel?

   (iii) How many arrangements begin with a vowel and end with a consonant?

   (iv) How many arrangements end with the two vowels side by side?

   (v) How many arrangements have the two vowels beside each other?

10. Sarah is a member of a 10-person committee. A subcommittee of four members must be chosen from these 10 people.

How many different subcommittees may be chosen:

   (i) If there are no restrictions

   (ii) If Sarah must be on the subcommittee

   (iii) If Sarah must **not** be on the subcommittee

11. A family of two adults and three children is seated in a row. In how many different ways can they be seated if:

   (i) There are no restrictions on the order of seating.

   (ii) A child must be seated at the beginning of the row.

   (iii) A child must be seated at the beginning of the row and an adult at the end of the row.

   (iv) The two adults must be seated beside each other at the end of the row.

   (v) The two adults must be seated beside each other.

12. (i) How many different four-digit numbers can be made from the digits 2, 3, 4 and 5 (if no digit may be used more than once)?

How many of these numbers are:

   (ii) Less than 3,000

   (iii) Even

   (iv) Divisible by 5

   (v) Divisible by 5 and less than 3,000

13. There are seven girls and three boys on the student council in a school. A committee of four students is formed from the students on the council. In how many different ways can the committee be selected if:

   (i) There are no restrictions.

   (ii) A particular student must be on the committee.

   (iii) The committee must consist of one girl and three boys.

   (iv) The committee must have more girls than boys.

14. (i) How many ways are there of arranging the letters of the word MICROBES?

How many of these arrangements:

   (ii) Begin with R

   (iii) Begin with a vowel

   (iv) Have the three vowels as the first three letters

   (v) Have the three vowels together

15. Nine students (four girls and five boys) are to be lined up for a photo.

   (i) How many arrangements are possible?

   (ii) How many arrangements are possible if all the boys stand on the left and all the girls on the right?

   (iii) How many arrangements are possible if no two boys may stand side by side?

16. (i) How many different five-digit numbers can be formed from the digits 3, 4, 5, 6 and 8 (if no digit may be used more than once)?

   (ii) How many of the numbers are less than 4,000?

   (iii) How many of the numbers are divisible by 2?

   (iv) How many of the numbers are less than 4,000 and divisible by 2?

17. From a standard pack of 52 cards, a hand of four cards is chosen. How many different hands are possible:

   (i) If any card can be picked

   (ii) If a hand must contain only Clubs

   (iii) If a hand must contain only Kings

   (iv) If a hand must contain two Kings and two Aces

   (v) If a hand must contain at least two Kings

18. Find the value of the natural number n in each of the following:

   (i) $\binom{11}{0} = \binom{11}{n}, n \neq 0$

   (ii) $\binom{n}{5} = \binom{n}{6}$

   (iii) $\binom{n}{2} = 21$

3 chapter

Probability

Learning Outcomes

In this chapter you will learn to:

➲ Describe the likelihood that everyday events will happen

➲ Put probabilities in order on a probability scale

➲ Use the language of probability to discuss events

➲ Predict and investigate the frequency of a specific outcome in a simple probability experiment

➲ Associate the probability of an event with its long-run, relative frequency

➲ Compare expected frequencies and actual frequencies

➲ Predict and determine probabilities of one or more events

➲ Calculate expected value and understand that this does not need to be one of the outcomes

➲ Discuss basic rules of probability through the use of set theory

➲ Find the probability of intersection of two independent events

➲ Construct and use a sample space such as a two-way table

➲ Construct and use tree diagrams

➲ Solve problems involving experiments whose outcome is random and can have two possibilities

➲ Recognise the role of expected value in decision-making with a focus on fair games

3.1 INTRODUCING PROBABILITY

Probability is a branch of mathematics that studies the chance or likelihood of something occurring.

We encounter probability in some form or another in everyday life...

...from the chance of a horse winning a race to the chance of someone winning the lottery.

Probability is also involved in determining car insurance premiums and forecasting the weather.

> The ancient Greek gods Zeus, Poseidon and Hades divided up the universe by drawing lots.

Probability tries to determine the chance of something occurring using words or, more commonly, a numerical value.

3.2 PROBABILITY

When you cross a road or make a guess in a multiple-choice test, you are using probability to determine your chance of success or failure. Probability, or chance, deals with the likelihood that something called an 'event' might occur.

In probability we encounter many common terms that have special meanings we must be aware of.

> A **trial** is the act of doing an experiment in probability.

> An **outcome** is one of the possible results of the trial.

The flipping of a coin is an example of a **trial**.

When flipping a coin, the **outcomes** are that you could flip a head or a tail.

Head   Tail

PROBABILITY

> The set or list of all possible outcomes in a trial is called the **sample space**.

> An **event** is the occurrence of one or more **specific outcomes**.

For a coin, the **sample space** is {head, tail}.

The tossed coin landing on a head would be the **event**.

3.3 LIKELIHOOD SCALE

The probability of an event can be described using certain words such as:

Impossible	Unlikely	Evens	Likely	Certain

Many different sayings that we use in everyday life can be used to describe certain probabilities.

'We figured the odds as best we could, and then we rolled the dice.'

Former U.S. President Jimmy Carter

ACTIVITIES 3.1, 3.2

Exercise 3.1

Describe each of the following as: impossible, unlikely, evens, likely or certain to occur.

1. A **fair** coin will land on a head.

> A **fair** coin is where the chance of landing on a head or a tail is equally likely to occur.

2. Roll a normal die once and get a 5.

3. The sun will set today.

4. A card chosen from a standard pack of 52 cards will be red.

5. A fair coin is tossed three times and lands heads up each time.

6. It will rain in August.

7. Roll an odd number on a single throw of a fair die.

8. A card chosen from a pack of cards will be a Diamond.

9. A ball thrown up in the air will fall back to the ground.

10. It will not rain for the whole of July.

11. A fair coin is tossed three times and lands heads up at least once.

12. The next baby born in Ireland will be a girl.

13. Roll a normal die and get a prime number.

14. A card chosen from a pack of cards will be the Ace of Diamonds.

15. Roll a 7 on a single throw of a fair die.

> Loaded dice are unfair dice that have been altered to give a more predictable outcome. Loaded dice have been found in the ruins of Pompeii.

3.4 PROBABILITY SCALE

In mathematics, we need to use a scale that is more precise and less open to different interpretations.

The chances of an event occurring can be shown on a probability scale. The scale goes from 0 to 1 or 0% to 100%.

A probability of 0 or 0% means that the event will never happen – **impossible**.

A probability of 1 or 100% means that the event will definitely happen – **certain**.

A probability of a $\frac{1}{2}$, 0.5 or 50% means that the event has an **even chance** of happening.

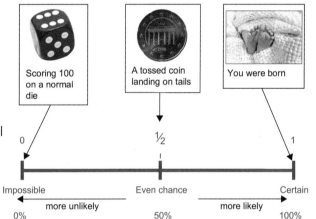

Scoring 100 on a normal die

A tossed coin landing on tails

You were born

Probability is a numerical measure of the chance of an event happening.

Events whose probabilities are close to 1 are likely to happen, whereas events whose probabilities are close to 0 are unlikely to happen.

The closer you move to 1, the more likely an event is to occur.

The closer you move to 0, the less likely an event is to occur.

It is also important to remember that the probabilities of **all** outcomes of a particular experiment will add up to 1.

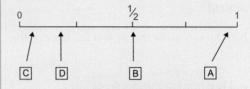

Worked Example 3.1

For each event below, mark on the probability scale an estimate of its probability.

A: It will rain in Ireland this year.

B: A die will land on an even number.

C: You will win the lottery.

D: You will grow to be over 2 m in height.

Solution

```
0               ½               1
|       |       |       |       |
↑       ↑       ↑              ↗
C       D       B              A
```

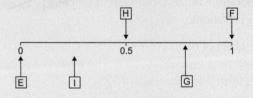

Exercise 3.2

1. Draw a probability scale. Mark each event with its letter on the scale.

   A: It will be sunny tomorrow.

   B: You will get a 7 on a single throw of a fair die.

   C: A fair coin will land on tails on a single flip.

   D: You will watch television tonight.

2. Draw a probability scale. Mark each event with its letter on the scale.

   A: You will pick a number divisible by two when selecting at random a number between 1 and 10.

   B: The Atlantic Ocean will disappear tomorrow.

   C: You will go home after school.

   D: You will get a 1 or a 2 on a single roll of a fair die.

3. Draw a probability scale. Mark each event with its letter on the scale.

   A: A rugby team will win the soccer World Cup.

   B: Everyone in the class will be present on the next school day.

   C: You will pick a number divisible by 3 when selecting at random a number between 1 and 30.

   D: You are 10 years or older.

4. The probabilities of five events are shown on the probability scale below.

```
              H                   F
0                 0.5                 1
|       |       |       |       |
↑       ↑               ↑
E       I               G
```

   (i) Which event is impossible?

   (ii) Which event is more than likely going to occur?

   (iii) Which event is unlikely to happen?

   (iv) Which event is certain to occur?

   (v) Which event has a 50–50 chance of happening?

5. Mark the probability of each event on a probability scale, when a single card is drawn at random from a normal pack of cards:

   (i) A Diamond, Heart, Club or Spade

   (ii) A red card

   (iii) A Diamond

   (iv) A Diamond picture card

   (v) The King of Diamonds

6. Explain what is wrong with each of the following statements:

   (i) The probability of rain today is 1.5.

   (ii) The chance of winning a lottery is –1.

   (iii) The probability of rolling a 1, 2, 3, 4, 5 or 6 on a normal die is 0.9.

3.5 RELATIVE FREQUENCY (EXPERIMENTAL PROBABILITY)

The probability of an event occurring can be found from statistical data derived from experiments or observations. The question of whether your school team will win their next match can be used as an example.

You can look at the previous results of the team and then determine the experimental probability that the team will win their next match.

This is referred to as **relative frequency** or experimental probability.

> **Relative frequency** is an estimate of the probability of an event.

FORMULA

$$\text{Relative frequency} = \frac{\text{frequency or number of times the event happens in trials}}{\text{total number of trials}}$$

Worked Example 3.2

A coin was flipped 1,000 times. It landed on tails 450 times.
Find the relative frequency of getting a tail.

Solution

$$\text{Relative frequency} = \frac{\text{number of times a tail was flipped}}{\text{number of times coin was flipped}}$$

$$= \frac{450}{1,000}$$

$$= \frac{9}{20} \text{ or } 0.45 \text{ (or } 45\%)$$

Worked Example 3.3

A spinner with five equal sectors was spun 20 times. The spinner landed on the green sector five times.
What is the experimental probability that the spinner lands on a green sector?

Solution

$$\text{Relative frequency} = \frac{\text{number of times spinner landed on green}}{\text{number of times spinner was spun}} = \frac{5}{20} = 0.25$$

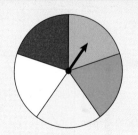

ACTIVITIES 3.4, 3.5

John Kerrich was interned in Denmark during the Second World War. He wanted to see if a coin was fair (unbiased). He tossed a coin 10,000 times and recorded his results.

Heads	Tails
5,067	4,933

He then worked out the relative frequency for both results:

Relative frequency for heads = $\frac{5,067}{10,000}$ = 0.5067

Relative frequency for tails = $\frac{4,933}{10,000}$ = 0.4933

While not exactly 50–50, they were so close to the theoretical values that he concluded that the coin was fair or unbiased.

> It is important to note that, in general, as the number of trials carried out increases, the more reliable the relative frequency will be in estimating the probability.

Worked Example 3.4

An experiment is conducted to show how the number of trials improves the accuracy of the relative frequency.

Mick rolls a die and notes the number of times a 1 is rolled.
He records his results every six throws of the die. (Note: 2 d.p. = two decimal places.)

	Total times 1 is rolled	Relative frequency (2 d.p.)
6 throws	0	0
12 throws	1	0.08
18 throws	2	0.11
24 throws	5	0.21
30 throws	5	0.17
36 throws	6	0.17
42 throws	8	0.19
48 throws	9	0.19
54 throws	9	0.17
60 throws	11	0.18

Mick then plots his results on a graph.

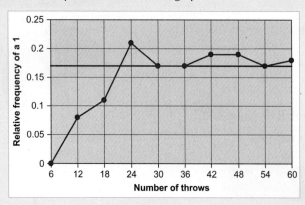

He notices that the more the experiment is repeated, the closer the relative frequency is to the estimated probability (in this $\frac{1}{6}$ or 0.17 to two decimal places).

ACTIVITY 3.6

PROBABILITY

1. A die is rolled 100 times. The number 1 shows 25 times. What is the relative frequency of rolling a 1?

2. A coin is flipped 1,000 times. It lands on heads 350 times. What is the relative frequency of the coin landing on:

   (i) Heads   (ii) Tails

3. A deli sells 75 lunches in one day. Ten of these lunches are vegetarian. What is the relative frequency of selling a non-vegetarian lunch?

4. In a local raffle 5,500 tickets are sold. Ten tickets are chosen as prize winners. Find the experimental probability that someone wins.

5. In a survey of 570 people, it was found that 190 people had a college degree. If a person is selected at random, find the relative frequency that the person does not have a college degree.

6. 55,000 students sit a maths exam. Ten thousand of these students get a B grade. What is the relative frequency of a student getting a B grade?

7. A spinner is spun and the number of times it lands on one of its five sectors is recorded as shown:

Spinner sector	A	B	C	D	E
Frequency	5	10	12	10	13

Find the relative frequency of the spinner landing on each sector.

8. A survey was carried out asking all Fifth Year students in a school who they would vote for in the next general election. All students answered the survey. The results are shown in the table below.

Party X	Party Y	Party Z	Undecided
50	40	10	20

   (i) How many students are in Fifth Year in the school?

   (ii) What is the relative frequency of selecting a student who would vote for Party X?

   (iii) What is the relative frequency of selecting a student who is undecided?

9. A die is rolled and the relative frequency for each possible outcome is recorded in the table below.

Number on die	1	2	3	4	5	6
Relative frequency	0.1	0.15	0.2	0.18	0.12	

   (i) Work out the relative frequency of rolling a 6 on the die.

   (ii) What outcome occurred the least often?

   (iii) What outcome occurred the most often?

   (iv) How many times did the die show a 4 if the die was rolled 200 times in total?

10. A survey of teachers' ages in a school found the following data. All teachers in the school answered the survey.

Age	20–24	25–34	35–44	45–54	55–64	>64
Number of teachers	1	10	13	12	8	2

   (i) How many teachers are in the school?

   If a teacher is selected at random, find the experimental probability that the teacher is:

   (ii) Under 35 years old

   (iii) Over 55 years old

   (iv) Between 25 and 44 years old

11. One thousand teenagers were asked about their plans for the following week.

Work	Study	Holiday abroad	Holiday in Ireland	Undecided
245	215	100	415	25

Calculate the relative frequency of picking a student who planned to:

(i) Work

(ii) Study

(iii) Holiday

12. The results of games played by three children are shown in the table.

Child	Games won	Games lost	Games drawn
Megan	5	1	4
Alex	2	2	3
Jack	0	1	1

(i) What is the relative frequency of a win for each child?

(ii) Who, according to their relative frequencies, is the best player? Explain what might be wrong in picking the best player using the highest relative frequency.

13. A bag contains three different coloured tokens. A token is picked at random from the bag, its colour noted and then returned to the bag. This experiment is done 100 times. Every 20th time, the relative frequency of picking a pink token is calculated. The graph of the results is shown below.

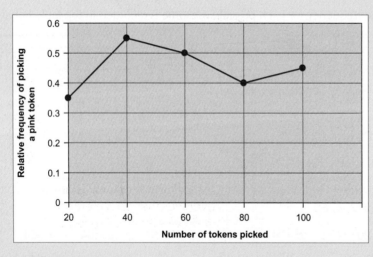

(i) Estimate how many times a pink token was picked after 20 experiments.

(ii) Estimate how many times a pink token was picked after 40 experiments.

(iii) Estimate how many times a pink token was picked after 80 experiments.

(iv) In your opinion, is there an equal number of each coloured token in the bag? Give a reason for your answer.

3.6 PROBABILITY OF ONE EVENT

 ## Worked Example 3.5

A bag contains five red and 10 blue marbles. One marble is picked at random from the bag. What is the probability that it is blue?

Solution

There are 10 blue marbles.
There are 15 marbles in total.
The desired outcome is that we pick a blue marble from the bag.

Probability of getting a blue marble = $\frac{\text{number of blue marbles}}{\text{total number of marbles}} = \frac{10}{15} = \frac{2}{3}$

We use the following formula to calculate the probability of an event:

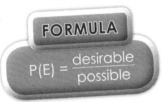

FORMULA

$$\text{Probability (Event)} = P(E) = \frac{\text{number of desirable outcomes}}{\text{total number of all possible outcomes}}$$

A good way to remember the formula is:

FORMULA

$$P(E) = \frac{\text{desirable}}{\text{possible}}$$

 ## Worked Example 3.6

A fair six-sided die is thrown.

What is the probability of rolling an even number?

Solution

There are six possible outcomes (1, 2, 3, 4, 5, 6).

Three of these outcomes are even (2, 4, 6).

The probability of rolling an even number on a die is:

> The probability of rolling an even number on a die can also be written as P(even).

$P(\text{even}) = \frac{\text{number of outcomes that are even}}{\text{total number of outcomes}} = \frac{3}{6} = \frac{1}{2}$ (fraction in its simplest form)

'Iacta alea est,'
'The die is cast.'

Attributed to Julius Caesar as he crossed the
Rubicon River.

(a) A card is drawn at random from a standard pack of 52 cards. What is the probability that the card drawn is:

    (i) A Jack   (ii) A Heart   (iii) A picture card

(b) A card is picked at random from all the red cards. What is the probability that it is a King?

Solution

(a) (i) A Jack

$$P(\text{Jack}) = \frac{\text{number of cards that are Jacks}}{\text{total number of cards in the pack}} = \frac{4}{52} = \frac{1}{13}$$

    (ii) A Heart

$$P(\text{Heart}) = \frac{\text{number of cards that are Hearts}}{\text{total number of cards in the pack}} = \frac{13}{52} = \frac{1}{4}$$

    (iii) A picture card

$$P(\text{picture card}) = \frac{\text{number of picture cards}}{\text{total number of cards in the pack}} = \frac{12}{52} = \frac{3}{13}$$

(b) A card is picked at random from all the red cards.

What is the probability that it is a King?

It is important to note that we are selecting a card out of all the red cards in a pack of cards.

$$P(\text{King}) = \frac{\text{number of RED Kings}}{\text{total number of RED cards in the pack}} = \frac{2}{26} = \frac{1}{13}$$

We know that the probabilities of all outcomes for a particular experiment add up to 1.

In a certain experiment, the probability of an event is 0.35.

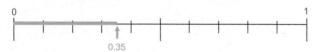

Therefore, the probability of the event NOT happening is $1 - 0.35 = 0.65$

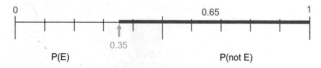

The probability of something **not** happening = 1 – the probability that it **will** happen.

Worked Example 3.8

A fair spinner shown is spun. What is the probability that the spinner will **NOT** land on a red sector?

Solution

There are four possible outcomes: green, red, orange or blue.

The probability of the spinner landing on a red sector $= \frac{1}{4}$ (one outcome out of four)

The probability of the spinner **not** landing on a red sector $= \frac{\text{number of outcomes not red}}{\text{total number of outcomes}} = \frac{3}{4}$

Alternatively:

If P(red) $= \frac{1}{4}$, then P(not red) $= 1 - $P(red)$ = 1 - \frac{1}{4} = \frac{3}{4}$

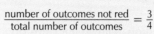

ACTIVITY 3.7

Exercise 3.4

1. A fair coin is flipped once. Calculate the probability of getting:

   (i)   A head   (iii) A head or a tail

   (ii) A tail

2. If the probability that it will rain tomorrow in Athlone is 0.75, what is the probability that it will not rain in Athlone tomorrow?

3. In a maths class there are eight boys and seven girls. A student is chosen at random. What is the probability that this student will be:

   (i)   A boy   (ii) Not a boy

4. A spinner with 20 equal sectors numbered 1–20 is spun. Calculate the probability that it lands on:

   (i)   10   (iv) An even number

   (ii)   5   (v)   A prime number

   (iii) 20   (vi) A composite number

5. A fair die is rolled once. Work out the probability that you roll:

   (i)   5   (v)   An even number

   (ii)   1   (vi)   A odd number

   (iii) 20   (vii) A number less than 4

   (iv)   1, 2, 3, 4, 5 or 6

6. A bag contains 14 red tokens and six white tokens. A token is taken from the bag at random. What is the probability (as a percentage) that this token will be:

   (i)   Red   (ii) Not red

7. A card is selected at random from a pack of 52 playing cards.
   Calculate the probability that it is:

   (i)   A red card   (iv) A black King

   (ii)   A black card   (v)   The King of Clubs

   (iii) The Ace of Spades

8. A bag contains 15 white marbles, six black marbles and four blue marbles. A marble is taken from the bag at random.
   Calculate the probability (as a percentage) that this marble will be:

   (i)   White   (iv) Not blue

   (ii)   Black   (v)   White or black

   (iii) Blue

9. A letter is selected at random from the word DISCOVERY. Work out the probability that the letter selected is:

   (i)   E   (iii) A vowel

   (ii) O   (iv)   A consonant

10. A bag contains 10 numbers. These numbers are 5, 7, 44, 45, 67, 68, 69, 100, 101 and 500. A number is drawn at random from the bag. What is the probability that it is:

    (i)   A one-digit number

    (ii)   A number that has a 4 in it

    (iii) An even number

    (iv)   A prime number

11. A fair spinner is spun once.

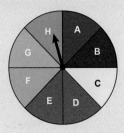

What is the probability that it lands on:

(i) Sector A

(ii) Sector B

(iii) A sector showing a vowel

12. Eight Scrabble tiles are placed in a bag. They are P, A, R, A, L, L, E, L. One tile is drawn out at random.
Work out the probability that the selected tile is:

(i) The letter L   (iii) A vowel

(ii) The letter P   (iv) Not a vowel

13. There are 20 students in a class. This table shows the number who are girls or boys and how many are left-handed or right-handed:

	Left-handed	Right-handed
Girls	2	10
Boys	3	5

A student is picked at random from the class. Find the probability that this student will be:

(i) A girl

(ii) A right-handed girl

A boy is picked at random from the class. Find the probability that this boy will be:

(iii) Left-handed

14. A person is stopped in the street at random and asked on what day of the week they were born. What is the probability that the person was born on:

(i) A Sunday

(ii) Not a Sunday

(iii) A Saturday or Sunday

(iv) A weekday (Monday to Friday)

(v) A day beginning with the letter T

15. A spinner with equal sectors labelled B, A, O and D is spun.

What is the probability of the spinner landing on:

(i) B

(ii) A vowel

(iii) A letter of the word BAD

16. A drop of water lands randomly on a rectangular counter 0.5 m wide and 1 m long. A bowl of radius 10 cm is placed on this counter.

(i) Calculate, to two decimal places, the probability that the drop lands in the bowl.

(ii) How many bowls would be needed in order to have an evens chance of the drop landing in a bowl?

17. A spinner has two red sectors, one of 45° and the other of 90°.

(i) Calculate the probability that the spinner does not land on a red sector.

(ii) The angle size of the bigger sector is changed so that the probability of landing on a red sector is now 70%.

What angle size is this new red sector?

18. A bag contains 13 tokens: three red, four blue and the remainder white. If one token is drawn at random from the bag, what is the possibility that it is:

(i) Blue   (ii) Not blue

A number of blue and white tokens are added, so that the probability of getting a red token is $\frac{1}{8}$.

(iii) How many tokens were added?

3.7 FAIRNESS AND FREQUENCY

Fairness

> If all outcomes are equally likely to occur, then the trial or experiment is considered to be **fair** or **unbiased**.

Worked Example 3.9

A coin is flipped. What percentage of the time would you expect it to land on tails if the coin is unbiased?

Solution

There should be an equal chance of each outcome occurring if the coin is fair. As there are only two outcomes, heads or tails, a fair or unbiased coin should land on tails around 50% of the time.

Worked Example 3.10

A spinner is made from a pentagon. Its sectors are labelled 1, 2, 3, 4 and 5. The spinner is spun and the number of the sector it lands on is noted after each spin. The results are recorded and shown in this table.

Is the spinner fair?

Number on spinner	Results
1	20
2	45
3	20
4	21
5	14

Solution

Total number of spins = 20 + 45 + 20 + 21 + 14 = 120.
Relative frequency of landing on 2 $= \frac{45}{120} = 0.375$.
If the spinner is fair, we would expect a relative frequency close to $\frac{1}{5}$ or 0.2.

Conclusion: The spinner is not fair, as the relative frequency is not close to the theoretical frequency even after 120 trials.

Expected Frequency

If we know the relative frequency or probability of an event, we can then estimate how many times that event would happen over a certain number of trials. This is called the **expected frequency**.

FORMULA

> Expected frequency = number of trials × relative frequency or probability

PROBABILITY

Worked Example 3.11

A die is thrown 900 times. How many times would you expect to roll a 1?

Solution

The probability of rolling a 1 on a normal die: $P(1) = \frac{1}{6}$
Number of times 1 would be expected to appear after rolling a die 900 times:
$$900 \times \frac{1}{6} = 150$$

Worked Example 3.12

A random survey of shoppers was carried out in a supermarket. It was found that the relative frequency of a shopper buying the supermarket's own toilet paper brand is 28%. If the supermarket had 1,500 customers that day, what is the expected number who bought the supermarket-branded toilet paper?

Solution

$$1,500 \times \frac{28}{100} = 420 \text{ shoppers}$$

ACTIVITIES 3.8, 3.9, 3.10

Exercise 3.5

1. A spinner is spun 500 times and shows red 75 times. How many times would you expect it to show red after 1,000 spins?

2. Decide if each of the following events are fair and give a reason for your answer:

   (i) A coin flip to start a game

   (ii) A game won on rolling an even number on a single throw of a die

   (iii) A game won on rolling a 1, 3, 5 or 6 on a single throw of a die

3. A die is rolled 400 times and lands on a 5 40 times. In your opinion, is the die fair? Give a reason for your answer.

4. A coin is flipped 100 times. It lands on tails 30 times.

   (i) Do you think the coin is biased? Explain the reasons for your answer.

   (ii) If the coin was flipped another 20 times, how often would you expect it to land on tails?

5. A card is drawn from a pack of cards and replaced. This is done 260 times. How many times would you expect to get:

   (i) A black card

   (ii) A picture card

   (iii) The King of Clubs

6. The experimental probability of scoring from a penalty in the World Cup final is 0.77.

   If 46 penalties are awarded during the next World Cup final, how many (to the nearest whole number) would you expect to be saved?

7. A company determines that the probability of a television developing a fault is 0.05% over a period of one year. If the company sells 50,000 televisions, how many would you expect to develop a fault over the first year?

8. A spinner as shown is spun 120 times.

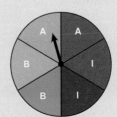

   How many times would you expect the spinner to land on:

   (i) An A   (ii) A vowel

9. An unfair die is rolled and the relative frequency that it lands on 3 is calculated to be 0.28. Estimate the number of times the die will land on a 3 if it is rolled 600 times.

10. A random survey of 50 adults is carried out, asking what mode of transport they use to go to work in a certain town. The results are shown below.

Mode	Walk	Car	Bus
Number	10	25	15

If there are 5,000 adults working in the town, how many would we expect to use each mode of transport listed to get to work?

11. A spinner is divided into four sections: blue, red, green and orange. The spinner is spun 1,000 times and the results are recorded.

Colour on spinner	Blue	Red	Green	Orange
Frequency	100	550	200	150

(i) What is the relative frequency of the spinner landing on each colour?

(ii) John plays a game where a person bets on the colour the spinner will land on. Which colour should John bet on and why?

12. A bag contains a number of discs lettered A, B, C and D. An experiment is conducted in which a disc is taken from the bag, its letter is recorded, and it is then returned to the bag. Two students conduct the experiment and record their results.

Letter on disc	A	B	C	D
Mark	50	10	20	40
Gayle	16	3	5	13

(i) Mark argues that Gayle's results are not as reliable as his own. State, giving a reason, whether you agree with Mark.

(ii) Using Mark's results, find the relative frequency for each lettered disc.

(iii) Does the bag contain the same number of each lettered disc? Explain.

3.8 SET THEORY AND PROBABILITY

Set theory, especially Venn diagrams, is very useful when trying to solve questions on probability.
A Venn diagram is used to represent the sample space, and individual probabilities can then be easily read from the diagram. Sets are represented as circles. If they have no elements in common, they are represented as shown. These are sometimes referred to as **mutually exclusive** or disjoint sets.

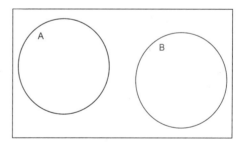

Mutually exclusive events have no elements or outcomes in common. This means that the events cannot occur at the same time. Two events are mutually exclusive if their intersection is empty.

If the sets have elements in common, then we represent the sets using overlapping circles.

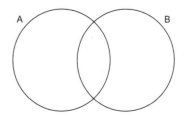

PROBABILITY

If we look at a Venn diagram with two sets:

The area shaded red indicates elements that are in Set A. ∪ is the universal set (the set of all elements under consideration) and is represented by a rectangle:

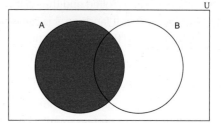

The area shaded blue indicates elements that are in Set B:

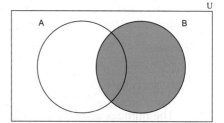

The area shaded grey indicates elements that are shared by Set A and Set B (i.e. the intersection A∩B):

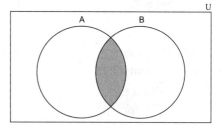

The area shaded green indicates elements that are in Set A or Set B (written A∪B):

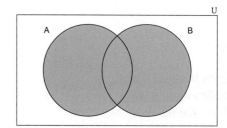

The area shaded yellow indicates elements that are in neither Set A nor Set B [written (A∪B)′]:

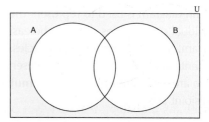

The area shaded red indicates elements that are in Set A but not in Set B (i.e. A \ B):

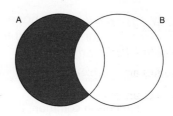

The area shaded green indicates elements that are in Set B but not in Set A (i.e. B \ A):

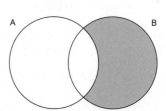

Worked Example 3.13

This Venn diagram shows the teenagers in a group who like tea and/or coffee.

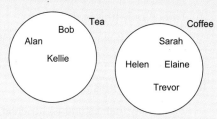

What is the probability that a teenager chosen at random:

   (i)   Likes tea

  (ii)   Likes tea or coffee

 (iii)   Likes tea and coffee

Solution

   (i)   The probability that a teenager picked at random likes tea (Set T)

       The number of teenagers in Set T is 3. The number of teenagers in the Universal Set is 7.

$$P(T) = \frac{3}{7}$$

  (ii)   The probability that a teenager picked at random likes tea or coffee

       This is the Union of the two sets.

$$P(T \text{ or } C) = \frac{7}{7} = 1$$

The next solution shows an example of **mutually exclusive** events.

 (iii)   The probability that a teenager picked at random likes tea and coffee

       This is the intersection of the two sets. As this is empty:

$$P(T \text{ and } C) = \frac{0}{7} = 0$$

Worked Example 3.14

Thirty students in a college were asked if they studied art or biology. The Venn diagram below shows the results of the survey.

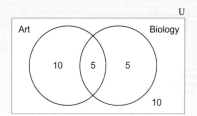

What is the probability that a student chosen at random:

   (i)   Studies art

  (ii)   Studies biology

 (iii)   Studies art and biology

 (iv)   Studies art or biology

Solution

#U → the sample space, total number of the possible outcomes of the experiment → 30

#A → the number of students who study art → 15 (10 + 5)

#B → the number of students who study biology → 10 (5 + 5)

#(A∩B) → the number of students who study art **AND** biology → 5

#(A∪B) → the number of students who study art **OR** biology → 20 (10 + 5 + 5)

#(A∪B)′ → the number of students who study neither art nor biology → 10

   (i)   What is the probability that a student studies art?

$$P(A) = \frac{\#A}{\#U} = \frac{15}{30} = \frac{1}{2}$$

  (ii)   What is the probability that a student studies biology?

$$P(B) = \frac{\#B}{\#U} = \frac{10}{30} = \frac{1}{3}$$

 (iii)   What is the probability that a student studies art and biology?

$$P(A \cap B) = \frac{\#(A \cap B)}{\#U} = \frac{5}{30} = \frac{1}{6}$$

 (iv)   What is the probability that a student studies art or biology?

$$P(A \cup B) = \frac{\#(A \cup B)}{\#U} = \frac{20}{30} = \frac{2}{3}$$

Worked Example 3.15

In a class of 22 students, 15 study French, eight study Spanish and four study neither of these subjects.

A Venn diagram is drawn to show this information.

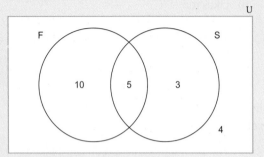

What is the probability that a student chosen at random studies:

   (i) French only

  (ii) Not Spanish

 (iii) Neither of these subjects

Solution

   (i) French only [this is #(F \ S)]

Probability that a student chosen at random studies French only $= \frac{10}{22} = \frac{5}{11}$

  (ii) Not Spanish [this is #(S')]

Probability that a student chosen at random does not study Spanish $= \frac{14}{22} = \frac{7}{11}$

 (iii) Neither of these subjects
[this is #[(F∪S)']]

Probability that a student chosen at random studies neither subject $= \frac{4}{22} = \frac{2}{11}$

We may sometimes encounter set questions on probability in which we are given the actual probabilities of certain events.

 Worked Example 3.16

Kerrie conducts a survey to discover how many students in her college participate in either soccer or Gaelic football. She discovers that the probability that a student plays soccer is 0.25 and the probability that a student plays Gaelic football is 0.4. The probability that they play neither of these sports is 0.45.

   (i) Draw a Venn diagram to show this data.

A student is picked at random.

  (ii) Find the probability that the student plays both soccer and Gaelic football.

 (iii) Find the probability that the student plays soccer only.

Solution

   (i) The probabilities should all add up to 1.

0.25 + 0.4 + 0.45 = 1.1

∴ 1.1 − 1 = 0.1

This is the probability that a student plays both sports.

Soccer only = 0.25 − 0.1 = 0.15

Gaelic football only = 0.4 − 0.1 = 0.3

We can now draw the Venn diagram.

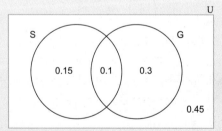

  (ii) The probability that the student plays both soccer and Gaelic football = 0.1.

 (iii) The probability that the student plays soccer only = 0.15.

 **ACTIVITIES 3.11, 3.12**

Exercise 3.6

1. Look at the Venn diagram.

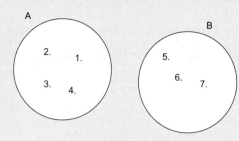

(i) List the elements of Set A.

(ii) List the elements of Set B.

A student picks a number at random from the numbers 1 to 7 inclusive. Find the probability that this number is in:

(iii) Set A

(iv) Set B

2. A Venn diagram shows Set C and Set D.

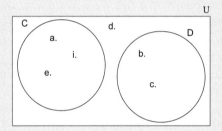

(i) List the elements of Set C.

(ii) List the elements of Set D.

(iii) What name is given to sets that have no elements in common?

(iv) Find the probability of picking a letter from Set C in a single pick.

(v) Find the probability of picking a letter from Set D in a single pick.

3. A Venn diagram shows Set X and Set Y.

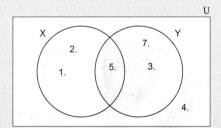

(i) Write down #X.

(ii) Write down #Y.

(iii) Find the probability of picking a number from Set X in a single pick.

(iv) Find the probability of picking a number from Set X or Set Y in a single pick.

(v) Find the probability of picking a number from Set X and Set Y in a single pick.

4. A Venn diagram shows Set E and Set F. The number of elements in each region is given.

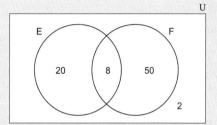

One element is selected at random.

(i) Find the probability of picking an element from Set E.

(ii) Find the probability of picking an element from Set E or Set F.

(iii) Find the probability of picking an element from Set E and Set F.

5. For each of the cardinal Venn diagrams below, find the probability of randomly selecting in a single pick an element from:

(i) P∪Q   (iii) P \ Q

(ii) P∩Q   (iv) (P∪Q)′ [or U\(P∪Q)]

(a)
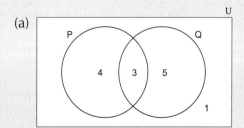

(b)
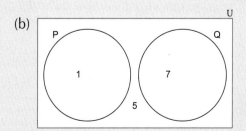

6. The Venn diagram below shows the response to a survey carried out in a supermarket. Two hundred customers were asked what coffee brand they had purchased.

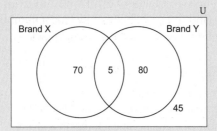

A customer is selected at random. What is the probability that:

(i) The customer purchased Brand X.

(ii) The customer did not purchase Brand X.

(iii) The customer did not purchase either brand.

7. Students are asked which strand of the new maths syllabus they like. The Venn diagram shows the results.

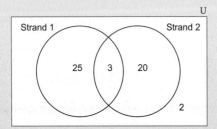

What is the probability that a student selected at random likes:

(i) Strand 1

(ii) Strand 1 and Strand 2

(iii) Strand 1 or Strand 2

(iv) Neither of the strands

8. In a survey the probability that a household has a dog for a pet is 0.6. The probability that a household has a cat for a pet is 0.3. The probability that the households surveyed did not have a dog or a cat is 0.35.

(i) Draw a Venn diagram to show this data.

(ii) Find the probability that a household has a cat and a dog.

(iii) Find the probability that a household has a cat only.

9. Thirty per cent of the students at a school have a part-time job. Ten per cent of students have a part-time job and attend evening study in school. Twenty-five per cent of students do neither.

(i) Draw a Venn diagram to show this data.

(ii) Find the probability that a student selected at random attends evening study but does not have a part-time job.

10. On a museum tour, the probability that a visitor visits the Egyptian exhibit only is $\frac{1}{5}$. The probability that they visit the African exhibit only is $\frac{1}{3}$. The probability that they visit neither exhibit is $\frac{1}{10}$.

(i) Draw a Venn diagram to show this data.

A visitor is selected at random. What is the probability that they:

(ii) Visited both exhibits

(iii) Visited the African exhibit

11. Twenty people in a club were asked what they did the previous week for entertainment. Ten went to a movie and seven went to a concert. Four did neither. A person is selected at random from the club. What is the probability that the person selected:

(i) Went to a movie only

(ii) Went to a movie and a concert

12. Of 70 people surveyed, 35 were members of a soccer club, 50 were members of a rugby club and three were not members of either of the two clubs. What is the probability that a person picked at random is a member of:

(i) The soccer club only

(ii) Both the soccer and rugby clubs

(iii) At least one club

13. Out of 40 students, 14 are taking English composition and 29 are taking chemistry.

(i) If five students are in both classes, how many students are in neither class?

(ii) How many are in English composition or chemistry class?

(iii) What is the probability that a randomly chosen student from this group is taking the chemistry class only?

14. First Year students in a school were asked what types of calculator they owned. Of the 100 students surveyed, 60 owned a Casio, 45 owned a Sharp and 20 owned both. What is the probability that a student selected at random:

   (i)   Did not own a calculator

   (ii) Owned a Casio only

   (iii) Owned at least one calculator

15. A teacher gave two maths problems to a class of 30 students. The next day 25 students said they had got the first question right and 10 had got the second question right. Five students said they got both questions wrong. A student is selected at random from the class. What is the probability that the student:

   (i)   Got both questions right

   (ii) Got only Question 2 right

   (iii) Got at least one question right

3.9 OR / AND: SINGLE EVENT

In many cases, probability deals with a single event where one outcome **OR** another outcome is desirable. Another type of probability case is that in a single event one outcome **AND** another is desirable.

We can use set theory, sample spaces and counting outcomes to help explain what happens in these cases.

'OR' Events

Worked Example 3.17

What is the probability of getting a King **OR** a Queen when selecting a single playing card from a normal deck?

Solution: Using a Venn Diagram

Let #U be the number of cards in a normal deck of cards.

Let #K be the number of Kings in a normal deck of cards.

Let #Q be the number of Queens in a normal deck of cards.

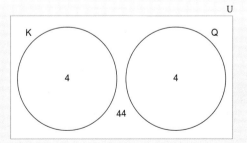

From the Venn diagram the Set K has 4 elements and the Set Q has 4 elements.

The number of Kings or Queens is $\#(K \cup Q) = 8$.

The probability of getting a King or Queen when selecting a playing card $= \frac{8}{52} = \frac{2}{13}$.

Solution: Using Sample Space Diagrams

We can list all the cards in a normal deck.

We remember that we looking for a King or a Queen, which in set theory means we are selecting either a King or a Queen, so we highlight both types of cards.

♥ Heart	♦ Diamond	♣ Club	♠ Spade
Ace	Ace	Ace	Ace
King	King	King	King
Queen	Queen	Queen	Queen
Jack	Jack	Jack	Jack
10	10	10	10
9	9	9	9
8	8	8	8
7	7	7	7
6	6	6	6
5	5	5	5
4	4	4	4
3	3	3	3
2	2	2	2

We have highlighted eight cards out of a possible 52.

The probability of getting a King or Queen when selecting a playing card $= \frac{8}{52} = \frac{2}{13}$.

Solution: By Counting Outcomes

Possibly the easiest way is to count the number of outcomes that would give us a King or a Queen.

- King: 4 outcomes
- Queen: 4 outcomes

The total number of desirable outcomes is 8.

The total number of possible outcomes is 52.

The probability of getting a King or a Queen when selecting a playing card $= \frac{8}{52} = \frac{2}{13}$.

> From this example, it is clear that, when dealing with OR events, we add.

> Of course, we may deal with problems that are not mutually exclusive, i.e. they have events in common.

Worked Example 3.18

What is the probability of getting a King or a Club when selecting a single playing card from a normal deck?

Solution: Using a Venn Diagram

Let #U be the number of cards in a normal pack of cards.

Let #K be the number of Kings in a normal deck of cards.

Let #C be the number of Clubs in a normal pack of cards.

We must pay particular attention to the intersection, as we have one card that is a King of Clubs. We must not count this card twice (this is referred to as double counting).

From the Venn diagram, the number of Kings or Clubs is $\#(K \cup C) = 16$.

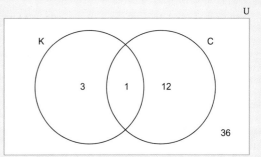

The probability of getting a King or a Club when selecting a playing card $= \frac{16}{52} = \frac{4}{13}$.

Solution: Using Sample Space Diagrams

We can list all the cards in a normal deck.

Remember that we are looking for a King or a Club, which in set theory means we are selecting either a King or a Club, so we highlight both types of cards.

♥ Heart	♦ Diamond	♣ Club	♠ Spade
Ace	Ace	Ace	Ace
King	King	King	King
Queen	Queen	Queen	Queen
Jack	Jack	Jack	Jack
10	10	10	10
9	9	9	9
8	8	8	8
7	7	7	7
6	6	6	6
5	5	5	5
4	4	4	4
3	3	3	3
2	2	2	2

We have highlighted 16 cards out of a possible 52.

The probability of getting a King or a Club when selecting a playing card $= \frac{16}{52} = \frac{4}{13}$.

Solution: By Counting Outcomes

We can count the number of outcomes that would give us a King or a Club.

- King: 4 outcomes
- Club: 13 outcomes
- King of Clubs: 1 outcome (we must subtract this from our total so as not to double count)

The total number of desirable outcomes is 16 [13 Clubs + 4 Kings – 1 King of Clubs].
The total number of possible outcomes is 52.
The probability of getting a King or a Club when selecting a playing card $= \frac{16}{52} = \frac{4}{13}$.

'AND' Events

 Worked Example 3.19

What is the probability of getting a King **AND** a Queen when selecting a single playing card?

Solution

These are mutually exclusive events. There is no single card that is both a King and a Queen.
Therefore, the probability of selecting a single card that is a King and a Queen is 0.

Worked Example 3.20

What is the probability of getting a card that is a King **AND** a Heart when selecting a single playing card from a normal deck?

These are not mutually exclusive events.

Solution: Using a Venn Diagram

Let #U be the number of cards in a normal deck of cards.

Let #K be the number of Kings in a normal deck of cards.

Let #H be the number of Hearts in a normal deck of cards.

We must pay particular attention to the intersection, as this is the outcome we are interested in.

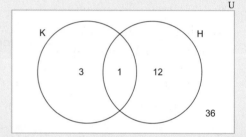

From the Venn diagram, the number of cards that are Kings and Hearts is $\#(K \cap H) = 1$.

The probability of getting a King and a Heart when selecting a single playing card $= \frac{1}{52}$.

Solution: Using Sample Space Diagrams

We can list all the cards in a normal deck.

Remember that we are looking for a single playing card that is both a King and a Heart.

♥ Heart	♦ Diamond	♣ Club	♠ Spade
Ace	Ace	Ace	Ace
King	King	King	King
Queen	Queen	Queen	Queen
Jack	Jack	Jack	Jack
10	10	10	10
9	9	9	9
8	8	8	8
7	7	7	7
6	6	6	6
5	5	5	5
4	4	4	4
3	3	3	3
2	2	2	2

PROBABILITY

We have highlighted one card out of a possible 52.

The probability of getting a King and a Heart when selecting a single playing card $= \frac{1}{52}$.

Solution: By Counting Outcomes

It is probably easier if we can count the number of outcomes that would give us a King and a Heart, which is one outcome – the King of Hearts.

The total number of desirable outcomes is 1.

The total number of possible outcomes is 52.

The probability of getting a King and a Heart when selecting a single playing card $= \frac{1}{52}$.

> The four suits – Spades, Hearts, Diamonds and Clubs – originated in France in the 15th century. The standard deck we use is called a French deck. However, the history of card playing can be traced back to 10th-century Asia.

 ACTIVITIES 3.13, 3.14

 Exercise 3.7

1. A bag contains one red token, four blue tokens and five yellow tokens.

   A token is taken out of the bag at random. What is the probability that it is:

   (i) Red   (iii) Yellow   (v) Blue or yellow

   (ii) Blue   (iv) Red or blue   (vi) Red or yellow

2. In a pencil case there are a number of pens: one red, three blue, two black and one green. If a student picks a pen at random, find the probability that the pen is:

   (i) A blue pen

   (ii) A red pen

   (iii) A red or a blue pen

   (iv) A green or black pen

   (v) Not a green or a black pen

3. A spinner with nine equal sectors as shown is spun once.

   What is the probability that the spinner lands on:

   (i) 1

   (ii) 1 or 4

   (iii) Not 1 or 4

   (iv) A prime number

   (v) A prime number or an even number

4. A fair six-sided die is rolled once. What is the probability that you obtain:

   (i) 3

   (ii) 3 or 5

   (iii) An even number

   (iv) An even number or an odd number

   (v) A number that is prime and even

   (vi) 1, 2, 3 or 4

   (vii) An number that is even and divisible by 6

5. A single card is selected at random from a normal pack of playing cards. What is the probability that the card selected is:

   (i) Red

   (ii) Red or black

   (iii) A Jack and red

   (iv) A Jack and not red

   (v) A King or a Spade

   (vi) An Ace or numbered

PROBABILITY

6. A spinner with 20 equal sectors numbered 1–20 is spun. What is the probability that it lands on:

(i) 5 or 11

(ii) 12 or an odd number

(iii) A single-digit number or an even number

(iv) A single-digit number and an even number

(v) A prime number or a number greater than 15

(vi) A prime number and a number greater than 15

(vii) An number that is even and divisible by 6

7. A bag contains 20 red marbles, three blue marbles and two white marbles. A marble is taken from the bag at random. What is the probability that this marble will be:

(i) White

(ii) Blue

(iii) White or blue

(iv) Red or white

(v) Not red or white

8. The following coins are in a money box: two 5c coins, ten 20c coins, five €1 coins and three €2 coins. A single coin is taken at random from the box. What is the probability that it is:

(i) A 5c coin

(ii) A 20c or 5c coin

(iii) A €2 or €1 coin

(iv) Not a €2 or €1 coin

3.10 COMBINED EVENTS

When dealing with more complicated questions involving probability, it can be advisable to use a two-way table or a tree diagram. This is especially the case when dealing with the probability of **combined events** that are equally likely to occur.

> A **combined event** is where two or more experiments occur and their outcomes are combined together.

 ## Worked Example 3.21

Two fair dice are thrown and the scores are added together.
Draw a two-way table to show all possible outcomes.
Find the probability that the sum of the scores on the two dice is:

(i) 7

(ii) Less than 5

(iii) 5 or greater

(iv) Even **OR** divisible by 3

(v) Even **AND** divisible by 3

Solution

We must first draw a two-way table (or sample space diagram) to show all the outcomes.
Put the outcomes of the first die along the side.
Put the outcomes of the second die along the top.

Find all possible outcomes by adding the two scores, e.g. 6 + 5 = 11.

		Second die					
		1	**2**	**3**	**4**	**5**	**6**
First die	**1**	2	3	4	5	6	7
	2	3	4	5	6	7	8
	3	4	5	6	7	8	9
	4	5	6	7	8	9	10
	5	6	7	8	9	10	11
	6	7	8	9	10	11	12

We then count the total number of possible outcomes, which in this case is 36.

(i) Probability of a score of 7

A total of six outcomes add up to 7 (coloured green).

		Second die					
		1	**2**	**3**	**4**	**5**	**6**
First die	**1**	2	3	4	5	6	7
	2	3	4	5	6	7	8
	3	4	5	6	7	8	9
	4	5	6	7	8	9	10
	5	6	7	8	9	10	11
	6	7	8	9	10	11	12

The probability of a score of 7

$$= \frac{\text{number of outcomes that total 7}}{\text{total number of possible outcomes}} = \frac{6}{36} = \frac{1}{6}.$$

(ii) Probability of a score less than 5

A total of six outcomes are of a score less than 5 (coloured red).

		Second die					
		1	**2**	**3**	**4**	**5**	**6**
First die	**1**	2	3	4	5	6	7
	2	3	4	5	6	7	8
	3	4	5	6	7	8	9
	4	5	6	7	8	9	10
	5	6	7	8	9	10	11
	6	7	8	9	10	11	12

The probability of a score less than 5

$$= \frac{\text{number of outcomes that are less than 5}}{\text{total number of possible outcomes}}$$

$$= \frac{6}{36} = \frac{1}{6}.$$

(iii) Probability of a score of 5 or greater

Six outcomes are less than 5 and there are 36 possible outcomes. Therefore, the number of outcomes that will give us a score of 5 or greater is 36 − 6 = 30.

The probability of a score of 5 or greater

$$= \frac{30}{36} = \frac{5}{6}.$$

(Alternatively, we could count the outcomes in the two-way table.)

(iv) Probability of a score that is even **OR** divisible by 3

A total of 24 outcomes are either even or divisible by 3 (coloured orange).

		Second die					
		1	**2**	**3**	**4**	**5**	**6**
First die	**1**	2	3	4	5	6	7
	2	3	4	5	6	7	8
	3	4	5	6	7	8	9
	4	5	6	7	8	9	10
	5	6	7	8	9	10	11
	6	7	8	9	10	11	12

The probability of score that is even or divisible by 3

$$= \frac{\text{number of outcomes that even or divisible by 3}}{\text{total number of possible outcomes}}$$

$$= \frac{24}{36} = \frac{2}{3}.$$

(v) Probability of a score that is even **AND** divisible by 3

A total of six outcomes are even and divisible by 3 (coloured blue).

		Second die					
		1	**2**	**3**	**4**	**5**	**6**
First die	**1**	2	3	4	5	6	7
	2	3	4	5	6	7	8
	3	4	5	6	7	8	9
	4	5	6	7	8	9	10
	5	6	7	8	9	10	11
	6	7	8	9	10	11	12

The probability of score that is even and divisible by 3

$$= \frac{\text{number of outcomes that even and divisible by 3}}{\text{total number of possible outcomes}}$$

$$= \frac{6}{36} = \frac{1}{6}.$$

Worked Example 3.22

A spinner as shown is spun three times. Using a tree diagram, determine the probability of the spinner landing on:

(i) Three red sectors

(ii) A red sector followed by two green sectors

(iii) A red and two green sectors in any order

(iv) At least one green sector

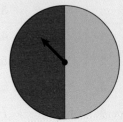

Solution

We first draw a tree diagram to show all our outcomes.
We can count that there are eight possible outcomes.

1st Spin	2nd Spin	3rd Spin	Outcome
		G	G, G, G
	G	R	G, G, R
G		G	G, R, G
	R	R	G, R, R
		G	R, G, G
R	G	R	R, G, R
	R	G	R, R, G
		R	R, R, R

(i) Probability of getting three red sectors

Red, Red, Red appears only once as an outcome:

$P(R, R, R) = \frac{1}{8}$

(ii) Probability of a red sector followed by two green sectors

Red, Green, Green appears only once as an outcome:

$P(R, G, G) = \frac{1}{8}$

(iii) Probability of a red and two green sectors in any order

We count how many times Red, Green, Green appears in the outcomes, ignoring order. There are three outcomes out of eight in which this occurs:

$P(R, G, G$ in any order$) = \frac{3}{8}$

(iv) Probability of at least one green sector

'At least one' means that we are looking for one or more of the required outcomes.

We count how many outcomes have one or more Green in them:

$P($at least one $G) = \frac{7}{8}$

Alternatively, this could have been found as:

$P($at least one Green$) = 1 - P($no Green$)$
$= 1 - P($all Red$)$
$= 1 - \frac{1}{8}$
$= \frac{7}{8}$

FORMULA

Probability of getting at least one required outcome = 1 – Probability of not getting that outcome.

 **ACTIVITIES 3.15, 3.16, 3.17**

PROBABILITY

Exercise 3.8

1. A fair coin is flipped and a fair die is rolled. Use a two-way table to show all possible outcomes.

		Die					
		1	**2**	**3**	**4**	**5**	**6**
Coin	**H**		H2				
	T					T5	

What is the probability of getting:

(i) A head and a 1

(ii) A tail and an even number

(iii) A head and an even number

(iv) A head or an even number

2. A spinner as shown is spun three times. Use a tree diagram to show all possible outcomes.

What is the probability that:

(i) The spinner lands on red three times.

(ii) The spinner lands on green, blue and red in that order.

(iii) The spinner lands on green, blue and red in any order.

(iv) The spinner doesn't land on red.

(v) The spinner lands on red only once.

3. A die is rolled twice. Complete the following two-way table:

		Second die					
		1	**2**	**3**	**4**	**5**	**6**
First die	**1**	(1, 1)					
	2						
	3					(3, 5)	
	4			(4, 3)			
	5						
	6						

What is the probability that:

(i) An even number is obtained on both rolls of the die.

(ii) An odd number is obtained on both rolls of the die.

(iii) The same number is obtained on both rolls of the die.

(iv) A different number is obtained on both rolls of the die.

4. Two dice, one coloured red and the other black, are thrown. The score from the red die is added to the score from the black die. Use a two-way table to show all the possible outcomes.

		Black die					
		1	**2**	**3**	**4**	**5**	**6**
Red die	**1**	2					
	2						
	3						
	4						
	5					10	
	6		8				

What is the probability that the score on the two dice will add up to:

(i) 5

(ii) An even number

(iii) A number divisible by 5 or even

(iv) A number that is greater than 10 and odd

5. A game is played with a spinner with four quarters labelled A, B, C and D. The spinner is spun twice and a point is scored if the spinner lands on the same letter twice. Complete the following two-way table to show all possible outcomes:

		Second spin			
		A	**B**	**C**	**D**
First spin	**A**	AA			
	B			BC	
	C				
	D				

Find the probability that:

(i) The spinner lands on the same letter twice.

(ii) A point will not be scored.

6. Two dice are thrown. The score on the second die is subtracted from the score on the first die. Complete the following two-way table:

		Second die					
		1	2	3	4	5	6
First die	**1**	0					
	2	1		−1			
	3					−2	
	4						
	5						
	6						

Find the probability that the final score on the two dice is:

(i) 1

(ii) A negative number

(iii) An integer

(iv) A positive whole number

(v) A number greater than 5

7. In a year of 100 students, each student studies one of the following subjects: art, biology or technical graphics.

(a) Complete the following two-way table:

	Art	Biology	Tech. graphics	Total
Boy		12		33
Girl			15	
Total	30		23	

(b) A student is selected at random. What is the probability that the student:

(i) Is a boy

(ii) Studies art

(iii) Is a girl studying biology

(iv) Does not study biology

A girl is selected at random. What is the probability that she:

(v) Studies art

(vi) Does not study technical graphics

8. A four-sided die and a six-sided die are rolled. The outcomes for the first die are 1, 2, 3 or 4. The outcomes for the second die can be 1, 2, 3, 4, 5 or 6. After rolling the dice, a student calculates the product of the two outcomes (by multiplying them). Complete the following table, by working out the products each time:

		Second die					
		1	2	3	4	5	6
First die	**1**	1					
	2		4				
	3					15	
	4						

What is the probability that the product of the outcomes will be:

(i) Even

(ii) A prime number

(iii) Odd and a prime number

(iv) Divisible by both 2 and 5

(v) Less than 7 and even

9. A spinner has four equal sectors numbered 10, 11, 12, 13. Another spinner has three equal sectors numbered 3, 4, 5. Draw a two-way table for the outcomes when both spinners are spun together and their scores multiplied.

What is the probability of obtaining:

(i) The maximum score

(ii) An even score

(iii) A number greater than 60

(iv) A prime number

(v) A number greater than 5

10. An unbiased coin is flipped three times. Use a tree diagram to list all the possible outcomes. Find the probability that:

(i) The coin will land on a tail three times.

(ii) The coin will land on a tail exactly twice.

(iii) The coin will land on a tail at least twice.

(iv) The coin will not land on a tail.

11. The blood groups of 150 patients in a hospital are as follows:

- Twenty patients have blood group A.
- Twenty-five female patients have blood group B.
- Thirty male patients have blood group O.

$\frac{4}{5}$ of all patients with blood group A are women.

There are a total of 60 male patients in the hospital.

(a) Complete the following table:

	A	B	O	Total
Male				
Female				
Total				

(b) A patient is selected at random. What is the probability that this patient:

   (i) Belongs to blood group A

   (ii) Belongs to blood group B or O

   (iii) Is male and belongs to blood group B

   (iv) Is female and belongs to blood group A or B

A male patient is selected at random. What is the probability that this patient:

   (v) Belongs to blood group O

A female patient is selected at random. What is the probability that this patient:

   (vi) Does not belong to blood group O

12. A fair die is rolled and a fair coloured spinner is spun. The die is numbered 1, 1, 2, 2, 2, 6 and the spinner has three equal sectors of green, white and orange as shown.

(a) Draw a two-way table to show all possible outcomes.

(b) What is the probability of getting:

   (i) 1 and any colour

   (ii) An even number and orange colour

   (iii) An odd number and white colour

13. Two fair dice are rolled. A score is calculated by recording the larger of the two numbers and ignoring the smaller number. If the numbers are the same, a score of 0 is recorded.

   (i) Draw a two-way table to show all possible outcomes.

   (ii) What is the most likely outcome?

   (iii) What is the least likely outcome?

   (iv) What is the probability of getting a score of 5?

   (v) What is the probability of getting a score of 3?

14. A table-tennis tournament has eight players taking part. There are two groups. Alan, Barbara, Claire and Declan are in Group 1. Eric, Fred, Gerry and Holly are in Group 2. Every player has an equal chance of winning their group. The winner from each group plays in the final.

   (i) Draw a two-way table to show the possible outcomes for the final.

   (ii) What is the probability that Alan plays Holly in the final?

   (iii) What is the probability that Fred does not play in the final?

   (iv) What is the probability that Gerry plays in the final?

   (v) What is the probability that Gerry or Holly play in the final?

15. A library does a survey of all its books out on loan on a particular day. For the purpose of the survey, it divides its books into the following categories: fiction, non-fiction or children's books, and hardback or paperback books.

The survey showed that on that particular day:

- 1,250 books were out on loan.

- 56% of all books on loan were paperback.

- $\frac{3}{5}$ of the paperback books on loan were fiction.

  This was $\frac{2}{3}$ of the total number of fiction books out on loan for that day.

- $\frac{1}{5}$ of all hardback books on loan were in the children's category.

- A total of 200 non-fiction paperback books were out on loan.

(a) Complete the following table:

	Hardback	Paperback	Totals
Fiction			
Non-fiction			
Children's books			
Total			

(b) A library record for a book on loan is chosen at random.

Calculate the probability that the book chosen is:

(i) Non-fiction

(ii) Hardback

(iii) Children's paperback

(iv) Fiction hardback or non-fiction paperback

(c) How many of the first 300 books taken out on loan the following day would you expect to be non-fiction paperbacks?

3.11 AND/OR: MULTIPLE EVENTS

When finding the probability of two or more events, we may not wish to, or be able to, use a two-way table to find the probability.

 ## Worked Example 3.23

A fair six-sided die is rolled twice.
What is the probability that a score of 1 will show on the die both times?

Solution

It is important to think of this as getting a 1 on the first roll AND getting a 1 on the second roll.

The probability of getting a 1 on the first roll is $\frac{1}{6}$.

The probability of getting a 1 on the second roll is also $\frac{1}{6}$.

We know from the fundamental principle of counting that we multiply when we encounter the word AND.

First roll **Second roll**

P(1) P(1)

$\frac{1}{6}$ × $\frac{1}{6}$ = $\frac{1}{36}$

These types of events are called **independent events**. The score on the second roll is not affected by the score on the first roll.

> **Independent events** are events in which the outcome of the first event does not affect the outcome of the second event.

Worked Example 3.24

A bag contains 15 marbles: six blue marbles and nine yellow marbles. A player picks a marble at random out of the bag, its colour is noted and the marble is returned to the bag. Another marble is then picked at random.
Find the probability of getting:

(i)   Two blue marbles

(ii) A blue marble and then a yellow marble

(iii) A blue marble and a yellow marble in any order

(iv) At least one blue marble

(v)   Two marbles that are both the same colour

Solution

> After each event, the marble is returned. This means that the outcome of the first event does not affect the outcome of the second event. These are referred to as **independent events**. Therefore, the probability of picking a certain marble for each event will not change.

We draw our tree diagram with blue and yellow as our two outcomes.

1st pick	2nd pick	Outcome
B	B	B, B
	Y	B, Y
Y	B	Y, B
	Y	Y, Y

We next fill in our probabilities for the two events on the tree diagram and multiply the two events to find the probability for each branch. We are looking for the probability of getting one marble AND another marble.

A blue marble → $\frac{6}{15} = \frac{2}{5}$ or 0.4

A yellow marble → $\frac{9}{15} = \frac{3}{5}$ or 0.6

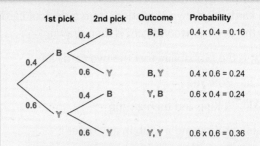

1st pick	2nd pick	Outcome	Probability
0.4 B	0.4 B	B, B	0.4 × 0.4 = 0.16
	0.6 Y	B, Y	0.4 × 0.6 = 0.24
0.6 Y	0.4 B	Y, B	0.6 × 0.4 = 0.24
	0.6 Y	Y, Y	0.6 × 0.6 = 0.36

> Notice that 0.16 + 0.24 + 0.24 + 0.36 = 1.

Find the probability of getting:

(i)   Two blue marbles

$P(B, B) = 0.4 \times 0.4 = 0.16$

(ii) A blue marble and then a yellow marble

$P(B, Y) = 0.4 \times 0.6 = 0.24$

(iii) A blue marble and a yellow marble in any order

This means we could have Blue, Yellow OR Yellow, Blue as our outcomes:

$P(B, Y)$ or $P(Y, B) = (0.4 \times 0.6) + (0.6 \times 0.4)$

$= 0.24 + 0.24 = 0.48$

> Remember that OR means to add.

(iv) At least one blue marble (one OR more blue marbles)

We add the probabilities of the outcomes that have one or more blue marbles:

B, B	B, Y	Y, B		
0.16	+ 0.24	+ 0.24	=	0.64

We could also use the other method:

1− P(none blue)

$= 1 - P(\text{both yellow}) = 1 - 0.36 = 0.64$

(v)   Both marbles the same colour

The marbles picked could be Blue, Blue OR Yellow, Yellow:

B, B	Y, Y		
0.16	+ 0.36	=	0.52

Sometimes it can be a good idea to use a tree diagram.

Sometimes a tree diagram is not required or is not the best method to use.

 Worked Example 3.25

Two cards are drawn at random from a deck of cards. The first card is drawn, recorded and replaced back into the deck. A second card is then drawn.

What is the probability that the two cards are:

   (i) Both red

   (ii) A King and then a Club

   (iii) A King and a Club in any order

Solution

   (i) Both red

      This means that the first card is red (26 outcomes out of 52) and the second card is red (26 outcomes out of 52).

First card		Second card	
Red		Red	
$\dfrac{26}{52}$	$\times$	$\dfrac{26}{52}$	$= \dfrac{1}{4}$

   (ii) A King and then a Club

      This means that the first card is a King (four outcomes out of 52) and the second card is a Club (13 outcomes out of 52).

First card		Second card	
King		Club	
$\dfrac{4}{52}$	$\times$	$\dfrac{13}{52}$	$= \dfrac{1}{52}$

   (iii) A King and a Club in any order

      This means that the cards drawn could have been a King followed by a Club or a Club followed by a King.

King	AND	Club	OR	Club	AND	King
$\dfrac{4}{52}$	$\times$	$\dfrac{13}{52}$	$+$	$\dfrac{13}{52}$	$\times$	$\dfrac{4}{52}$
$\dfrac{1}{52}$			$+$			$\dfrac{1}{52}$

$$= \frac{2}{52} = \frac{1}{26}$$

We may also come across questions that involve **dependent events**.

Generally, this means that the number of possible outcomes is one less for the second event. We can spot these type of events, as replacement does not occur.

> **Dependent events** are events in which the second event is affected by the first event.

PROBABILITY

Worked Example 3.26

A bag contains three red tokens and five white tokens. A token is drawn at random from the bag **but not replaced**. Another token is then drawn from the bag. Find the probability that:

  (i)   Both tokens are red.

  (ii) The first token is red and the second token is white.

  (iii) One token is red and the other token is white.

Solution

  (i) Both tokens are red

  This means that the first token picked is red (three outcomes out of eight) and then the second token picked is red as well.

  It is now that the issue of non-replacement arises. As a token has been removed, there are seven tokens to choose from in the second pick. There are now two red tokens left.

First token		Second token	
P(Red)		P(Red)	
$\dfrac{3}{8}$	×	$\dfrac{2}{7}$	$= \dfrac{3}{28}$

  (ii) The first token is red and the second token is white

  This means that the first token picked is red (three outcomes out of eight), and then the second token picked is white (five outcomes out of seven).

First token		Second token	
P(Red)		P(White)	
$\dfrac{3}{8}$	×	$\dfrac{5}{7}$	$= \dfrac{15}{56}$

  (iii) One token is red and the other token is white

  The possibilities are Red followed by White OR White followed by Red.

Red	AND	White	OR	White	AND	Red
$\dfrac{3}{8}$	×	$\dfrac{5}{7}$	+	$\dfrac{5}{8}$	×	$\dfrac{3}{7}$
$= \dfrac{15}{56}$			+			$\dfrac{15}{56}$

$$= \frac{30}{56} = \frac{15}{28}$$

ACTIVITIES 3.18, 3.19

 Exercise 3.9

1. A bag contains 12 blue balls and five white balls. A student picks a ball at random out of the bag. She then returns the ball to the bag and picks another ball at random. What is the probability that she picks a blue ball on her first pick and a white ball on her second pick?

2. A fair spinner numbered 1–10 is spun three times.
   What is the probability that it lands on a 3 each time?

PROBABILITY

3. An urn contains 10 red tokens and 12 green tokens. A token is selected at random and its colour is noted. It is then replaced and another token is selected and its colour is noted.

Find the probability of:

(i) Picking two red tokens

(ii) Picking a red token and then a green token

(iii) Picking a red and a green token in any order

4. A white die and a black die are thrown. Find the probability of getting:

(i) 2 on the white die and 4 on the black die

(ii) 2 on the white die and any number on the black die

(iii) An even number on the white die and an odd number on the black die

5. The probability that Lucy scores a penalty in a camogie game is $\frac{4}{5}$. During a match, she takes two penalties. Find the probability that:

(i) She scores both penalties.

(ii) She misses both penalties.

(iii) She scores at least one penalty.

6. A bag contains 10 red tokens and eight black tokens. A token is picked at random from the bag and then returned. A second token is then picked at random.
What is the probability of picking:

(i) A black token followed by a red token

(ii) A red token followed by a black token

(iii) Two red tokens

(iv) Two tokens of the same colour

7. A bag contains twenty €1 coins and thirteen €2 coins. A coin is taken at random from the bag and then put back. A second coin is then taken out. What is the probability of selecting:

(i) Two €1 coins

(ii) Two €2 coins

(iii) Two coins of the same value

(iv) Two coins of different value

8. A student plays two snooker matches. The probability that he wins the first match is 0.35 and the probability of winning the second match is 0.25.
What is the probability that he:

(i) Wins the first match and loses the second match

(ii) Loses the first match and wins the second match

(iii) Wins one match and loses another match

(iv) Wins at least one match

9. The spinner shown is spun twice.

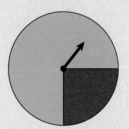

Find the probability that:

(i) The spinner will land on red both times.

(ii) The spinner lands first on red and then on green.

(iii) The spinner lands on red and green in any order.

10. Two people are chosen at random and say in what month their birthday lies. Taking each month as equally likely, find the probability that:

(i) Both were born in December.

(ii) Both were born in the same month.

(iii) They were not born in the same month.

11. A family has nine children: four girls and five boys. A child is chosen at random to do the washing up. Another child is chosen at random from the remaining group to do the drying. Find the probability that:

(i) Both are boys.

(ii) Both are girls.

(iii) At least one is a boy.

12. Two cards are drawn at random from a pack of cards. The first card is removed and recorded but not replaced. A second card is then removed. What is the probability that the two cards are:

  (i)   Both red

  (ii) Both Spades

  (iii) A Queen and then a King

  (iv) A Queen and a King

13. A bag contains five blue and seven yellow marbles. A marble is drawn at random from the bag but is not replaced. Another marble is then drawn from the bag.
Find the probability that:

  (i)   The marbles drawn are both blue.

  (ii) The marbles drawn are both yellow.

  (iii) The first marble is blue and the second marble is yellow.

  (iv) One marble is blue and the other marble is yellow.

  (v)   Both marbles are the same colour.

  (vi) At least one of the marbles is blue.

3.12 BERNOULLI TRIALS

In real life, we deal with many examples where we are interested only in the probability of two outcomes: success or failure. An example would be passing or failing a driving test.

When dealing with experiments whose outcomes are random and have two possible outcomes – success or failure – we are dealing with a type of trial called a **Bernoulli trial**.

The properties of a Bernoulli trial are:

  ■ Two possible outcomes: success or failure, hit or miss, yes or no.

  ■ The trials are independent of each other. The outcome of one trial has no effect on the outcome of another trial.

  ■ The probability of success or failure does not change from one trial to another.

Examples of Bernoulli trials include:

  ■ Flipping a coin where getting a tails is a success

  ■ Rolling a die where it landing on a 3 is a success

 Worked Example 3.27

In a game, a die is rolled. To win, a player must score a 3.
What is the probability that a player first gets a 3 on the second roll?

Solution

In this case, the player must fail on the first throw of the die and then get a 3 on the second throw.

We first draw our tree diagram as normal, noting that there are two possible outcomes that we are interested in:

Rolling a 3 (Success)   or   Not rolling a 3 (Failure).

We next fill in the probability of the two events on the tree diagram at every branch where these events occur.

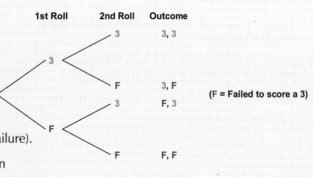

Success: Rolled a 3 → $\frac{1}{6}$

Failure: Did not roll a 3 → $\frac{5}{6}$

The outcome we are looking for is F, 3
(Failed to roll a three, Succeeded in rolling a 3).

We follow the branches of the tree diagram,
noting the probabilities from the start to the
desired outcome:

$$P(F, 3) = \frac{5}{6} \times \frac{1}{6} = \frac{5}{36}$$

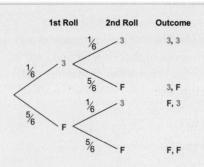

1st Roll	2nd Roll	Outcome
	$\frac{1}{6}$ → 3	3, 3
$\frac{1}{6}$ → 3		
	$\frac{5}{6}$ → F	3, F
	$\frac{1}{6}$ → 3	F, 3
$\frac{5}{6}$ → F		
	$\frac{5}{6}$ → F	F, F

ACTIVITY 3.20

Worked Example 3.28

A car drives through three sets of traffic lights. The probability of the traffic lights showing a red light is $\frac{1}{5}$.
What is the probability that the car will **first stop** at a red light at the:

    (i) First light   (ii) Second light   (iii) Third light

Solution

We fill in our probabilities for the two events:

Success or Red (R): A red traffic light → $\frac{1}{5}$

Failure or Not red (F): $1 - \frac{1}{5} = \frac{4}{5}$

    (i) First light (R)

        We are looking for a Red as an outcome.

        The probability of stopping at the first
        light = $\frac{1}{5}$.

    (ii) Second light (F, R)

        The desired outcome is Not red, Red.

        $P(F, R) = \frac{4}{5} \times \frac{1}{5} = \frac{4}{25}$

    (iii) Third light (F, F, R)

        The desired outcome is Not red, Not red,
        Red.

        $P(F, F, R) = \frac{4}{5} \times \frac{4}{5} \times \frac{1}{5} = \frac{16}{125}$

Worked Example 3.29

A game is played with 10 marbles in a bag: seven
blue marbles and three yellow marbles.

A player picks a marble at random out of the bag.
If a yellow marble is picked, the player wins the
game. If a blue marble is picked, it is returned to
the bag (replaced) and the player tries again.

What is the probability, in percentages, that the
player wins the game on the:

    (i) Second go   (ii) Third go

Solution

The probability of picking a certain marble for
each event will not change.

We must now recognise what has happened if we
win on the:

    (i) Second go

        For the player to win on their second
        go, they must have picked a blue marble
        first. The outcome we are looking for is
        Blue, Yellow (B, Y).

(ii) **Third go**

For the player to win on the third go, they must have picked a blue marble on their first and second go. The outcome we are looking for is Blue, Blue, Yellow (B, B, Y).

We next calculate our probabilities for the two events:

A blue marble $\rightarrow \frac{7}{10}$ or 0.7

A yellow marble $\rightarrow \frac{3}{10}$ or 0.3

(i) Second go (B, Y)

$P(B, Y) = 0.7 \times 0.3 = 0.21$ or 21%

(ii) Third go (B, B, Y)

$P(B, B, Y) = 0.7 \times 0.7 \times 0.3$
$= 0.147$ or 14.7%

 ACTIVITY 3.21

 Exercise 3.10

1. A coin is flipped three times.
What is the probability that it lands on heads for the first time on the third flip?

2. The probability that an Olympic archer hits a bullseye is 0.6. What is the probability that she hits the target for the first time on her third arrow?

3. A spinner with equal sectors numbered 1 to 10 is spun twice. What is the probability that:

    (i) It lands on an even number both times.

    (ii) It lands on an odd number first and then on an even number.

4. A coin is flipped three times. A player wins if the coin lands on a tail. What is the probability that the player wins for the first time on the:

    (i) First flip

    (ii) Second flip

    (iii) Third flip

    What is the probability that the player doesn't win?

5. A fair die is rolled up to three times. A player wins if a roll of 5 is scored. What is the probability that the player wins on the:

    (i) First turn

    (ii) Second turn

    (iii) Third turn

    What is the probability that the player doesn't win?

6. The probability that Liam will be on time for school on any given day is 0.85.

    (i) What is the probability that he will be late for school?

    What is the probability that Liam will be late for the first time on:

    (ii) The second day

    (iii) The third day

7. A game is played with a deck of cards. A card is picked at random from the deck, recorded and then put back into the deck. The game is won when a player picks an Ace card. What is the probability that the player wins on the:

    (i) First card

    (ii) Second card

    (iii) Third card

    What is the probability that the player doesn't win?

8. A spinner with equal sectors numbered 1 to 5 is spun. What is the probability that it lands on an odd number for the first time on the:

    (i) First spin

    (ii) Second spin

    (iii) Third spin

PROBABILITY

3

9. A game is played with an unfair coin. The coin is biased so that the probability of getting heads is 0.8 and the probability of getting tails is 0.2. The game is won if the player gets two tails.
   What is the probability of winning the game on the third flip of the coin?

10. A bag contains four balls: three yellow balls and one orange ball. A ball is taken from the bag at random, its colour is noted and it is then replaced. If an orange ball is picked, the person wins a prize. What is the probability that a prize is first won:

    (i) On the second go   (ii) On the third go

    Five more yellow and two more orange balls are added. Does a person have a better chance of winning a prize now? Explain your answer.

3.13 EXPECTED VALUE

In many cases, it can be useful to calculate the average or mean outcome of an experiment.
This is referred to as **expected value**.

> The **expected value**, E(X), is the average outcome of an experiment.

To calculate the expected value, we multiply every possible outcome by the probability for that outcome occurring and then add these values together.
The table below shows expected value of a die roll:

Outcome		Probability		
1	×	$\frac{1}{6}$	=	$\frac{1}{6}$
2	×	$\frac{1}{6}$	=	$\frac{2}{6}$
3	×	$\frac{1}{6}$	=	$\frac{3}{6}$
4	×	$\frac{1}{6}$	=	$\frac{4}{6}$
5	×	$\frac{1}{6}$	=	$\frac{5}{6}$
6	×	$\frac{1}{6}$	=	$\frac{6}{6}$

Adding these values together gives us the expected value E(X):

$$E(X) = \frac{1}{6} + \frac{2}{6} + \frac{3}{6} + \frac{4}{6} + \frac{5}{6} + \frac{6}{6} = 3.5$$

> The expected value does not have to be an actual outcome.

FORMULA

$$E(X) = \sum x \cdot P(x)$$

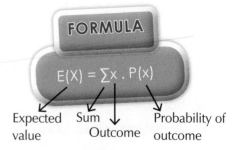

Expected value   Sum   Outcome   Probability of outcome

The expected value of a die roll is 3.5. Consider playing a game where each roll of the die paid out that value in euro (for example, if a 2 is rolled then €2 is won). We would expect to win (on average) €3.50 per game.

We can use expected value to determine whether an experiment is fair or not and whether a bet is good or bad value.

In general:

If the expected value > 0, we would expect to gain that amount.

If the expected value of a game is €10, then we would expect to win €10 per game on average.

If the expected value = 0, the game is fair. We are equally likely to win or lose.

If the expected value of a game is €0, then we would expect to win €0 per game on average.

If the expected value < 0, we would expect to lose that amount.

If the expected value of a game is –€3, then we would expect to lose €3 per game on average.

Worked Example 3.30

The spinner shown is used to play a game.

The game costs €5 to play. A player wins whatever amount the spinner lands on.

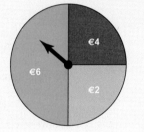

   (i)   Calculate the expected value.

   (ii) Would you advise a person to play this game? Justify your answer.

Solution

We fill in the following table.

   (i)   Calculate the expected value:

Outcome		Probability		
€4	×	$\frac{1}{4}$	=	€1
€6	×	$\frac{1}{2}$	=	€3
€2	×	$\frac{1}{4}$	=	€0.50
			Total	€4.50

We must now include the fact that the game costs €5 to play.

$E(X) = 4.5 - 5$

$E(X) = -€0.50$

   (ii) As we would expect to lose €0.50 per game on average, this is not good value.

      Therefore, I would advise the person not to play the game.

PROBABILITY

Worked Example 3.31

A game is played by rolling a fair six-sided die. The winnings for each outcome are shown below.

Die roll	Outcome
1	Win €9
2, 3 or 4	Money back
5 or 6	Lose

(i) Find the expected value of the game if it costs €2 to play.

(ii) Explain what this value represents.

Solution

(i) We fill in the following table:

Die roll	Outcome		Probability		€
1	€9	×	$\frac{1}{6}$	=	1.50
2, 3 or 4	€2	×	$\frac{3}{6}$	=	1.00
5 or 6	€0	×	$\frac{2}{6}$	=	0
			Total	=	2.50

We put in an outcome of 0 when we lose, as we have won nothing.

We must now factor in the cost of the game.

E(X) = €2.50 − €2.00

∴ E(X) = €0.50

The expected value of this game is 50 cent.

(ii) On average, a player would expect to win 50 cent per game.

 Worked Example 3.32

Shane and Jackie play a game where a die is rolled and the winner is decided by referring to the following table:

Number on die	Result
1	Jackie gives Shane €4
2	Shane gives Jackie €2
3	No one wins or loses
4	Jackie gives Shane €1
5	Jackie gives Shane €2
6	Shane gives Jackie €10

Which person will expect to win more per game: Shane or Jackie?

Solution

We must first decide who we will 'play' as: Shane or Jackie.

If we decide to play as Shane, we assign a positive value to the outcomes or values that favour Shane and a negative value to outcomes that don't favour him.

Die roll	Outcome		Probability		
1	€4	×	$\frac{1}{6}$	=	$\frac{2}{3}$
2	−€2	×	$\frac{1}{6}$	=	$-\frac{1}{3}$
3	0	×	$\frac{1}{6}$	=	0
4	€1	×	$\frac{1}{6}$	=	$\frac{1}{6}$
5	€2	×	$\frac{1}{6}$	=	$\frac{1}{3}$
6	−€10	×	$\frac{1}{6}$	=	$-\frac{5}{3}$

The expected value for Shane:

$$E(X) = \frac{2}{3} - \frac{1}{3} + 0 + \frac{1}{6} + \frac{1}{3} - \frac{5}{3}$$

$$= -\frac{5}{6} \text{ or } -€0.83 \text{ (to the nearest cent)}$$

∴ The game favours Jackie, who would expect to win €0.83 per game on average.

 ACTIVITY 3.22

The earliest examples of dice were made from the knucklebones of animals.

Exercise 3.11

1. Find the expected value when this spinner is spun.

2. A game with a spinner as shown is played.

If the spinner lands on red, you lose €3.

If the spinner lands on blue, you win €8.

(i) Calculate the expected value for this game.

(ii) Is this game fair? Explain your answer.

3. A card is drawn from a normal pack of cards. If an Ace is drawn, €20 is won; if a Club card is drawn, €5 is won. It costs €3 to draw a card. One prize only may be won. Is it worthwhile to play this game? Explain your answer with reference to the expected value.

4. Five thousand tickets are sold for a raffle at €10 each for a single prize of €20,000. What is the expected value if a person purchases one ticket? Is this good value?

5. A die is rolled and the winnings for each outcome are as follows:

- Roll a 6: Win €5
- Roll a 3: Win €1
- Roll any other number: Win nothing

   (i) Calculate to the nearest cent the expected value for this game.

It is then decided to charge €5 per game.

   (ii) Calculate the expected value for this game.

6. For €5, the following spinner is spun and the amount it lands on is won.

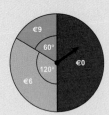

Is this a fair game? Give a reason, using the expected value in your answer.

7. A friend offers to play a game by picking a card from a pack of cards at random. The rules of the game are as follows:

- It costs €1 to play.
- If you pick a Heart, you get your €1 back.
- If you pick a King, you win €2.
- If you pick the Ace of Spades, you win €13.
- One prize only may be won.

Is this a fair game? Explain your answer.

8. A €50, a €20, a €10 and a €5 note are placed in a bag. A person draws a note at random and wins that amount.

   (i) What is the expected value for this game?

   (ii) Six more €5 notes are placed in the bag. A person draws a note at random and wins that amount.

What is the expected value for this game?

9. Ten thousand tickets are to be sold for a prize draw. There is a first prize of €1,000, a second prize of €250 and a third prize of €50. A winning ticket will not be put back for the next draw.

   (i) Vera buys one ticket. What is the probability that she wins a prize?

   (ii) What price do you think that Vera would be willing to pay for her ticket?

Explain your answer, making sure to refer to expected value.

10. John and Caroline decide to play a game to divide up a bag of sweets. A single die is rolled and the sweets are divided up as follows:

Roll a 1: John gets five sweets.

Roll a 2: Both get no sweets.

Roll a 3: Caroline gets eight sweets.

Roll a 4: John gets five sweets.

Roll a 5: Caroline gets two sweets.

Roll a 6: Caroline gets one sweet.

   (i) Who would expect to get the most sweets?

   (ii) Give one example of how you would change the rules to make this a fair game.

11. It costs €10 to play a game in which a coin is flipped four times. If the coin lands on heads four times, the player wins €100. Otherwise the player wins nothing.

   (i) Find the expected value for this game.

   (ii) The game is played again but with new rules.

- It costs €10 to play.
- If the coin lands on heads at least twice in the four flips, €50 will be paid.
- Otherwise the player wins nothing.

Is this a fair game to play?

   (iii) If a person played this game 20 times, how much would they expect to win or lose, to the nearest cent?

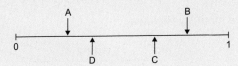

1. (a) The events A, B, C and D have probabilities as shown on this probability scale:

   A   B

   0   D   C   1

   (i) Which event is the most likely to happen?

   (ii) Which event is the least likely to happen?

   (b) Match each term to its correct definition.

Term	Definition
Relative frequency	One of the possible results of the trial
Fairness	The act of doing an experiment in probability
Trial	All outcomes are equally likely to occur
Sample space	The occurrence of one or more specific outcomes
Event	An estimate of the probability of an event
Outcome	The set or list of all possible outcomes in a trial

   (c) A card is drawn at random from a normal deck of cards. Find the probability that the card is:

   (i) An Ace of Clubs   (iv) A King or a Heart

   (ii) An Ace   (v) A Queen or a Diamond

   (iii) A King   (vi) A Jack and a Club

2. (a) A bag contains one blue token, two red tokens, three black tokens and four yellow tokens.

   One token is taken at random from the bag.
   What is the probability that the token drawn is:

   (i) Blue   (v) Blue or black

   (ii) Red   (vi) Red or yellow

   (iii) Yellow   (vii) Not red or yellow

   (iv) Not yellow   (viii) Red and blue

   (b) A fair coin is flipped and a fair die is rolled.

   (i) Draw a two-way table to show all possible outcomes.

   Find the probability of obtaining:

   (ii) A tail on the coin and a 5 on the die

   (iii) A head on the coin and a 1 on the die

   (iv) A tail on the coin and an odd number on the die

   (v) A tail on the coin and a number less than 4 on the die

3. (a) Give an example of each of the following events and show them on a likelihood scale:

(i) Impossible   (ii) Certain   (iii) Likely   (iv) Unlikely   (v) Evens

(b) What is meant by the term 'mutually exclusive events'?
In each case below, state whether the events are mutually exclusive.

Event 1	Event 2
Picking a student who is a girl	Picking a student who is a boy
Picking a red top	Picking a cotton top
Rolling a die and getting an odd number	Rolling a die and getting a prime number
Flipping a coin and getting a head	Flipping a coin and getting a tail
Picking a Spade from a deck of cards	Picking a Heart from a deck of cards
Picking a King from a deck of cards	Picking a Diamond from a deck of cards

(c) What is meant by the term 'independent events'?
In each case below, state whether the events are independent of each other.

(i) A die being rolled and a coin being flipped

(ii) Two tokens taken from a bag, one after another with replacement

(iii) Two tokens taken from a bag, one after another without replacement

(iv) Checking six smoke alarms to see if any are defective

4. (a) A spinner as shown is spun three times.

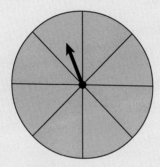

(i) Draw a tree diagram to show all possible outcomes.

What is the probability that the spinner lands on:

(ii) Green three times

(iii) Green the first two times and orange on the third

(iv) Green twice and orange once

(v) Orange at least once

(b) A box contains 15 sweets: five chocolate-flavoured and 10 toffee-flavoured. Two sweets are taken at random from the bag one at a time (no replacement). Find the probability that:

(i) Both sweets are chocolate-flavoured.

(ii) The first sweet is toffee-flavoured and the second chocolate-flavoured.

(iii) Both sweets have the same flavour.

(iv) The sweets have different flavours.

5. (a) A student plays a game of chess and a game of draughts. The probability that she wins the game of chess is 0.5. The probability that she wins the game of draughts is 0.3. The probability that she wins both games is 0.15.

(i) Draw a Venn diagram to show this data.

(ii) Find the probability that she wins only at draughts.

(iii) Find the probability that she loses both games.

(b) A game is played with two dice. A player wins if the scores on both dice are the same.

   (i) Draw a two-way table for the outcomes of rolling two dice.

   (ii) Megan suggests that this is not a fair game. Do you agree? Explain your answer.

   (iii) Jack suggests a rule to make the game fair. Give an example of such a rule and refer to the two-way table to explain how this rule would make the game fair.

6. (a) Helen is trying to decide if she wishes to buy a raffle ticket that costs €1. The grand prize is €5,000 and there are 20 additional prizes worth €100 each. Only 10,000 tickets are to be sold for this lottery.

   (i) Find the expected value if Helen buys one ticket.

   (ii) Explain the term 'expected value' in relation to this lottery.

   (iii) Find the expected value if Helen buys 20 tickets.

(b) The probability that a tennis player will fault on her first serve is 0.5. The probability that she will fault on her second serve is 0.25.

   Calculate the probability that she:

   (i) Faults on her first serve but not on her second serve

   (ii) Faults on both serves

7. (a) A game is played in which a die is rolled. If an odd number is rolled, you lose the amount on the die. If an even number is rolled, you gain the amount on the die.

   (i) Find the expected value.

   (ii) Is this a fair game?

   (iii) Would you play this game given the opportunity? Explain.

(b) A game is played by rolling a fair six-sided die three times. A player wins if the die rolls a 1 on any of the rolls.

   (i) Find the probability that a player wins on the first roll of the die.

   (ii) Find the probability that a player wins on the third roll of the die.

   (iii) Find the probability that a player doesn't win.

   (iv) It is decided to change the rules so the player wins only if he rolls a 1 twice.

   If the die is rolled three times, find the probability that a player wins.

8. (a) Two cards are drawn at random from a normal deck of cards. The first card is drawn, recorded and then replaced. A second card is then chosen. Find the probability that:

   (i) The first card is a Club and the second card is a Diamond.

   (ii) Both cards are Hearts.

   (iii) Both cards are not Hearts.

   (iv) Neither card is a picture card (Jack, King or Queen).

   (v) At least one card is a King.

(b) A courier firm delivers 80% of all packages the next day. Two packages are posted. The deliveries are independent of each other.

   (i) Explain what the term 'independent' means in this context.

   (ii) Draw a tree diagram to show all the possible outcomes.

   Find the probability that:

   (iii) Both packages are delivered the next day.

   (iv) Neither package is delivered the next day.

   (v) One package only is delivered the next day.

9. (a) A game involves rolling two dice. The scores from the two dice are added together.

    (i) Draw a two-way table to show all possible outcomes.

A score of 2, 3, 9, 10, 11 or 12 will win €10. A roll of anything else will cost you €10.

    (ii) With reference to expected value, explain why this game is not fair.

    (iii) Explain one rule change that would make this game fair.

(b) Laura works in a factory, checking to see if a component the factory makes is faulty or not. The probability that any one component is faulty is $\frac{1}{20}$. She checks three components in a row.

    (i) Draw a tree diagram to show all the possible outcomes.

Calculate the probability that:

    (ii) The first component she checks is faulty.

    (iii) No component is faulty.

    (iv) At least one component is faulty.

Laura checks 10,000 components in a week. How many of these would you expect not to have a fault?

10. (a) One hundred students in First Year of college take maths. Twenty of those students taking maths also take science. There are 220 First Year students in the college and 70 take neither of these subjects.

    (i) Draw a Venn diagram to represent the students in First Year at this college.

    (ii) Find the probability that a student picked at random studies science only.

    (iii) Find the probability that a student picked at random studies maths but not science.

(b) A motorist drives through three sets of traffic lights on her way to work each day. The probability that she has to stop at the first light is 0.25. The probability that she will have to stop at the second light is 0.35. The probability that she will have to stop at the third light is 0.5. What is the probability that the car will first stop at the:

    (i) First set of traffic lights

    (ii) Third set of traffic lights

What is the probability that the driver has to stop at:

    (iii) All sets of traffic lights

    (iv) No set of traffic lights

If the driver makes this journey 300 times a year, how many times would she expect to stop at at least one of these sets of traffic lights?

11. (a) A roulette wheel with 38 numbers – 18 black, 18 red and two green – is spun. If €1 is bet and the ball lands on the number picked, €35 is won.

    (i) Calculate the expected value of this game.

    (ii) Is this a fair game? Give a reason for your answer.

    (iii) €1 is bet and the player wins €1 if the ball lands on black. They also get their €1 bet back. Is this a fair game to play?

(b) A container contains 1,000 light bulbs, of which 200 are broken. A light bulb is chosen at random from the container, checked and then put back. A second bulb is then chosen. What is the probability of selecting:

  (i) Two broken lights bulbs

  (ii) Two working light bulbs

  (iii) One broken and one working light bulb

12. (a) A person is selected at random. If there is an equal likelihood of being born on any day of the week, what is the probability that the person selected:

  (i) Was born on a Monday

  (ii) Was **not** born on a Monday

  Two people are selected at random. What is the probability that:

  (iii) Both were born on a Monday.

  (iv) Only one of them was born on a Monday.

  (v) They were born on different days of the week.

(b) The independent probabilities that three different species of animal – A, B and C – will be extinct in 100 years are 0.8, 0.1 and 0.2, respectively. Calculate the probability that in 100 years' time:

  (i) All three species will be extinct.

  (ii) All three species will survive.

  (iii) Species A will be extinct, but species B and C will still survive.

  (iv) Only one species will survive.

  (v) At least one species will survive.

13. (a) A fair coin is flipped once. What is the probability that the coin will land on:

  (i) Heads   (ii) Tails

(b) A coin is flipped 20 times and the results are recorded.

H	H	H	T	T	T	T	H	H	H
H	H	T	H	T	T	H	H	H	H

  (i) Show these results on a bar chart.

  Using these results, calculate the experimental probability that the coin will land on:

  (ii) Heads   (iii) Tails

  Joe concludes that, based on these results, the coin is not fair.

  (iv) Explain what is meant by 'fair'. Give a reason why Joe thinks the coin is not fair.

  (v) Ann points out that the coin may still be a fair coin. Give one reason why Ann might think the coin is still fair.

(c) A fair coin is flipped three times.

  (i) Show the sample space of this experiment using an appropriate method.

  Using this sample space, calculate the probability that the coin lands on:

  (ii) Three heads and one tail

  (iii) Three tails

  (iv) Two heads

  (v) One head only

  (vi) At least one tail

  (vii) No tails

14. A census is done in a town to find the most popular first names for girls. The total number of girls surveyed is 300. The following data is collected, which shows the 11 most popular names.

Name	Amy	Aoife	Chloe	Emily	Katie	Lauren	Leah	Lucy	Mia	Sarah	Sophie
Number	41	33	29	48	17	20	13	18	15	10	21

(a)　(i)　What is meant by the term 'census'?

　　(ii)　Use the most appropriate method to graph this data.

　　(iii)　Redraw the table so that the names are now ranked in descending order.

　　(iv)　Explain why it is impossible, based on the given data, to determine the least popular name for a girl.

　　(v)　What percentage of girls have a name that is in the top five of the most popular names (to the nearest whole number)?

(b)　The next day, a researcher wishes to determine the experimental probability of picking a girl from the town with a certain name.

　　(i)　What assumption must first be made in order to determine the experimental probability?

　　A girl from the town is picked at random. What is the experimental probability, to the nearest whole number, that the girl picked:

　　(ii)　Is named Amy

　　(iii)　Has one of the three most popular names

　　(iv)　Has a name that is not included in the table

(c)　One hundred girls are picked at random from the town.
　　How many would you expect to be called Lauren?

15. (a)　A fair six-sided die is rolled. Calculate the probability that you roll:

　　(i)　A prime number

　　(ii)　A number divisible by 3

　　What is the expected value of the die?

(b)　A fair spinner with equal sectors is spun.

　　Calculate the probability that you roll:

　　(i)　An even number

　　(ii)　A composite number

　　What is the expected value of this spinner?

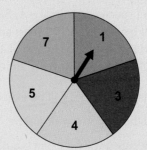

(c)　A game is played where the spinner is spun and the die is rolled. The scores from each are added together.

　　Complete a two-way table to show all possible outcomes.

PROBABILITY

The rules of the game are as follows:

- The game costs €1 to play.

- A score divisible by 4 means you get your money back.

- A score of 11 means you win €6.

- Any other score means you win nothing.

    (i) Calculate the average amount lost or won per game.

    (ii) Tom has €10 to spend on this game. How many games on average would he expect to play before he runs out of money?

   By only changing the amount won, the game's expected value is now 50 cent.

    (iii) Calculate the amount that needs to be won to give this expected value.

16. (a) There are 20 people in a committee: 14 men and six women. A subcommittee is formed that consists of three members from the committee.

    (i) How many different subcommittees can be chosen?

    (ii) How many different subcommittees can be chosen if they must contain two women and one man?

    (iii) How many different subcommittees can be chosen if the subcommittee must be made up entirely of women?

    (iv) How many different subcommittees can be chosen if they must contain more women then men?

Copy and complete the following table:

Total number of three-member subcommittees possible	
Number of subcommittees that contain two women and one man	
Number of subcommittees that contain three women and no men	
Number of subcommittees that contain more women than men	

Using this information, if three people are selected at random to be on the subcommittee, find the probability, to two decimal places, that:

    (v) Two women and one man are selected.

    (vi) Three women are selected.

    (vii) More women then men are selected.

(b) In how many ways can the letters of the word CASTLE be arranged if:

    (i) There are no restrictions.

    (ii) The arrangements must begin with the letter T.

    (iii) The first two letters are vowels.

    (iv) The vowels are beside each other.

The letters of the word CASTLE are randomly arranged in a row. What is the probability that:

    (v) The letter T will come first.

    (vi) The vowels will be beside each other.

17. The table below gives motor insurance information for fully licensed 17–20-year-old drivers in Ireland in 2007. All drivers who had their own insurance policy are included.

	Number of drivers	Number of claims	Average cost per claim
Male	9,634	977	€6,108
Female	6,743	581	€6,051

(Source: Adapted from: Financial Regulator. Private Motor Insurance Statistics 2007.)

Questions (a) to (e) below refer to drivers in the table above only.

(a) What is the probability that a randomly selected male driver made a claim during the year?
Give your answer correct to three decimal places.

(b) What is the probability that a randomly selected female driver made a claim during the year?
Give your answer correct to three decimal places.

(c) What is the expected value of the cost of claims on a male driver's policy?

(d) What is the expected value of the cost of claims on a female driver's policy?

(e) The male drivers were paying an average of €1,688 for insurance in 2007 and the female drivers were paying an average of €1,024. Calculate the average surplus for each group and comment on your answer.

(Note: the surplus is the amount paid for the policy minus the expected cost of claims.)

(f) A 40-year-old female driver with a full license has a probability of 0.07 of making a claim during the year. The average cost of such claims is €3,900. How much should a company charge such drivers for insurance in order to show a surplus of €175 per policy?

SEC Project Maths Paper 2, Leaving Certificate Ordinary Level, 2010

chapter 4

Statistics II

Learning Outcomes

In this chapter you will learn:

- About measures of central tendency: mean, median and mode
- About measures of spread: range, interquartile range and standard deviation
- About the normal distribution and the empirical rule
- How to use a spreadsheet to generate charts and provide summary statistics
- How to analyse, interpret and draw conclusions from data
- How to recognise misuses of statistics

4.1 MEASURES OF CENTRAL TENDENCY: MEAN, MODE AND MEDIAN

When statisticians describe and compare data sets, they often look for one number to represent each data set. This number is known as an **average** or a **measure of centre**. Measures of centre are sometimes called **measures of location**. There are different ways of working out the average. We will look at three averages: the mean, the mode and the median.

YOU SHOULD REMEMBER...

- How to construct a bar chart
- How to construct a pie chart
- How to construct a histogram
- How to construct a stem-and-leaf plot
- How to find percentage error

The **average** is the measure of centre in a data set.

KEY WORDS

- **Mean, median and mode**
- **Range**
- **Quartiles**
- **Interquartile range**
- **Standard deviation**
- **Mid-interval values**
- **The normal distribution**
- **The empirical rule**

The Mean

The **mean** of a set of values is the sum of all the values divided by the number of values.

For example, the **mean** of the set {2, 2, 3, 5, 9, 9} is:

$$\text{Mean} = \frac{2 + 2 + 3 + 5 + 9 + 9}{6} = \frac{30}{6} = 5$$

The Mode

The **mode** of the set {2, 2, 2, 3, 3, 3, 3, 5, 5} is 3, as 3 occurs more often than any other value.

The **mode** of a set of values is the value that occurs most often.

The Median

Ranking the set {4, 7, 11, 9, 12, 10, 8, 11, 14, 2, 6}

gives {2, 4, 6, 7, 8, 9, 10, 11, 11, 12, 14}.

The number in the middle of the ranked set is called the **median**, which in this case equals 9.

The **median** of a set of values is the middle value when the values are arranged in order.

What happens if the set contains an even number of values?
For example, the set {1, 2, 3, 4} contains an even number of values.
The median is the mean of the middle two numbers. In this case, we sum the two middle numbers, 2 and 3, and divide our result by 2:

$$\text{Median} = \frac{2 + 3}{2} = \frac{5}{2} = 2.5$$

Arranging the values of a set in order is known as **ranking**.

Worked Example 4.1

A golfer keeps a record of his scores in competitions during 2009.

Score	75	76	77	78	79
Frequency	4	3	4	7	2

Find:

(i) His mean score for 2009   (iii) His median score for 2009

(ii) His modal score for 2009

Solution

(i) Mean $= \dfrac{\text{Total of all scores}}{\text{Total number of competitions}}$

$= \dfrac{4(75) + 3(76) + 4(77) + 7(78) + 2(79)}{4 + 3 + 4 + 7 + 2}$

$= \dfrac{1{,}540}{20}$ $\therefore$ Mean score $= 77$

(ii) Mode = most common score = 78 (78 has the highest frequency).

(iii) There are 20 scores. The middle two numbers of the ranked data are the 10th and 11th numbers. Both these numbers are 77.

Median $= \dfrac{77 + 77}{2} \Rightarrow$ Median score $= 77$

Worked Example 4.2

The stem-and-leaf diagram below displays the predicted high-water tides at the North Wall, Dublin, for 15 consecutive days in April 2010.

Find the median predicted high-water mark at the North Wall during this period.

Stem	Leaf
3.2	7, 7
3.3	6, 9
3.4	9
3.5	7
3.6	1
3.7	0, 3, 7
3.8	1, 5, 6
3.9	6
4.0	1 Key: 3.3|6 = 3.36 m

Solution

To find the median, cross out the smallest and the largest number (3.27 and 4.01), then the second largest and the second smallest, and so on until you are left with the number in the middle. This number is the median.

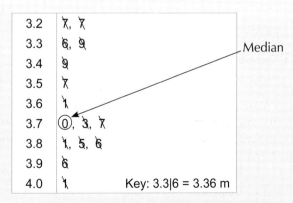

The median predicted high-water mark is 3.70 m.

Sampling Variability

In Chapter 1 Statistics I, we learned how to select random samples from a population. The value of the mean, median or mode of the random sample depends on the particular values in the sample, and it generally varies from sample to sample. This variation is called **sampling variability**.

 Exercise 4.1

1. Find the mean of these sets of numbers:

   (i) {3, 4, 8, 9, 9}

   (ii) {7, 8, 9, 10, 11, 12, 13}

   (iii) {8.2, 7.9, 8.1, 7.8}

   (iv) {−1, −2, −3, −8, −8}

   (v) {5, 8, 6, 4, 5, 3, 4}

   (vi) {0, 1, 0, 1, 0, 1, 0, 1, 0, 1}

2. Find the median and mode of these sets:

   (i) {6, 7, 7, 4, 5, 6, 7}

   (ii) {3, 5, 7, 3, 4, 9, 10}

   (iii) {6, 2, 2, 2, 6}

   (iv) {6, 7, 8, 6, 7, 8, 9, 6, 7, 8, 9, 10}

   (v) {0, 0, 0}

3. Aoife is doing a study on the relationship between time (in minutes per day) spent playing computer games and success in exams. She surveys a random sample of students in her school. One question on her survey generated the following data:

2	1, 2, 4, 5, 5, 5, 5, 6, 7, 7, 8
3	0, 0, 1, 1, 1, 2, 2, 3, 3, 6, 7, 8, 8
4	1, 1, 1, 2, 2, 3, 3, 4, 8, 9
5	0, 1, 1, 2, 7, 7
6	1, 2, 2, 6, 6 Key 4|1 = 41 min

   (i) Suggest a question that generated this data.

   (ii) What is the size of the sample?

   (iii) Find the mode of the data.

   (iv) Find the median of the data.

4. The table below shows average monthly sea temperatures, in degrees Celsius, at Malin Head, Co. Donegal, for the year 2009. Average monthly readings for the period 1961–1990 are also given.

Month	2009	1961–1990
January	7.3	7.3
February	6.9	6.7
March	7.6	7
April	8.8	8.1
May	10.4	9.9
June	12.4	12
July	14.3	13.8
August	15.3	14.6
September	14.4	14
October	13.0	12.4
November	11.1	10.2
December	8.8	8.5

Source: http://www.met.ie/marine/marine_climatology.asp

   (i) Using the monthly averages, estimate the mean annual sea temperature at Malin Head for 2009. (Give your answer correct to two decimal places.)

   (ii) Using the monthly averages, estimate the mean annual sea temperature at Malin Head for the period 1961 to 1990. Comment on the difference between the 2009 figure and the 1961–1990 figure. (Give your answer correct to two decimal places.)

   (iii) Is the comparison made in part (ii) a fair comparison? Explain.

5. A teacher marks a test for 20 students and summarises the results in a stem-and-leaf diagram.

Stem	Leaf
0	6
1	3
2	1
3	6, 7
4	3, 3, 3, 5, 5
5	3, 8, 9
6	3, 7
7	7, 8
8	2, 5
9	9 Key 6|3 = 63

(i) Find the mode of the data.

(ii) Find the median of the data.

(iii) How many students scored higher than the median?

(iv) Explain how the median of a data set divides the set.

6. There are 16 students taking part in a school play. Here is a list of their ages:

12, 15, 16, 15, 16, 14, 16, 12, 14, 15, 12, 15, 12, 13, 12, 14

(i) Find the mode of the data.

(ii) Rank the data.

(iii) Find the median.

(iv) Find the mean.

7. The foot lengths (to the nearest centimetre) of a group of students is given below.

20, 22, 23, 25, 26, 25, 22, 25, 24, 25, 25, 24, 22, 24, 23, 25

(i) Find the mode of the data.

(ii) Rank the data.

(iii) Find the median.

(iv) Find the mean.

8. The table below gives the number of vehicles licensed in Ireland for the first time from 2000 to 2009.

Vehicles licensed for the first time (number) by year					
Year	2000	2001	2002	2003	2004
New private cars	225,269	160,908	150,485	142,992	149,635
Year	2005	2006	2007	2008	2009
New private cars	166,270	173,273	180,754	146,470	54,432

Source: http://www.cso.ie/

(i) In what year was the highest number of vehicles registered?

(ii) In what year was the lowest number of vehicles registered?

(iii) What was the mean number of vehicles registered for the first time during these 10 years?

(iv) What was the median number of vehicles registered for the first time during these 10 years?

9. The following are the goals scored by 20 teams in a soccer league:

0, 2, 0, 2, 3, 2, 5, 2, 6, 2

4, 1, 1, 2, 5, 2, 5, 4, 1, 1

(i) Find the mode of the data.

(ii) Rank the data.

(iii) Find the median.

(iv) Find the mean.

10. The stem-and-leaf diagram below displays the weights, in kilograms, of 10-week-old babies.

Stem	Leaf
3	7, 9
4	2, 4, 7, 8, 8, 8
5	0, 1, 3, 6, 7, 7, 9
6	0, 1, 2, 3, 5
7	1, 2 Key 4|2 = 4.2 kg

(i) Find the mode of the data.

(ii) Find the median.

(iii) Find the mean.

11. The frequency table below shows the grades achieved by a Fifth Year maths class in an end-of-term test.

Grade	A	B	C	D	E
Number	3	7	7	2	1

(i) What is the mode of this distribution?

(ii) Explain why you cannot write down the mean of this distribution.

12. Four girls and six boys received text messages. The mean number of messages received by the four girls was 42, and the mean number of messages received by the six boys was 40.

(i) How many messages in total were received by the girls?

(ii) How many messages in total were received by the boys?

(iii) What was the mean number of messages received by the entire group (girls and boys)?

(iv) Is it possible to say that a girl must have received the most messages? Explain.

13. Alice removes all the Aces and picture cards from a deck of playing cards. She then deals out six cards. She reveals four of the cards to her audience. The four cards are the 3 of Clubs, the 3 of Hearts, the 3 of Spades and the 3 of Diamonds.

   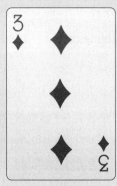

(a) Is it possible for Alice's audience to give:

(i) The median of the six numbers on the cards

(ii) The mode of the six numbers

(iii) The mean of the six numbers

Explain your reasoning.

(b) Alice then reveals that the number on one of the hidden cards is less than 3 and the number on the other hidden card is greater than 3. If the mean of the six numbers is 4, find the numbers on the hidden cards.

Deciding Which Average to Use

The mean, median and mode of a set of data are all averages, but each one has a different meaning. The average, or measure of central tendency, that we choose depends on the characteristics of the data set we are studying. The following table will help you decide when to use the mean, the median or the mode.

Average	When to use	Advantages/Disadvantages
Mode	■ If data is **categorical**, then the mode is the only sensible measure of centre to use. Therefore, for data on hair colour, eye colour, gender, etc., use only the mode. ■ The mode can also be used with **numerical** data.	*Advantages* ■ It can be used with any type of data. ■ It is easy to find. ■ It is not affected by extreme values. *Disadvantage* ■ There is not always a mode, or there are several modes.
Median	■ Used **only** with **numerical** data. ■ If there are **extreme values** in the data set, then use the median.	*Advantages* ■ It is easy to calculate. ■ It is not affected by extreme values.
Mean	■ Used **only** with **numerical** data. ■ If there are **not extreme values** in the data set, use the mean.	*Advantage* ■ It uses all the data. *Disadvantage* ■ It is affected by extreme values.

Worked Example 4.3

Eight European professional soccer players are selected at random. They are asked the following question: 'What is the most money any club has paid for you in transfer fees?' Below is the data generated by the question. All amounts are in sterling.

£3 million	£80 million	£5.8 million	£18.25 million
£3.5 million	£3.7 million	£8 million	£7 million

(i) Find the mean transfer fee for the sample (correct to two decimal places).

(ii) Find the median transfer fee.

(iii) Which of the above averages is the most typical of transfer fees?

Solution

(i) Mean $= \dfrac{3 + 80 + 5.8 + 18.25 + 3.5 + 3.7 + 8 + 7}{8} = \dfrac{129.25}{8} = $ £16.16 million

(ii) Median $= \{3, 3.5, 3.7, 5.8, 7, 8, 18.25, 80\}$

$= \dfrac{5.8 + 7}{2} = $ £6.4 million

(iii) The median is the most typical. The extreme value of £80 million affects the mean.

STATISTICS II

Exercise 4.2

1. Decide which average you would use for each of the following. Give a reason for your answer.

    (i) The average height of students in your class

    (ii) The average eye colour of all teachers in the school

    (iii) The average mark in a maths exam

    (iv) The average colour of all cars in the school car park

    (v) The average wage of 100 workers in a company, given that 90 of the workers earn between €30,000 and €40,000 per annum, five workers earn between €60,000 and €80,000, and the remaining five workers earn over €600,000 per annum

2. Write down the type of average in each case:

    (i) This average uses all values of the data.

    (ii) This average is used with categorical data.

    (iii) This average is useful with data that contains extreme values.

3. Below is some data selected at random from the CensusAtSchools database. The data gives the different modes of transport a group uses to go to school.

Walk	Bus	Walk	Walk	Walk
Bus	Walk	Car	Car	Bus
Walk	Bus	Car	Walk	Walk
Car	Rail	Bus	Walk	Rail

    (i) What type of data is contained in this sample?

    (ii) What average are you using when you refer to the most popular mode of transport used by these students?

4. Rex has just been given the result of his last maths test. He does not know the results his classmates received, but would like to know how his result compares with those of his friends. The teacher has given the class the modal mark, the mean mark and the median mark for the test.

    (i) Which average tells Rex whether he is in the top half or the bottom half of the class?

    (ii) Is the modal mark useful to Rex? Explain.

    (iii) Which average tells Rex how well he has done in comparison to everyone else?

5. Find the mean and the median of the following set of numbers:

    1, 2, 12, 12, 18, 19, 20, 24, 188

    Which average would you use to describe these numbers? Give a reason for your answer.

6. Generate some primary data from within your class.
   Find the average of the data using a suitable measure.

Mean of a Grouped Frequency Distribution

Consider the grouped frequency table below. The table summarises the resting pulse rates of 82 adults in beats per minute.

Pulse rate	60–70	70–80	80–90	90–100	100–110	110–120
Frequency	5	8	22	29	13	5

Note: 60–70 means that 60 is included but 70 is not, and so on.

We can see from the table that five people had a pulse rate of 60–70 beats per minute. However, the table does not tell us the exact pulse rates of each person. In order to estimate the mean resting pulse rate, we must assign each person a resting pulse rate. We choose the mid-interval values as the rate for each group.

Here is how we calculate the mid-interval values (M.I.V.):

M.I.V.	$\frac{60 + 70}{2}$	$\frac{70 + 80}{2}$	$\frac{80 + 90}{2}$	$\frac{90 + 100}{2}$	$\frac{100 + 110}{2}$	$\frac{110 + 120}{2}$
Frequency	5	8	22	29	13	5

We can now continue and estimate the mean:

M.I.V.	65	75	85	95	105	115
Frequency	5	8	22	29	13	5

$$\text{Mean} = \frac{(65)(5) + (75)(8) + (85)(22) + (95)(29) + (105)(13) + (115)(5)}{(5 + 8 + 22 + 29 + 13 + 5)} = \frac{7,490}{82}$$

$$\approx 91 \text{ beats per minute}$$

This answer is correct to the nearest beat.

 Exercise 4.3

1. The length (in minutes) of 20 phone calls made to a school switchboard is shown in the grouped frequency distribution below.

Length	0–2	2–4	4–6	6–8	8–10
Frequency	3	5	6	4	2

Note: 0–2 means 0 is included but 2 is not, etc.

(i) Using mid-interval values, estimate the mean length of a phone call.

(ii) What is the maximum number of calls that could have been longer than 6.2 minutes?

2. The following frequency distribution shows the time (in minutes) taken by a group of people to complete a 5-km run:

Time	30–35	35–40	40–45	45–50	50–55
Frequency	13	13	24	20	4

Note: 30–35 means 30 is included but 35 is not, etc.

(i) Using mid-interval values, estimate the mean time taken to complete the 5-km run.

(ii) What is the maximum number of people who could have completed the run in less than 37 minutes?

3. The following frequency distribution shows the amounts spent by 30 customers in a shop:

Amount (€)	0–5	5–10	10–15	15–20
Frequency	12	8	6	4

Note: 0–5 means 0 is included but 5 is not, etc.

(i)   Using mid-interval values, estimate the mean amount spent.

(ii) What percentage of shoppers spent €10 or more?

4. The frequency distribution below shows the ages of people living in a street.

Age	0–20	20–30	30–50	50–80
Frequency	24	16	41	15

Note: 0–20 means 0 is included but 20 is not, etc.

(i)   How many people are living in the street?

(ii) Estimate the mean age.

(iii) What percentage of the people are less than 20 years old?

5. The heights of a random sample of 1,000 women are given in the frequency distribution below.

Height	140–145	145–150	150–155	155–160	160–165	165–170	170–175	175–180
Frequency	9	65	177	325	253	133	31	7

Note: 140–145 means 140 is included but 145 is not, etc.

(i) Estimate the mean height.

(ii) Construct a histogram to represent the data.

6. The table below shows the amount of money that a group of people spent one year on Christmas presents.

Amount (€)	0–20	20–40	40–60	60–100
Frequency	20	5	25	60

Note: 0–20 means 0 is included but 20 is not, etc.

Estimate the mean amount of money spent by the group.

7. The number of hours per day that the secretary of a construction firm spends on the phone is recorded. The following data shows the number of hours per day over a 30-day period:

4.21   1.12   0.33   1.1   3.3   3.2   5.2   1.5   3.1   0.5

1.22   2.51   0.8   0.7   1.8   6   1.2   2.5   5.2   1.6

4   1.4   0.9   2.8   5   0.2   1.9   2.3   1.79   4

(i)   Is this data discrete or continuous? Explain.

(ii) Complete the frequency table below.

Hours	0–1	1–2	2–3	3–4	4–5	5–6
Tally						
No. of days						

Note: 0–1 means 0 is included but 1 is not, etc.

(iii) Draw a histogram of the distribution.

(iv) Describe the distribution.

(v) Rank the raw data and find the median.

(vi) Using mid-interval values, estimate the mean of the distribution.

(vii) Now, using the raw data, calculate the mean.

(viii) What is the percentage error in the estimated mean?

(ix) Which is the better measure of centre, the mean or the median? Explain.

8. The following are the daily maximum temperatures in Dubai for the month of June (in degrees Celsius):

29.2   29.4   34.1   36.3   36.5   32.1   32.0   35.7   35.6   34.9

36.2   32.3   32.6   36.5   33.8   32.1   32.2   38.8   36.5   35.7

31.1   33.9   34.7   34.3   37.3   41.0   33.8   32.2   41.0   34.2

(i) Is this data discrete or continuous? Explain.

(ii) Complete the frequency table below.

Hours	29–31	31–33	33–35	35–37	37–39	39–41
Tally						
No. of days						

Note: 29–31 means 29 is included but 31 is not, etc.

(iii) Draw a histogram of the distribution.

(iv) Describe the distribution.

(v) Rank the raw data and find the median.

(vi) Using mid-interval values, estimate the mean of the distribution.

(vii) Now, using the raw data, calculate the mean.

(viii) What is the percentage error in the estimated mean?

4.2 MEASURES OF SPREAD 1: RANGE AND INTERQUARTILE RANGE

The mean, median and mode supply us with one number to describe a set of data. However, such numbers give no indication of data spread.

Consider the sets A = {8, 8, 9, 11, 14} and B = {1, 3, 8, 17, 21}.

- The mean of set A = $\dfrac{8 + 8 + 9 + 11 + 14}{5} = \dfrac{50}{5} = 10$.

- The mean of set B = $\dfrac{1 + 3 + 8 + 17 + 21}{5} = \dfrac{50}{5} = 10$.

Both sets have the same mean, but the members of set A are more tightly bunched around the mean than the members of set B. To measure the spread of values, we could use the **range**.

> The **range** of a set of data is the difference between the maximum value and the minimum value in the set:
> Range = Maximum value – Minimum value.

$Range_A = 14 - 8 = 6$ $Range_B = 21 - 1 = 20$

This indicates that the elements of set B may have a greater spread of values.

STATISTICS II

Quartiles and the Interquartile Range

Quartiles divide a data set into four parts. There are three quartiles: the lower quartile, the median and the upper quartile. The interquartile range is the difference between the first, or lower, quartile (Q_1) and the third, or upper, quartile (Q_3). The interquartile range is more reliable than the range as a measure of spread, as it is not affected by extreme values, also called **outliers**.

Outliers are extreme values that are not typical of the other values in a set.

Q_1, the **lower quartile** of a ranked set of data, is a value such that one-quarter of the values are less than or equal to it.

Q_2, the **second quartile**, is the median of the data.

Q_3, the **upper quartile** of a ranked set of data, is a value such that three-quarters of the values are less than or equal to it.

FORMULA

Interquartile range = $Q_3 - Q_1$

Worked Example 4.4

The stem-and-leaf plot below gives the ages of 31 people attending a meeting about a government proposal not to grant medical cards to all people over the age of 70.

Stem	Leaf
5	1, 4, 4, 4
5	5, 9, 9, 9, 9
6	3, 3, 3, 4
6	5, 6, 6, 7, 7, 8, 8, 9
7	1, 1, 2, 3, 3, 3, 3, 3, 4
7	5 Key: 6|6 = 66

Calculate:

(i) Q_1, the lower quartile

(ii) Q_3, the upper quartile

(iii) The interquartile range

Solution

(i) **Step 1**

Count the number of leaves on the stem-and-leaf plot. There are 31 leaves in total.

Step 2

Find $\frac{1}{4}$ of 31, which is 7.75. As this is not a whole number, we round up to the nearest whole number (always round up), which is 8. We then find the eighth value in the plot, which is 59. This is the lower quartile.

$Q_1 = 59$ years

Lower quartile

Upper quartile

(ii) Find $\frac{3}{4}$ of 31, which is 23.25. As this is not a whole number, round up to the nearest whole number, which is 24. We then find the 24th value in the plot, which is 72. This is the upper quartile.

$Q_3 = 72$ years

(iii) The interquartile range is $Q_3 - Q_1 = 72 - 59 = 13$ years.

Worked Example 4.5

Set B is a list of the ages of a group of people at a birthday party.

$$B = \{6, 7, 8, 9, 9, 10, 10, 12, 14, 15, 15, 22\}$$

(i) Represent the data on a stem-and-leaf plot.

(ii) Find Q_1, the lower quartile, and Q_3, the upper quartile, of the data.

(iii) What is the interquartile range?

Solution

(i) Stem-and-leaf plot

0	6, 7, 8, 9, 9
1	0, 0, 2, 4, 5, 5
2	2 Key: 1|2 = 12

(ii) **Step 1**

Count the leaves in the stem-and-leaf plot. The number of leaves in this plot is 12.

Step 2

0	6, 7, 8, ⌄, 9, 9	— Lower quartile
1	0, 0, 2, 4, •, 5, 5	
2	2	Upper quartile

Find $\frac{1}{4}$ of 12, which is 3. This is a whole number, so the lower quartile will lie midway between the third and fourth value in the stem-and-leaf plot. So the lower quartile is:

$$\frac{8 + 9}{2} = 8.5 \quad \Rightarrow Q_1 = 8.5 \text{ years}$$

Step 3

Now, find $\frac{3}{4}$ of 12, which is 9, a whole number. In this case, the upper quartile will lie midway between the ninth and 10th value. So, the upper quartile is:

$$\frac{14 + 15}{2} = 14.5 \quad \Rightarrow Q_3 = 14.5 \text{ years}$$

(iii) The interquartile range is $Q_3 - Q_1 = 14.5 - 8.5 = 6$ years.

 **ACTIVITY 4.3**

 ## Exercise 4.4

1. Find the lower quartile, the upper quartile and the interquartile range for the following sets:

   Note: You should first rank the data.

   (i) $\{2, 5, 7, 3, 3, 2, 8\}$

   (ii) $\{5, 8, 6, 4, 5, 3, 4, 12\}$

   (iii) $\{8, 7, 6, 5, 4, 3, 2, 1\}$

   (iv) $\{8, 7, 8, 7, 6, 5, 6, 5, 4, 3, 4, 3\}$

   (v) $\{-3, -2, -1, 0, 1, 2, 3\}$

   (vi) $\{1, 2, -3, 8, 7, -5, -2\}$

2. The ages of a group of people entering a shopping centre are summarised in the following stem-and-leaf plot:

Stem	Leaf
2	1, 2, 4, 5, 5, 5, 5, 6, 7, 7, 8
3	0, 0, 1, 1, 1, 2, 2, 3, 3, 6, 7, 8, 8
4	1, 1, 1, 2, 2, 3, 3, 4, 8, 9
5	0, 1, 1, 2, 7, 7
6	1, 2, 2, 6, 6 Key 4|1 = 41

Calculate:

(i) Q_1, the lower quartile

(ii) Q_3, the upper quartile

(iii) The interquartile range

3. The stem-and-leaf diagram shows the time (in seconds) it took contestants to answer a general knowledge question. All contestants answered in less than 7 seconds.

Stem	Leaf
2	1, 2, 2
3	2, 4, 8, 9
4	1, 3, 4, 6, 7
5	1, 5
6	8 Key 3|2 = 3.2 s

Calculate:

(i) Q_1, the lower quartile

(ii) Q_3, the upper quartile

(iii) The interquartile range

4. Twenty people attend a fancy dress party. Their ages are summarised in the following stem-and-leaf diagram:

Stem	Leaf
1	1, 3, 4, 5, 6, 9
2	1, 3, 5
3	3, 8
4	4, 5, 6, 7, 8
5	1, 6, 7
6	2 Key: 1|4 = 14

Calculate:

(i) Q_1, the lower quartile

(ii) Q_3, the upper quartile

(iii) The interquartile range

5. Here is a back-to-back stem-and-leaf diagram showing the marks obtained by 30 girls and 30 boys in the same maths test. The girls marks are on the left-hand side of the diagram.

Leaf (Girls)	Stem	Leaf (Boys)
9	0	7, 9
7, 2	1	3, 4
8	2	9
9, 6, 6	3	5, 7, 9
8, 8, 6, 6, 6, 4, 2, 2	4	3, 4, 4
8, 6, 4	5	2, 2, 3, 5, 7, 7, 8
8, 2	6	1, 2, 5, 8, 9
9, 6, 4	7	3, 4, 5, 9
8, 5, 2, 0	8	4, 7
Key: 3|9 = 93 9, 8, 3	9	1 Key: 3|7 = 37

Calculate for both sets:

(i) The median mark

(ii) Q_1, the lower quartile

(iii) Q_3, the upper quartile

(iv) The interquartile range

6. Here are the IQ scores for a group of Sixth Year students:

100	113	126	110	99	106	109	117	121	116
97	108	103	115	119	125	132	93	87	130
88	116	102	119	130	110	123	109	119	132

(i) Draw a stem-and-leaf diagram to illustrate the data.

(ii) Describe the distribution.

(iii) Find the range.

(iv) Find the median.

(v) Find the interquartile range.

7. John has done a survey of the cost of bed-and-breakfast in his town. The results are summarised in the following stem-and-leaf diagram:

Stem	Leaf
2	1, 2, 2, 2, 2, 2, 6, 6, 7, 8, 9
3	0, 0, 0, 0, 0, 5, 5, 5, 5, 5, 5, 8, 8
4	0, 0, 0, 0, 0, 0, 5, 5, 5, 5, 9, 9, 9, 9
5	0, 0, 0, 0, 0, 0, 0, 0, 5, 5
6	2, 3, 8, 8, 8, 8, 8
7	5, 5, 9, 9, 9 Key: 6|2 = €62

(i) Write down the median of these costs.

(ii) Find the lower and upper quartiles.

(iii) Find the interquartile range.

8. The number of hours per day that the secretary of a construction firm spends on the phone is recorded. The following data indicates the number of hours per day spent on the phone over a 30-day period:

4.2	1.1	0.3	1.1	3.3	3.2	5.2	1.5	3.1	0.5
1.2	2.5	0.8	0.7	1.8	6	1.2	2.5	5.2	1.6
4	1.4	0.9	2.8	5	0.2	1.9	2.3	1.7	4

(i) Draw a stem-and-leaf diagram to illustrate the data.

(ii) Describe the distribution.

(iii) Find the range.

(iv) Find the median.

(v) Find the interquartile range.

9. The following data indicates the electricity consumption (in kilowatt-hours) for 20 typical two-bedroom apartments in Dublin:

9	11	16	10	11	9	8	13	11	9
13	11	7	9	7	12	14	13	11	7

(i) Draw a stem-and-leaf diagram to illustrate the data.

(ii) Describe the distribution.

(iii) Find the range.

(iv) Find the median.

(v) Find the interquartile range.

4.3 MEASURES OF SPREAD 2: STANDARD DEVIATION

Standard deviation measures the **average deviation or spread from the mean of all values in a set**. It is a reliable measure of spread, as it takes account of all values in the set, unlike the range or interquartile range. However, if there are extreme values in the data set, it is best to use the interquartile range as a measure of spread.

FORMULA

Standard deviation

$$\sigma = \sqrt{\sum \frac{(x - \bar{x})^2}{n}}$$

Note:

σ is the standard deviation.

Σ means 'sum of'.

x is the variable.

$\bar{x}$ is the mean.

n is the number of variables.

Worked Example 4.6

Consider the sets A = {8, 8, 9, 11, 14} and B = {1, 3, 8, 17, 21}.

Calculate for both sets:

(i) The mean   (ii) The range   (iii) The standard deviation

Solution

(i) The mean of set A = $\bar{x}_A = \dfrac{8 + 8 + 9 + 11 + 14}{5} = \dfrac{50}{5} = 10$.

The mean of set B = $\bar{x}_B = \dfrac{1 + 3 + 8 + 17 + 21}{5} = \dfrac{50}{5} = 10$.

(ii) Both sets have the same mean, but the members of set A are more tightly bunched around the mean than the members of set B. To measure the spread of values, we could use the range:

Range$_A$ = 14 − 8 = 6   Range$_B$ = 21 − 1 = 20

(iii) This gives an indication of spread and indicates that set B has a much greater spread than set A. However, as a measure of spread, the range is limited to using just two values in the set, the maximum value and the minimum value. The standard deviation uses **all** values in the set to calculate the spread and is therefore a much better measure. Here is how the standard deviation is calculated for set A.

Step 1: Write down the difference between each member and the mean:

(8 − 10) = −2, (8 − 10) = −2, (9 − 10) = −1, (11 − 10) = 1, (14 − 10) = 4

Step 2: Square these numbers:

$(−2)^2 = 4$, $(−2)^2 = 4$, $(−1)^2 = 1$, $(1)^2 = 1$, $(4)^2 = 16$

Step 3: Find the mean of the squares: $\dfrac{4 + 4 + 1 + 1 + 16}{5} = \dfrac{26}{5} = 5.2$

Step 4: Find the square root of this number: $\sqrt{5.2} \approx 2.28$

The standard deviation of set A is $\sigma_A \approx 2.28$.

Similarly, by following the procedure above, we can find the standard deviation of set B: $\sigma_B \approx 7.80$.

Set B has the greater standard deviation because the members of set B are more widely dispersed than the members of set A: 7.80 > 2.28.

Finding the standard deviation for set A can be summarised as follows:

x	$\bar{x}$	d	d^2
8	10	−2	4
8	10	−2	4
9	10	−1	1
11	10	1	1
14	10	4	16
			26

$$\sigma = \sqrt{\frac{26}{5}}$$

$$\sigma = \sqrt{5.2}$$

$$\sigma \approx 2.28$$

ACTIVITY 4.4

 ## Worked Example 4.7

One hundred students are given a maths problem to solve. The times taken to solve the problem are tabled as follows:

Time (minutes)	10–14	14–18	18–22	22–26	26–30
Number of students	13	28	26	21	12

Note: 14–18 means 14 is included and 18 is not, etc.

Using mid-interval values, estimate the mean of the distribution, and hence, estimate the standard deviation from the mean. Give your answers to two decimal places.

Solution

We can summarise our work as follows:

M.I.V. x	Number f	Number xf	Mean $\bar{x}$	Deviation d	Deviation² d^2	fd^2
12	13	156	19.64	−7.64	58.3696	758.8048
16	28	448	19.64	−3.64	13.2496	370.9888
20	26	520	19.64	0.36	0.1296	3.3696
24	21	504	19.64	4.36	19.0096	399.2016
28	12	336	19.64	8.36	69.8896	838.6752
	100	1964				2371.04

Estimated mean $\bar{x} = \dfrac{1,964}{100} = 19.64$

Standard deviation $\sigma = \sqrt{\dfrac{2,371.04}{100}} = \sqrt{23.7104} \approx 4.87$

The statistics functions on your calculator can also be used to find standard deviation. Here are the keystrokes for this problem. Note that individual calculators may differ.

Exercise 4.5

1. Find, correct to one decimal place, the standard deviation of the following sets of numbers:

   (i) {5, 8, 9, 10}

   (ii) {1, 0, 2, 5, 7}

   (iii) {3, 5, 6, 8, 8}

   (iv) {9, 13, 14, 4, 7}

   (v) {3.1, 3.2, 3.3, 3.4}

2. A = {4, 5, 5, 6, 10}   B = {1, 2, 7, 9, 11}

   (i) Verify that sets A and B have a mean of 6.

   (ii) Find the standard deviation in each case, correct to one decimal place.

3. A = {0, 1, 3, 4, 7, 15}

   (i) Verify that A has a mean of 5.

   (ii) Verify that the standard deviation = 5.

4. The ages of children in a crèche were tabled as follows:

Age	1	2	3	4	5
Frequency	1	0	2	2	5

   Show that 4 is the mean age, and calculate the standard deviation.

5. Twenty households were asked the number of pets they kept. Their responses were tabled as follows:

Number	0	1	2	3	4
Frequency	2	4	8	4	2

   Calculate the standard deviation of the data.

6. The grouped frequency table below refers to the number of minutes it took 20 people to solve a problem.

Time	2–4	4–8	8–10	10–16
Frequency	2	7	8	3

   (i) Estimate the mean of the distribution.

   (ii) Calculate the standard deviation.

7. The following frequency distribution shows the pocket money of 100 students:

Pocket money (€)	0–1	1–2	2–5	5–10
Frequency	4	23	42	31

   (i) Estimate the mean pocket money.

   (ii) Find the standard deviation from the mean.

8. Twenty students were asked how many minutes they spent watching television on a particular day. The following frequency distribution summarises their replies:

Time	0–40	40–60	60–80	80–100	100–120
Frequency	2	6	5	3	4

    (i) Estimate the mean time spent watching television.

    (ii) Find, to the nearest minute, the standard deviation from the mean.

9. The frequency distribution below shows the ages of 100 people.

Age (years)	0–10	10–20	20–30	30–50	50–80
Frequency	10	19	25	30	16

    (i) Estimate the mean age.

    (ii) Find, to the nearest integer, the standard deviation from the mean.

10. A garage owner recorded the amount of money spent by customers on petrol over a day. The following frequency distribution shows the results:

Amount (€)	0–10	10–20	20–30	30–50	50–100
Frequency	50	150	400	300	100

    (i) How many customers spent money on petrol over the day?

    (ii) Estimate the mean amount spent.

    (iii) Find, to the nearest euro, the standard deviation from the mean.

4.4 SPREADSHEETS

Spreadsheets are a very useful tool for generating charts and providing summary statistics. We can generate bar charts, pie charts and histograms, as well as finding measures of central tendency and variation using a spreadsheet such as Excel. Students are expected to be familiar with the procedures outlined in this section.

Worked Example 4.8

All the cars in a car park were surveyed to find their country of origin. The results were tabulated in a spreadsheet as follows:

	A	B	C	D	E	F	G
1	**Country**	Ireland	Poland	UK	Lithuania	France	
2	**Number**	24	6	2	5	1	
3							

Sheet1 / Sheet2 / Sheet3 /
Ready   NUM

    (i) Copy this table into a spreadsheet of your own.

    (ii) Use the spreadsheet to generate a bar chart.

    (iii) Use the spreadsheet's SUM function to find the total number of cars in the car park.

Solution

(i)

	A	B	C	D	E	F	G
1	**Country**	Ireland	Poland	UK	Lithuania	France	
2	**Number**	24	6	2	5	1	
3							

Sheet1 / Sheet2 / Sheet3 /
Ready   NUM

(ii) ▪ Highlight cells B1:F2.

▪ Using the mouse, click on the following:
INSERT → CHART → COLUMN → NEXT → NEXT

▪ Enter 'Cars in a car park' in the chart title box. Enter 'Country' in the x-axis box. Enter 'Number of cars' in the y-axis box.

▪ Click on FINISH.

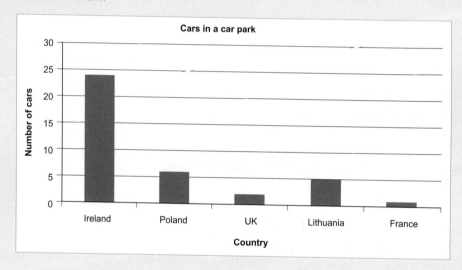

(iii) Here we need to sum the numbers in the cells B2 to F2, and we would like to put our answer in cell G2. So we type '=SUM(B2:F2)' into cell G2. Here is the result:

	A	B	C	D	E	F	G
1	**Country**	Ireland	Poland	UK	Lithuania	France	Total
2	**Number**	24	6	2	5	1	=SUM(B2:F2)
3							

Sheet1 / Sheet2 / Sheet3 /
Ready   NUM

	A	B	C	D	E	F	G
1	**Country**	Ireland	Poland	UK	Lithuania	France	Total
2	**Number**	24	6	2	5	1	38
3							

Sheet1 / Sheet2 / Sheet3 /
Ready   NUM

STATISTICS II

Worked Example 4.9

A committee holds an election for a leader. The votes for the four candidates were counted and tabulated in a spreadsheet.

	A	B	C	D	E	F	G
1	Candidate	Allison	Brian	Cathy	Dermot		
2	No. of votes	4	3	5	6		
3							

Sheet1 / Sheet2 / Sheet3 /

Ready   NUM

(i) Copy the data into your own spreadsheet.

(ii) Use the spreadsheet to generate a pie chart.

(iii) Use the SUM command to find the total number of votes cast.

Solution

(i)

	A	B	C	D	E	F	G
1	Candidate	Allison	Brian	Cathy	Dermot		
2	No. of votes	4	3	5	6		
3							

Sheet1 / Sheet2 / Sheet3 /

Ready   NUM

(ii) ■ Highlight cells B1:E2.

   ■ Using the mouse, click on the following:

   INSERT → CHART → PIE → NEXT → NEXT

   ■ Enter 'Election result' in the chart title box.

   ■ Click on FINISH.

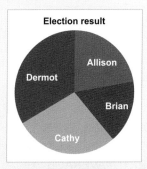

(iii) Here we need to sum the numbers in the cells B2 to E2, and we would like to put our answer in cell F2. So, we type '=SUM(B2:E2)' into cell F2. Here is the result:

	A	B	C	D	E	F	G
1	Candidate	Allison	Brian	Cathy	Dermot	Total	
2	No. of votes	4	3	5	6	18	
3							

Sheet1 / Sheet2 / Sheet3 /

Ready   NUM

The following spreadsheet shows student results in four tests:

	A	B	C	D	E
1	Student	Test 1	Test 2	Test 3	Test 4
2					
3	K Murphy	51	55	68	60
4	A Browne	74	82	79	80
5	C Guerin	40	70	48	55
6	D Keane	90	94	89	100
7	E O'Shea	56	60	82	85
8	F Long	12	41	58	60
9	G Moran	51	82	46	85

Sheet1 / Sheet2 / Sheet3 /

Ready   NUM

(i) Copy the data into your own spreadsheet.

(ii) Using the spreadsheet's MAX and MIN commands, find the maximum and minimum result for each test.

(iii) Find the mean mark for each test.

(iv) Find the median mark for each test.

(v) Find the lower quartile and upper quartile for each test.

(vi) Find the interquartile range.

Solution

	A	B	C	D	E
1	Student	Test 1	Test 2	Test 3	Test 4
2					
3	K Murphy	51	55	68	60
4	A Browne	74	82	79	80
5	C Guerin	40	70	48	55
6	D Keane	90	94	89	100
7	E O'Shea	56	60	82	85
8	F Long	12	41	58	60
9	G Moran	51	82	46	85
10	Max	=MAX(B3:B9)	=MAX(C3:C9)	=MAX(D3:D9)	=MAX(E3:E9)
11	Min	=MIN(B3:B9)	=MIN(C3:C9)	=MIN(D3:D9)	=MIN(E3:E9)
12	Mean	=AVERAGE (B3:B9)	=AVERAGE (C3:C9)	=AVERAGE (D3:D9)	=AVERAGE (E3:E9)
13	Median	=MEDIAN (B3:B9)	=MEDIAN (C3:C9)	=MEDIAN (D3:D9)	=MEDIAN (E3:E9)
14	Lower Quartile	=QUARTILE (B3:B9,1)	=QUARTILE (C3:C9,1)	=QUARTILE (D3:D9,1)	=QUARTILE (E3:E9,1)
15	Upper Quartile	=QUARTILE (B3:B9,3)	=QUARTILE (C3:C9,3)	=QUARTILE (D3:D9,3)	=QUARTILE (E3:E9,3)
16	IQR	=B14-B13	=C14-C13	=D14-D13	=E14-E13

Sheet1 / Sheet2 / Sheet3 /

Ready   NUM

	A	B	C	D	E
1	Student	Test 1	Test 2	Test 3	Test 4
2					
3	K Murphy	51	55	68	60
4	A Browne	74	82	79	80
5	C Guerin	40	70	48	55
6	D Keane	90	94	89	100
7	E O'Shea	56	60	82	85
8	F Long	12	41	58	60
9	G Moran	51	82	46	85
10	Max	90	94	89	100
11	Min	12	41	46	55
12	Mean	53.43	69.14	67.14	75
13	Median	51	70	68	80
14	Lower Quartile	45.5	57.5	53	60
15	Upper Quartile	65	82	80.5	85
16	IQR	19.5	24.5	27.5	25

Sheet1 / Sheet2 / Sheet3 /
Ready   NUM

Exercise 4.6

1. The spreadsheet below gives the marks out of 10 scored by a class in a maths test.

	A	B	C	D	E	F	G	H	I	J	K	L
1	Mark	0	1	2	3	4	5	6	7	8	9	10
2	Freq.	0	1	1	2	4	6	8	4	2	1	1

Sheet1 / Sheet2 / Sheet3 /
Ready   NUM

   (i) Copy the data into your own spreadsheet.

   (ii) Use the spreadsheet to generate a bar chart.

   (iii) Using the SUM command, find the number of students in the class and place your answer in cell B3.

2. Elaine, a Leaving Certificate student, has logged in a spreadsheet the number of hours she has spent studying over the past week. Below is a section of the spreadsheet Elaine used.

	A	B	C	D	E	F	G
1	Day	Mon	Tue	Wed	Thu	Fri	
2	Hours	3	2	4	1	0	
3							

Sheet1 / Sheet2 / Sheet3 /
Ready   NUM

(i) Copy the data into your own spreadsheet.

(ii) Use the spreadsheet to generate a bar chart.

(iii) Using the SUM command, find how many hours' study Elaine did over the past week.

3. John works out how he spends a typical 24-hour day and tabulates his findings in a spreadsheet.

	A	B	C	D	E	F	G
1	Activity	School	Study	Play	TV	Sleep	
2	No. of hours	7	3	x	2	10	
3							

Sheet1 / Sheet2 / Sheet3 /
Ready   NUM

(i) Find the value of x.

(ii) Copy this information into your own spreadsheet.

(iii) Use your spreadsheet to generate a pie chart.

4. There are 72 people on a campsite: 27 are Irish, 33 are from mainland Europe, and the rest are British.

(i) What percentage of the campsite population is British?

(ii) Put the information in a spreadsheet and generate a pie chart.

5. Collect the following data from your class: (a) wrist circumference and (b) eye colour.

(i) Enter the data in a spreadsheet.

(ii) Generate appropriate charts to represent the data.

(iii) Find the mean and median wrist measurements for the class.

(iv) Find the maximum and minimum wrist measurements.

(v) Find the lower quartile, upper quartile and IQR for the wrist measurements.

(vi) Print your spreadsheet.

4.5 THE NORMAL DISTRIBUTION AND THE EMPIRICAL RULE

In nature there are many continuous distributions that are symmetric. For example, if we measure the heights of all adult males in Ireland, we will find a high proportion of the adult male population with heights close to the mean height of the population. As measurements increase or decrease away from the mean, the proportion of the population with these heights begins to decrease. This results in a **symmetric distribution**.

If the distribution is very large and we allow the class intervals (base widths of the rectangles) to become small enough, the distribution forms a smooth, symmetrical, bell-shaped curve called the **normal distribution curve**.

The French mathematician Abraham de Moivre (1667–1754) discovered a mathematical formula for constructing the normal curve. If we wish to find the equation of the normal curve for a particular normal distribution, we substitute (i) the mean and (ii) the standard deviation from the mean into de Moivre's formula.

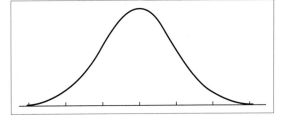

In any normal distribution:

(i) Approximately 68% of the population lies within one standard deviation of the mean, i.e. 68% lies within the range $[\bar{x} - \sigma, \bar{x} + \sigma]$.

(ii) Approximately 95% of the population lies within the range $[\bar{x} - 2\sigma, \bar{x} + 2\sigma]$.

(iii) Approximately 99.7% of the population lies within the range $[\bar{x} - 3\sigma, \bar{x} + 3\sigma]$.

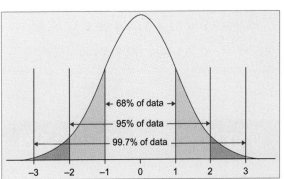

Worked Example 4.11

The frequency table below shows the number of hits a website received each day during a particular week:

Day	Mon	Tue	Wed	Thu	Fri
Number of hits	50	80	120	40	20

(i) Calculate $\bar{x}$, the mean number of hits per day during that week.

(ii) Calculate σ, the standard deviation from the mean.

(iii) Calculate $\bar{x} - \sigma$.

(iv) Calculate $\bar{x} + \sigma$.

(v) Now find the range $[\bar{x} - \sigma, \bar{x} + \sigma]$.

Solution

(i) $\bar{x} = \dfrac{50 + 80 + 120 + 40 + 20}{5} = \dfrac{310}{5} = 62$ hits

(ii)

x	d	d^2
50	−12	144
80	18	324
120	58	3,364
40	−22	484
20	−42	1,764
		6,080

$$\sigma = \sqrt{\dfrac{6,080}{5}} = \sqrt{1,216}$$

$$\approx 34.9$$

$$\sigma \approx 34.9$$

You may also use your calculator to do this. Note that individual calculators may differ.

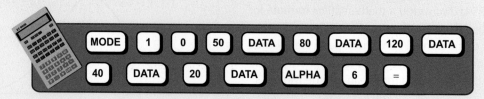

(iii) $\bar{x} - \sigma = 62 - 34.9 = 27.1$

(iv) $\bar{x} + \sigma = 62 + 34.9 = 96.9$

(v) $[\bar{x} - \sigma, \bar{x} + \sigma] = [27.1, 96.9]$

Worked Example 4.12

The distribution of heights of a large group of students is normal, with a mean of 158 cm and a standard deviation from the mean of 10 cm. The empirical rule says that approximately 68% of a normally distributed population lies within one standard deviation of the mean.

(i) Using the empirical rule, find the range of heights within which 68% of this population lies.

(ii) If a student is chosen at random from the population, find the probability that the student has a height between 148 cm and 168 cm.

Solution

(i) Range $= [\bar{x} - \sigma, \bar{x} + \sigma]$

$= [158 - 10, 158 + 10] = [148 \text{ cm}, 168 \text{ cm}]$

(ii) From part (i), we know that 68% of the population has heights in the range [148 cm, 168 cm]. Therefore, the probability that the student has a height between 148 cm and 168 cm is 0.68.

Worked Example 4.13

Washers are produced so that their inside diameter is normally distributed with a mean of 1.25 cm. If 95% of the diameters are between 1.2375 cm and 1.2625 cm, then what is the approximate standard deviation from the mean?

Solution

The empirical rule tells us that approximately 95% of the diameters will be in the range $[1.25 - 2\sigma, 1.25 + 2\sigma]$.

Therefore, $1.25 - 2\sigma = 1.2375$

$-2\sigma = 1.2375 - 1.25$

$-2\sigma = -0.0125$

$\sigma = 0.00625 \text{ cm}$

Exercise 4.7

1. In a normal distribution:

   (i) Approximately what proportion of observations lies within one standard deviation of the mean?

   (ii) Approximately what proportion of observations lies within two standard deviations of the mean?

   (iii) Approximately what proportion of observations lies within three standard deviations of the mean?

2. The principal of Fermat High School records the number of pupils absent each day during a week in December. The results are displayed in the table below.

Day	Monday	Tuesday	Wednesday	Thursday	Friday
Number	12	19	17	25	20

   (i) Calculate $\bar{x}$, the mean number of students absent per day during that week.

   (ii) Calculate σ, the standard deviation from the mean.

   (iii) Now find the range $[\bar{x} - \sigma, \bar{x} + \sigma]$.

3. In each of the following, the mean ($\bar{x}$) and the standard deviation (σ) of the normal distributions are given. For each distribution, find the range within which 68% of the distribution lies.

   (i) $\bar{x} = 200, \sigma = 25$ (iii) $\bar{x} = 20, \sigma = 2$

   (ii) $\bar{x} = 100, \sigma = 20$ (iv) $\bar{x} = 25, \sigma = 2.5$

4. In each of the following, the mean ($\bar{x}$) and the standard deviation (σ) of the normal distributions are given. For each distribution, find the range within which 95% of the distribution lies.

   (i) $\bar{x} = 280, \sigma = 35$ (iii) $\bar{x} = 25, \sigma = 2$

   (ii) $\bar{x} = 120, \sigma = 30$ (iv) $\bar{x} = 35, \sigma = 5.5$

5. In each of the following, the mean ($\bar{x}$) and the standard deviation (σ) of the normal distributions are given. For each distribution, find the range within which 99.7% of the distribution lies.

   (i) $\bar{x} = 150, \sigma = 25$ (iii) $\bar{x} = 20, \sigma = 2$

   (ii) $\bar{x} = 300, \sigma = 15$ (iv) $\bar{x} = 100, \sigma = 5$

6. In each of the following, the mean ($\bar{x}$) and the standard deviation (σ) of the normal distributions are given. For each distribution, find the range within which 95% of the distribution lies.

   (i) $\bar{x} = 200, \sigma = 25$ (iii) $\bar{x} = 20, \sigma = 2$

   (ii) $\bar{x} = 100, \sigma = 20$ (iv) $\bar{x} = 25, \sigma = 2.5$

7. In each of the following, the mean ($\bar{x}$) and standard deviation (σ) of the normal distributions are given. For each distribution, find the range within which 99.7% of the distribution lies.

   (i) $\bar{x} = 40, \sigma = 5$ (iii) $\bar{x} = 22, \sigma = 6$

   (ii) $\bar{x} = 100, \sigma = 15$ (iv) $\bar{x} = 30, \sigma = 2$

8. IQ scores are normally distributed with a mean of 100 and a standard deviation of 15. Isaac de Moivre has taken an IQ test and scored 145. His friend Eoin has remarked that Isaac's score is in the top 5% of all IQ scores. Isaac disagrees and says that he is in the top 2.5%. Is Eoin's remark correct? Explain your reasoning.

9. Men's heights are normally distributed with a mean of 172.5 cm and a standard deviation from the mean of 7 cm. Séamus the statistician has designed a house with doorways high enough to allow all men, except the tallest 2.5%, to pass through without bending. What doorway height has Séamus used?

10. Human body temperatures are normally distributed with a mean of 36.8°C and a standard deviation from the mean of 0.2°C. Rita has a body temperature of 40.5°C. Should Rita be concerned? Explain your reasoning using statistics.

11. Birth weights in Ireland are normally distributed with a mean of 3.42 kg and a standard deviation of 0.5 kg. What percentage of babies born will weigh between 2.92 kg and 3.92 kg? Explain your answer.

STATISTICS II

4.6 MISUSES OF STATISTICS

Statistics presented in newspapers, on TV, on websites and in other media can sometimes be misleading. It is important that we, as consumers, are able to spot errors and exaggerations in such statistics. The following is a list of possible errors and exaggerations that may mislead the consumer.

1. *Arithmetic errors or omissions.* Always check that everything adds up. Do all percentages add up to 100? Does the number in each group add up to the total number surveyed?

2. *Sample size.* Many advertisements or newspaper articles contain statements such as 'Four out of five owners said their cats preferred KAT food.' How many cat owners were surveyed? If only 10 cat owners were surveyed and 8 said that their cats preferred KAT, we cannot say that this number is representative of all cat owners, as the number surveyed is too small.

3. *Misleading comparisons.* Newspaper articles and TV reports sometimes make misleading comparisons. For example:

   > The unemployment situation in the country at present is twice as bad as it was in the 1980s. There are twice as many unemployed now as at any time in the 1980s.

   However, there is a larger workforce now than in the 1980s. Unemployment figures should always be given as a percentage of the workforce. This is an example of a misleading comparison.

4. *Sources.* Always check the source of the information. Surveys are sometimes sponsored by companies with vested interests to promote. Very often, the sponsor can gain financially from the results of the survey.

5. *Misleading graphs.* The chart below summarises the results of 500 throws of a die. Do you think the die is biased?

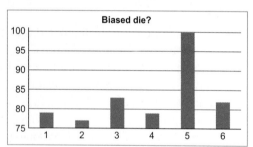

What makes the chart exaggerate the difference between the number of times a 5 was thrown and the number of times a 3 was thrown?

Now look at a different chart that summarises the same results:

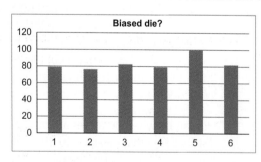

The second graph is more correct, as it starts with zero at the bottom of each bar.

6. *Non-representative samples.* A sample should always be representative of the population from which it is taken, otherwise the results will be misleading. For example, suppose you want to find the average height of 16-year-olds in your school, and you wish to do it by taking a sample. You decide to randomly choose thirty 16-year-olds. However, you limit your sample to girls only. This is not a representative sample, as boys have been deliberately omitted from the sample. This will lead to misleading results.

7. *Response bias.* This occurs when people can choose whether or not to take part in a survey. For example, a television show might ask people to call in and vote on some issue. First, the people who watch that particular show may not be representative of the overall population; second, people who do phone in might be more likely or less likely to vote 'Yes' than people who don't phone in.

ACTIVITY 4.5

Revision Exercises

1. The following are the pulse rates (beats per minutes) of a group of 30 adults:

68	64	88	72	64	72	66	88	76	56
64	60	96	72	56	64	60	64	86	74
74	72	64	60	56	56	64	56	88	84

(i)   Is this data discrete or continuous? Explain.

(ii) Complete the frequency table below.

No. of beats	56–60	60–64	64–68	68–72	72–76	76–80	80–84	84–88
Tally								
Frequency								

Note: 56–60 means 56 is included but 60 is not, etc.

(iii) Draw a bar chart of the distribution.

(iv)   Describe the distribution.

(v)   Rank the raw data and find the median.

(vi)   Using mid-interval values, estimate the mean of the distribution.

(vii) Now, using the raw data, calculate the mean.

(viii) What is the percentage error in the estimated mean?

(ix)   Using the raw data, find the standard deviation from the mean.

2. A class was asked to estimate the height of a tall building adjacent to the school. The following table gives their estimates. All estimates are in metres.

(i)   Is this data categorical data or numerical data? Explain.

(ii) How many students are in the class?

(iii) Represent the data on a stem-and-leaf plot.

(iv) Describe the shape of the distribution.

(v)   What is the median estimate?

(vi) Calculate the mean estimate.

(vii) What is the difference between the mean and median estimates?

(viii) Explain why the difference between the mean and the median is small.

36	41	60	53	75	83
43	54	64	79	86	47
56	64	49	48	58	66
58	59	38	79	52	31
21	22				

STATISTICS II

3. The following frequency table shows the time spent by a group of students on a difficult maths problem:

Time (min)	0–4	4–8	8–12	12–16
Number	8	12	10	7

Note: 0–4 means 0 is included but 4 is not, etc.

(i) How many students worked on the problem?

(ii) Construct a histogram for the data.

(iii) Describe the shape of the distribution.

(iv) Using mid-interval values, calculate the mean time taken to solve the problem.

(v) Using mid-interval values, find the standard deviation from the mean.

4. Twenty people attend a meeting on healthy diets. Their ages are summarised in the following stem-and-leaf diagram:

Stem	Leaf
1	1, 1, 1, 4, 5
2	1, 3, 5
3	3, 8
4	4, 5, 6, 7, 8
5	9, 9
6	8, 9, 9 Key: 1|4 = 14

Using the stem-and-leaf diagram, calculate:

(i) The median age

(ii) Q_1, the lower quartile

(iii) Q_3, the upper quartile

(iv) The interquartile range

(v) The range

(vi) The mean age

5. There are 15 boys and 13 girls in a maths class. The mean time spent on homework each week for the boys is 5.5 hours. The mean time spent on homework for the girls is 7.2 hours.

(i) Find the mean time spent on homework for all students in the class.

(ii) 'All girls study more than all boys.' Is this a true statement based on the given information? Explain your answer.

(iii) Can we conclude that girls will do better in exams than boys based on the mean time spent on homework? Explain.

6. The table below shows the monthly salaries (in euro) of 20 families living in a particular neighbourhood.

2,451	2,580	2,595	2,635
2,635	2,530	2,550	1,680
2,654	2,520	2,560	2,575
2,462	2,540	2,690	2,740
2,635	2,635	2,673	2,480

(i) Complete the grouped frequency distribution below.

Salary	2,450–2,500	2,500–2,550	2,550–2,600	2,600–2,650	2,650–2,700	2,700–2,750
Number						

Note: 2,450–2,500 includes 2,450 but excludes 2,500.

(ii) Draw a histogram to represent the distribution.

(iii) Comment on the shape of the histogram.

(iv) Using the original table, calculate the mean and the median salary.

(v) Estimate the mean salary from the grouped frequency distribution.

(vi) Find the lower quartile, upper quartile and interquartile range for the above data.

Another family have moved into the neighbourhood. One member of the family is a very successful writer and earns €10,000 a month.

(vii) Comment on how this will affect the mean salary for the neighbourhood.

(viii) Which average will now be more representative of salaries for the neighbourhood? Explain.

(ix) Will the interquartile range be affected? Explain.

7. In 1798 Henry Cavendish, using a piece of equipment known as a torsion balance, obtained measurements for the density of the earth. A random sample of the measurements is given below. Measurements are in g/cm^3.

5.10	5.30	5.42	5.53
5.26	5.34	5.44	5.55
5.27	5.34	5.46	5.57
5.29	5.36	5.47	5.58
5.29	5.39	5.50	5.61

(i) Display the data on a stem-and-leaf diagram.

(ii) Comment on the shape of the distribution.

(iii) Find the mean and median measurements.

(iv) Find the lower quartile, upper quartile and interquartile range for the above data.

8. The size, mean and standard deviation from the mean of four different data sets are given below.

	A	B	C	D
Size	500	100	50	20
Mean	50	120	5	34
Standard deviation	15	10	7	3

Complete the sentences below by inserting the relevant word in each space.

(i) The biggest data set is _____ and the smallest data set is _____.

(ii) In general, the data in set _____ are the biggest and the data in set _____ are the smallest.

(iii) The data in set _____ are more spread out than the data in the other sets.

(iv) Set _____ must contain some negative numbers.

9. Women's heights are normally distributed with a mean of 159 cm and a standard deviation from the mean of 6.25 cm. Find the range of heights within which:

(i) Approximately 99.7% of the female population lie

(ii) Approximately 68% of the female population lie

(iii) Approximately 95% of the female population lie

10. (a) Write down the most likely value of the correlation coefficient for each of the following scatter graphs. Choose from the following list:

−0.4   0.95   −0.76   −2.1   0.75   −0.97

(i)
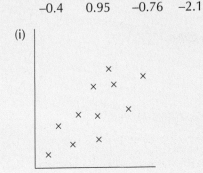

(ii)
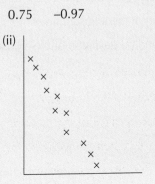

(b) Alice carried out a survey to determine how accurately a group of primary school children measured the perimeter of a rectangle.

The rectangle measured 35 mm by 5 mm. The results of the survey are shown in the stem-and-leaf plot below.

7	3, 6, 6, 8, 9
8	0, 0, 0, 1, 2, 2, 3, 6 Key: 7|6 = 76 mm

Alice then constructed another stem-and-leaf plot to show the same data.

7	3
7	6, 6, 8, 9
8	0, 0, 0, 1, 2, 2, 3
8	6 Key: 8|0 = 80 mm

(i) How many students were surveyed?

(ii) What is the advantage of using the second plot rather than the first?

(iii) Find the mean, the median and the mode of the data.
Give your answers correct to the nearest whole number.

(iv) What is the correct length of the perimeter?

(v) Are the measures of centre a good approximation of the perimeter length? Explain.

11. During a go-kart competition, Seán recorded the lap times of some competitors during a 30-minute period. His results are shown in the table below.

Time (secs)	0–10	10–20	20–30	30–40	40–50	50–60
Number	6	11	36	21	8	3

Note: 10–20 means 10 is included but 20 is not, and so on.

(i) Draw a histogram of the distribution.

(ii) Describe the shape of the distribution.

(iii) Using mid-interval values, estimate the mean of the distribution.

(iv) Now estimate the standard deviation of the distribution.

(v) Seán randomly selects one of the competitors he has timed.
What is the probability that this competitor has posted a time of 30 seconds or less?

Seán has just discovered that the times he recorded belong to an elite group of competitors. The organisers have decided to add 10 seconds onto the times of all elite competitors.

(vi) Represent the adjusted times in a grouped frequency table.

(vii) What is the mean of the adjusted times? Explain.

(viii) Calculate the standard deviation of the adjusted times.

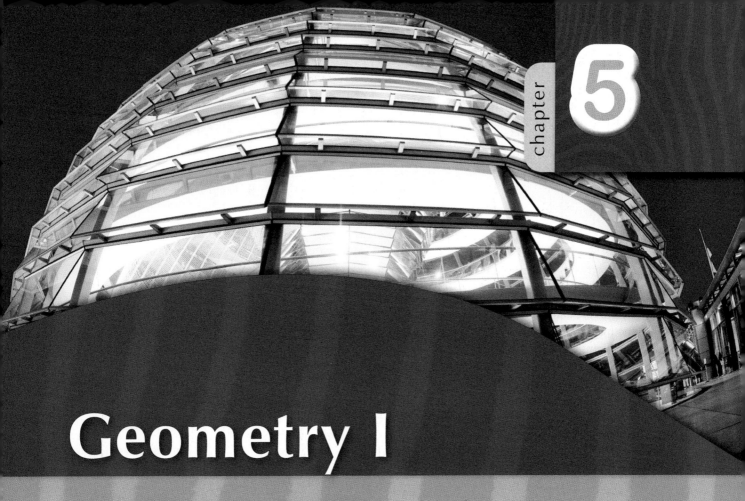

chapter 5

Geometry I

Learning Outcomes

In this chapter you will learn:

- ➲ To understand the basic concepts of geometry and geometry notation.

- ➲ To understand what an axiom is and be able to use them to solve problems.

- ➲ Theorem 1. Vertically opposite angles are equal in measure.

- ➲ Theorem 2. In an isosceles triangle the angles opposite the equal sides are equal. Conversely, if two angles are equal, then the triangle is isosceles.

- ➲ Theorem 3. If a transversal makes equal alternate angles on two lines then the lines are parallel (and converse).

- ➲ Theorem 4. The angles in any triangle add to 180°.

- ➲ Theorem 5. Two lines are parallel if and only if, for any transversal, the corresponding angles are equal.

- ➲ Theorem 6. Each exterior angle of a triangle is equal to the sum of the interior opposite angles.

- ➲ Theorem 7. In a triangle, the angle opposite the greater of two sides is greater than the angle opposite the lesser. Conversely, the side opposite the greater of two angles is greater than the side opposite the lesser angle.

- ➲ Theorem 8. Two sides of a triangle are together greater than the third.

- ➲ Theorem 9. In a parallelogram, opposite sides are equal and opposite angles are equal.

- ➲ Theorem 10. The diagonals of a parallelogram bisect each other.

5.1 GEOMETRY

Geometry comes from the Greek word meaning 'earth measurement' (γεωμετρία; *geo* = earth, *metria* = measure). It is the study of figures and their properties in two- and three-dimensional space.

Geometry has applications from laying tiles on a floor to building a space station.

One of the earliest uses of geometry was in the measurement of area and height. Thales of Miletus (c.620–c.546 BC) supposedly used the properties of similar triangles to measure the height of the pyramids.

Another famous geometer was Pythagoras, who is credited with discovering the famous theorem on right-angled triangles.

FORMULA

$$c^2 = a^2 + b^2$$

Euclid of Alexandria, a Greek mathematician, is famous for his book *The Elements*, written around 300 BC. It is from this book that we derive many of our concepts and ideas on geometry.

In many careers, from carpentry to engineering and from computer game design to astronomy, a good understanding of geometry is required.

YOU SHOULD REMEMBER...

- Geometry notation
- Types of angles
- Types of triangles
- Parallel
- Perpendicular
- Junior Certificate geometry theorems

KEY WORDS

- **Axiom**
- **Theorem**
- **Vertically opposite**
- **Alternate**
- **Corresponding**
- **Isosceles triangle**
- **Interior angle**
- **Exterior angle**
- **Opposite angle**
- **Inequality**
- **Quadrilateral**
- **Parallelogram**

5.2 BASIC CONCEPTS

The Plane

A **plane** stretches on to infinity. Points and lines are shown on a plane.

> A plane is a flat two-dimensional surface. It has length and width, but it has no thickness.

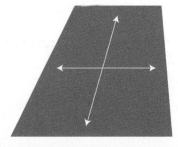

Points on the Plane

> A **point** is a position on a plane. It has no dimensions.

A **point** is denoted by a capital letter and a dot.

This is the point B.

> If points lie on the same plane they are said to be **coplanar**.

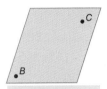

Here, B and C are **coplanar**.

Lines

> A **line** is a straight, infinitely thin line that continues forever in both directions; it has no endpoints.

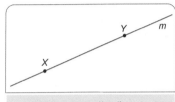

The line XY or the line m.

A **line** can be named by any two points on the line or by a lower-case letter. It has an infinite number of points on it.

> Points that lie on the same line are called **collinear points**.

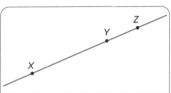

The points X, Y and Z are **collinear**.

Perpendicular and Parallel Lines

> **Perpendicular lines** are lines that are at right angles or 90° to each other.

> **Parallel lines** are lines that are the same distance apart. They never meet.

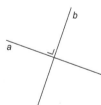

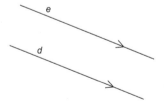

The line a is **perpendicular** to the line b. We denote this as a ⊥ b.

The line d is **parallel** to the line e. We denote this as d ∥ e.

Line Segment

A **line segment** is part of a straight line. It has two endpoints and can be measured using a ruler.

The **line segment** shown has one endpoint A and another endpoint B. This is the line segment $[AB]$ or $[BA]$. We can use a ruler to measure a line segment.

$$|AB| = 5 \text{ cm.}$$

When we write an actual measurement, we use the $|\quad|$ symbols to show this. For example: $|AB| = 5$ cm.

Ray

A **ray** is part of a line that originates at a point and goes on forever in only one direction.

The other end of a **ray** goes on to infinity. It is sometimes called a half-line.

A single square bracket is used to denote where the ray originates from.

This is the ray $[AB$.

This is the ray $[BA$.

ACTIVITY 5.1

5.3 ANGLES

An **angle** is a measure of rotation. The measure or size of the angle is how much one ray rotates or turns around the **vertex**.

When two rays meet at a point called the **vertex**, they make an **angle**.

The rotation of the **arms** of the angle determines the size of the angle.

The two rays that make up the angle are called the **arms** of the angle.

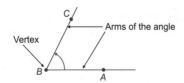

Both these angles are the same. The length of the arms of the angle does not change the size of the angle.

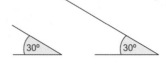

Angle Notation

There are many different ways to label an angle:

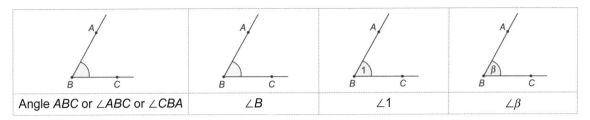

Angle *ABC* or ∠*ABC* or ∠*CBA*	∠*B*	∠1	∠*β*

Identifying Different Types of Angles

Angles can be divided into many different types.

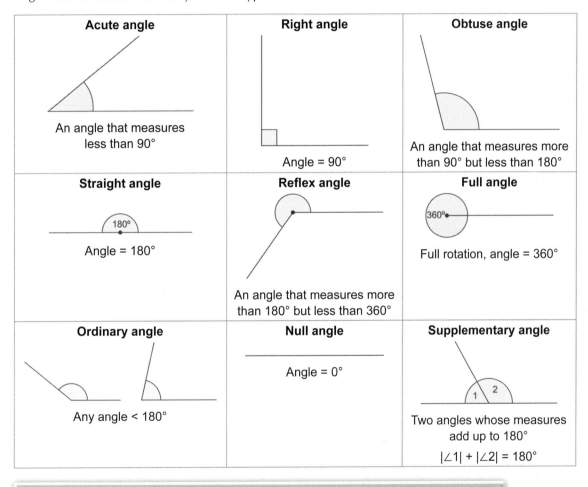

Acute angle	Right angle	Obtuse angle
An angle that measures less than 90°	Angle = 90°	An angle that measures more than 90° but less than 180°
Straight angle	**Reflex angle**	**Full angle**
Angle = 180°	An angle that measures more than 180° but less than 360°	Full rotation, angle = 360°
Ordinary angle	**Null angle**	**Supplementary angle**
Any angle < 180°	Angle = 0°	Two angles whose measures add up to 180° $|∠1| + |∠2| = 180°$

Supplementary angles do not need to be beside or adjacent to each other.

For example, the two angles shown are supplementary.

Measuring Angles

Angles on our course are usually measured in **degrees**, although there are other ways to measure angles.

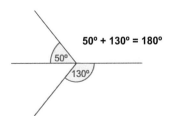

50° + 130° = 180°

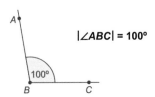

$|∠ABC| = 100°$

GEOMETRY I

We use a **protractor** to measure an angle accurately.

A protractor has two scales, a centre point and a baseline.

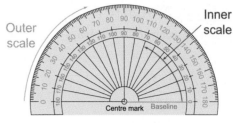

We must be careful to use the right scale. The **inner scale** of the protractor is used if the arm of the angle that is lined up with the baseline of the protractor passes through the zero of the inner scale.

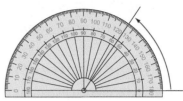

The **outer scale** of the protractor is used if the arm of the angle that is lined up with the baseline of the protractor passes through the zero of the outer scale.

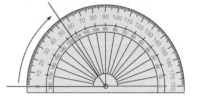

5.4 AXIOMS

An **axiom** is a statement that we accept **without any proof**. Knowing axioms is essential to understanding geometry.

Axiom 1 (Two Points Axiom)
There is exactly one line through any two given points.

We can draw only one line through the points A and B.

Axiom 2 (Ruler Axiom)
The properties of the distance between points.

The distance between two points has the following properties:

1. The distance is never a negative number.
   We can't write $|DE| = -7$ cm.

2. $|DE| = |ED|$.

3. If F lies on DE, between D and E, then $|DE| = |DF| + |FE|$.

4. Given any ray from the point A and a distance $d \geqslant 0$, there is exactly one point B on the ray whose distance from A is d.

   This property means that we can mark off a distance of, say, 5 cm on a ray from a point A and call this point B. The length of the line segment [AB] will also be 5 cm.

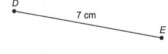

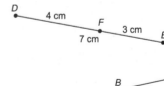

Axiom 3 (Protractor Axiom)

The properties of the degree measure of an angle.

The number of degrees in an angle is always a number between 0 and 360. This axiom has the following properties:

1. A straight angle has 180°.

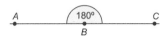

All the angles at a point add up to 360°.

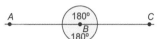

2. Given a ray [AB and a number between 0 and 180, there is exactly one ray from A, on each side of the line AB, that makes an (ordinary) angle having d degrees with the ray [AB.

   This property of the protractor axiom means that there is, for example, only one 60° angle on each side of the line AB, having A as a vertex.

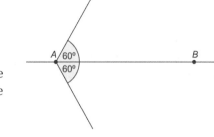

3. If an angle is divided into two smaller angles, then these two angles add up to the original angle.

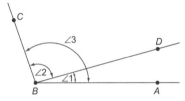

$$|\angle 1| + |\angle 2| = |\angle 3|$$

Axiom 5 (Axiom of Parallels)

Given any line *l* and a point *P*, there is exactly one line through *P* that is parallel to *l*.

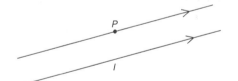

Only one line can be drawn through the point *P* that is parallel to the line *l*.

ACTIVITIES 5.3, 5.4, 5.5, 5.6

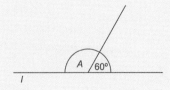

Worked Example 5.1

Without using a protractor, find the measure of the angle A.

Solution

Remember to show as much work as possible.

A straight angle = 180°.

$$|\angle A| = 180° - 60°$$

$$|\angle A| = 120°$$

Worked Example 5.2

Without measuring, find the measure of ∠ABC.

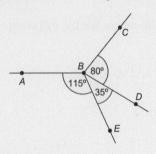

Solution

Full angle = 360°.

|∠ABC| = 360° − 80° − 35° − 115°

|∠ABC| = 360° − 230°

|∠ABC| = 130°

Exercise 5.1

1. Identify in the following figure:

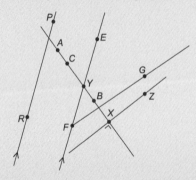

   (i)   A point

   (ii) A line

   (iii) A ray

   (iv) A pair of parallel lines

   (v)   A pair of perpendicular lines

   (vi) Four collinear points

   (vii) A point of intersection of two lines

2. Explain each of the following terms used in geometry. Use diagrams if necessary.

   (i)   Obtuse angle

   (ii) Right angle

   (iii) Acute angle

   (iv) Straight angle

   (v)   Reflex angle

   (vi) Null angle

3. Use a protractor to measure the following angles. In each case, name and identify the type of angle.

   (i)

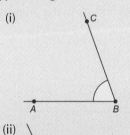

   (ii)

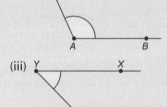

   (iii)

   (iv)

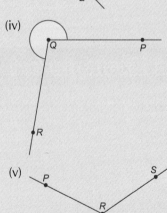

   (v)

4. Use a protractor to draw the following angles:

(i) 65°   (iii) 210°   (v) 90°

(ii) 135°   (iv) 335°   (vi) 172°

5. Consider the following angles:

(i) Estimate which angle is the smallest.

(ii) Explain how you estimated your answers.

(iii) Check your answer using a protractor.

(iv) Does the length of the arm of the angle affect the measure of the angle? Give a reason for your answer.

6. Find the measure of each of the unknown angles without measuring them.

(i)

(ii)

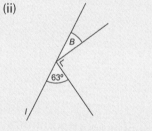

(iii)

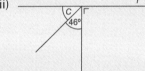

(iv)

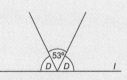

(v)

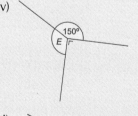

(vi)

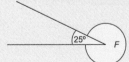

(vii)

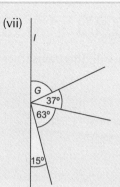

7. Solve for x in each of the following diagrams:

(i)

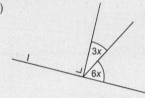

(ii)

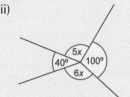

(iii)

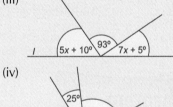

(iv)

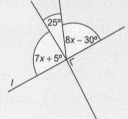

8. Solve for x and y in each of the following diagrams:

(i)

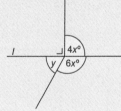

(ii)

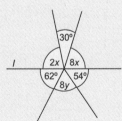

5.5 THEOREM TERMS

When dealing specifically with **theorems**, there are some terms that we need to understand.

> A **theorem** is a rule that has been proved by following a certain number of logical steps or by using a previous theorem or axiom that you already know.

Theorem 14 (Theorem of Pythagoras)

In a right-angled triangle, the square of the hypotenuse is the sum of the squares of the other two sides.

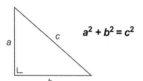

$$a^2 + b^2 = c^2$$

You should be able to use each of the theorems that you learn to solve various geometry questions.

$|\angle A| = ?$

Here we use the theorem that states that the angles in any triangle add up to $180°$. This gives $|\angle A| = 180° - (70° + 60°) \Rightarrow |\angle A| = 50°$.

Theorem

Step 1...
Step 2...
Step 3...

> A **proof** is a series of logical steps that we use to prove a theorem.

Corollary 4

If the angle standing on a chord [BC] at some point of the circle is a right angle, then [BC] is a diameter of that circle.

> A **corollary** is a statement that follows readily from a previous theorem.

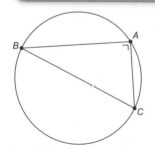

> The **converse** of a theorem is the reverse of the theorem.

A theorem is a mathematical statement that can be proved.

Statement: In an isosceles triangle the angles opposite the equal sides are equal in measure.

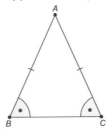

The **converse** of a theorem is made by switching the statement around.

Converse: If two angles in a triangle are equal in measure, then the triangle is isosceles.

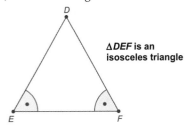

△*DEF* is an isosceles triangle

Statement: Dogs do not like cats.

Converse: Cats do not like dogs.

A converse of a statement may not be true. For example:
Statement – The interior angles of a square each measure 90° (True).
Converse – If the interior angles each measure 90°, then the figure is a square (False).

The angles of a triangle *ABC* are all 60°.

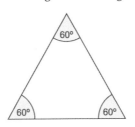

Implies is a term we use in a proof when we can write down a fact we have proved from our previous statements. The symbol for implies is ⇒.

⇒ Triangle *ABC* is an equilateral triangle.

ACTIVITY 5.7

5.6 VERTICALLY OPPOSITE ANGLES

Vertically opposite angles are angles that have the same vertex and are directly opposite each other.

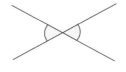

ACTIVITY 5.8

Theorem 1

Vertically opposite angles are equal in measure.

A way to spot **vertically opposite angles** is to look for the X shape.

$|\angle 1| = |\angle 2|$

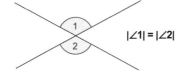

Worked Example 5.3

Find the measure of the angle *ABC* and the angle *DBC*.

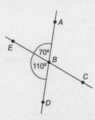

Solution

$|\angle ABC| = 110°$ (angle vertically opposite is 110°)

$|\angle DBC| = 70°$ (angle vertically opposite is 70°)

Worked Example 5.4

Find $|\angle A|, |\angle B|$ and $|\angle C|$.

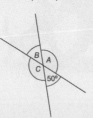

Solution

$|\angle A| = 130°$ (180° − 50°)

$|\angle B| = 50°$ (vertically opposite angle)

$|\angle C| = 130°$ (vertically opposite angle A)

Exercise 5.2

1. Find the measure of angle *A* in each of the following diagrams that show intersecting lines. Make sure to show all your work and give a reason for your answer. Do not use a protractor.

(i)   (ii) 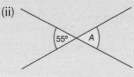 (iii) 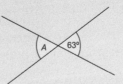 (iv)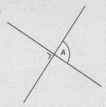

2. Find the value of *B* and *C* in each of the following diagrams that show intersecting lines. Make sure to show all your work. Do not use a protractor.

(i) 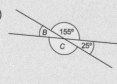 (ii)  (iii) 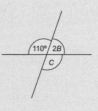 (iv)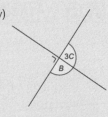

3. Find the value of *x* and *y* in each of the following diagrams. (Diagrams are not drawn to scale.)

(i) 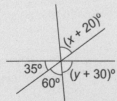 (ii)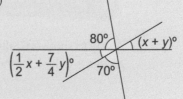

5.7 ALTERNATE AND CORRESPONDING ANGLES IN PARALLEL LINES

When a line cuts across two or more other lines, certain angles are formed.

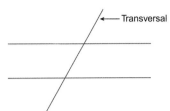
← Transversal

> A line that cuts two or more (usually parallel) lines is called a transversal.

Alternate Angles

Alternate angles are on opposite sides of the **transversal** that cuts two lines but are between the two lines.

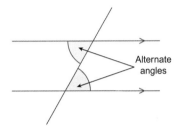
Alternate angles

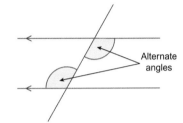
Alternate angles

Remember to look for the Z shape.

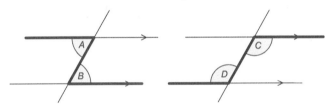

We can now explore the properties of alternate angles.

ACTIVITY 5.9

From Activity 5.9, we can conclude that:

Theorem 3

If a transversal makes equal alternate angles on two lines, then the lines are **parallel** (and converse).

$|\angle A| = |\angle B|$

Corresponding Angles

Corresponding angles are on the same side of the transversal that cuts two lines. One angle is between the lines and the other angle is outside the lines.

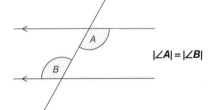
Corresponding angles

Corresponding angles

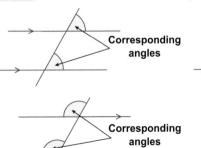
Corresponding angles

Corresponding angles

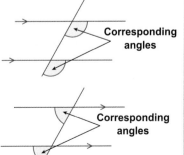
Corresponding angles

Corresponding angles

Remember to look for the F shape.

We can now investigate the properties of corresponding angles.

From Activity 5.10, we can show that:

Theorem 5

Two lines are parallel if, and only if, for any transversal, the corresponding angles are equal.

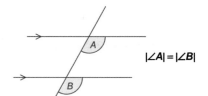

$|\angle A| = |\angle B|$

Worked Example 5.5

Without measuring, find the value of $|\angle A|$, $|\angle B|$, $|\angle C|$ and $|\angle D|$.

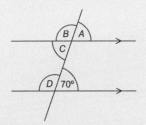

Solution

$|\angle D| = 180° - 70°$ (straight angle)

$\therefore |\angle D| = 110°$

$|\angle C| = 70°$ (alternate angle)

$|\angle A| = 70°$ (corresponding angle or vertically opposite to C)

$|\angle B| = 110°$ (corresponding angle to D)

Worked Example 5.6

Without measuring, find the value of $|\angle 1|$.

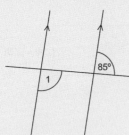

This question is more difficult, as we must determine ourselves which angles to use.

Solution

Fill in Angle 2.

$|\angle 2| = 85°$ (corresponding angle)

$|\angle 1| = 180° - 85°$ (straight angle)

$\Rightarrow |\angle 1| = 95°$

Remember: Many questions have more than one way in which to find the measure of the required angle.

Exercise 5.3

1. Find $|\angle 1|$ and $|\angle 2|$ in each of the following diagrams. Make sure to show all your work and give a reason for your answer.

(i)

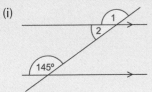

(ii)

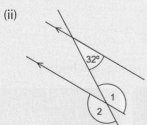

(iii)

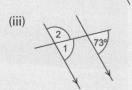

(iv)

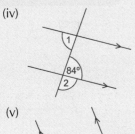

(v)

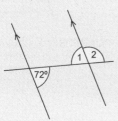

2. Investigate if the each of the following pairs of lines are parallel. Explain your answer in each case.

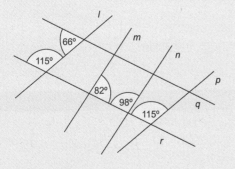

(i) *m* and *n*

(ii) *p* and *l*

(iii) *r* and *q*

3. Find the size of each of the unknown angles marked in each of the following diagrams. Make sure to show all your work and give a reason for your answer.

(i)

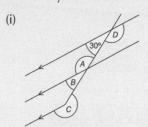

(ii)

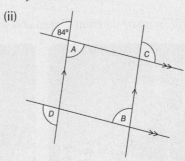

(iii)

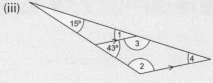

(iv)

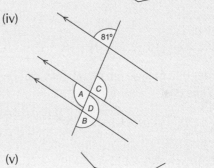

(v)

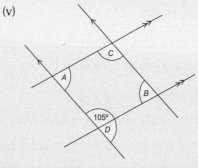

(vi)

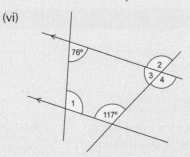

4. Find the value of *x* and *y* in each of the following diagrams. (Diagrams are not drawn to scale.)

(i)

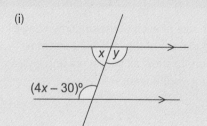

(ii)

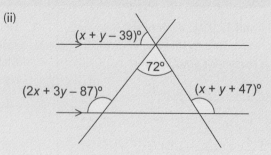

5.8 TRIANGLES

Triangles come in many different shapes and sizes. They are often seen in buildings and bridges.

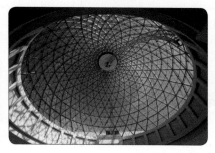

Triangle Notation

The triangle below could be called the triangle *ABC* or $\triangle ABC$.

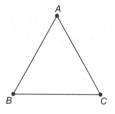

If the sides of a triangle are equal, they can be marked like this:

Two sides are equal.	All sides are equal.

If the angles of a triangle are equal, they can be identified as shown:

Two angles are equal.	All angles are equal.

Types of Triangles

Triangles are usually divided into three types according to the sides and angles.

The different triangles and their properties are:

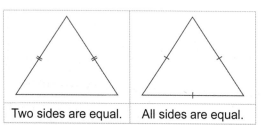
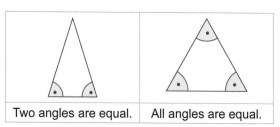

Equilateral	Isosceles	Scalene
All sides the same length	Two sides the same length	Three sides different in length
All angles the same size (60°)	Two angles the same size	Three angles different in measure

A special type of triangle is a **right-angled triangle**.
We can now look at the various properties of triangles.

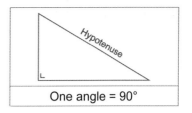

One angle = 90°

Isosceles Triangle

From our investigations, it is clear that:

Theorem 2

In an isosceles triangle the angles opposite the equal sides are equal in measure. Conversely, if two angles are equal in measure, then the triangle is isosceles.

Angles in a Triangle

From Activity 5.12, we know that:

Theorem 4

The angles in any triangle add to 180°.

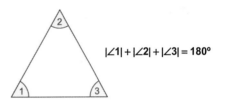

$|\angle 1| + |\angle 2| + |\angle 3| = 180°$

Exterior Angles of a Triangle

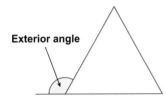

Exterior angle

An **exterior angle** of a triangle is the angle between one side of a triangle and the extension of an adjacent side.

We can now investigate the properties
of **exterior angles** of a triangle.

From our investigations of these angles, it is clear that:

Theorem 6

Each exterior angle of a triangle is equal to the sum of the interior opposite angles.

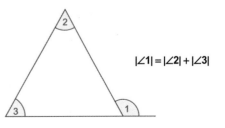

$|\angle 1| = |\angle 2| + |\angle 3|$

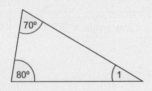

Worked Example 5.7

Without measuring, find the value of $|\angle 1|$.

Solution

$|\angle 1| + 80° + 70° = 180°$ (sum of the angles in a triangle)

$\therefore |\angle 1| = 180° - 80° - 70°$

$|\angle 1| = 30°$

Worked Example 5.8

Find $|\angle X|$.

Solution

$|\angle X| + 45° = 150°$ (exterior angle of a triangle)

$\therefore |\angle X| = 150° - 45°$

$\Rightarrow |\angle X| = 105°$

Worked Example 5.9

Find $|\angle A|$ and $|\angle B|$ without measuring the angles.

Solution

As the triangle is an isosceles triangle, we can fill in another angle A.

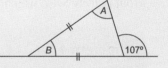

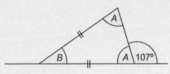

$|\angle A| = 180° - 107°$ (straight angle)

$\therefore |\angle A| = 73°$

$|\angle B| + |\angle A| + |\angle A| = 180°$ (sum of the angles in a triangle)

$|\angle B| + 73° + 73° = 180°$

$|\angle B| = 180° - 73° - 73°$

$\therefore |\angle B| = 34°$

or $|\angle B| + |\angle A| = 107°$ (exterior angle of a triangle)

$|\angle B| + 73° = 107°$

$|\angle B| = 107° - 73°$

$\therefore |\angle B| = 34°$

Exercise 5.4

1. Find the measure of the angles A and B in each of the following triangles. Do not use a protractor.

(i)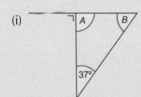

(ii)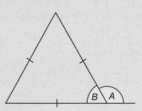

(iii)

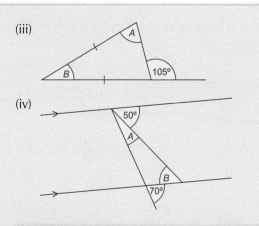

(v)

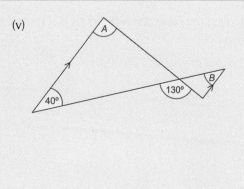

(iv)

> The following questions will require you to use the knowledge that you gained in the previous sections of this chapter.

2. Find the size of the angles marked with letters in each of the following triangles:

(i)

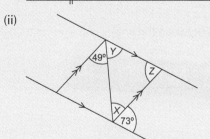

(v)

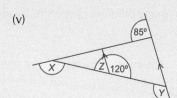

(ii)

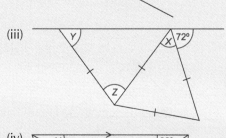

(vi)

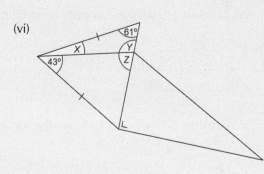

(iii)

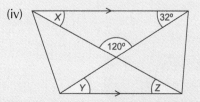

(vii)

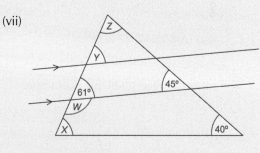

(iv)

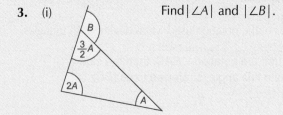

3. (i)   Find $|\angle A|$ and $|\angle B|$.

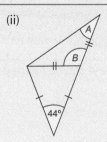

(ii)   Find $|\angle A|$ and $|\angle B|$.

4. Find the value of *x* and *y* in each of the following diagrams. (Diagrams are not drawn to scale.)

(i)

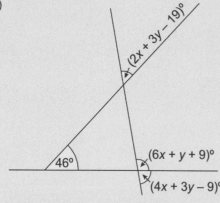

(ii)

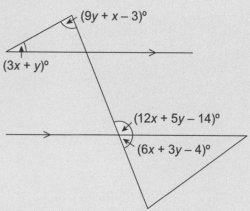

5.9 MORE TRIANGLES

Triangles have many different properties in addition to the ones already mentioned.

$|\angle A| + |\angle B| + |\angle C| = 180°$

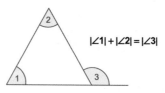

$|\angle 1| + |\angle 2| = |\angle 3|$

We can now deal with one property concerning the relationship between the angles and sides of triangles.

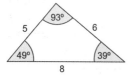

ACTIVITY 5.14

From Activity 5.14 we can clearly see that for any triangle:

> The largest angle is opposite the largest side.
>
> The smallest angle is opposite the smallest side.

The converse (reverse) of this is also true.

> The largest side is opposite the largest angle.
>
> The smallest side is opposite the smallest angle.

When dealing with this property, we must remind ourselves of the notation used when dealing with triangles.

The side opposite angle *A* can be referred to as side *a*.	If we use the notation $\angle BAC$, then the side opposite this angle is referred to as [*BC*].
	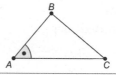

From our investigations we can now state:

Theorem 7

In a triangle, the angle opposite the greater of two sides is greater than the angle opposite the lesser. Conversely, the side opposite the greater of two angles is greater than the side opposite the lesser angle.

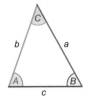

If ∠A is the largest angle, side a is the largest side.

Another property of triangles can help determine if three lengths can form the three sides of a triangle.

 **ACTIVITY 5.15**

From Activity 5.15 we can see that:

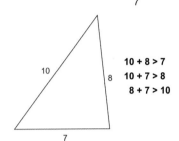

> The sum of the lengths of any two sides of a triangle **have to be** greater than the length of the third side.

$$10 + 8 > 7$$
$$10 + 7 > 8$$
$$8 + 7 > 10$$

This allows us to state the following theorem:

Theorem 8

Two sides of a triangle are together greater than the third. This theorem is sometimes referred to as the **triangle inequality theorem**.

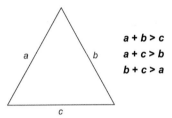

$$a + b > c$$
$$a + c > b$$
$$b + c > a$$

This theorem implies that one side of a triangle must always be smaller than the other two sides added together.

Worked Example 5.10

Consider △ABC.

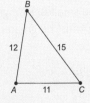

(i) Which is the smallest angle?

(ii) Which is the largest angle?

Solution

(i) Which is the smallest angle?

|∠ABC| is the smallest angle (opposite smallest side).

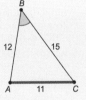

(ii) Which is the largest angle?

|∠BAC| is the largest angle (opposite largest side).

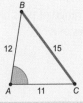

Worked Example 5.11

List the sides of the triangle *DEF* in ascending order of length.

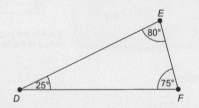

Solution

[*EF*] is the smallest side (opposite smallest angle).

[*DF*] is the largest side (opposite the largest angle).

⇒ [*DE*] is the middle length side.

So the sides of the triangle *DEF* in ascending order (smallest to highest) are: [*EF*], [*DE*], [*DF*].

 Worked Example 5.12

Determine if a triangle can be constructed with the following side measurements:

    (i) 3, 7 and 11 cm   (ii) 3, 6 and 8 cm

Solution

(i) 3, 7 and 11 cm

> It is a good idea to draw out a table and to start with the smaller sides first.

3 + 7 = 10	10 is not > 11	∴ Triangle can't be constructed.

(ii) 3, 6 and 8 cm

> The two sides must add to a value greater than (and not equal to) the other side.

3 + 6 = 9	9 > 8	
3 + 8 = 11	11 > 6	∴ Triangle can be constructed.
6 + 8 = 14	14 > 3	

Sometimes we might be asked to find the range of values that a side of a triangle could have when given the other two sides.

 Worked Example 5.13

The sides of a triangle are 12, 7 and *n*, where $n \in N$.

> $n \in N$ means that *n* is a natural number, which is any whole number greater than 0.

Find:

  (i) The minimum possible value of *n*

  (ii) The maximum possible value of *n*

  (iii) The range of possible values of *n*

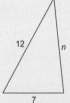

Solution

(i) The minimum possible value of *n*:

    n and the smallest side given, added together, must be greater than the given larger side.

    $n + 7 > 12$

           $n > 12 - 7$

    ∴ $n > 5$

> Minimum possible value of triangle side > Largest side given – smallest side given.

As $n \in N$, the minimum value of *n* is the next natural number greater than 5.

∴ $n = 6$

(ii) The maximum possible value of n:
The two sides given, added together, must be greater than n. This means that n must be smaller than the sum of the two sides.

$n < 12 + 7$

> Maximum possible value of triangle side < Sum of other two sides.

$\therefore n < 19$

As $n \in N$, the largest value of n is the next natural number less than 19.

$\therefore n = 18$

(iii) The range of the possible values of n:

Minimum possible value of triangle side is $n = 6$.

Maximum possible value of triangle side is $n = 18$.

$\therefore 6 \leqslant n \leqslant 18, n \in N$

> When writing a range of values for the sides of the triangle, we usually write it in the form min $\leqslant n \leqslant$ max.

Exercise 5.5

1. In each of the following triangles identify the smallest and largest angles:

(i)

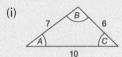

(ii)

(iii)

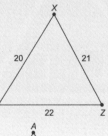

(iv)

(v)

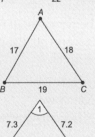

2. In each of the following triangles identify the smallest and largest sides:

(i)

(ii)

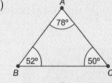

(iii)

(iv)

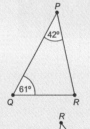

(v)

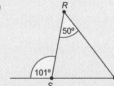

3. Explain, in each case, if it is possible to construct triangles with sides of the following lengths:

(i) 2, 3, 6

(ii) 10, 6, 15

(iii) 17, 14, 26

(iv) 3, 5, 4

(v) 6, 2, 10

(vi) 11, 3, 3

(vii) 6, 7, 8

(viii) 11, 13, 24

(ix) 52, 72, 95

(x) 1.1, 0.8, 2

4. Is it possible to construct the triangle shown below? Explain your answer.

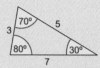

5. The sides of a triangle are of lengths 6.1, 7.2 and n, where $n \in N$. What is the:

    (i) Smallest possible value of n

    (ii) Largest possible value of n

6. The sides of a triangle are of lengths 11.7, 6.4 and a, where $a \in N$. What is the:

    (i) Smallest possible value of a

    (ii) Largest possible value of a

7. Danielle is building a triangular enclosure for her chicken coop. She decides that two of the sides of the pen must be 8 m and 10 m, respectively.

    (i) What is the smallest and the largest length the third side could be to the nearest centimetre?

    (ii) If the fence costs €5 per metre, calculate the minimum and maximum cost of building this fence.

8. In an exam, four answers are given for the possible sides of a scalene triangle. Which two answers are correct?

    A: (4, 6, 2) *B*: (3, 5, 4) *C*: (8, 7, 7) *D*: (4, 5, 6)

9. Jamie starts to set up the triangular front of his tent. He has four tent poles, from which he must choose three.

Each pole has a different size: 50 cm, 60 cm, 1 m and 1.5 m.

How many different ways can he build the front of his tent?

10. A triangular end wall is shown.

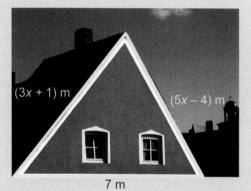

Sheena works out the perimeter of the end wall to be 12 m. Elle works out the perimeter of the end wall to be 16 m.

Which answer is correct?
Give a reason for your answer.

11. The sides of a triangle are of lengths 9, 14 and b, where $b \in N$. What is the:

    (i) Smallest possible value of b

    (ii) Largest possible value of b

    (iii) Range of possible values of b

12. The side of a triangle are of lengths 10, 16 and c, where $c \in N$. What is the:

    (i) Smallest possible value of c

    (ii) Largest possible value of c

    (iii) Range of possible values of c

5.10 QUADRILATERALS

Many two-dimensional shapes can be described as being **polygons**.

A **polygon** is a closed shape (no gaps or openings) with straight sides. A polygon has at least three sides.

This is the polygon *PQRTS*.

A polygon is labelled from its vertices, following a circular path around the polygon.

A type of polygon commonly encountered is that of a **quadrilateral**.

A **quadrilateral** is a four-sided polygon.

Special Quadrilaterals

We can now investigate common types of quadrilateral.
The different quadrilaterals and their properties are:

Type of quadrilateral	Sides	Parallel sides	Angles	Diagonals
Square	Four equal sides	Opposite sides are parallel	All angles the same size (90°)	Bisect each other – angle of 90° formed
Rectangle	Opposite sides are equal	Opposite sides are parallel	All angles the same size (90°)	Bisect each other
Parallelogram	Opposite sides are equal	Opposite sides are parallel	Opposite angles are equal	Bisect each other
Rhombus	Four equal sides	Opposite sides are parallel	Opposite angles are equal	Bisect each other – angle of 90° formed

A square, rectangle and rhombus could all be described as being **parallelograms**.

A **parallelogram** is a quadrilateral that has two pairs of parallel sides.

GEOMETRY I

From our investigations, we can now state:

Theorem 9

In a parallelogram, opposite sides are equal and opposite angles are equal.

Conversely, for a quadrilateral, if opposite sides or opposite angles are equal, the quadrilateral is a parallelogram.

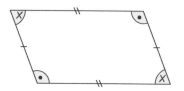

We also know that:

Theorem 10

The diagonals of a parallelogram bisect each other.

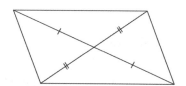

Worked Example 5.14

In the following parallelogram, find:

   (i) |AB|

   (ii) |XC|

   (iii) |AC|

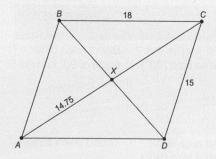

Solution

(i) |AB|

   |AB| = 15 (opposite side to [CD])

(ii) |XC|

   |XC| = 14.75 (diagonals of a parallelogram bisect each other)

(iii) |AC|

   |AC| is twice the length of [AX].

   $\Rightarrow$ |AC| = 2(14.75)

   $\therefore$ |AC| = 29.5

Worked Example 5.15

In the following parallelogram, find:

   (i) |∠1|

   (ii) |∠2|

   (iii) |∠3|

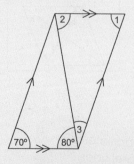

Solution

(i) |∠1|

   |∠1| = 70° (opposite angles in a parallelogram)

(ii) |∠2|

   |∠2| = 80° (alternate angle)

(iii) |∠3|

   |∠1| + |∠2| + |∠3| = 180° (sum of the angles in a triangle)

   70° + 80° + |∠3| = 180°

   $\therefore$ |∠3| = 180° − 70° − 80°

   $\therefore$ |∠3| = 30°

Worked Example 5.16

In the following rhombus, find:

(i) $|\angle A|$ (iii) $|\angle C|$

(ii) $|\angle B|$ (iv) $|\angle D|$

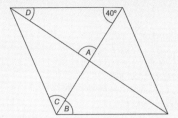

Solution

(i) $|\angle A|$

     $|\angle A| = 90°$ (right angles at point of diagonals' intersection)

(ii) $|\angle B|$

     $|\angle B| = 40°$ (alternate angle)

(iii) $|\angle C|$

     $|\angle C| = 40°$ (diagonals in a rhombus bisect angle)

(iv) $|\angle D|$

     $|\angle D| + 40° + |\angle A| = 180°$

     $|\angle D| + 40° + 90° = 180°$

     $\therefore |\angle D| = 180° - 90° - 40°$

     $\therefore |\angle D| = 50°$

Exercise 5.6

1. Find the measure of the angles A, B and C in each of the following parallelograms:

(i)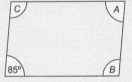

(ii)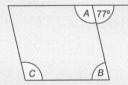

(iii)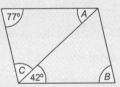

(iv)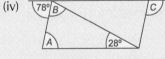

(v)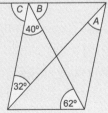

2. $ABCD$ is a parallelogram.

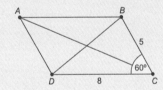

Find:

(i) $|\angle BAD|$

(ii) $|AB|$

(iii) $|\angle ADC|$

3. $DEFG$ is a parallelogram.

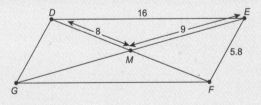

Find:

(i) $|GF|$

(ii) $|EG|$

(iii) $|DF|$

(iv) $|DG|$

4. Find the size of each of the angles marked with letters in the given diagrams.
Make sure to show all your work and give a reason for your answer.

(i)

(iii)

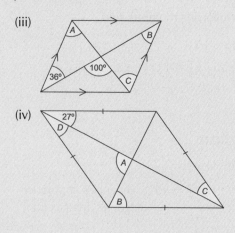

(iv)

(ii)

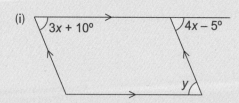

---

5. Find the value of *x* and *y* in each of the following polygons. (Diagrams are not drawn to scale.)

(i) $3x + 10°$ $4x - 5°$

   y

(ii) $(5x + 2y + 40)°$ $(3x + 6y + 8)°$

   $100°$ $(10x + 11y + 9)°$

6. The quadrilateral *PQRS* is shown. Seán explains that the quadrilateral is in fact a trapezoid.
Is Seán correct? Give an explanation of how he came to this conclusion.

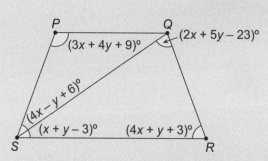

P   Q $(2x + 5y - 23)°$
$(3x + 4y + 9)°$

$(4x - y + 6)°$

$(x + y - 3)°$ $(4x + y + 3)°$
S   R

Revision Exercises

1. (a) Consider the following diagram:

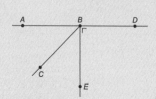

Identify and name:

(i) An acute angle

(ii) An obtuse angle

(iii) An ordinary angle

(iv) A right angle

(v) A ray

(vi) A line

(vii) The supplementary angles

(b) In the following line segment [AB], the point Y is the midpoint of [AB] and $|AX| = \frac{1}{3}|AB|$.

State whether each of the following is true or false. Give a reason for your answer.

(i) $|AX| > |AY|$

(ii) $|AX| > |XY|$

(iii) $|AX| + |AY| > 2|AX|$

(iv) $|AX| + |XY| + |YB| = |AB|$

(v) $|AB| - |YB| = |YB|$

2. (a) Consider the following diagram:

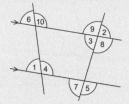

$|\angle 1| = 70°$ and $|\angle 2| = 85°$.
Find the measure of all the angles numbered below.

(i) $|\angle 3|$

(ii) $|\angle 4|$

(iii) $|\angle 5|$

(iv) $|\angle 6|$

(v) $|\angle 7|$

(vi) $|\angle 8|$

(vii) $|\angle 9|$

(viii) $|\angle 10|$

(b) In your own words, explain the difference between each of the following:

Use diagrams to help your explanations where necessary.

(i)   A line and a line segment

(ii) A line and a ray

(iii) Coplanar and collinear

(iv) Perpendicular lines and parallel lines

(v)   Theorem and corollary

3. (a) Classify the relationship between each pair of angles using the diagram below. The first pair of angles has been done for you.

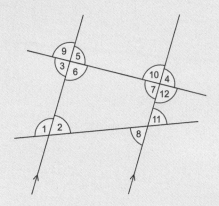

(i) $\angle 2$ and $\angle 11$: *Corresponding angles*

(ii) $\angle 3$ and $\angle 7$:

(iii) $\angle 8$ and $\angle 11$:

(iv) $\angle 9$ and $\angle 5$:

(v) $\angle 7$ and $\angle 5$:

(vi) $\angle 4$ and $\angle 5$:

(b) Investigate if:

(i) $p \parallel q$

(ii) $m \parallel n$

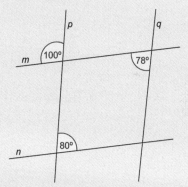

(c)

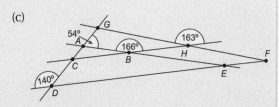

Investigate if:

(i) $CB \parallel DF$

(ii) $GF \parallel AE$

4. (a) Find the measure of the missing angles. Show as much work as possible.

(i)
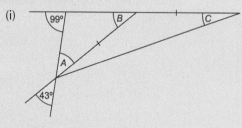

(ii)
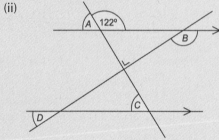

(iii)
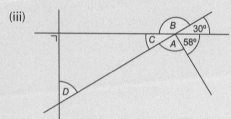

(iv)
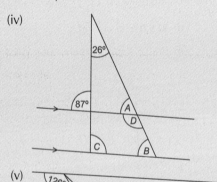

(v)
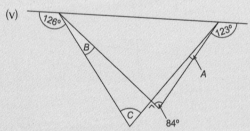

(b) Investigate if it is possible to construct a triangle using the three side lengths given:

(i) 2, 3 and 5

(ii) 10, 7 and 18

(iii) 15, 15 and 13

(iv) 8, 6.6 and 9

(v) $\sqrt{2}$, $\sqrt{5}$ and 6

5. (a) Find the measure of the missing angles in each of the following parallelograms. Show as much work as possible.

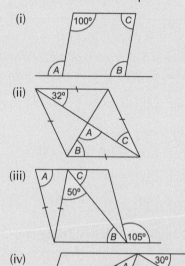

(i)

(ii)

(iii)

(iv)

(b) Consider the parallelogram *ABCD*:

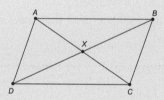

State if each of the following is true or false:

(i) $|AX| = |DX|$

(ii) $|DX| = |XC|$

(iii) $|AD| = |BC|$

(iv) $|\angle AXD| = |\angle BXC|$

(v) $|\angle DAX| = |\angle DBC|$

(c) State two properties of rectangles that are not properties of all parallelograms.

6. (a) Find the value of *x* and *y* in each of the following diagrams:

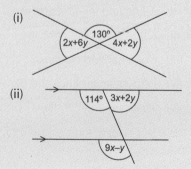

(i)

(ii)

(iii)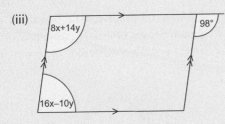

(b)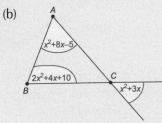

(i) Find two values for x.

(ii) If x > 0, find the measure of all the angles in the triangle ABC.

7. (a) List the sides of each of the triangles below in ascending order of length.

(i)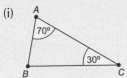

(ii)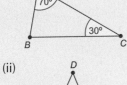

(iii)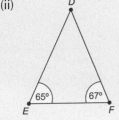

(b) The parallelogram ABCD is divided up using parallel lines as shown.

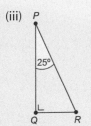

How many parallelograms in total are there? Name each one.

(c) A carpenter is given the dimensions of four different triangular roof beams that are to be constructed for use in a building:

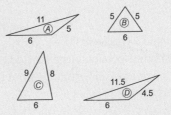

The carpenter complains that only two are actually possible to construct.

(i) Explain how the carpenter came to this decision.

(ii) Which two triangular roof beams could be constructed?

8. (a) State if each of the following statements is 'Always', 'Sometimes' or 'Never' true:

(i) A rectangle is a parallelogram.

(ii) A square is a rhombus.

(iii) A rhombus is a square.

(iv) A parallelogram is not a rectangle.

(v) A circle is a polygon.

(vi) A quadrilateral is any four-sided shape.

(vii) A parallelogram is a four-sided shape.

(b) An orienteering competition is run on a course as shown in the diagram below. Opposite sides are parallel.

The runners run from A to B to C to D and then back to A.

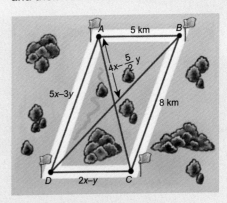

(i) How long is the course?

(ii) A runner cheats by running from A to C and then completes the course as normal.

What is the length of this route?

ACTIVE MATHS 2

GEOMETRY I

(c) The direct distance from town *A* to town *B* is 100 km.

The direct distance from town *B* to town *C* is 75 km.

   (i) If the towns are collinear, what is the shortest possible distance and the longest possible distance from town *B* to town *C*?

  (ii) If the towns are **not** collinear, write the range of distances that are possible from town *B* to town *C*.

9. (a) What is the measure of the ordinary angle formed by the two hands of the 12-hour clock at:

   (i) 4.00 a.m.   (ii) 12.30 a.m.

(b) Consider the following geometrical shape:

   (i) How many sides does this shape have?

  (ii) Name this shape.

 (iii) Find the sum of all the interior angles in this shape. Explain your answer.

(c) A jeweller is asked to fix a brooch as shown below. One side of the brooch is 16 mm and the other side is 25 mm in length.

16 mm   25 mm

It is decided to connect the two ends of the brooch with a gold bar to form a triangle. This bar can be of different lengths.

- 1 cm of this gold bar costs $25.
- The exchange rate is €1 = $1.25.
- The jeweller charges €50 for labour.

Calculate to the nearest euro the highest and lowest price the jeweller could charge to fix this brooch.

chapter 6

Constructions

Learning Outcomes

In this chapter, you will learn to construct the following:

- ➲ Constructions as specified on Junior Certificate Ordinary Level Syllabus
- ➲ The circumcentre and circumcircle of a given triangle, using only a straight edge and a compass
- ➲ The incentre and incircle of a given triangle, using only a straight edge and a compass
- ➲ An angle of 60°, without using a protractor or a set square
- ➲ A tangent to a given circle at a given point on it
- ➲ A parallelogram, given the length of the sides and the measure of the angles
- ➲ The centroid of a triangle

6.1 INTRODUCTION

From cave drawings to modern blueprints, geometry has always held a certain fascination.

- Why do the angles of a triangle add up to 180°?
- Why should a building's walls be built at right angles?
- What properties do different shapes have?

Constructions are an important tool in understanding many aspects of geometry that you have studied. From the earliest days of formal education thousands of years ago, geometry and constructions have been an integral part of the curriculum. By studying these constructions, you continue in a tradition begun by the Greek mathematician Euclid more than 2,000 years ago. His famous book *The Elements* deals with geometry and constructions, and is considered by many to be the first mathematics textbook ever written. It is still in use today, so Euclid may be the most successful maths teacher of all time!

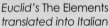

Euclid's The Elements translated into Italian

This painting shows an Italian mathematician called Fra Luca Pacioli (1445–1517), known as the Father of Accounting because he wrote the first book to deal with double-entry book-keeping. Pacioli also translated Euclid's Elements into Latin. He is shown here drawing a geometry construction on a board; the open book on which his hand is resting may well be The Elements.

6.2 CONSTRUCTION EQUIPMENT

When asked to construct a triangle or bisect a line segment, it is vital that you are as accurate as possible. Many builders and architects from ancient to modern times have learned to their cost what a difference even half a degree can make! We use the following equipment to ensure that our constructions are as accurate as possible.

Compass

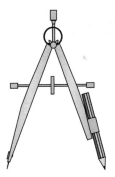

The compass is a very important tool for constructions.

It is used to draw arcs…

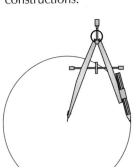

…and circles.

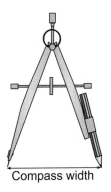

Compass width

By adjusting the compass width, we can change the size of the arcs or circles that we draw.

Protractor

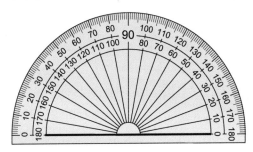

The protractor is used to construct angles. It can also be used to check the accuracy of some constructions.

Straight Edge

A straight edge is a tool which is used to draw a straight line. It has no markings, so it cannot be used for measuring lines. In practice, we just use the ruler found in the construction set.

Ruler

A ruler is used to construct line segments of certain lengths.

Set Square

Set squares are simply rulers in the shape of triangles. We can use two common set squares to draw lines and certain angles. Two set squares are used:

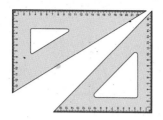

- The 45° set square, which has the angles 45°, 45° and 90°
- The 30° or 60° set square, which has the angles 30°, 60° and 90°

Pencil

Ensure that your pencil has a sharp point. Remember to NEVER rub out any lines, arcs, etc. that you have used in your constructions. These construction lines are very important, as they show that you have followed the correct method.

ACTIVITY 6.1

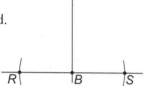

6.3

The following constructions were studied at Junior Certificate Ordinary Level and must also be known for Leaving Certificate Ordinary Level.

CONSTRUCTION 1

A Bisector of Any Given Angle Using Only a Compass and a Straight Edge

Worked Example 6.1

Construct the **bisector** of ∠ABC.

> To **bisect** is to cut into two equal parts. The **bisector** is the line that cuts an angle in two.

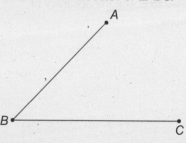

Solution

1 Place the compass point on the angle's **vertex** B.

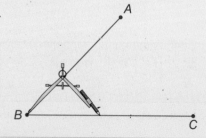

> The **vertex** of an angle is the point where the two rays (or arms) of an angle meet.

2 Draw an arc of the same width across each ray of the angle. Label X, Y.

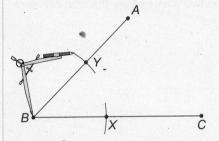

5 Mark the point where the two arcs intersect.

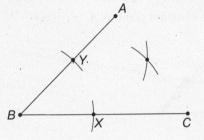

3 Place the compass on the point X and draw an arc.

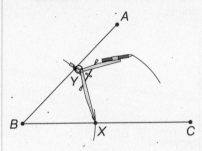

6 Using a straight edge, draw a line from this point to the vertex B.

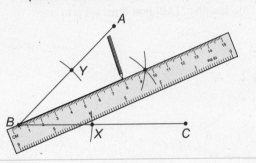

4 Without changing the compass width, place the compass on the point Y and draw an overlapping arc.

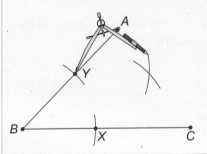

7 This line is the bisector of the angle ABC.

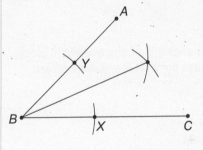

CONSTRUCTION 2

A Perpendicular Bisector of a Line Segment, Using Only a Compass and a Straight Edge

Worked Example 6.2

Construct the **perpendicular bisector** of the line segment [AB], where |AB| = 4 cm.

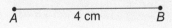

A **perpendicular bisector** cuts the line segment into two equal parts and meets the line segment at an angle of 90°.

Solution

1 Place the compass point on *A*.

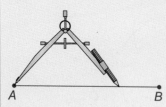

2 Set the compass width to **more than half** the length of [*AB*] and draw an arc.

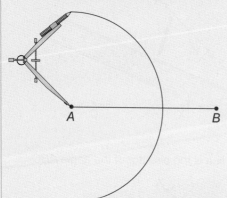

3 Without changing the compass width, place the compass point on *B* and draw an arc.

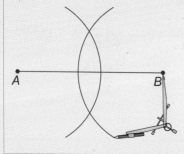

4 Mark the two points where the arcs intersect.

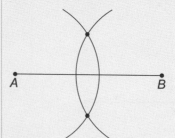

5 Using a straight edge, draw a line through these two points.

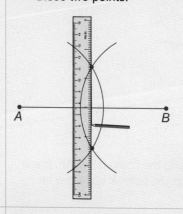

6 This line is the perpendicular bisector of the line segment [*AB*].

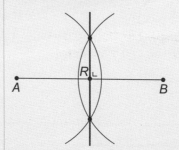

Constructing the perpendicular bisector of a line segment also finds the **midpoint** of the line segment. In the example above, *R* is the midpoint of [*AB*].

CONSTRUCTION 4

A Line Perpendicular to a Given Line *l*, Passing Through a Given Point on *l*

Two methods are shown, **both of which must be known**.

Note: Constructions 3 and 7 are not included on the Ordinary Level course.

Construct a line perpendicular to the line *l*, passing through the point *B* on the line *l*.

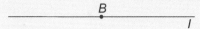

Solution Using a Compass and a Straight Edge

1 Place the compass point on the point *B*. 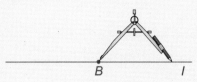	**5** Mark the point where the arcs intersect. 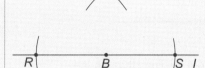
2 Using a small compass width, draw an arc that intersects the line *l* at two points. Label *R*, *S*. 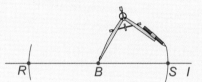	**6** Using a straight edge, draw a line through this point and the point *B*. 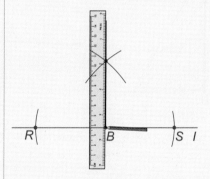
3 Increase the compass width, place the compass point on *R*, and draw an arc. 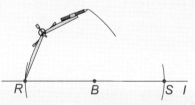	**7** This line is perpendicular to the line *l* and passes through the point *B*. 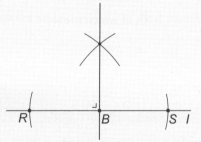
4 Without changing the compass width, place the compass point on *S* and draw an overlapping arc. 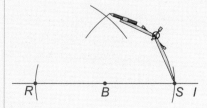	

Solution Using a Set Square or Protractor

1 Line up one side of the right angle of the set square at point *B* and the other side on the line *l*.

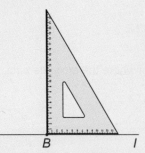

3 This line is perpendicular to the line *l* and passes through the point *B*.

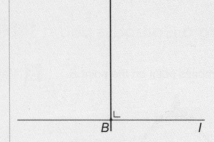

2 Draw a line from the line *l* through the point *B*.

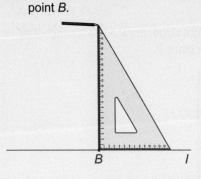

CONSTRUCTION 5

A Line Parallel to a Given Line, Passing Through a Given Point

Two methods are shown, **both of which must be known**.

Worked Example 6.4

Construct a line parallel to the line *m*, passing through the point *C*.

Ċ

_____
m

Solution Using a Compass and a Straight Edge

1 Draw a line through the point C to the line m. Label the intersection of these two lines D.

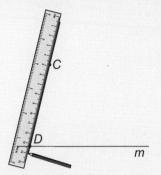

5 Use the compass to measure the distance between X and Y.

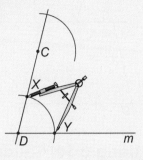

2 Place the compass point on D, and draw an arc across both lines. Ensure that the arc does not go above the point C.

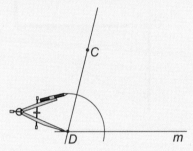

6 Using this compass width, place the compass point where the upper arc and line meet. Draw a new arc across the upper arc.

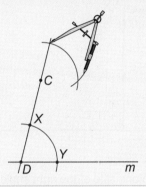

3 Label the points of intersection X and Y.

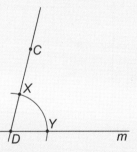

7 Mark the point where the arcs intersect.

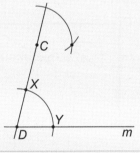

4 Without changing the compass width, place the compass point on C and draw an arc.

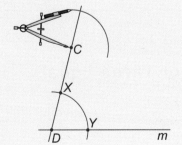

8 Using a straight edge, draw a line from this point through the point C.

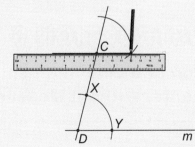

9 This line is parallel to the line *m* and passes through the point *C*.

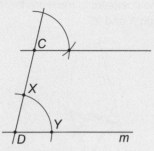

Solution Using a Set Square

1 Using a set square, draw a perpendicular line through the point *C* to the line *m*.

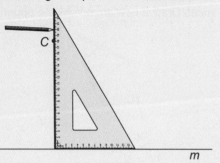

3 Draw a line through the point *C*.

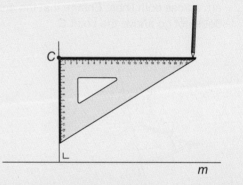

2 Line up one side of the right angle of the set square at point *C* and the other side on the perpendicular line.

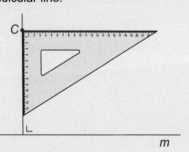

4 This line is parallel to the line *m* and passes through the point *C*.

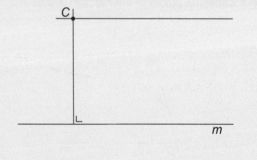

CONSTRUCTION 6

Division of a Line Segment into Two or Three Equal Segments, Without Measuring It

Divide the line segment [AB] into **three** equal parts, where |AB| = 10 cm.

A •————————————————————• B

Solution

1 From point A (or B), draw a ray at an acute angle to the given line segment.

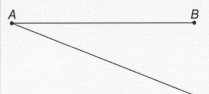

2 Place the compass point on A.

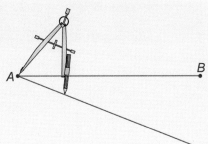

3 Using the same compass width, mark off **three** equal distances along the ray. (Use a small compass width.)

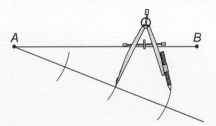

4 Label the points of intersection R, S and T.

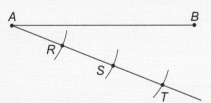

If asked to divide into two equal parts, mark off two equal distances along the ray.

5 Join the last point T to the point B on the line segment.

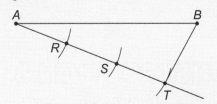

6 Using a set square and straight edge, line the set square up with the line segment [TB].

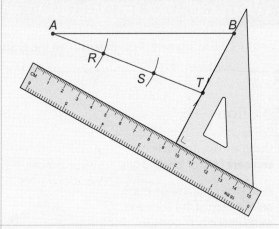

7 Slide the set square along, using the straight edge as a base. Using the set square, draw a line segment from S and R to the line segment [AB].

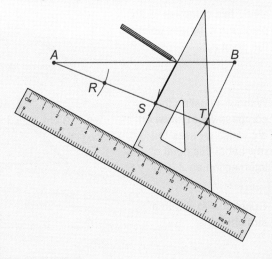

8 Label the points of intersection with the line segment [AB] as points C and D.

The line segment [AB] has now been divided into three equal segments.

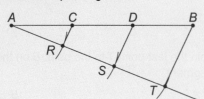

Note: Another method to divide a line segment into two equal parts is to use Construction 2: A perpendicular bisector of a line segment, using only a compass and a straight edge.

CONSTRUCTION 8

A Line Segment of a Given Length on a Given Ray

 Worked Example 6.6

Construct a line segment 3 cm in length on the given ray.

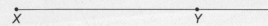

X   Y

Solution

Using a ruler, draw a line segment [AB] of length 3 cm.	A B 3 cm
Place the compass on the point A. Adjust the compass width until it is at point B, i.e. 3 cm.	A 3 cm B X Y
Using this compass width, place the compass point on the point X.	A 3 cm B X Y
Without adjusting the compass width, draw an arc which crosses the ray. Label this point of intersection as Z.	A 3 cm B X Z Y
Connect X to Z with a straight edge.	A B X Z Y

The line segment of a given length has been constructed on the given ray. $|XZ| = 3$ cm	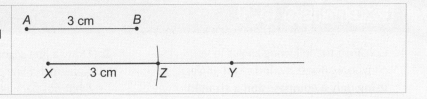

CONSTRUCTION 9

An Angle of a Given Number of Degrees With a Given Ray as One Arm

Worked Example 6.7

Construct an angle of 65° on the ray [AB.

Solution

1 Place the centre of the protractor on the point A. 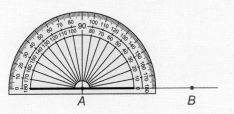	**3** Draw a ray from A through C with a straight edge. 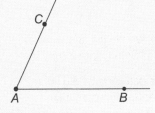
2 At the required angle, mark a point C using the protractor. 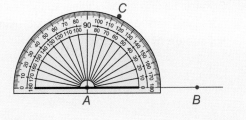	**4** Write in the required angle value, i.e. 65°. An angle of the given length has been constructed on the given ray. $|\angle BAC| = 65°$. 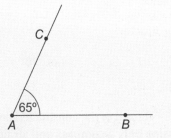

ACTIVITY 6.2

Exercise 6.1

1. Construct the following angles in your copybook. Bisect the indicated angles, **using only a compass and a straight edge**. Remember that you can check your construction with a protractor.

   (i)
   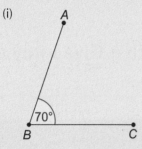

   (ii)
   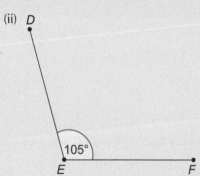

   (iii)
   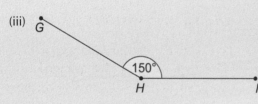

   (iv)
   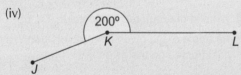

2. (a) Construct the following angles **using a protractor**:

       (i) 20°   (iii) 70°

       (ii) 180°   (iv) 330°

   (b) Bisect each of the constructed angles, **using only a compass and straight edge**.

3. Draw a line segment [AB] of length 9.5 cm. Construct the perpendicular bisector of [AB].

4. Draw a line segment [CD] of length 6.2 cm. Construct the perpendicular bisector of [CD].

5. Draw a line segment [EF] of length 100 mm. Construct a line that is equidistant from E and F but not parallel to EF. (Note: Equidistant means the same distance)

6. Copy the following lines into your copybook. In each case, construct a line perpendicular to the given line passing through the given point, **using only a compass and a straight edge**.

   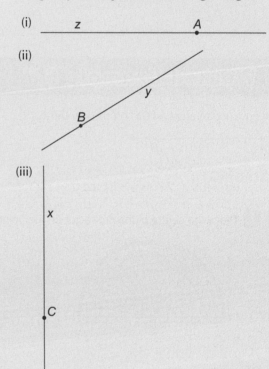

7. Copy the following lines into your copybook. Construct a line perpendicular to the given lines passing through the given point, **using a set square or protractor**.

   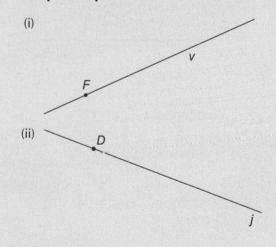

8. Copy the following figures into your copybook. In each case, construct a line parallel to the given line passing through the given point, **using only a compass and a straight edge**.

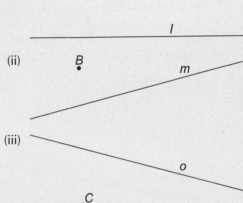

(i)

(ii)

(iii)

9. Copy the following figure into your copybook. Construct a line parallel to the given line passing through the given points, **using a set square**.

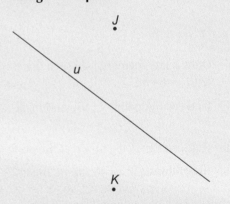

10. Draw a line segment [CD] of length 8.5 cm. Divide this line segment into three equal segments, without measuring it.

11. Draw a line segment [AB] of length 90 mm. Divide this line segment into two equal parts without measuring it.

12. Draw a line segment [GH] of length 5 cm. Divide this line segment into three equal parts without measuring it.

13. Draw a line segment [KL] of length 112 mm. Divide this line segment into two equal parts without measuring it.

14. Draw a triangle using a straight edge only (ensure that the triangle is not too small). Label the vertices of the triangle ABC.

   (i) Construct the perpendicular bisectors of all three sides.

   (ii) Mark the point where all three bisectors meet. Label as the point O.

   (iii) Measure |OA|, |OB| and |OC|. What do you notice?

   (iv) Draw a circle with centre O and radius length |OA|.

15. Copy the following figure into your copybook.

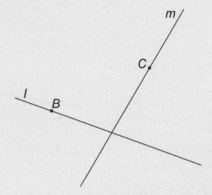

Using only a compass and straight edge:

   (i) Construct a line perpendicular to the line *l* passing through the point *B*.

   (ii) Construct a line perpendicular to the line *m* passing through the point *C*.

   (iii) Mark the point of intersection of these two constructed lines and label it *D*.

   (iv) Using your protractor, measure angle *BDC*.

16. (i) Draw the line segment [CD] such that |CD| = 8 cm.
Draw the line segment [DE] such that |DE| = 4 cm and |∠CDE| = 110°.

   (ii) Construct a line through the point C which is parallel to DE **using only a compass and straight edge**.

   (iii) Construct a line through the point E which is parallel to CD **using a set square**.

   (iv) Label the point of intersection of these two lines as the point F.

   (v) What type of shape is CDEF? Give reasons for your answer.

17. (i) Draw a line segment [AB] where |AB| = 12 cm. Divide this line segment into three equal parts without measuring it. Label [AB] as shown.

(ii) Construct ∠BAX such that |∠BAX| = 90° and |AX| = 7 cm

(iii) Divide [AX] into three equal parts without measuring it.

(iv) Label [AX] as shown.

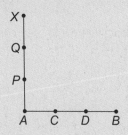

(v) Draw [PC], [QD] and [XB]. What can be said about these line segments?

18. (i) Draw a triangle using a straight edge only (make it reasonably big).

(ii) Bisect all three angles of the triangle.

(iii) Mark where the bisectors meet. What do you notice?

19. Copy the following figures into your copybook. In each case, construct the given line segment on the given ray. Note that figures are not drawn to scale.

(i)

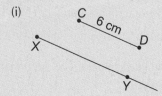

(ii)

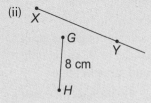

(iii)

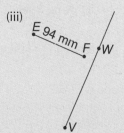

20. Construct the following angles **using a protractor**.

(i) |∠ABC| = 50°

(ii) |∠DEF| = 125°

(iii) |∠JKL| = 260°

21. Construct the following angles with the given ray as one arm of the angle.

(i) |∠PQR| = 70°

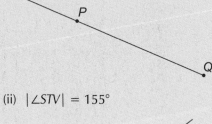

(ii) |∠STV| = 155°

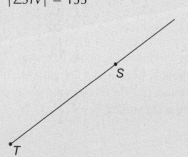

22. (i) Draw a line segment [AB] such that |AB| = 8 cm.

(ii) Find the midpoint of [AB], and mark as point C.

(iii) Construct an angle of 45° at the point C.

(iv) Bisect this angle of 45° at the point C.

23. Construct a line segment [EF] such that |EF| = 12 cm. Construct a line that is equidistant from E and F.

24. (i) Draw a line segment [CD] such that |CD| = 150 mm.

(ii) Without measuring, divide the line segment [CD] into three equal parts.

(iii) Copy one-third of the line segment [CD] onto a ray.

(iv) Label this line segment [XY].

(v) Divide the line segment [XY] into two equal parts.

25. (i) Using a protractor, construct the angle ABC such that |∠ABC| = 60°.

  (ii) Using only a compass and a straight edge, construct an angle DEF where |∠DEF| is equal to |∠ABC|.

  (iii) Using only a compass and a straight edge, construct an angle XYZ where |∠XYZ| is twice as large as |∠ABC|.

26. (i) Draw the line segment [AB] such that |AB| = 10 cm.

  (ii) Construct the angle ABC such that |∠ABC| = 55°.

  (iii) Mark a point D on the angle arm [BC] such that |DB| = 5 cm.

  (iv) Construct a line through D parallel to [AB].

  (v) Construct a line through A parallel to [BC].

  (vi) What is the resulting four-sided figure called?

  (vii) Confirm your answer to part (vi) by listing the measurements of angles and line segments from your construction.

6.4   Junior Certificate Ordinary Level Constructions continued.

When dealing with more complicated constructions, it is always better to follow a certain approach before you begin the actual construction.

- Draw a rough sketch of the shape.

- Label the corners or vertices.

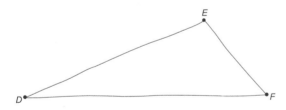

- We put the length of the side of the triangle given in the question at the bottom of the sketch.
  If two sides are given, we usually put the longest side on the bottom of the sketch.

  Fill in any other information given about the triangle.

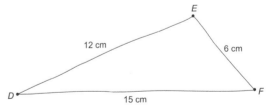

> When you have finished your construction, don't forget to label all the angles and side lengths that were given in the question. Also, it is a good idea to check that your construction has the same dimensions as given in the question.

CONSTRUCTION 10

A Triangle, Given the Lengths of Three Sides (SSS)

> **SSS** means **Side, Side, Side.**

Worked Example 6.8

Construct a triangle ABC where $|AB| = 7$ cm, $|BC| = 9$ cm and $|AC| = 5$ cm.

Solution

1 Draw a rough sketch of the construction. 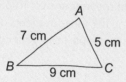	**6** Using this width, place the compass point on C and draw an overlapping arc. 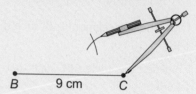

| **2** Using a ruler, draw the line segment $[BC]$. This will be the base of the triangle, as it is the longest side. 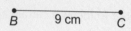 | **7** Label the intersection of the two arcs as point A. 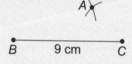 |

| **3** Next, use $|AB| = 7$ cm. Set the compass width to 7 cm. 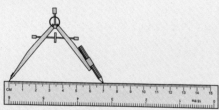 | **8** Join A to B and A to C. 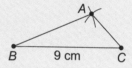 |

| **4** Using this width, place the compass point on B and draw an arc. 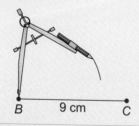 | **9** Fill in the remaining lengths. The triangle is now constructed as required. 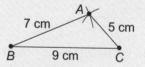 |

| **5** Now use $|AC| = 5$ cm. Set the compass width to 5 cm.  | |

CONSTRUCTION 11

A Triangle, Given SAS Data (Side, Angle, Side)

SAS means **Side, Angle, Side**.

Worked Example 6.9

Construct a triangle *EDF* where |*ED*| = 10 cm, |∠*FED*| = 50° and |*EF*| = 6 cm.

Solution

1 Draw a rough sketch of the construction, putting the longest side as the base.

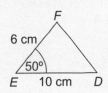

2 Using a ruler, draw the line segment [*ED*] where |*ED*| = 10 cm.

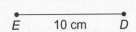

3 Using a protractor, construct an angle of 50° at the point *E*.

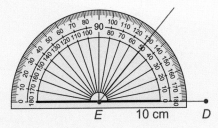

4 Set the compass width to 6 cm.

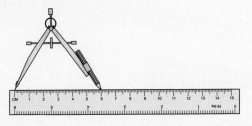

5 Using this width, place the compass point on *E* and draw an arc on the arm of the angle.

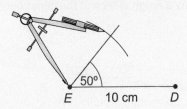

6 Mark and label this intersection as the point *F*.

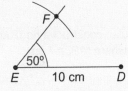

7 Join *F* to *D*.

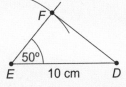

8 Fill in the remaining lengths and the angle.

The triangle is now constructed as required.

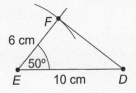

ACTIVE MATHS 2

189

CONSTRUCTION 12

A Triangle, Given Two Angles and the Side Between These Two Angles (ASA)

ASA means **Angle, Side, Angle**.

Worked Example 6.10

Construct a triangle ABC where $|AB| = 7$ cm, $|\angle ABC| = 30°$ and $|\angle BAC| = 50°$.

Solution

1 Draw a rough sketch of the construction.

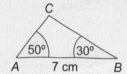

2 Using a ruler, construct a horizontal line segment where $|AB| = 7$ cm.

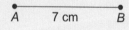

3 Using a protractor, construct an angle of 50° at the point A.

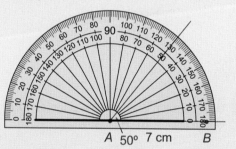

4 Using a protractor, construct an angle of 30° at the point B.

Mark and label the intersection of these angles' arms as the point C.

The triangle is now constructed as required.

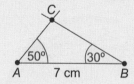

CONSTRUCTION 13

A Right-Angled Triangle, Given the Length of the Hypotenuse and One Other Side

Remember that the hypotenuse is the side opposite the right angle.

Construct a triangle *EDF* where |*ED*| = 5 cm, |∠*EDF*| = 90° and |*EF*| = 8 cm.

Solution

1 Make a rough sketch of the triangle. It is important to identify where the right angle is and generally not use the hypotenuse as the horizontal line.

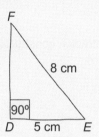

2 Using a ruler, construct the horizontal line segment where |*ED*| = 5 cm.

3 Using your protractor or set square, draw an angle of 90° at *D*.

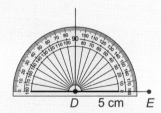

4 Set the compass width to the length of the hypotenuse. |*EF*| = 8 cm.

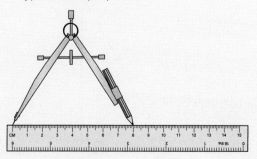

5 Using this width, place the compass point on *E* and draw an arc.

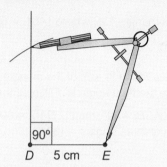

6 Mark and label where the arc meets the vertical line as point *F*.

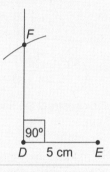

7 Using a ruler, join *F* to *E*.

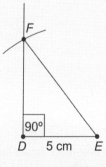

8 The triangle is now drawn as required. Label all given measurements.

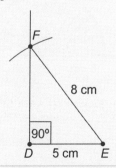

CONSTRUCTION 14

A Right-Angled Triangle, Given One Side and One of the Acute Angles (Several Cases)

 Worked Example 6.12

Construct a triangle ABC where $|AB| = 6$ cm, $|\angle ABC| = 90°$ and $|\angle ACB| = 30°$.

Solution

1 Make a rough sketch of the triangle. Identify where the right angle is. Fill in all the angles.

As $|\angle ACB| = 30°$, then $|\angle BAC| = 60°$
[Sum of three angles = 180°]

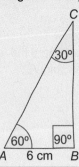

2 Using a ruler, construct the line segment $[AB]$ of length 6 cm.

A　6 cm　B

3 Using your protractor or set square, draw an angle of 90° at B.

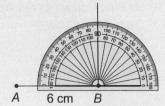

4 Using a protractor, construct an angle of 60° at the point A.

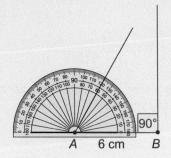

5 Mark and label where this angle's arm meets the right angle's arm as the point C.

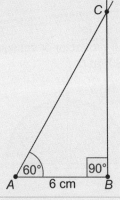

6 Fill in $|\angle ACB| = 30°$.

The triangle is now constructed as required.

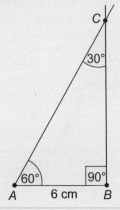

Worked Example 6.13

Construct a triangle *EDF* where |*EF*| = 8 cm, |∠*EDF*| = 90° and |∠*FED*| = 50°.

> This triangle is more difficult, as the only side length we are given is the hypotenuse. It is simpler to use the hypotenuse as the base of our triangle.

Solution

1 Make a rough sketch of the triangle. Identify where the right angle is. Fill in all the angles.

|∠*EFD*| = 40° [180° − 90° − 50°]

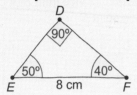

2 Using a ruler, construct the horizontal line segment [*EF*] where |*EF*| = 8 cm (hypotenuse).

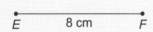

3 Using a protractor, construct an angle of 50° at the point *E*.

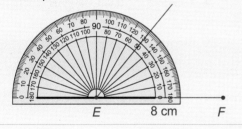

4 Using a protractor, construct an angle of 40° at the point *F*.

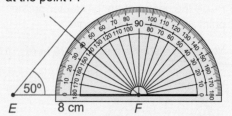

5 Mark and label where the arms of these two angles meet as point *D*.

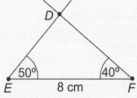

6 Fill in the remaining lengths and angles.

The triangle is now constructed as required.

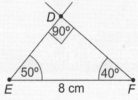

CONSTRUCTION 15

A Rectangle, Given Side Lengths

Worked Example 6.14

Construct a rectangle *ABCD*, where |*AB*| = 9 cm and |*BC*| = 4 cm.

Solution

1 Make a rough sketch of the rectangle.

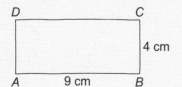

2 Draw a line *l*.

_____
                                    l

3 Construct the line segment [AB] where |AB| = 9 cm.

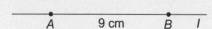

4 Place the centre of the protractor on the point A and draw a 90° angle.

You could also use a set square here.

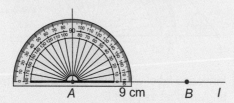

5 Using your compass, mark a point on this line at the given distance from A (4 cm). Label this point D.

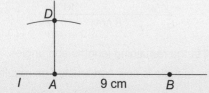

6 Place the centre of the protractor on the point B and draw a 90° angle.

You could also use a set square here.

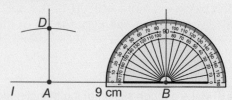

7 Using your compass, mark a point on this line at the given distance from B (4 cm). Label this point C.

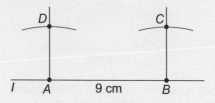

8 Join C to D. Label all given measurements.

The rectangle ABCD is now drawn.

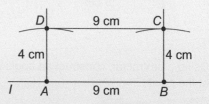

Exercise 6.2

Construct the following triangles. Don't forget to check to see if your construction has the correct dimensions. Diagrams are not to scale.

1. Triangle ABC where |AB| = 8 cm, |BC| = 12 cm and |AC| = 9 cm.

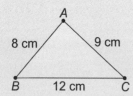

2. Triangle GHI, using the measurements shown in the diagram.

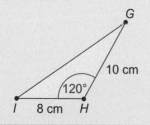

3. The triangle STU using the measurements as shown in the diagram.

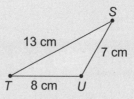

4. Triangle ABC where |∠BAC| = 40°, |AC| = 8 cm and |∠BCA| = 55°.

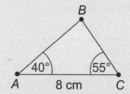

5. The triangle *PQR* using the measurements as shown in the diagram.

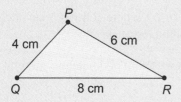

6. Triangle *ABC* where |*AB*| = 8 cm, |*AC*| = 7 cm and |∠*CAB*| = 40°.

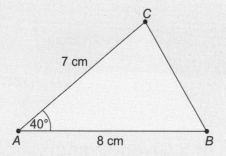

7. Triangle *GHI*, using the measurements shown in the diagram.

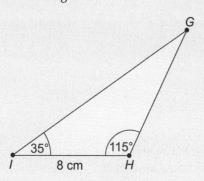

8. Triangle *MNO* where |∠*MON*| = 95°, |*NO*| = 7 cm and |*MO*| = 4 cm.

9. Triangle *JKL* where |*JK*| = 6 cm, |*KL*| = 5 cm and |*JL*| = 8 cm.

10. Triangle *MNO* where |*MN*| = 7.5 cm, |*MO*| = 7.5 cm and |*NO*| = 5 cm.

11. Triangle *PQR* where |*QR*| = 6 cm, |*PR*| = 3 cm and |∠*QRP*| = 140°.

12. Triangle *MNO* where |∠*OMN*| = 20°, |∠*MNO*| = 70° and |*MN*| = 4 cm.

13. Triangle *PQR* where |∠*QPR*| = 110°, |*PQ*| = 7.5 cm and |∠*PQR*| = 30°.

14. Triangle *XYZ* where |*XY*| = 6 cm, |*XZ*| = $\frac{3}{2}$|*XY*| and |*YZ*| = $\frac{4}{3}$|*XZ*|.

15. Triangle *ABC* where |∠*ACB*| = 90°, |*AC*| = 5 cm and |*AB*| = 7 cm.

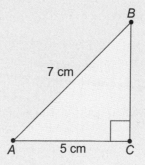

16. Triangle *GHI*, using the measurements shown in the diagram.

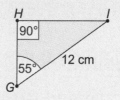

17. Triangle *ABC* where |∠*ABC*| = 90°, |*AB*| = 6 cm and |∠*BAC*| = 35°.

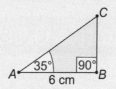

18. Triangle *DEF* where |∠*DEF*| = 55°, |∠*EFD*| = 90° and |*EF*| = 6 cm.

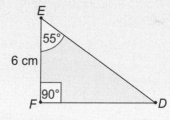

19. Triangle *GHI*, using the measurements shown in the diagram.

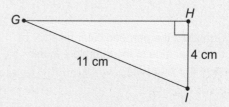

20. Triangle *MNO* where |*NO*| = 3 cm, |∠*MNO*| = 90° and |*MO*| = 6.5 cm.

21. Triangle *PQR* where |∠*RPQ*| = 90°, |*QR*| = 90 mm and |∠*QRP*| = 30°.

22. Triangle *MNO* where $|\angle MNO| = 90°$, $|\angle MON| = 70°$ and $|MN| = 7.5$ cm.

23. Triangle *XYZ* where $|XY| = 4$ cm, $|XZ| = 9$ cm and $XY \perp ZY$.

24. Triangle *STU* where $|ST| = 3.5$ cm, $|\angle STU| = 90°$ and $|\angle SUT| = 45°$.

25. Rectangle *ABCD* where $|AB| = 10$ cm and $|BC| = 3$ cm.

26. Rectangle *QRST* where $|QR| = 7.5$ cm and $|QT| = 3.5$ cm.

27. Rectangle *UVWX* where $|UV| = 5$ cm and the area of the rectangle *UVWX* is 30 cm².

28. Square *EFGH* whose perimeter is 240 mm.

6.5 The following constructions were not studied at Junior Certificate Ordinary Level but must be known at Leaving Certificate Ordinary Level.

CONSTRUCTION 16

The Circumcentre and Circumcircle of a Given Triangle, Using Only a Straight Edge and a Compass

 Worked Example 6.15

Construct the circumcentre and circumcircle of the triangle *ABC*.

Solution

1 Construct the perpendicular bisector of [*AC*].

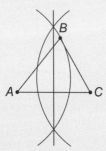

2 Construct the perpendicular bisector of any other side of the triangle – in this case the side [*BC*].

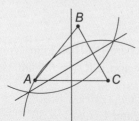

3 Mark the point of intersection of the perpendicular bisectors and label as point *O*.

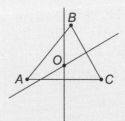

4 Point *O* is the **circumcentre** of the triangle *ABC*.

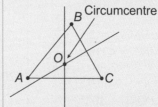

Circumcentre

The **circumcentre** is the point where a triangle's three perpendicular bisectors meet.

5 Place the compass point on O and draw a circle of radius length $|OA|$. This circle is the **circumcircle** of the triangle ABC.

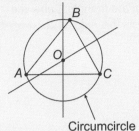

Circumcircle

The circumcircle of a triangle is a circle that passes through all three vertices of the triangle.

ACTIVITY 6.3

 Exercise 6.3

Construct the following triangles in your copybook. Construct the circumcentre and circumcircle of each one.

1. Triangle ABC where $|AB| = 8$ cm, $|BC| = 4$ cm and $|AC| = 6$ cm.

2. Triangle EDF having $|ED| = 7$ cm, $|\angle FED| = 55°$ and $|EF| = 6$ cm.

3. Triangle GHI where $|GH| = 5$ cm, $|\angle IGH| = 30°$ and $|\angle IHG| = 100°$. What do you notice about the position of the circumcentre?

4. Triangle JKL where $|JK| = 7$ cm, $|\angle JKL| = 90°$ and $|JL| = 10$ cm. What do you notice about the position of the circumcentre?

5. Triangle MNO where $|\angle MON| = 90°$, $|\angle MNO| = 45°$ and $|MN| = 7$ cm.

6. Triangle PQR where $|\angle QPR| = 120°$, $|QP| = 5$ cm and $|PR| = 3$ cm.

7. The circumcentre of a triangle can be inside, on or outside the triangle, depending on the type of triangle given. Match the correct position of the circumcentre (inside, on, outside) with its corresponding triangle (right-angled, obtuse, acute) in the following table:

Position of circumcentre	Type of triangle

CONSTRUCTION 17

Incentre and Incircle of a Given Triangle, Using Only a Straight Edge and a Compass

 Worked Example 6.16

Construct the incentre and incircle of the triangle PQR.

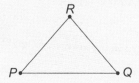

Solution

1 Construct the bisector of the angle *PQR*.

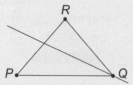

2 Construct the bisector of any other angle in the triangle, e.g. ∠*RPQ*.

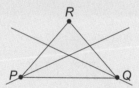

3 Mark the point of intersection of the angle bisectors, and label as point *O*.

Point *O* is the **incentre** of the triangle *PQR*.

Incentre

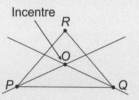

> The **incentre** is the point where a triangle's three angle bisectors meet.

4 Using your set square, draw a perpendicular from *O* to a side of the triangle. Label the point where it meets this side as *S*.

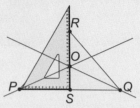

5 Place the compass point on *O* and the pencil on *S*, and draw a circle. This circle should touch all three sides of the triangle.

This is the **incircle** of the triangle *PQR*.

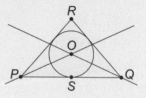

> The **incircle** of a triangle is the largest circle that will fit inside the triangle. Each of the triangle's three sides is a tangent to the circle.

 **ACTIVITIES 6.4, 6.5**

Exercise 6.4

Construct the following triangles in your copybook. Construct the incentre and incircle of each one.

1. Triangle *ABC* where |*AB*| = 7 cm, |*BC*| = 7 cm and |*AC*| = 9 cm.

2. Triangle *DEF* where |∠*EDF*| = 40°, |*DE*| = 8 cm and |*FD*| = 5 cm.

3. Triangle *GHI* where |*HI*| = 10 cm, |∠*GHI*| = 40° and |*GIH*| = 70°.

4. Triangle *JKL* where |*JK*| = 3 cm, |∠*LJK*| = 90° and |*JL*| = 4 cm.

5. Triangle *TUV* where |*TU*| = 7 cm, |*UV*| = 3 cm and |∠*UVT*| = 90°.

6. Triangle *XYZ* where |*XY*| = 12 cm, |∠*XYZ*| = 100° and |∠*ZXY*| = 35°.

CONSTRUCTION 18

An Angle of 60° Without Using a Protractor or a Set Square

Worked Example 6.17

Construct an angle of 60° without using a protractor or a set square.

Solution

1 Draw a line segment [AB]. 	**4** Mark the point of intersection of the arcs and label as point C. 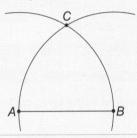
2 Place the compass point at A, and draw an arc of radius length |AB|. 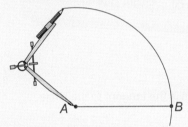	**5** Join C to A. Label |∠CAB| as 60°. [Note: |∠CAB| = 60°, as △ABC is equilateral and all angles are therefore 60°.] 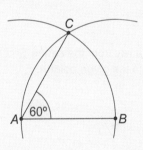
3 Place the compass point at B, and draw an arc of radius length |AB|. 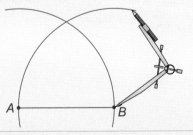	 ACTIVITY 6.6

Exercise 6.5

1. Copy the following line segments into your copybook. Construct an angle of 60° on each line segment without using a protractor or set square.

(i)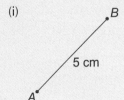

(ii)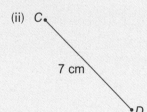

2. Construct an equilateral triangle of side length 5 cm using only a ruler and compass.

3. Using only a compass and straight edge, construct an angle of 30°. (*Hint:* First construct a 60° angle.)

CONSTRUCTION 19

A Tangent to a Given Circle at a Given Point on It

Worked Example 6.18

Construct a **tangent** to the given circle at the point A.

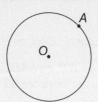

> A **tangent** is a line that touches the circle at a single point.

Solution

1 Draw a ray from the centre O of the circle through the given point A.

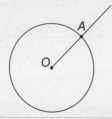

2 Construct a line perpendicular to the ray [OA through the point A.

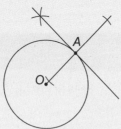

3 This is the tangent to the circle.

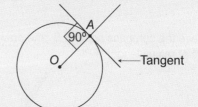

Tangent

ACTIVITIES 6.7, 6.8

Exercise 6.6

1. Construct a circle of radius 5 cm, and draw a tangent to this circle at any point on the circle.

2. Construct a circle of diameter 12 cm, and draw a tangent to this circle at any point on the circle.

3. Construct the following circles with centre *O* in your copybook, and construct a tangent to each circle at the given point.

(i)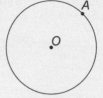

|OA| = 4 cm

(ii)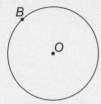

|OB| = 45 cm

(iii)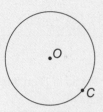

|OC| = 55 cm

CONSTRUCTION 20

A Parallelogram, Given the Length of the Sides and the Measure of the Angles

 Worked Example 6.19

Construct a parallelogram *ABCD* where |*AB*| = 7 cm, |*BC*| = 4 cm and |∠*ABC*| = 60°.

Solution

1 Draw a rough sketch of the parallelogram.

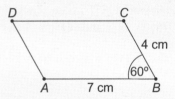

3 At point *B*, construct an angle of 60°, using the line segment [*AB*] as one arm of the angle.

Use your protractor for this angle.

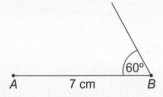

2 Construct the line segment [*AB*] where |*AB*| = 7 cm.

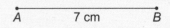

4 Mark the point *C* on this angle such that |*BC*| = 4 cm.

Use your compass (or ruler) for this measurement.

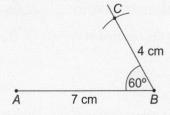

5 At point *A*, construct a ray parallel to *BC*.

Use your protractor to measure the correct angle.

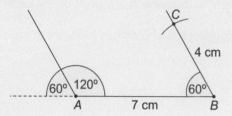

6 Mark the point *D* on this ray such that |*AD*| = 4 cm.

Use your compass (or ruler) for this measurement.

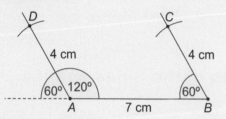

7 Using a ruler, join *C* to *D*.

Label all given measurements.

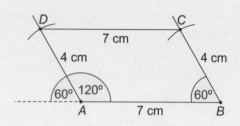

ACTIVITY 6.9

 Exercise 6.7

Construct the following quadrilaterals:

1. Parallelogram *ABCD* where |*AB*| = 10 cm, |*BC*| = 4 cm and |∠*ABC*| = 50°.

2. Parallelogram *EFGH* where |*EF*| = 7 cm, |*FG*| = 3 cm and |∠*EFG*| = 80°.

3. Parallelogram *IJKL* where |*IJ*| = 9 cm, |*JK*| = 5 cm and |∠*IJK*| = 110°.

4. Rhombus *MNOP* where |*MN*| = 50 mm and |∠*MNO*| = 40°.

5. Parallelogram *QRST* where |*QR*| = 6.5 cm, |∠*QTS*| = 135° and |*QT*| = 5 cm.

6. Rhombus *UVWX* where |*UX*| = 8 cm and |∠*XWV*| = 60°.

CONSTRUCTION 21

The Centroid of a Triangle

 Worked Example 6.20

Construct the centroid of the triangle *PQR*.

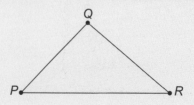

Solution

1 Construct the perpendicular bisector of the side [PQ].

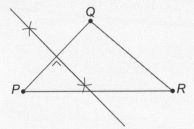

2 Label the midpoint of [PQ] as the point X.

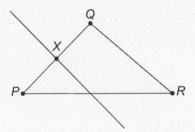

3 Using a straight edge, draw a line from X to R, the opposite vertex of the triangle.

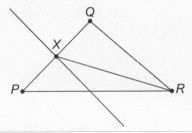

4 This line is a **median** of the triangle PQR.

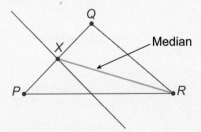

Median

> A **median** of a triangle is a segment that goes from one of the triangle's vertices to the midpoint of the opposite side.

5 Construct the perpendicular bisector of [PR] and label the midpoint Y.

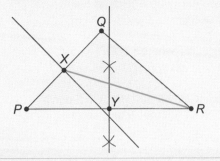

6 Using a straight edge, join Y to the opposite vertex, Q.

This is a second median.

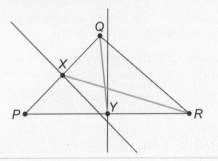

7 Where the medians intersect is the centroid of the triangle PQR.

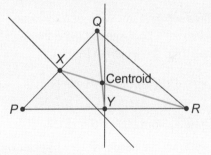

Centroid

> The **centroid** is the triangle's balance point or centre of gravity, i.e. the point where the three medians of the triangle meet.

 **ACTIVITIES 6.10, 6.11**

Exercise 6.8

Construct the centroid of each triangle.

1. Triangle *ABC* where $|AB| = 5$ cm, $|BC| = 6$ cm and $|AC| = 7$ cm.

2. Triangle *DEF* where $|\angle EDF| = 30°$, $|DE| = 8$ cm and $|FD| = 5$ cm.

3. Triangle *GHI* where $|HI| = 6.5$ cm, $|\angle GHI| = 30°$ and $|GIH| = 110°$.

4. Triangle *JKL* where $|JK| = 7$ cm, $|\angle LJK| = 90°$ and $|JL| = 8$ cm.

5. Triangle *TUV* where $|TU| = 10$ cm, $|UV| = 3$ cm and $|\angle UVT| = 90°$.

6. Equilateral triangle *XYZ* where $|XY| = 5.5$ cm.

Revision Exercises

1. (i) Draw a line *l*. Label a point *X* on this line *l*.

   (ii) Construct a line perpendicular to *l* and passing through *X* **using a compass and straight edge**. Label this line *m*.

   (iii) Mark a point *Y* on *m* such that $|XY| = 5$ cm.

   (iv) Construct a line through *Y* parallel to *l*.

2. (i) Draw the line segment [*AB*] such that $|AB| = 3$ cm.

   (ii) Without measuring, construct a line segment [*XY*] on a ray that is four times the length of [*AB*].

   (iii) On a separate ray, without measuring, construct a line segment [*MN*] that is one-third the length of [*AB*].

3. (i) Draw a circle of radius 5 cm with a centre *O*.

   (ii) Draw a chord [*AB*] of this circle.

   (iii) Construct the perpendicular bisector of [*AB*].

   (iv) Is the centre *O* on this line?

4. (i) Draw any triangle using a straight edge. Label the triangle *XYZ*.

   (ii) Bisect all three interior angles of the triangle.

   (iii) What do you notice about the three lines that bisect the angles in the triangle?

5. (i) Draw any quadrilateral using a straight edge. Label the vertices *P*, *Q*, *R* and *S*.

   (ii) Construct the perpendicular bisector of all four sides of the quadrilateral.

   (iii) Starting at [*PQ*], join the midpoint of each side to form a new quadrilateral.

   (iv) What type of quadrilateral is formed?

6. (i) Using a protractor, construct an angle *ABC* such that $|\angle ABC| = 90°$.

   (ii) Using the same diagram from part (i), and using only a compass and straight edge, construct the following angles:

   (a) $|\angle CBD| = 45°$

   (b) $|\angle DBE| = 22\frac{1}{2}°$

7. (i) Construct a triangle *ABC* as shown where $|AB| = 6$ cm, $|\angle ABC| = 30°$ and $|BC| = 5$ cm.

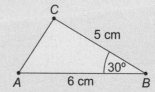

   (ii) Construct the circumcentre of the triangle *ABC*.

   (iii) Construct the circumcircle of the triangle *ABC*.

8. (i) Construct a triangle *PQR* where $|PQ| = 7$ cm, $|\angle RPQ| = 110°$ and $|\angle RQP| = 20°$.

   (ii) Construct the incentre of the triangle *PQR*.

   (iii) Construct the incircle of the triangle *PQR*.

9. (i) Construct an equilateral triangle *XYZ* of side 7 cm.

   (ii) Measure the angles at each vertex of the triangle.

6

CONSTRUCTIONS

10. (i)   Construct a triangle *RST* where
          |*RT*| = 12 cm, |∠*RST*| = 90° and
          |∠*STR*| = 35°.

     (ii) Find the length of the sides [*RS*]
           and [*ST*] using a ruler.

11. (i)   Construct the triangle *ABC* where
          |*BC*| = 7 cm, |∠*ABC*| = 40° and
          |∠*ACB*| = 30°.

     (ii) By measuring, find the longest side and
           biggest angle.

     (iii) Construct the triangle *DEF* where
           |*DE*| = 7 cm, |*FD*| = 10 cm and
           |∠*FED*| = 90°.

     (iv) By measuring, find the longest side and
           biggest angle.

     (v)   What do you notice about the longest side
           and biggest angle in these two triangles?

12. (i)   Construct the rectangle *LMNO* where
          |*LM*| = 5 cm and |*MN*| = 7 cm.

     (ii) Construct the diagonal [*OM*].

     (iii) Find the area of the triangles *OLM* and
           OMN. What do you notice?

     (iv) Are the triangles *OLM* and *OMN*
           congruent? If so, why?

13. Using only a compass and a straight edge,
     construct the following angles:

     (i)   60°   (iii) 30°

     (ii) 120°   (iv)   15°

14. (i)   Construct a circle of radius 5 cm.

     (ii) Draw a diameter of the circle and write
           down its length.

     (iii) Construct a triangle with its three vertices
           on the circle such that the longest side is
           10 cm and another side is 6 cm long.

     (iv) Write down the length of the third side.

     (v)   Using a protractor, find the measure of
           all three angles of the triangle.

     (vi) What type of triangle have you
           constructed?

15. (i)   Construct a square *DEFG* of side length
           10 cm.

     (ii) Draw all the axes of symmetry of this
           square.

     (iii) How many axes of symmetry did you
           draw?

16. The diagram shows two circles inscribed in a
     rectangle. The radius of each circle is 3 cm.

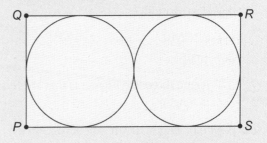

     (i)   Construct the rectangle *PQRS*.

     (ii) Construct the two circles inscribed in the
           rectangle.

17. (i)   Construct the triangle shown in the
           diagram.

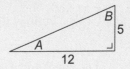

     (ii) Using a protractor, find the measure of
           angles *A* and *B*.

     (iii) Construct the circle that circumscribes
           the triangle.

     (iv) Measure the radius of this circle.

18. Construct the parallelogram *UVWX* as shown
     in the diagram.

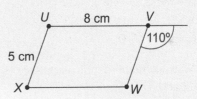

19. (i)   Construct the following shape using the
           measurements shown in the diagram.
           The circle has a diameter of 10 cm with
           O as its centre.

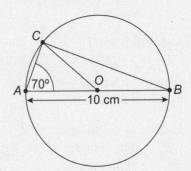

Using measurements taken from your construction, find:

(ii) $|\angle ACB|$

(iii) $|\angle COB|$

(iv) $|CB|$

(v) Name three line segments that are 5 cm in length.

20. A wire of length 100 m is bent to form a rectangle, one side of which is 30 m.

(i) Using a scale of 1 cm = 10 m, construct this rectangle.

It is then decided to use the same wire length to construct an isosceles triangle with one side of 30 m.

(ii) Using the same scale, construct this triangle.

21. (i) Draw a circle of centre *O* and with diameter length 14 cm.

(ii) For your circle, draw a chord [*AB*] and a chord [*CD*] as shown in the diagram.

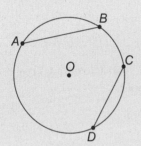

(iii) Construct the perpendicular bisectors of [*AB*] and [*DC*].

(iv) What point do these perpendicular bisectors have in common?

22. (i) Construct a triangle *XYZ* in which $|XY| = 10$ cm, $|XZ| = 5$ cm and $|YZ| = 8$ cm.

(ii) Construct the centroid of the triangle. Label as the point *P*.

(iii) Construct a line segment equal in length to [*XZ*] on the ray [*PY*.

23. (i) Construct a parallelogram *ABCD* where $|AB| = 8$ cm, $|\angle ABC| = 130°$ and $|BC| = 5$ cm.

(ii) Measure all four interior angles of the parallelogram to the nearest degree; which angles, if any, are equal in measure?

(iii) Draw the diagonals [*AC*] and [*BD*], and label the point of intersection of the diagonals as *X*.

(iv) Find, using a ruler, $|AX|$ and $|XC|$. What do you notice?

(v) Find $|BX|$. What length should $|XD|$ be?

24. (i) Construct the triangle *DEF* where $|DF| = 9$ cm and the perpendicular height of the triangle is 5 cm, as shown in the diagram.

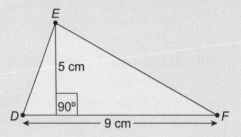

(ii) Calculate the area of the triangle *DEF*.

(iii) Using a ruler, measure [*ED*]. Using your set square, draw a perpendicular from *F* to [*ED*].
Measure this perpendicular height.

(iv) Find the area of Δ*DEF* using [*ED*] as the base. Did you get the same answer as in part (ii)?

25. A cable 13 m long joins the top of an antenna 12 m high as shown on the diagram.

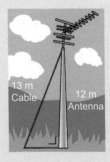

(i) Construct the triangle shown in the diagram using an appropriate scale.

(ii) Find the horizontal distance between the cable and the antenna, using a ruler.

(iii) What other method could you use to find this horizontal distance?

26. (i) Construct a circle of radius 6 cm.

(ii) Construct two tangents to this circle which are parallel to each other, using only a compass and ruler.

27. Using only a ruler and compass, construct the shape shown below.

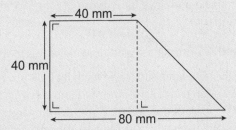

28. Using the given diagram, construct the circle inscribed in a square of length 8 cm, using only a ruler and compass.

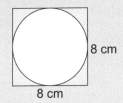

29. (i) Construct the quadrilateral as shown.

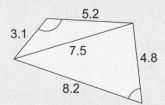

(ii) Use your protractor to measure the shaded angles.

30. (i) A tree is 10 m high and casts a shadow of 4 m. Using a scale of 1 cm to represent 1 m, construct the triangle shown in the diagram.

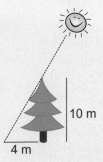

(ii) Use your protractor to measure the angle that the sun's rays make with the ground.

(iii) Write the scale you used as a ratio.

31. Copy the following diagram into your copybook.

Using only a compass and a straight edge, construct a circle that passes through the points *A* and *B*.

32. (i) Construct the parallelogram *ABCD* where |*AB*| = 80 mm, |*BC*| = 55 mm and |∠*ABC*| = 125°.

(ii) Construct a ray from point *B* that is equidistant from [*AB*] and [*BC*].

33. An advertising company wants to design a logo of a circle inside an equilateral triangle as shown.

(i) If the equilateral triangle has sides of length 6 cm, construct this logo.

(ii) It is then decided that it would be better if the equilateral triangle was inside the circle for the logo. The circle is to pass through all three vertices of the triangle. Construct this new logo.

34. A town planner wishes to build a shopping centre that is the same distance from three towns.

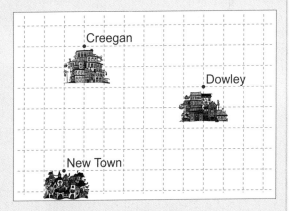

(i) Show by construction, and using an appropriate scale, how this could be achieved. (Note: You can set your own figures for the distance between the towns.)

(ii) Using your construction, find the distance between the shopping centre and any one of these towns.

35. Two new houses are being built. A pipeline from a local well is to be laid to supply water to both houses. This pipe must always be the same distance from each house.

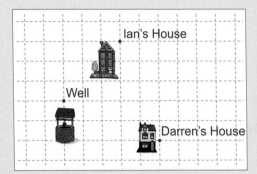

Show by construction, and using an appropriate scale, how this could be achieved.

36. A landscaper is given a design for a lawn. The lawn should be in the shape of a triangle and have dimensions of 6 m, 7.5 m and 5 m.

  (i) Construct a scaled drawing of this lawn.

  (ii) The landscaper wishes to include a large circular flower-bed in the lawn as part of the design. Construct the largest flower-bed possible into your drawing in part (i).

  (iii) Find the area of this flower-bed using the measurements from your construction.

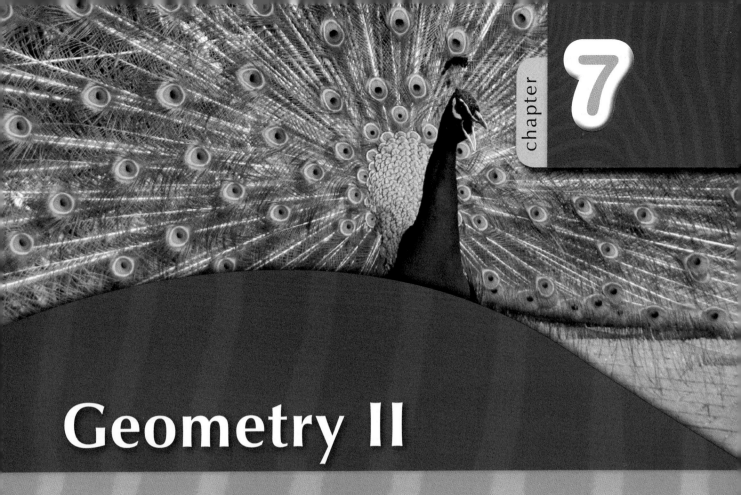

Geometry II

Learning Outcomes

In this chapter you will learn the following axioms, theorems and corollaries:

- Axiom 4. Congruent triangles (SSS, SAS, ASA and RHS).

- Theorem 11. If three parallel lines cut off equal segments on some transversal line, then they will cut off equal segments on any other transversal.

- Theorem 12. Let *ABC* be a triangle. If a line *l* is parallel to *BC* and cuts [*AB*] in the ratio *m* : *n*, then it also cuts [*AC*] in the same ratio.

- Theorem 13. If two triangles are similar, then their sides are proportional, in order.

- Theorem 14. The theorem of Pythagoras: In a right-angled triangle the square of the hypotenuse is the sum of the squares of the other two sides.

- Theorem 15. If the square of one side of a triangle is the sum of the squares of the other two sides, then the angle opposite the first side is a right angle.

- Theorem 16. For a triangle, base times height does not depend on the choice of base.

- Theorem 17. A diagonal of a parallelogram bisects the area.

- Theorem 18. The area of a parallelogram is the base times the height.

- Corollary 3. Each angle in a semicircle is a right angle.

- Corollary 4. If the angle standing on a chord [*BC*] at some point of the circle is a right angle, then [*BC*] is a diameter.

- Theorem 20. Each tangent is perpendicular to the radius that goes to the point of contact. If *P* lies on *s*, and a line *l* is perpendicular to the radius to *P*, then *l* is a tangent to *s*.

- Corollary 6. If two circles intersect at one point only, then the two centres and the point of contact are collinear.

- Theorem 21. (i) The perpendicular from the centre to a chord bisects the chord. (ii) The perpendicular bisector of a chord passes through the centre.

7.1 CONGRUENT TRIANGLES

If two shapes are exactly the same size and shape, they are said to be **identical**.

If two triangles are identical to each other, they can also be described as being **congruent**.

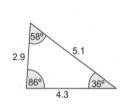 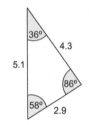

> **Congruent triangles** are triangles where all the corresponding sides and interior angles are equal in measure.

> **Corresponding angles** are the angles that match each other in the two triangles.

There are four different methods or cases to show that two triangles are congruent.

These methods are listed in Axiom 4:

> **Axiom 4**
>
> Congruent triangles (SSS, SAS, ASA and RHS).

Congruent Triangles: Side, Side, Side (SSS)

> **SSS** means **Side, Side, Side**.

$\triangle ABC$ is congruent to $\triangle XYZ$.

The side lengths in $\triangle ABC$ are the same as the side lengths in $\triangle XYZ$.

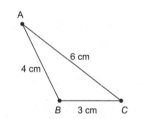 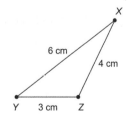

> The symbol $\equiv$ is a shorthand way of describing two triangles as congruent, e.g. $\triangle ABC \equiv \triangle XYZ$.

Congruent Triangles: Side, Angle, Side (SAS)

ΔDEF is congruent to ΔPQR **or** $\Delta DEF \equiv \Delta PQR$.

Two sides and the angle in between them are equal.

> The **in-between** angle can also be called the **included angle**.

> SAS means **Side, Angle, Side.**

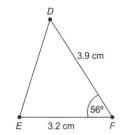
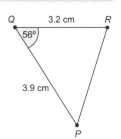

Congruent Triangles: Angle, Side, Angle (ASA)

ΔGHI is congruent to ΔMNO **or** $\Delta GHI \equiv \Delta MNO$.

Two angles and the included side are equal.

> The **included side** is the side in between the vertices of the two given angles.

> ASA means **Angle, Side, Angle.**

Congruent Triangles: Right Angle, Hypotenuse, One Other Side (RHS)

> The **hypotenuse** is the side opposite the right angle; it is also the longest side in the triangle.

ΔRST is congruent to ΔUVW **or** $\Delta RST \equiv \Delta UVW$.

Both of these triangles are right-angled, their hypotenuse is the same length, and they have one other side that is equal.

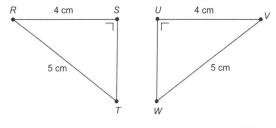

> The areas of congruent triangles are equal as well.

ACTIVITY 7.1

Worked Example 7.1

Verify that the triangles ABC and ABD are congruent.

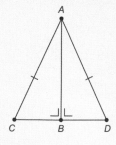

Solution

$|AC| = |AD|$ (given)

$|AB| = |AB|$ (common)

$|\angle ABC| = |\angle ABD|$ (both 90°)

$\therefore \Delta ABC \equiv \Delta ABD$ (RHS)

> The same side is used in both triangles. This is known as the **common side.**

Always remember to state which case you used to show congruency.

Worked Example 7.2

Is △PQR ≡ △RST?

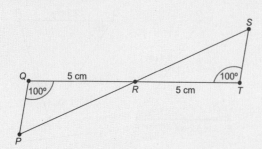

Solution

|QR| = |RT| (both 5 cm)

|∠PQR| = |∠RTS| (both 100°)

|∠QRP| = |∠SRT| (vertically opposite)

> We realise that these angles are equal, as they are vertically opposite to each other.

∴ △PQR ≡ △RST (ASA)

Exercise 7.1

1. State if any of the following triangles are congruent. Explain your answer fully.

(i)

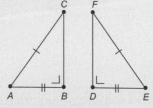

Is △ABC ≡ △DEF?

(ii)

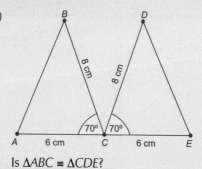

Is △ABC ≡ △CDE?

(iii)

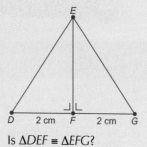

Is △DEF ≡ △EFG?

(iv)

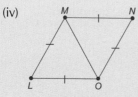

Is △LMO ≡ △MNO?

(v)

Is △RST ≡ △TUV?

(vi)

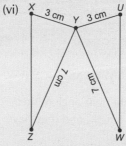

Is △XYZ ≡ △UYW?

(vii)

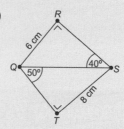

Is △QRS ≡ △QTS?

(viii)

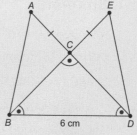

Is △ABC ≡ △CDE?

ACTIVE MATHS 2

(ix) Note: *DEFG* is a parallelogram.

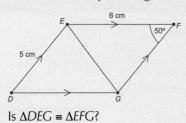

Is Δ*DEG* ≡ Δ*EFG*?

(x)

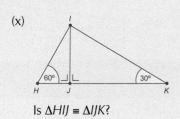

Is Δ*HIJ* ≡ Δ*IJK*?

2. Consider the following diagram:

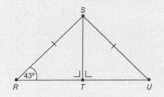

(i) Find |∠*RST*| and |∠*SUT*|.

(ii) What type of triangle is Δ*RSU*?

(iii) Investigate if the triangle *RST* is congruent to the triangle *STU*.

3. In the following diagram, |*AX*| = |*XB*|, |*BY*| = |*YC*|, and |∠*BXC*| = |∠*BYA*|.

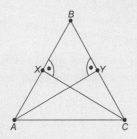

(i) If |*BX*| = 5 cm, find |*AX*|.

(ii) If |*BY*| = 5 cm, what type of triangle is Δ*ABC*?

(iii) Show that Δ*ABY* ≡ Δ*BXC*.

4. In the following diagram, *ABCD* is a parallelogram.

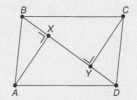

(i) Show that Δ*ABD* is congruent to Δ*BCD*.

(ii) Show that Δ*ABX* is congruent to Δ*CYD*.

7.2 PARALLEL LINES

We already know some properties of parallel lines that deal with the angles formed by a transversal. We will now consider:

(a) what happens when three parallel lines intersect a transversal, and specifically,

(b) what happens when that transversal is cut into two equal segments.

From our investigations, we can determine that:

ACTIVITY 7.2

> If a transversal is cut into two equal parts by three parallel lines, then any other transversal drawn between these parallel lines will also be cut into two equal parts.

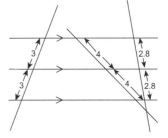

We can now state this as a theorem:

Theorem 11

If three parallel lines cut off equal segments on some transversal line, then they will cut off equal segments on any other transversal.

Worked Example 7.3

Find the value of $|EF|$.

Solution

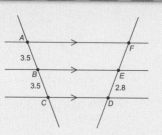

If three parallel lines divide up one of the transversals into two equal segments, they must do the same for the other transversal.

$\therefore |EF| = 2.8$

Worked Example 7.4

Find the value of a and b.

Solution

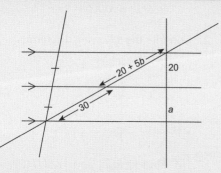

We can see that one transversal is cut into equal parts. Therefore, all other transversals will be cut into equal parts as well.

(i) To find a:

$\therefore a = 20$ (from above)

(ii) To find b:

$20 + 5b = 30$

$5b = 30 - 20$

$5b = 10$

$\therefore b = 2$

Exercise 7.2

1. In each of the following diagrams, find the value of x.

   (i)

   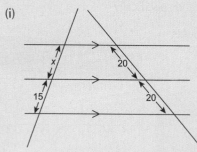

   (ii)

   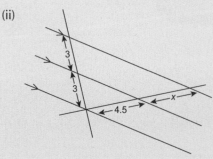

2. In each of the following diagrams, the three parallel lines cut a transversal into equal segments.
   Find the value of x and y.

   (i)

   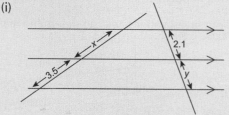

   (ii)

   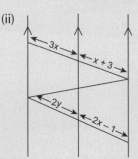

3. In each of the following diagrams, find the value of x and y.

(i)

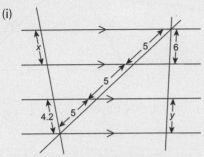

(ii)

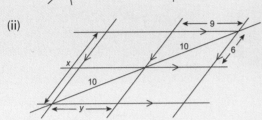

4. The new logo for the clothes company N is shown on graph paper of 1 cm².

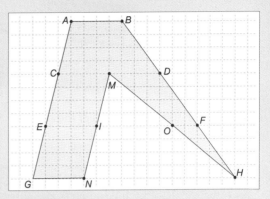

If $|AG| = 12.4$ cm, $|BD| = 5$ cm and $|OH| = 6.4$ cm, find the perimeter of this shape.

7.3 PARALLEL LINES AND TRIANGLES

We will now investigate what happens when a line that is parallel to one side of a triangle divides another side of the triangle in a certain ratio.

ACTIVITIES 7.3, 7.4

From our investigations, we know that:

> A line that is parallel to one side of a triangle cuts the other two sides of the triangle in the same ratio. This ratio is often referred to as $m : n$.

$$m:n = s:t$$

Consider the triangle shown on the bottom right:

If the ratio $|AX|:|XB|$ is equal to 3 : 2, then the ratio $|AY|:|YC|$ is also 3 : 2.

> This ratio is often referred to as $m : n$.

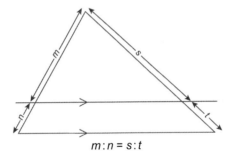

This can be written more formally as:

Theorem 12

Let ABC be a triangle. If a line *l* is parallel to BC and cuts [AB] in the ratio $m : n$, then it also cuts [AC] in the same ratio.

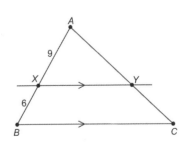

Ratios can be written as fractions. So, this theorem can also be written as:

$$\frac{|AX|}{|XB|} = \frac{|AY|}{|YC|} \quad \text{or} \quad \frac{\text{Top length}}{\text{Bottom length}} = \frac{\text{Top length}}{\text{Bottom length}}$$

FORMULA

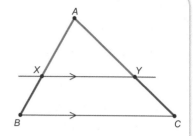

It is important to realise that all of these ratios can be inverted or turned upside down:

FORMULA

$$\frac{|XB|}{|AX|} = \frac{|YC|}{|AY|} \quad \text{or} \quad \frac{\text{Bottom length}}{\text{Top length}} = \frac{\text{Bottom length}}{\text{Top length}}$$

This theorem by itself cannot be used to find the length of the triangle side which is parallel to the intersecting line.

The theorem means that the following is also true:

FORMULA

$$\frac{|AB|}{|XB|} = \frac{|AC|}{|YC|} \quad \text{or} \quad \frac{\text{Overall length}}{\text{Bottom length}} = \frac{\text{Overall length}}{\text{Bottom length}}$$

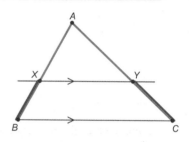

And:

FORMULA

$$\frac{|AB|}{|AX|} = \frac{|AC|}{|AY|} \quad \text{or} \quad \frac{\text{Overall length}}{\text{Top length}} = \frac{\text{Overall length}}{\text{Top length}}$$

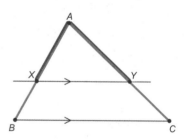

The converse of Theorem 12 can be used to show that two lines are parallel:

If a line cuts two sides of a triangle in the same ratio, then the line is parallel to the side not cut by the line.

Worked Example 7.5

Find the length of [AD], given that DE ∥ BC.

Solution

We need to find |AD|, so we first identify what ratio we will use.

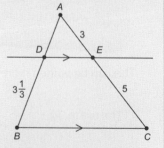

We start with the side we are looking for when writing the ratio, as this makes our calculations much easier.

$$\frac{\text{Top length}}{\text{Bottom length}} = \frac{\text{Top length}}{\text{Bottom length}}$$

$$\frac{|AD|}{3\frac{1}{3}} = \frac{3}{5}$$

We cross-multiply to eliminate fractions:

$$5|AD| = 10$$

$$\therefore |AD| = 2$$

Worked Example 7.6

In the triangle *PRT*, |*RT*| = 10.4. Find the length of [*RS*].

Solution

We need to find |*RS*|, so we again identify which ratio we are using.

> We are looking for the top length, and we have been given the overall length of one side.

First, find |*RP*|.

$|RP| = |RQ| + |QP|$

$\qquad = 5 + 1.5$

$\therefore |RP| = 6.5$

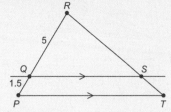

$$\frac{\text{Top length}}{\text{Overall length}} = \frac{\text{Top length}}{\text{Overall length}}$$

$$\frac{|RS|}{10.4} = \frac{5}{6.5}$$

Cross-multiply:

$$6.5\,|RS| = 5 \times 10.4$$

$$6.5\,|RS| = 52$$

$$\therefore |RS| = 8$$

Exercise 7.3

1. For each of the line segments below, find the following ratios:

   (i) |*AB*| : |*BC*|

   (ii) |*AC*| : |*AB*|

   (iii) |*BC*| : |*AC*|

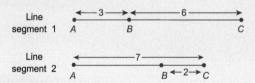

2. Find the value of *x* in each case.

   (i)

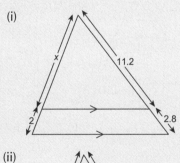

   (ii)

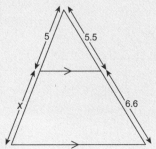

   (iii)

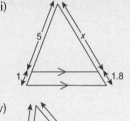

   (iv)

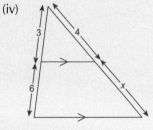

   (v)

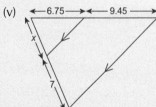

3. Find the value of *y* in each case.

   (i)

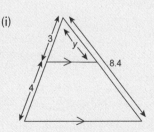

(ii)

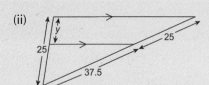

25, y, 25, 37.5

(iii)

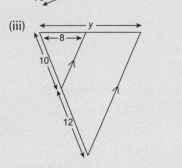

y, 8, 10, 12

(iv)

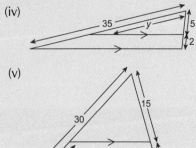

35, y, 5, 2

(v)

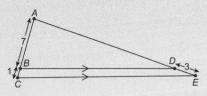

15, 30, 10, y

4. In the diagram $BD \parallel CE$.

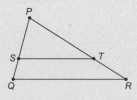

A, 7, B, 1, C, D, 3, E

Find: (i) $|AD|$

      (ii) $|AE|$

      (iii)   The ratio $|AB| : |AC|$

5. In the diagram, $ST \parallel QR$. $|PS| : |SQ| = 5 : 2$

P, S, T, Q, R

Find the following ratios:

   (i) $|PT| : |TR|$

   (ii) $|PR| : |PT|$

   (iii) $|PQ| : |PS|$

   (iv)   Gemma writes, '$|SQ| = 2$'.

       Could $[SQ]$ have a different length?

       Give a reason for your answer.

6. In the diagram, $XZ \parallel AB$. Also, $|XY| : |AY| = 7 : 3$.

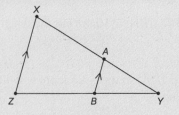

X, A, Z, B, Y

Write down the following ratios:

(i) $\dfrac{|XA|}{|AY|}$ (ii) $\dfrac{|ZB|}{|BY|}$ (iii) $\dfrac{|YZ|}{|BY|}$

If $|AX| = 8$ cm and $|ZB| = 7$ cm, find:

(iv) $|AY|$ (v) $|BY|$ (vi) $|ZY|$

7. Investigate if $XY \parallel PQ$.

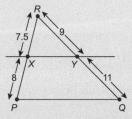

R, 7.5, 9, X, Y, 8, 11, P, Q

8. Investigate if $PQ \parallel AC$.

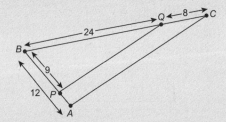

Q, 8, C, 24, B, 9, 12, P, A

9. Find the value of x in each case.

(i)

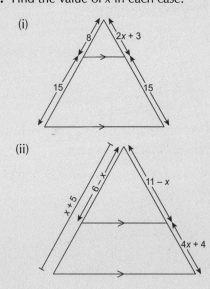

8, $2x + 3$, 15, 15

(ii)

$x + 5$, $6 - x$, $11 - x$, $4x + 4$

7.4 SIMILAR TRIANGLES

Another relationship that two triangles can have is that of similarity. We can see from the example below that the two triangles have the same angles but are not the same size.

The triangles *ABC* and *DEF* are said to be **similar** to each other.

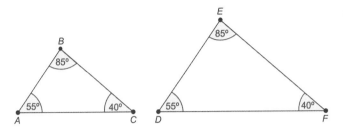

In **similar** or equiangular triangles, all three angles in one triangle have the same measurement as the corresponding three angles in another triangle.

It is important to remember that while the angles are equal, the sides are not. However, the sides of two similar triangles do have a special property.

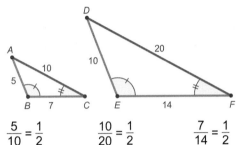

It is clear that when we have two similar triangles:

$$\frac{5}{10} = \frac{1}{2} \qquad \frac{10}{20} = \frac{1}{2} \qquad \frac{7}{14} = \frac{1}{2}$$

> The corresponding sides of similar triangles are in the same ratio.

> Corresponding sides are the sides that match each other in the two triangles. In the above example, for the side [*AB*], the corresponding side is [*DE*].

This now allows us to state the following theorem:

Theorem 13

If two triangles are similar, then their sides are proportional, in order.

In the following similar triangles the corresponding sides are proportional:

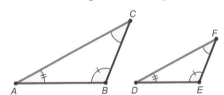

FORMULA

$$\frac{|AB|}{|DE|} = \frac{|AC|}{|DF|} = \frac{|BC|}{|EF|}$$

Usually, we only need to use two of the ratios to determine the missing side.

As before, these ratios can be inverted or turned upside down.

The converse of Theorem 13 also applies:

FORMULA

$$\frac{|DE|}{|AB|} = \frac{|DF|}{|AC|} = \frac{|EF|}{|BC|}$$

> If, in any two triangles, the sides (in order) are proportional, i.e. if $\frac{|AB|}{|DE|} = \frac{|AC|}{|DF|} = \frac{|BC|}{|EF|}$, then the two triangles are similar to each other.

Sometimes, we must first show that two triangles are similar.

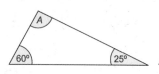 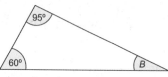

$|\angle A| = 180° - 25° - 60° = 95°$

$|\angle B| = 180° - 60° - 95° = 25°$

Both triangles have the same angles.

∴ The two triangles are similar or equiangular.

 Worked Example 7.7

Find the value of *y*.

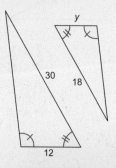

> When dealing with similar triangles, it is always a good idea to redraw the triangles so that the corresponding sides match on the diagram.

Solution

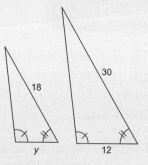

These triangles are similar.

Again, we start with the unknown side and put it over the corresponding side which we know:

$$\frac{y}{12} = \frac{18}{30}$$

Cross-multiply: $\quad 30y = 216$

$$\therefore y = 7.2$$

It is also apparent that:

> If a triangle is cut by a line parallel to one of its sides, this line divides the triangle into two similar triangles.

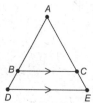

Worked Example 7.8

Find   (i) |AE| (ii) |DE|

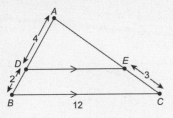

Solution

(i)   To find |AE|:

$$\frac{|AE|}{3} = \frac{4}{2}$$

$$\therefore \frac{|AE|}{3} = 2$$

Cross-multiply:

$$\therefore |AE| = 6$$

(ii)   To find |DE|:

It is a good idea to redraw the triangles, but this time into two separate similar triangles.

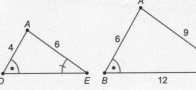

$$\frac{|DE|}{12} = \frac{4}{6}$$

$$\therefore \frac{|DE|}{12} = \frac{2}{3}$$

Cross-multiply:

$$\therefore 3|DE| = 24$$

$$\therefore |DE| = 8$$

Exercise 7.4

1. Identify the pairs of corresponding sides in each of the following similar triangles.

   Part (i) has been done for you to show how to lay out your answer.

   (i)
   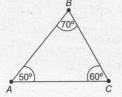

   Answer:

   [AB] corresponds to [DE].

   [AC] corresponds to [DF].

   [BC] corresponds to [EF].

   (ii)
   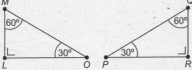

   (iii)
   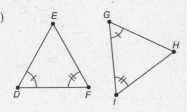

   (iv)
   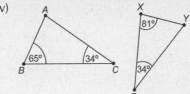

   (v)
   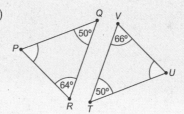

2. Find the value of x in each case.

   (i)
   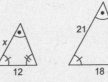

   (ii)
   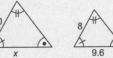

   (iii)

(iv)

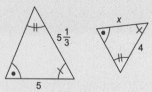

(v)

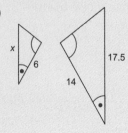

3. Find the value of x and y in each case.

(i)

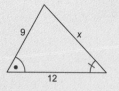

(ii)

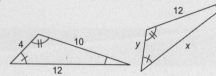

(iii)

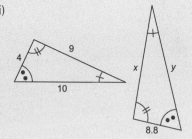

(iv)

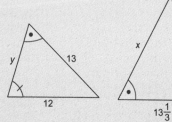

(v)

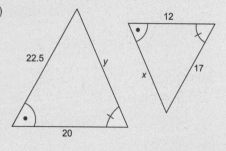

4. Investigate if the following pairs of triangles are similar to each other. Explain your answer.

(i) Is △PQR similar to △PST?

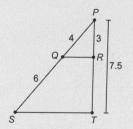

(ii) Is △DEF similar to △DGH?

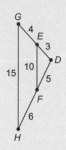

5. For each question, the triangles ABC and ADE are similar. Find the value of x and y in each case.

You can also use Theorem 12 to help find the required sides.

(i)

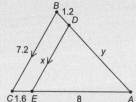

(ii)

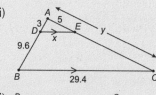

(iii)

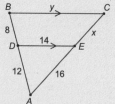

(iv)

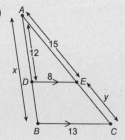

6. In the given diagram $AB \perp BC$ and $EC \perp ED$.

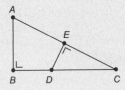

(i) Show that the two triangles ABC and EDC are similar.

Given that $|ED| = 3$, $|AB| = 6$ and $|DC| = 5$, find:

(ii) $|AC|$ (iii) $|BC|$ (iv) $|EC|$

7. In the triangle PQR, $ST \parallel QR$, and $|QS| = \frac{1}{3}|TR|$.

Find:

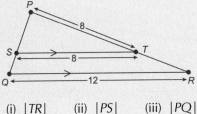

(i) $|TR|$ (ii) $|PS|$ (iii) $|PQ|$

8. In the $\triangle XYZ$, $AB \parallel YZ$.

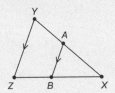

(i) In your own words explain why $\triangle XYZ$ and $\triangle XAB$ are similar.

If $|XB| : |XZ| = 3:5$, find the following ratios:

(ii) $|XB| : |BZ|$ (iv) $|XY| : |AY|$

(iii) $|XA| : |AY|$

9. Consider the triangles ABC and BEF, where $AC \parallel EF$.

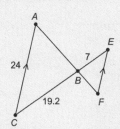

(i) Show that the two triangles ABC and BEF are similar.

(ii) Find $|EF|$.

10. A building casts a shadow of length 6.4 m. At the same time a 3 m high lamppost casts a shadow of length 2.5 m. How tall is the building?

11. For a school project, students measure the lengths of their shadows on a sunny day. Student A's shadow was 3 m long and student B's shadow was 3.4 m long.

(i) Which student is taller? Give a reason for your answer.

(ii) If student A is 1.6 m tall, how tall is student B? (Give your answer to two decimal places.)

(iii) A building close by has a height of 4 m. How long would its shadow be? (Give your answer to two decimal places.)

12. The diagram shows a person who is 1.74 m tall. Her shadow length is 4 m.

(i) Find the height of the nearby tree, if the person is standing 16.5 m away from the tree.

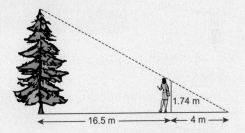

(ii) Another tree shadow is 23 m in length. Find the height of this tree to the nearest metre.

13. A firework is fired from the ground at an angle. It travels in a straight line and hits a target at a height of 15 m, 55 m in a horizontal line away from where it was fired. Along its path it just passed over a stone wall which is a distance of 47.5 m from the target.

(i) Draw a diagram to show the above information.

(ii) Using a suitable theorem, find the approximate height of the wall to the nearest centimetre.

14. Jane is 1.6 m tall. She stands in front of lamppost which is 3 m high. When she stands 15 m away from the lamppost, she can see that the top of the lamppost just lines up with the top of her office block. From where she is standing the lamppost is 85 m away from the office block.

  (i) Draw a suitable diagram to show the above information. (Include the fact that she is 1.6 m tall.)

  (ii) Hence, find the height of the office block (to the nearest metre).

7.5 THEOREM OF PYTHAGORAS

One of the most important angles used in construction is a 90° angle. Walls are usually at right angles to each other and to the ground. Egyptian surveyors were known as 'rope stretchers' and would use ropes knotted at intervals of 3, 4 and 5 to generate right-angled triangles.

While this was widely known in many ancient cultures, it is Pythagoras whose name is associated with the properties of right-angled triangles.

In the given triangle it was noticed that

$10^2 = 100$ and that $6^2 + 8^2$ is also equal to 100.

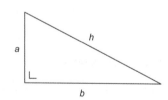

We can show that:

> **Theorem 14: The theorem of Pythagoras**
>
> In a right-angled triangle the square of the hypotenuse is the sum of the squares of the other two sides.

This leads to the equation:

FORMULA

$$h^2 = a^2 + b^2$$

> *h* is the hypotenuse: this is the longest side and also the side opposite the right angle.
> *a* and *b* are the other two sides of the triangle.

We can also show that the angle opposite the longest side is a right angle. This then leads us to the next theorem based on Pythagoras' theorem.

> **Theorem 15**
>
> If the square of one side of a triangle is the sum of the squares of the other two sides, then the angle opposite the first side is a right angle.

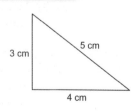

$$5^2 = 3^2 + 4^2$$

⇒ The angle opposite the side of 5 cm is a right angle.

GEOMETRY II

Worked Example 7.9

Find |AB|.

Solution

It is important to identify if we are trying to find the hypotenuse or another side.

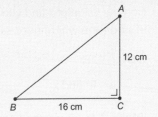

Write Pythagoras' theorem.	$h^2 = a^2 + b^2$
Write down the given values.	$a = 16,\ b = 12$
Put these values into the equation and solve.	$h^2 = 16^2 + 12^2$ $h^2 = 256 + 144$ $h^2 = 400$
Find the square root.	$h = \sqrt{400}$
$\therefore\ |AB| = 20$ cm	$h = 20$

Worked Example 7.10

Which of the following triangles are right-angled triangles? (Triangles are not drawn to scale.)

Triangle 1

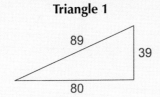

Triangle 2

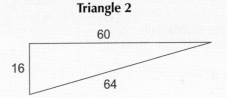

Solution

If a triangle is right-angled, then $c^2 = a^2 + b^2$.

We must first identify which side we will use as the hypotenuse. The hypotenuse is always the longest side.

Once we have identified one side as the hypotenuse, we call the two other sides a and b.

Triangle 1	Triangle 2
$c = 89$ (longest side) $\therefore\ c^2 = (89)^2 = 7{,}921$	$c = 64$ (longest side) $\therefore\ c^2 = (64)^2 = 4{,}096$
If the triangle is right-angled, then $a^2 + b^2$ will also be equal to 7,921: $a = 80 \rightarrow a^2 = (80)^2 = 6{,}400$ $b = 39 \rightarrow b^2 = (39)^2 = 1{,}521$	$a^2 + b^2$ should be equal to 4,096 if the triangle has a right angle: $a = 60 \rightarrow a^2 = (60)^2 = 3{,}600$ $b = 16 \rightarrow b^2 = (16)^2 = 256$
$6{,}400 + 1521 = 7{,}921$ $\therefore$ Triangle 1 is a right-angled triangle.	$3{,}600 + 256 = 3{,}856$ $3{,}856 \neq 4{,}096$ $\therefore$ Triangle 2 is **NOT** a right-angled triangle.

Find the value of x and y in the diagram, leaving your answer
in surd form where necessary.

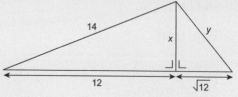

Solution

(i) To find x:

Write Pythagoras' theorem.	$h^2 = a^2 + b^2$
Write down the given values.	$h = 14, b = 12$
Put these values into the equation.	$14^2 = a^2 + 12^2$ $196 = a^2 + 144$
We now get the unknown on one side and everything else onto the other side.	$196 - 144 = a^2$ $52 = a^2$
Leave a in surd form (unless told otherwise).	$a = \sqrt{52}$
$\therefore x = \sqrt{52}$	

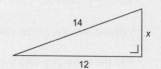

(ii) To find y:

Write Pythagoras' theorem.	$h^2 = a^2 + b^2$
Write down the given values.	$a = \sqrt{52}, b = \sqrt{12}$
Put these values into the equation and simplify.	$h^2 = (\sqrt{52})^2 + (\sqrt{12})^2$ $h^2 = 52 + 12$ $h^2 = 64$
Find the square root.	$h = \sqrt{64}$ $h = 8$
$\therefore y = 8$	

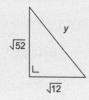

1. Find the value of x in each of the following triangles:

(i) 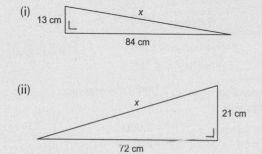 13 cm, x, 84 cm

(ii) x, 21 cm, 72 cm

(iii) 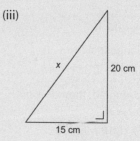 x, 20 cm, 15 cm

(iv) 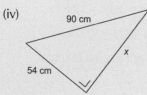 90 cm, x, 54 cm

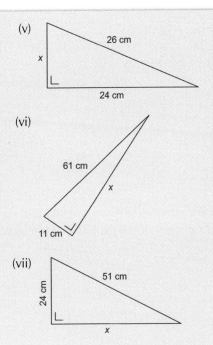

(v) 26 cm, x, 24 cm

(vi) 61 cm, x, 11 cm

(vii) 24 cm, 51 cm, x

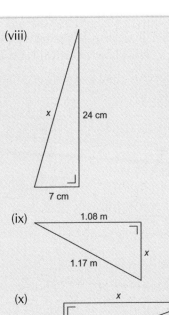

(viii) x, 24 cm, 7 cm

(ix) 1.08 m, x, 1.17 m

(x) x, 45 km, 205 km

2. Find the value of y correct to two decimal places.

(i)
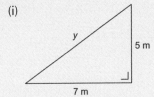
y, 5 m, 7 m

(ii)

11 cm, 8 cm, y

(iii)
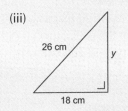
26 cm, y, 18 cm

(iv)
8 cm, 8 cm, y

(v)
22 cm, y

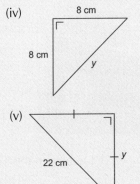

3. Find the length of the unknown side. Leave your answers in surd form where appropriate.

(i)
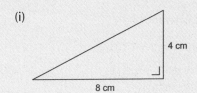
4 cm, 8 cm

(ii)
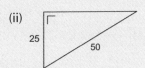
25, 50

(iii)
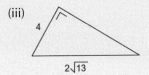
4, $2\sqrt{13}$

(iv)
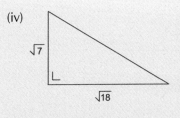
$\sqrt{7}$, $\sqrt{18}$

(v)
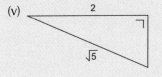
2, $\sqrt{5}$

4. Identify which of these triangles are right-angled triangles. Show clearly how you arrived at your answer.

(i)
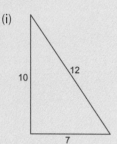

(ii)

(iii)
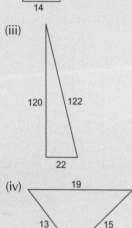

(iv)
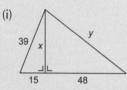

5. Find the length of x and y in each of the following triangles.

(i)
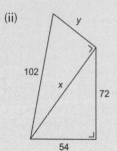

(ii)

(iii)
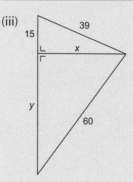

6. Using the theorem of Pythagoras, find the value of x in each of the right-angled triangles:

(i)
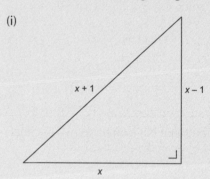

(ii)
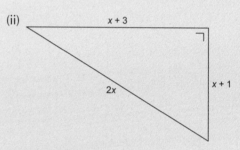

7. A ladder leans against a wall at a height of 2.5 m. The ladder's base is 0.75 m from the wall. The ladder slips down so that its base is now 90 cm away from the wall. How far did the ladder slip to the nearest centimetre?

8. The side view of a barn is shown. All measurements are in metres.

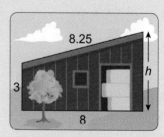

Calculate the height (h) of the barn to the nearest centimetre.

9. A diagram of a roof is shown. Find the perpendicular height of this roof to the nearest centimetre. (All lengths are in metres.)

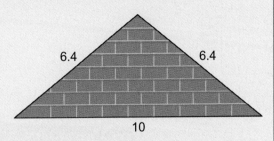

10. A builder is building rectangular frames 3.5 m by 5.2 m. To ensure that the sides are perpendicular to each other, what should the length of each diagonal measure to the nearest centimetre?

11. A sharpened pencil 19 cm long is placed in a rectangular pencil case. The pencil fits exactly when placed diagonally as shown.

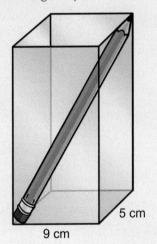

5 cm

9 cm

How long is the pencil case (to the nearest centimetre)?

12. A rectangular piece of land is shown adjoined by two triangular fields.

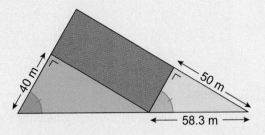

40 m

50 m

58.3 m

Find the area of the field system to the nearest square metre.

13. Rectangular blocks for a child's toy are to be packed as shown.

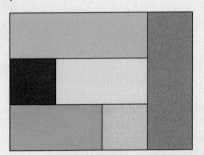

All blocks are the same width of x cm. The smaller rectangular blocks are twice as long as the square blocks. The larger rectangular blocks are three times as long as the square blocks.

The diagonal length of the rectangle formed by the packed blocks can be expressed as $\sqrt{x^2 + 10x + 25}$.
Find the dimensions of each block.

7.6 AREA OF A TRIANGLE AND AREA OF A PARALLELOGRAM

One of the earliest uses of geometry was to determine the area of a plot of land so as to calculate the amount of tax that had to be paid.

In ancient Egypt, officials would measure the area of the land that had been flooded by the Nile and use this to determine the tax payable by the farmer to the Pharaoh for that year.

Area of a Triangle

We are already aware that the area of a rectangle is its length multiplied by its width.

Area = $l \times b$

From this knowledge, we can determine the formula for the area of a triangle.

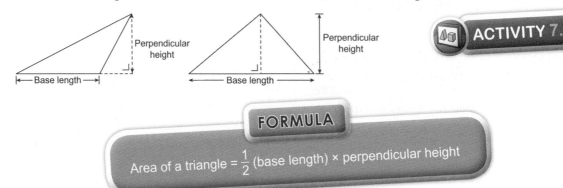

Perpendicular height

Base length

Perpendicular height

Base length

ACTIVITY 7.7

FORMULA

Area of a triangle = $\frac{1}{2}$ (base length) × perpendicular height

It is also clear from our investigation that in calculating the area of a triangle:

It does not matter which base of the triangle we choose as long as we know the perpendicular height from the corresponding base.

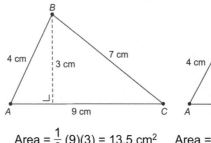

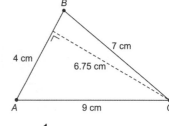

Area = $\frac{1}{2}$ (9)(3) = 13.5 cm²   Area = $\frac{1}{2}$ (4)(6.75) = 13.5 cm²

This is stated as:

Theorem 16

For a triangle, base times height does not depend on the choice of base.

Area of a Parallelogram

We can now consider how to find the area of a parallelogram.

ACTIVITY 7.8

We know from Activity 7.8 that a parallelogram is cut into two triangles of equal area by a diagonal.

This is known as:

Theorem 17

A diagonal of a parallelogram bisects the area.

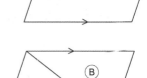

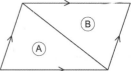

Area Triangle Ⓐ = Area Triangle Ⓑ

From Theorem 17, a parallelogram can be cut into two triangles of equal area.

Area triangle Ⓐ $= \frac{1}{2}$ base × height

$= \frac{1}{2} \times 8 \times 5 = 20$ cm²

Area triangle Ⓑ $= \frac{1}{2}$ base × height

$= \frac{1}{2} \times 8 \times 5 = 20$ cm²

Area of parallelogram (Area of triangles Ⓐ + Ⓑ)

Area of parallelogram $= 20$ cm² $+ 20$ cm²

$= 40$ cm² (or 8 × 5)

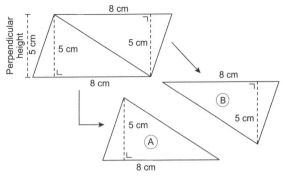

FORMULA

Area of parallelogram = base × height

This is known as:

Theorem 18

The area of a parallelogram is the base times the height.

 Worked Example 7.12

Find the area of each of the following shapes.

(i)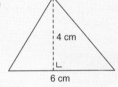

(ii)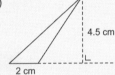

(iii)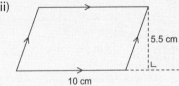

Solution

(i) Area $= \frac{1}{2} \times 6 \times 4 = 12$ cm²

(ii) Area $= \frac{1}{2} \times 2 \times 4.5 = 4.5$ cm²

(iii) Area $= 10 \times 5.5 = 55$ cm²

 Worked Example 7.13

The area of the parallelogram *ABCD* is equal to the area of the triangle *PQR*. Find the value of *x*, the height of the parallelogram.

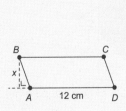

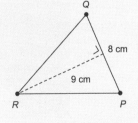

Solution

Area of parallelogram *ABCD*	Area of triangle *PQR*
= base × height	$= \frac{1}{2}$ (base) × height
= 12(x)	$= \frac{1}{2}(8)(9)$
= 12x	= 36 cm²

$12x = 36$

$x = 3$ cm

Exercise 7.6

GEOMETRY II

1. Find the area of each of the following triangles:

   (i)
   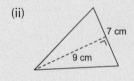
   9 cm
   10 cm

   (ii)
   7 cm
   9 cm

   (iii)
   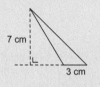
   7 cm
   3 cm

   (iv)
   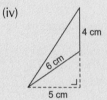
   4 cm
   6 cm
   5 cm

   (v)
   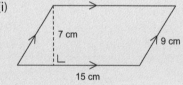
   20 cm
   5 cm
   12 cm

2. Find the area of each of the following parallelograms:

   (i)
   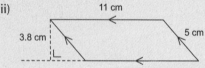
   7 cm
   9 cm
   15 cm

   (ii)
   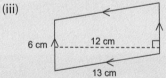
   11 cm
   3.8 cm
   5 cm

   (iii)
   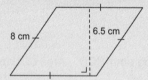
   6 cm
   12 cm
   13 cm

   (iv)
   8 cm
   6.5 cm

3. Find *h*, and hence find the area of the parallelogram.

   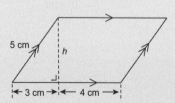
   5 cm
   h
   3 cm
   4 cm

4. Find the area of each of the following coloured shapes.

   (i)
   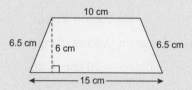
   10 cm
   6.5 cm
   6 cm
   6.5 cm
   15 cm

   (ii)
   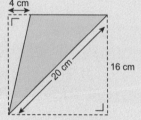
   4 cm
   20 cm
   16 cm

   (iii)
   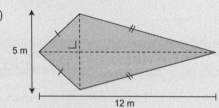
   5 m
   12 m

5. Find the area of the shaded region in each of the following diagrams:

   (i)
   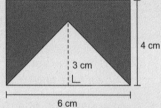
   4 cm
   3 cm
   6 cm

   (ii)
   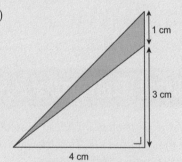
   1 cm
   3 cm
   4 cm

   (iii)
   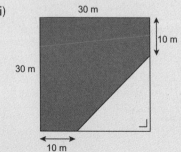
   30 m
   10 m
   30 m
   10 m

ACTIVE MATHS 2

(iv)
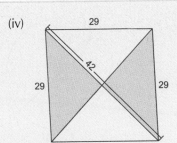

(v)
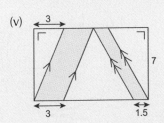

(ii)
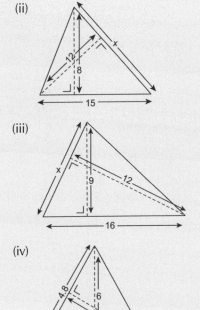

(iii)

(iv)

6. Find the value of x in each of the following triangles:

(i)
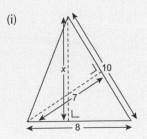

7.7 CIRCLES

A **circle** is a very common shape found in all aspects of everyday life. One of the most important uses we see for the circle is that of the wheel.

Some common terms associated with circles:

> A **circle** is a set of points in a plane that are all equidistant from a fixed point, its centre.

> **Radius** – the line segment from the centre of the circle to any point on the circle.

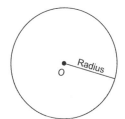

The centre of a circle is usually marked with a dot and sometimes the letter O.

The plural of radius is **radii**.

Chord – any segment that joins two points on a circle.

Diameter – a chord that passes through the centre of a circle. The diameter is twice the radius in length.

Circumference – the perimeter or length of the circle.

Arc – any part of the circumference or curve of the circle.

Tangent – a line which touches the circle at only one point. Where the tangent touches the circle is called the point of contact, or point of tangency.

Sector – the region of the circle enclosed by two radii and the arc between these radii.

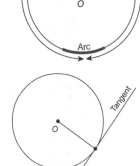

Circle Properties

It is clear from our explorations of circles that:

ACTIVITY 7.9

The angle opposite the diameter in a circle is a right angle or 90°.

This can be stated as:

Corollary 3

Each angle in a semicircle is a right angle.

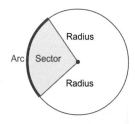

A **semicircle** is half a circle whose base is its diameter.

From this corollary, we can also show another property of a circle:

Corollary 4

If the angle standing on a chord [BC] at some point of the circle is a right angle, then [BC] is a diameter.

This corollary could be considered the converse of Corollary 3.

Worked Example 7.14

Find (i) |∠A|, (ii) |∠B|, (iii) |∠C| and (iv) |∠D| in the following diagram:

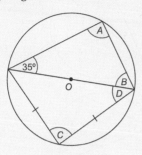

Solution

(i) |∠A| = 90° (angle in a semicircle)

(ii) |∠B| = 180° − 90° − 35° (angles in a triangle)

∴ |∠B| = 55°

(iii) |∠C| = 90° (angle in a semicircle)

(iv) |∠D| = (180° − 90°) ÷ 2 (isosceles triangle)

|∠D| = 90° ÷ 2

∴ |∠D| = 45°

Worked Example 7.15

Find (i) |∠OCA| and (ii) |∠OBC| in the following diagram:

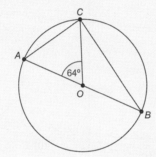

Solution

(i) |∠OCA|

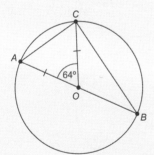

Triangle AOC is an isosceles triangle.
(|AO| = |CO| … radii)

∴ |∠OAC| and |∠OCA| are equal

|∠OCA| = (180° − 64°) ÷ 2

⇒ |∠OCA| = 116 ÷ 2

∴ |∠OCA| = 58°

(ii) |∠OBC|

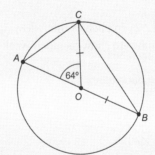

Triangle COB is an isosceles triangle.
(|OC| = |OB| … radii)

|∠BOC| = 180° − 64° (straight angle)

|∠BOC| = 116°

|∠OBC| = (180° − 116°) ÷ 2 (isosceles triangle)

|∠OBC| = 64 ÷ 2

|∠OBC| = 32°

This question could have also been solved using the exterior angles of a triangle.

Exercise 7.7

GEOMETRY II

7

1. In each of the following diagrams, identify and name the 90° angle. Also name the diameter of each of the circles.
   O is the centre in each case.

(i)

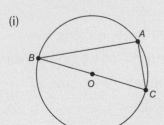

(ii)

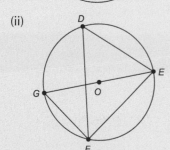

(iii)

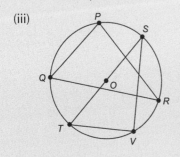

2. Find |∠1| and |∠2| in each of the following diagrams. Remember to show as much work as possible.
   O is the centre in each case.

(i)

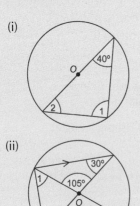

(ii)

(iii)

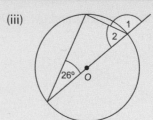

(iv)

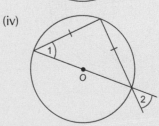

3. Find |∠A| and |∠B| in each of the following diagrams. Remember to show as much work as possible. O is the centre in each case.

(i)

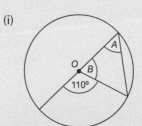

(ii)

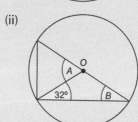

(iii)

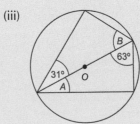

(iv)

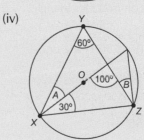

(v)

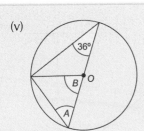

(vi)

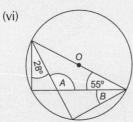

(vii)

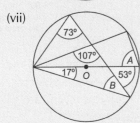

4. Find the length of the diameter of the given circle with centre O in each of the following diagrams.

(i)

(ii)

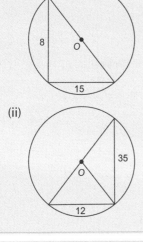

5. [AD] is the diameter of the circle with centre O.

FE ∥ AD.

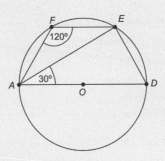

Find:

(i) |∠AED|

(ii) |∠EDA|

(iii) |∠FEA|

(iv) Explain why |AF| = |FE|.

6. [BD] is the diameter of the circle with centre O.

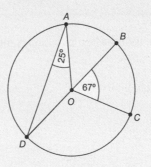

Find:

(i) |∠DOC|

(ii) |∠DCO|

(iii) |∠OBC|

(iv) |∠BAO|

7.8 FURTHER CIRCLE THEOREMS

Another important theorem based on a circle concerns a tangent to the circle.

Tangents

As we have already learned, a tangent is a line that touches the circle at only one point. This point is called the point of contact, or point of tangency.

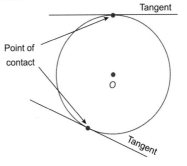

The tangent to a circle is at a right angle to the radius at the point of contact.

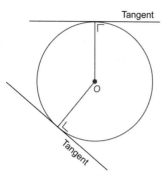

This is stated as the following theorem:

Theorem 20

Each tangent is perpendicular to the radius that goes to the point of contact.

This theorem also includes the converse of this statement:

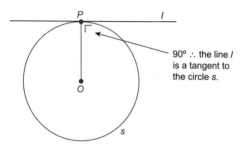

90° ∴ the line *l* is a tangent to the circle *s*.

If a point *P* lies on a circle *s*, and a line *l* which passes though the point *P* is perpendicular to the radius, then this line is a tangent to the circle at the point *P*.

This can be more formally stated as:

If *P* lies on *s*, and a line *l* is perpendicular to the radius to *P*, then *l* is tangent to *s*.

Tangents can also be found when two circles meet at one point only. Circles can meet internally or externally.

External:

Tangent

Point of contact

Internal:

Tangent

Point of contact

🔷 **ACTIVITY 7.11**

From our investigations, it is evident that:

Corollary 6

If two circles intersect at one point only, then the two centres and the point of contact are collinear.

Perpendicular to a Chord

We can also consider the relationship between any chord of a circle and the centre of the circle.

From Activity 7.12 we know that:

> If a line is drawn at right angles to a chord and this line goes through the centre of the circle, it will cut the chord in two equal segments.

This can more formally be written as:

Theorem 21 Part (i)

The perpendicular from the centre to a chord bisects the chord.

Theorem 21 Part (ii)

The perpendicular bisector of a chord passes through the centre.

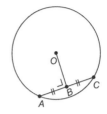

$|AB| = |BC|$

Perpendicular bisector of $[AB]$

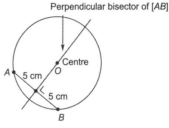

By constructing the perpendicular bisectors of two chords, this theorem can be used to find the centre of a given circle.

Worked Example 7.16

Consider the following circle with centre O and radius 5 cm. t is a tangent to the circle at the point P.

$|PS| = 12$ cm. Find $|RS|$.

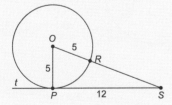

Solution

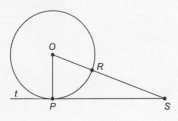

$|\angle OPS| = 90°$ (tangent)

$|OP| = |OR|$ (both radii)

Using the theorem of Pythagoras, we will find $|OS|$, the hypotenuse:

$h^2 = a^2 + b^2$
$a = 5, b = 12$
$h^2 = 5^2 + 12^2$
$h^2 = 25 + 144$
$h^2 = 169$
$\therefore h = 13$

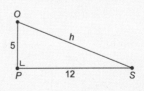

$|OS| = 13$ cm

$\therefore |RS| = 13 - 5$

$|RS| = 8$ cm

Worked Example 7.17

A circle with centre O has a radius of 29 cm. $[AB]$ is a chord. M is a point on $[AB]$ such that $OM \perp AB$. $|OM| = 21$ cm. Find $|AB|$.

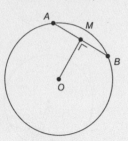

Solution

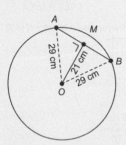

$|OA| = |OB|$ (both radii)

$|OM| = 21$ cm

Using the theorem of Pythagoras, we will find $|AM|$:

$h^2 = a^2 + b^2$
$h = 29, b = 21$
$29^2 = a^2 + 21^2$
$841 = a^2 + 441$
$841 - 441 = a^2$
$400 = a^2$
$\therefore a = 20$

$|AM| = 20$ cm

$\therefore |AB| = 2 \times 20$ cm (M is the midpoint of $[AB]$)

$\Rightarrow |AB| = 40$ cm

Exercise 7.8

1. O is the centre of the following circle. t is a tangent to the circle. Find:

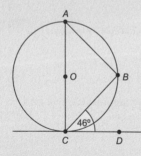

(i) $|\angle ABC|$

(ii) $|\angle ACD|$

(iii) $|\angle ACB|$

(iv) $|\angle CAB|$

2. O is the centre of the following circle. t is a tangent to the circle. Find:

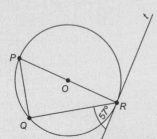

(i) $|\angle PQR|$

(ii) $|\angle PRQ|$

(iii) $|\angle QPR|$

3. In each diagram, O is the centre of the circle. P is the point of contact between a tangent and the circle. Find the value of x in each case.

(i)

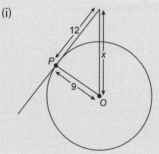

(ii)

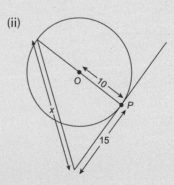

4. [AB] is the diameter of a circle with centre O. [CD] is a chord with a midpoint M. AB ⊥ CD.

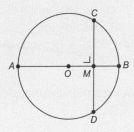

|CD| = 8 cm and |OM| = 3. Find:

(i) |OC| (ii) |AM| (iii) |MB| (iv) |AC|

5. [EF] is the diameter of a circle with centre O. The length of the diameter is 10 cm.

[QR] is a chord such that:

|QM| = |MR| = 4 cm and |EM| = 2 cm.

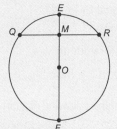

Find: (i) |QO|
(ii) |OM|
(iii) |FM|

6. The diagram shows a circle, with centre O and radius [OK].

T is a point on the circle.

PT is a tangent to the circle such that |PO| = 13 cm and |PT| = 12 cm.

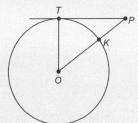

Find: (i) |OK|
(ii) |PK|

7. A circle with centre O has a tangent t. Their point of contact is the point P. R is a point such that |OR| = 10 cm and |PR| = 6 cm.
Find the radius length of the circle.

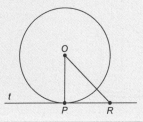

8. A circle with centre O has a radius of 13 cm. X is a point on the diameter [PQ] such that |OX| = 12 cm. The chord [RS] is perpendicular to the diameter [PQ].

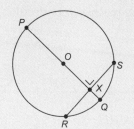

Find:

(i) |XS| (iv) |PX|
(ii) |RS| (v) |PR|
(iii) |XQ|

9. A circle with centre O has two chords [AB] and [CD]. It has a radius length of 20 cm.

OM ⊥ AB and ON ⊥ CD.

|OM| = 16 cm and |ON| = 12 cm.

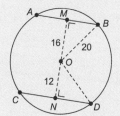

Find:

(i) |AB|

(ii) |CD|

(iii) Area of ΔMBO

(iv) Area of ΔNDO

10. A circle with centre O and radius [OP] is shown.

t is a tangent to the circle with a point of contact P.

|OP| = 7 cm and |PS| = $4\sqrt{2}$ cm.

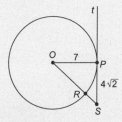

Find:

(i) |OS|

(ii) |RS|

(iii) Area of ΔOPS

GEOMETRY II

1. (a) State if each of the following pairs of triangles are congruent.
   Explain how you reached your decision.

   (i)
   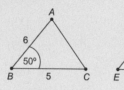

   Is ΔABC ≡ ΔDEF?

   (ii)
   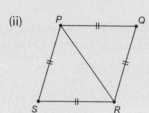

   Is ΔPSR ≡ ΔPQR?

   (iii)
   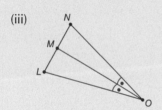

   Is ΔLMO ≡ ΔMON?

   (iv)
   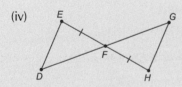

   Is ΔDEF ≡ ΔFGH?

   (v)
   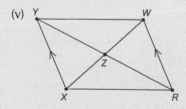

   Is ΔXYZ ≡ ΔWZR?

   (b) ABCD is a quadrilateral.

   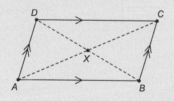

   (i) What type of quadrilateral is ABCD?

   (ii) Show that ΔAXD ≡ ΔCXB.

   (iii) Is ΔDXC ≡ ΔAXB?
   Give a reason for your answer.

   (iv) If |AB| = 15 cm and the area of ABCD = 90 cm², find the perpendicular distance between [AB] and [DC].

   (c) ABCD is a parallelogram. In the triangle DCE, |DC| = |CE|.

   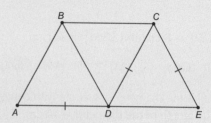

   (i) What type of triangle is DCE?

   (ii) Explain, using a theorem, why |∠BAD| is equal to |∠BCD|.

   (iii) Is ΔABD ≡ ΔDCE?
   State reasons for your answer.

   (iv) Show that ADCB is a rhombus.

2. (a) Find the value of x in the following diagrams.

   (i)
   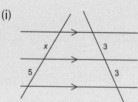

   (ii)
   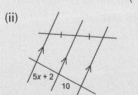

   (iii)
   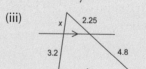

   (iv)

   (v)
   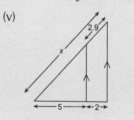

(vi)

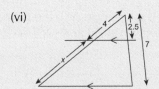

(b) Consider the triangle *ABC* with measurements shown.

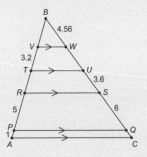

Find:

(i) |*QC*|

(ii) |*RT*|

(iii) |*UW*|

(iv) |*BV*|

(c) A surveyor is trying to measure the length of a pond, [*AB*]. As he is afraid of water, he does not wish to use a boat. With the aid of a measuring tape and protractor, he marks the points *A*, *B*, *C*, *D* and *X*, as shown on the diagram.

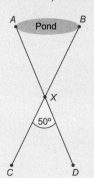

|*AX*| = |*XD*|, |*BX*| = |*XC*| and |∠*AXB*| = |∠*CXD*|.

If |*CD*| = 100 m, explain why the surveyor can state that the length of the pond, [*AB*], is also 100 m.

3. (a) Find the value of *x* and *y* in each case.

(i)

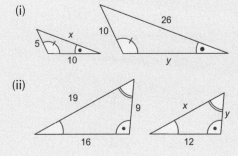

(ii)

(iii)

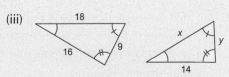

(iv)

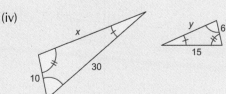

(v)

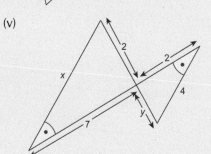

(b) In the triangle *PQR*, *PR* is parallel to *ST*.

|*QR*| = 10 cm, |*QS*| = 4 cm, |*ST*| = 8 cm and |*PR*| = 9 cm.

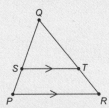

(i) Draw Δ*PQR* and Δ*SQT* separately.

(ii) Are Δ*PQR* and Δ*SQT* similar? Explain your answer.

(iii) Find |*QP*|.

(iv) Find |*QT*|.

(v) Find |*TR*|.

(c) Consider the following triangles *PQR* and *PST*.

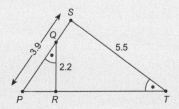

(i) Show that Δ*PQR* and Δ*PST* are similar.

If |*PT*| = 9.25 cm, find:

(ii) |*PR*| (iii) |*RT*| (iv) |*QS*|

GEOMETRY II

4. (a) Find the length of x and y in each of the following diagrams. Leave your answers in surd form where appropriate.

(i)

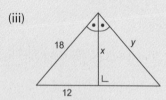

(ii)

(iii)

(iv)

(v)

(b) The triangle *ABC* is a right-angled triangle where $BD \perp AC$.
$|BD| = 10$ cm and $|DC| = 8$ cm.

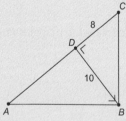

Find:

(i) $|BC|$

(ii) $|AB|$

(iii) $|AC|$

(c) *ABCD* is a rectangle. *M* is the midpoint of [*AD*]. $|AB| = 8$ cm and $|BC| = 12$ cm.

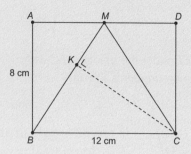

(i) Identify the isosceles triangle.

(ii) Identify three angles which are equal to $|\angle MCB|$.

(iii) Find $|BM|$.

(iv) Find the area of $\triangle BMC$.

(v) *K* is a point on [*BM*] such that $BM \perp CK$. Find $|CK|$.

5. (a) Find the area of each of the following shapes.

(i)

(ii)

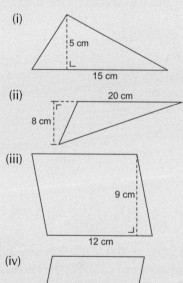

(iii)

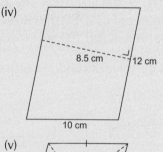

(iv)

(v)

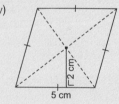

(b) Find the value of x in each of the following polygons, and hence, find the area of each polygon.

(i)

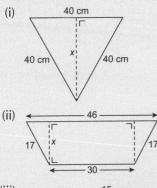

(ii)

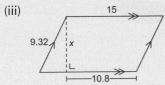

(iii)

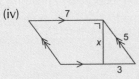

(iv)

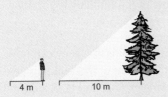

(c) Sharon measures the shadow of a tree and notices that it is 10 m long. She then measures the shadow of a friend and notices that it is 4 m long.

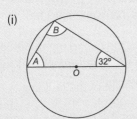

If her friend is 1.6 m tall, how tall is the tree?

6. (a) Find the value of A and B in each of the following diagrams. Remember to show as much work as possible.
O is the centre in each case.

(i)

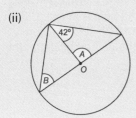

(ii)

(iii)

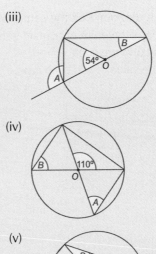

(iv)

(v)

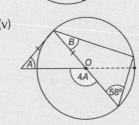

(b) Consider the following circle with centre O.

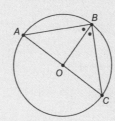

(i) What type of triangle is the ΔABC?

(ii) Show that ΔABO ≡ ΔBOC.

(iii) Find |∠ABO|.

(iv) If |OB| = 15 cm, find |AB|.

(c) A design for a piece of art is shown. The piece is made up of a solid metal circle with [AD] as its diameter. A glass rhombus ABCD is put on top of this circle.

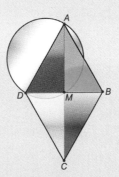

|AC| = 24 mm and |BD| = 10 mm.

(i) Find |AM| and |DM|.

(ii) Identify four right angles.

(iii) Find |AD|.

(iv) Is ΔADM congruent to ΔABM?

(v) Calculate the area of the glass rhombus.

7. (a) In each diagram, O is the centre of the circle. P is the point of contact between a tangent and the circle.
Find the value of x in each case.

(i)

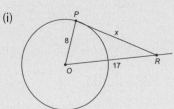

(ii)

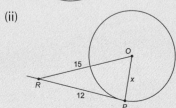

(iii)

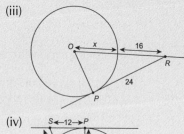

(iv)

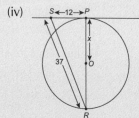

(b) In each diagram, O is the centre of the circle. Find the value of x in each case.

(i)

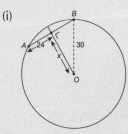

(ii)

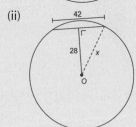

(iii)

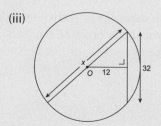

(c) A barrel of oil is tipped onto its side as shown.

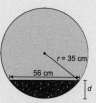

Calculate the depth (d) of the oil.

8. At a certain time, a group of students measure the length of the shadow of a building and the length of the shadow of a 1.5-m ranging pole.

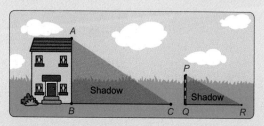

The shadow of the building is 5 m long, and that of the ranging pole is 2 m long.

The teacher explains that they can now calculate the height of the building. She states that the triangles ABC and PQR are similar.

(i) Give a reason for this statement.

(ii) Describe how you would check that the two triangles are similar.

The teacher asks the students to sketch the triangles ABC and PQR with all the measurements that were collected.

(iii) Sketch out the two triangles ABC and PQR with the measurements included.

(iv) Find the height of the building.

Megan measures the ranging pole and discovers that the pole is in fact 1.55 m long.

(v) Calculate the revised height of the building.

9. A new sewerage system is being laid in a housing estate as shown. It costs €20 per metre (including labour costs) to lay these pipes.

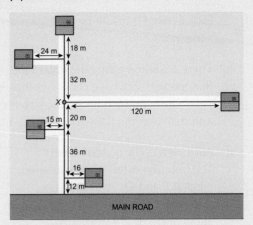

(i) Find the total length of pipe needed for this work.

(ii) Find the total cost to install this system.

To save money, it is decided to connect all the sewer pipes from each house directly to a central point *X* and then from this point to the main road.

(iii) Find the total length of pipe needed for this new layout (to the nearest metre).

(iv) Find the total cost to install this new layout (to the nearest euro).

(v) Which is the cheaper option and by how much?

10. A game is played in which the person who picks a point that is closest to the centre of a circle wins a prize. The circle has a radius length of 7 cm.

(i) State one theorem that could be used to locate the centre of the circle.

(ii) By drawing a circle of radius length 7 cm, demonstrate how the centre of the circle could be located using the theorem in part (i).

(iii) Describe another method that could be used to find the centre of a circle.

(iv) By drawing another circle of radius length 7 cm, demonstrate how the centre of this circle could be found using the method in part (iii).

11. A design for a garden is shown. The garden is in the shape of a triangle that is divided into four different areas.

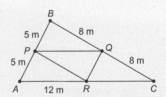

(i) Using a theorem from your geometry course, explain why *PQ* is parallel to *AC*.

(ii) If *QR* ∥ *PA*, find |*PQ*|.

(iii) Find |*AC*|.

(iv) Find the perimeter of *PQRA*.

(v) The area of Δ*PAR* is 26 cm². What is the total area of the garden? Give reasons for your answer.

12. (a) In the diagram below, *ABCF*, *ABEF*, and *ACDE* are parallelograms. The area of the shaded triangle *AFE* is 15 square units.

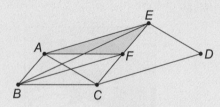

(i) State why the area of triangle *AFB* must also be 15 square units.

(ii) Find the area of the whole figure *ABCDE*. Show your work.

(iii) If the perpendicular distance from *D* to the line *EC* is 6, find |*AB*|. Show your work.

(b) Dónal is making a wooden pull-along toy.

He has disks to use as wheels, but the centres are not marked on them.
He needs to find the exact centre of each wheel in order to drill holes in them.

He knows that there is a geometrical method for finding the centre of a circle.

(i) State a theorem from your geometry course that could be used to locate the centre of a circle with geometrical instruments.

(ii) Find the centre of the circle below, by applying the theorem you mentioned above.
Show your construction lines clearly.

(iii) Describe another way that Dónal could find the centres of the wheels.

SEC Project Maths Sample Paper 2,
Leaving Certificate Ordinary Level, 2010

13. (a) Explain what is meant by the *converse* of a theorem.

(b) There are some geometric statements that are true, but have converses that are false. Give one such geometric statement, and state also the (false) converse.

(c) *ABCD* is a cyclic quadrilateral.
The opposite sides, when extended, meet at *P* and *Q*, as shown.
The angles α, β, and γ are as shown.
Show that $\beta + \gamma = 180° - 2\alpha$.

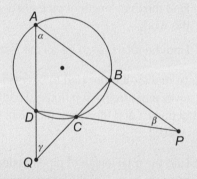

SEC Project Maths Sample Paper 2,
Leaving Certificate Ordinary Level, 2011

Length, Area and Volume

Learning Outcomes

In this chapter you will learn to:

- Find the area and perimeter of 2D shapes

- Find the area and circumference of circles and sectors of circles

- Solve problems involving area

- Investigate the nets of rectangular solids

- Find the surface area and volume of various 3D shapes

- Solve problems involving surface area and volume

- Use the trapezoidal rule to approximate area

8.1 AREA AND PERIMETER OF TWO-DIMENSIONAL (2D) SHAPES

What size wheel do you need for a car? How much paint is needed to paint a wall? How much will it cost to tile a kitchen floor?

These are examples of situations where we need to know the **area** and **perimeter** of certain objects.

> **Area** is the amount of flat space that a shape occupies.

> **Perimeter** is the sum of the length of all the sides of a shape.

The units of area will always be units², for example: mm², cm², m², km², etc. When finding the area of a shape, make sure that you use the **same** units: mm × mm, cm × cm, etc.

Rectangle	Square
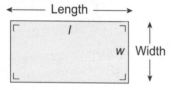 Area = (length × width) = $l \times w$ Perimeter = $2l + 2w$ or $2(l + w)$	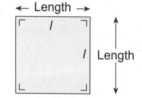 Area = (length)² = l^2 Perimeter = $4l$
Triangle	**Parallelogram**
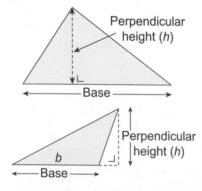 Area = $\frac{1}{2}$ × base × perpendicular height = $\frac{1}{2} bh$	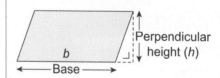 Area = base × perpendicular height = bh

YOU SHOULD REMEMBER...

- Area and volume from your Junior Certificate course
- The theorem of Pythagoras

KEY WORDS

- Triangle
- Rectangle
- Square
- Parallelogram
- Trapezium
- Disc (circle)
- Sector of a disc
- Rectangular block
- Cylinder
- Right cone
- Right prism
- Sphere
- Hemisphere
- Trapezoidal rule
- Perimeter
- Area
- Volume
- Surface area

Another 2D shape on our course is the **trapezium**.

A **trapezium** is a quadrilateral that has one pair of parallel sides.

ACTIVITY 8.1

Trapezium	Area = Half the sum of the lengths of the parallel sides (*a* and *b*) × perpendicular height between them
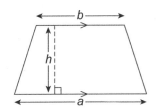	Area = $\frac{1}{2}(a + b)h$ **or** Area = $\left(\frac{a + b}{2}\right)h$ This formula appears on page 8 of *Formulae and Tables*.

Worked Example 8.1

Find the area of each of the following shapes:

(i)
7 cm
5 cm

(iii)
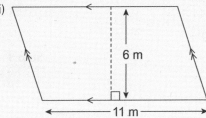
6 m
11 m

(ii)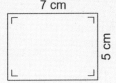
2.5 cm
4 cm

(iv)
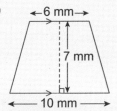
6 mm
7 mm
10 mm

Solution

(i) This shape is a rectangle.

∴ Area = $l \times w = 7 \times 5 = 35$ cm²

(ii) This shape is a triangle.

∴ Area = $\frac{1}{2}bh = \frac{1}{2} \times 4 \times 2.5 = 5$ cm²

(iii) This shape is a parallelogram.

∴ Area = $bh = 11 \times 6 = 66$ m²

(iv) This shape is a trapezium.

∴ Area = $\frac{1}{2}(a + b)h = \frac{1}{2}(10 + 6)(7) = \frac{1}{2}(16)(7) = 56$ mm²

Worked Example 8.2

Calculate the shaded area of this shape.

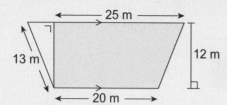

Solution

Step 1 Find the area of of the unshaded triangle first.

Use the theorem of Pythagoras to find the length of the triangle's base.

$$c^2 = a^2 + b^2$$
$$(13)^2 = (12)^2 + b^2$$
$$169 = 144 + b^2$$
$$169 - 144 = b^2$$
$$25 = b^2$$
$$5 = b$$

$\therefore$ Area of triangle $= \frac{1}{2}bh = \frac{1}{2}(5)(12) = 30 \text{ m}^2$

Step 2 We can now find the area of the whole shape, which is a trapezium.

Area $= \frac{1}{2}(a + b)h$

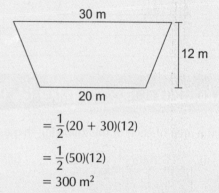

$$= \frac{1}{2}(20 + 30)(12)$$
$$= \frac{1}{2}(50)(12)$$
$$= 300 \text{ m}^2$$

Step 3

Area of shaded shape

$=$ total area $-$ unshaded area

$\therefore$ Shaded area $= 300 \text{ m}^2 - 30 \text{ m}^2$

$= 270 \text{ m}^2$

> Take care: 1 metre = 100 cm
> $\Rightarrow 1 \text{ m}^2 = (100)^2 \text{ cm}^2 = 10,000 \text{ cm}^2$
> also 1 cm^2 = 100 mm^2

Exercise 8.1

1. Find the area of each of the following shapes:

(i)

3 cm

(ii)

7 cm
13 cm

(iii)
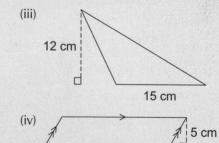
12 cm
15 cm

(iv)
5 cm
20 cm

LENGTH, AREA AND VOLUME

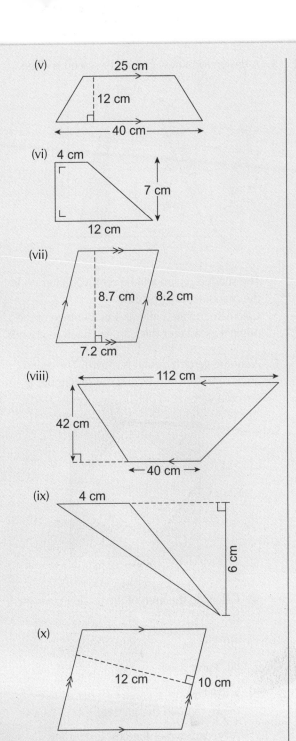

(v)

25 cm

12 cm

40 cm

(vi) 4 cm

7 cm

12 cm

(vii)

8.7 cm   8.2 cm

7.2 cm

(viii)

112 cm

42 cm

40 cm

(ix) 4 cm

6 cm

(x)

12 cm   10 cm

2. Find the area and perimeter of each of the following compound shapes:

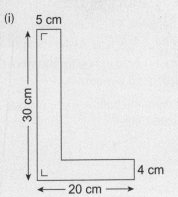

(i) 5 cm

30 cm

4 cm

20 cm

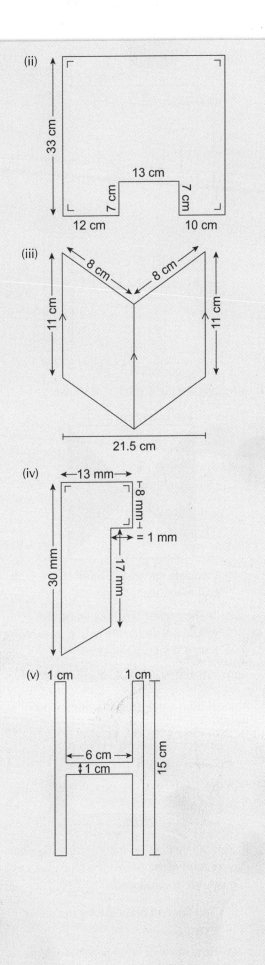

(ii)

33 cm

13 cm

7 cm   7 cm

12 cm   10 cm

(iii)

8 cm   8 cm

11 cm   11 cm

21.5 cm

(iv)

13 mm

8 mm

30 mm   = 1 mm

17 mm

(v) 1 cm   1 cm

6 cm

1 cm   15 cm

(vi)

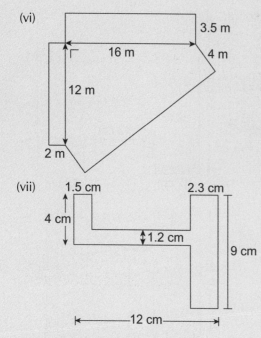

(vii)

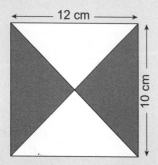

3. A rectangular tile is shaded as shown.

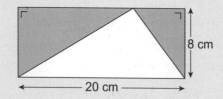

(i) Calculate the area covered by the pink part of the tile.

(ii) To the nearest tile, how many tiles will be needed to tile a room measuring 5 m × 4 m?

(iii) What area of this floor will be white?

4. A panel from a stained glass window panel is shown.

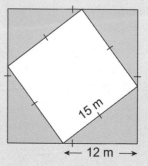

It costs 50c per cm² to manufacture the clear glass portion of the panel. The blue glass costs 20c per cm² to produce.

(i) Find the cost of producing the panel shown.

(ii) How many of these panels would be needed if the blue window glass used covers an area of 4.48 m²?

5. A design for a new computer screen is given.

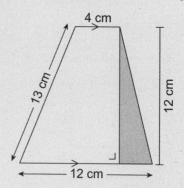

The shaded region will be removed later on in the manufacturing process.
Calculate the area left, as a percentage of the original area, after this part has been removed.

6. A square garden design is shown. The green areas represent shrubs and the remainder is covered with patio slabs.

(a) Calculate the area of the garden covered by:

(i) Shrubs

(ii) Patio slabs

(b) It will cost on average €19 per square metre to build this garden.

A breakdown of the cost (excluding labour) is given:

■ Patio: Slabs cost €10 per square metre + V.A.T. @ 21%

■ Shrubbery: €1.50 per square metre + V.A.T. @ 21%

■ Ground preparation for the whole garden: €5 per m².

What were the builder's labour costs, to the nearest euro?

8.2 AREA AND CIRCUMFERENCE OF A CIRCLE AND SECTOR OF A CIRCLE

There are many examples of circular shapes in everyday life.

In the next activity we will investigate some properties of circles.

$$\pi = \frac{\text{Circumference of Circle}}{\text{Length of Diameter}}$$

The length of the circumference (perimeter) of any circle divided by the length of its diameter is always the same. This number is π (pronounced 'pi'). We use π to help calculate the area and circumference (length) of a circle or sector of a circle.

Circles

FORMULA

Area of a circle = $\pi \times r^2$, usually written as πr^2.

FORMULA

Circumference of a circle = $2 \times \pi \times r$, usually written as $2\pi r$.

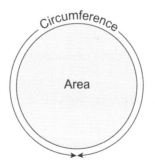
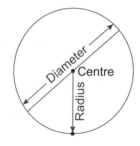

These formulae appear on page 8 of *Formulae and Tables*.

$\pi = 3.141592...$ is an infinite decimal which never ends and never repeats.

Therefore, in calculating the area or circumference of a circle, we may be told to use one of the following values for π:

- $\pi = 3.14$
- The value of π from the calculator $\boxed{\pi}$
- $\pi = \frac{22}{7}$

Sometimes we don't give π a value but just leave it as π. This is referred to as 'leaving our answer in terms of π'.

Worked Example 8.3

Find the area and circumference of each of the following circles:

(i) $r = 15$ cm ($\pi = 3.14$)   (iii) $r = 24$ m (leaving your answers in terms of π)

(ii) $r = 14$ mm $\left(\pi = \dfrac{22}{7}\right)$

Solution

> Remember that the circumference of a circle is also known as the length of a circle.

(i) $\pi = 3.14$

$$\begin{aligned}\text{Area of a circle} &= \pi \times r^2 \\ &= 3.14 \times (15)^2 \\ &= 3.14 \times 225 \\ &= 706.5 \text{ cm}^2\end{aligned}$$

$$\begin{aligned}\text{Circumference of circle} &= 2 \times \pi \times r \\ &= 2 \times 3.14 \times 15 \\ &= 6.28 \times 15 \\ &= 94.2 \text{ cm}\end{aligned}$$

(ii) $\pi = \dfrac{22}{7}$

$$\begin{aligned}\text{Area of a circle} &= \pi \times r^2 \\ &= \frac{22}{7} \times (14)^2 \\ &= \frac{22}{7} \times 196 \\ &= 616 \text{ mm}^2\end{aligned}$$

$$\begin{aligned}\text{Circumference of circle} &= 2 \times \pi \times r \\ &= 2 \times \frac{22}{7} \times 14 \\ &= 6\frac{2}{7} \times 14 \\ &= 88 \text{ mm}\end{aligned}$$

(iii) In terms of π

$$\begin{aligned}\text{Area of a circle} &= \pi \times r^2 \\ &= \pi \times (24)^2 \\ &= \pi \times 576 \\ &= 576\pi \text{ m}^2\end{aligned}$$

$$\begin{aligned}\text{Circumference of circle} &= 2 \times \pi \times r \\ &= 2 \times \pi \times 24 \\ &= 48 \times \pi \\ &= 48\pi \text{ m}\end{aligned}$$

Sectors

A **sector** is a specific slice of a circle (a pie-shaped part).

> A **sector** of a circle is the portion of a circle bounded by two radii and the included arc.

 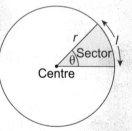

The sector angle, usually referred to as θ (theta), is needed to work out the area and length of arc of the sector.

FORMULA

Area of sector $= \pi r^2 \left(\dfrac{\theta}{360°}\right)$

FORMULA

Length of arc (circumference of arc)
$l = 2\pi r \left(\dfrac{\theta}{360°}\right)$

These formulae appear on page 9 of *Formulae and Tables*.

Note: θ must be in degrees.

Worked Example 8.4

Find the area, length of arc and perimeter of the following sector of a circle ($\pi = 3.14$).

Solution

54°
← 6 cm →

Length of arc

$l = 2\pi r\left(\dfrac{\theta}{360°}\right)$

$l = 2 \times 3.14 \times 6 \times \dfrac{54}{360}$

$l = 5.652$ cm

Area of sector

$\pi r^2\left(\dfrac{\theta}{360°}\right)$

$= 3.14 \times (6)^2 \times \dfrac{54}{360}$

$= 16.956$ cm²

Perimeter

Length of arc = 5.652 cm

Length of two radii = 6 × 2 = 12 cm

∴ Perimeter = 5.652 + 12 = 17.652 cm

Exercise 8.2

1. Taking $\pi = 3.14$, find the area and circumference of each of the following circles: $2\pi r$

   (i)   Radius length = 10 cm $2(3.14)(10)$

   (ii) Radius length = 1 m

   (iii) Radius length = 120 mm

   (iv) Diameter length = 320 cm

2. Taking $\pi = \frac{22}{7}$, find the area and circumference of each of the following circles:

   (i)   Radius length = 3 cm

   (ii) Radius length = 140 cm

   (iii) Radius length = 89 cm

   (iv) Diameter length = $11\frac{1}{5}$ cm

3. Find the area and circumference of each of the following circles, in terms of π:

   (i)   Radius length = 10 cm

   (ii) Radius length = 4 mm

   (iii) Radius length = 12 m

   (iv) Diameter length = 0.5 cm

4. Find the area, length of arc and perimeter of each of the following sectors:

   (i) $\pi = 3.14$

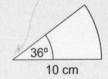

   36°
   10 cm

   (ii) $\pi = 3.14$

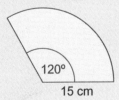

   120°
   15 cm

   (iii) $\pi = \frac{22}{7}$

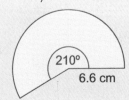

   210°
   6.6 cm

   (iv) $\pi = \frac{22}{7}$

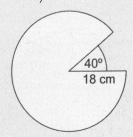

   40°
   18 cm

(v) $\pi = \frac{22}{7}$

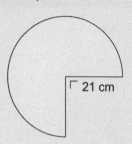

┌ 21 cm

5. Find the area and perimeter of each of the following compound shapes ($\pi = 3.14$):

(i)

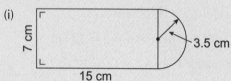

7 cm · 3.5 cm · 15 cm

(ii)

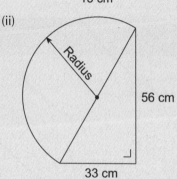

Radius · 56 cm · 33 cm

(iii)

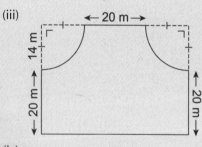

←— 20 m —→ · 14 m · 20 m · 20 m

(iv)

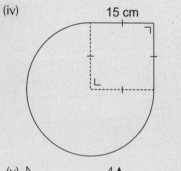

15 cm

(v)

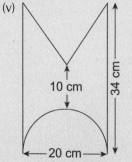

10 cm · 34 cm · ←— 20 cm —→

6. A satellite orbits a planet of radius 3,000 km as shown in the diagram.

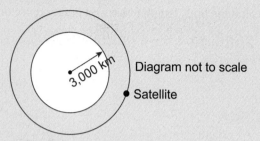

3,000 km · Diagram not to scale · Satellite

The satellite orbits the planet at a height of 100 km and a speed of 6,000 m/s. How long to the nearest minute does it take the satellite to complete one full orbit? ($\pi = 3.14$)

7. A circular design is cut into a square piece of wood using a computerised cutting saw.

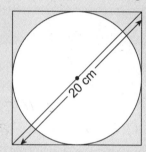

20 cm

(i) The operator of the saw must program in the radius of the circle required to four decimal places.

Find the radius of the required circle.

(ii) The time taken to cut out a design depends on the circumference of the circle. It takes 5 minutes to cut the above design. How long would it take to cut a circle that has a diameter of 20 cm? ($\pi = 3.14$) (Answer to the nearest second.)

8. A metal part of a machine is shown. The arcs shown are semicircles. This part is made from a sheet of metal 5 m by 3 m.

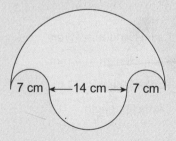

7 cm · ←—14 cm—→ · 7 cm

Find the number of complete parts that can be made from one sheet of metal, assuming that all the sheet of metal can be used. ($\pi = 3.14$)

8.3 FINDING DIMENSIONS WHEN GIVEN AREA OR PERIMETER

Sometimes we may be given the area or perimeter of a shape and have to work backwards to find a side or radius. To do this, we follow certain steps.

Worked Example 8.5

The area of a rectangle is 50 cm². Find its width if its side length is 5 cm.

Solution

Write down what we are given	Area of rectangle = 50
Write down formula	$lw = 50$
Fill in given dimensions	$5(w) = 50$ $5w = 50$
Solve	$w = 10$ cm

Don't forget the units of measurement in your answer.

Worked Example 8.6

The area of this triangle is 20 cm². Find the perpendicular height of the triangle.

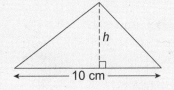

Solution

Write down what we are given	Area of triangle = 20
Write down formula	$\frac{1}{2}bh = 20$
Fill in given dimensions	$\frac{1}{2}(10)(h) = 20$ $5h = 20$
Solve	$h = 4$ cm

Worked Example 8.7

The area of a circle is 153.86 cm². Find the length of the radius of the circle ($\pi = 3.14$).

Solution

Write down what we are given	Area of circle = 153.86
Write down formula	$\pi r^2 = 153.86$
Fill in given dimensions	$(3.14)(r^2) = 153.86$ $3.14r^2 = 153.86$
Solve	$r^2 = \dfrac{153.86}{3.14} = 49$ $r = \sqrt{49}$ $r = 7$ cm

Worked Example 8.8

The circumference of a circle is 22π mm. Find the length of the radius of the circle.

Solution

The circumference of the circle is given in terms of π.

Write down what we are given	Circumference of circle = 22π
Write down formula	$2\pi r = 22\pi$
As **both** sides of the equation contain π, we can divide both sides by π.	
Solve	$2\pi r = 22\pi$ $2r = 22$ $r = 11$ mm

Worked Example 8.9

The area of a circle is $78\frac{4}{7}$ cm². Find the length of the diameter of the circle $\left(\pi = \frac{22}{7}\right)$.

Solution

Write down what we are given	Area of circle = $78\frac{4}{7}$
Write down formula	$\pi r^2 = 78\frac{4}{7}$
Fill in given dimensions	$\left(\frac{22}{7}\right)(r^2) = 78\frac{4}{7}$ $\frac{22}{7}r^2 = 78\frac{4}{7}$
Solve	$r^2 = \dfrac{78\frac{4}{7}}{\frac{22}{7}} = 25$ $r = \sqrt{25}$ $r = 5$ cm ∴ Diameter = 10 cm

ACTIVITY 8.3

Exercise 8.3

1. By using the information from each diagram below, find the value of x.
   Diagrams are not to scale.

(i)
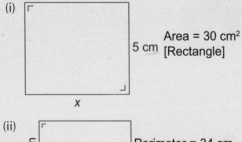
5 cm   Area = 30 cm²
[Rectangle]
x

(ii)
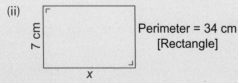
7 cm   Perimeter = 34 cm
[Rectangle]
x

(iii)
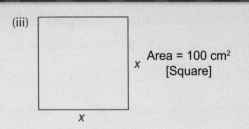
x Area = 100 cm²
[Square]
x

(iv)
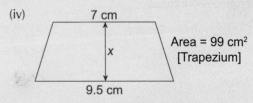
7 cm
x Area = 99 cm²
[Trapezium]
9.5 cm

LENGTH, AREA AND VOLUME

(v)

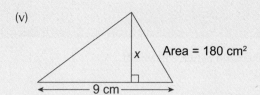

Area = 180 cm²

(vi) Area rectangle + Area triangle = 133 cm²

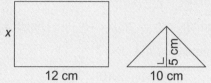

(vii) Area rectangle + Area trapezium
= 51.815 cm²

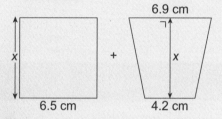

2. Fill in the table below by first finding the radius of each of the circles.

π	r	Area	Circumference
π		49π	
3.14			43.96
$\frac{22}{7}$		2,464	
π			70π
3.14		803.84	
$\frac{22}{7}$			$100\frac{4}{7}$
3.14		28.2	
π		$\frac{1}{81}\pi$	

3. Using the information given, find the measure of the unknown radius or the angle of each of the following sectors:

(i) Length of arc $=7\pi$ cm

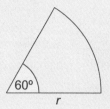

(ii) Area = 1,413 cm² (π = 3.14)

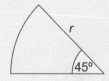

(iii) Area $= 78\frac{4}{7}$ cm² $\left(\pi = \frac{22}{7}\right)$

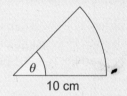

(iv) Length of arc $=23.8\pi$ cm

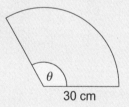

(v) Area = 841.52 cm² (π = 3.14)

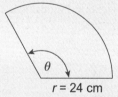

8.4 PROBLEMS INVOLVING AREA AND PERIMETER

Using what we have learned in the previous sections of this chapter, we can now try to solve real-life problems involving area and perimeter.

Worked Example 8.10

The area of a rectangular lawn is 50 m². The length of the lawn is twice its width. Find the perimeter of the lawn.

Solution

The length of the lawn is twice its width.

If the width $(w) = x$, then the length $(l) = 2x$.

Area of lawn $= lw = 50$ m².

Fill in the dimensions:

$(2x)(x) = 50$

$\quad 2x^2 = 50$

$\quad\quad x^2 = 25$

$\quad \therefore x = 5$

Width $(w) = x = 5$	Width $= 5$ m
Length $(l) = 2x = 2(5) = 10$	Length $= 10$ m

Perimeter $= 2(l) + 2(w)$

$\quad\quad\quad\quad = 2(5) + 2(10)$

$\therefore$ Perimeter $= 30$ m

Worked Example 8.11

A part for a machine, pictured below, is formed from a sheet of metal of 1 m². How many complete parts can be made from this sheet ($\pi = 3.14$)? (Assume no wastage.)

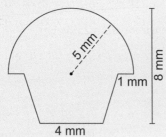

Solution

We work out all the relevant dimensions.

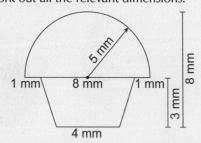

Step 1

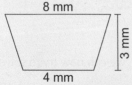

Area of trapezium $= \frac{1}{2}(a + b)h = \frac{1}{2}(4 + 8)3$

$\quad\quad\quad\quad\quad\quad = \frac{1}{2}(12)(3) = 18$ mm²

Step 2

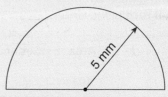

Area of semicircle $= \pi r^2\left(\frac{\theta}{360}\right) = 3.14 \times (5)^2 \times \frac{180}{360}$

$\quad\quad\quad\quad\quad\quad = 39.25$ mm²

Step 3

The area required to make one part is
18 mm² + 39.25 mm² = 57.25 mm².

Step 4

The sheet of metal is 1 m².
We need to convert this into mm².

1 m² $= 1$ m $\times 1$ m

$\quad\quad\quad = 100$ cm $\times 100$ cm

$\quad\quad\quad = 1{,}000$ mm $\times 1{,}000$ mm

$\quad\quad\quad = 1{,}000{,}000$ mm²

$\frac{1{,}000{,}000}{57.25} = 17{,}467.24891$

$\therefore$ 17,467 complete parts can be made from this sheet.

1. An A4 sheet of paper is 30 cm long and 21 cm wide. Find:

   (i) Its perimeter   (ii) Its area

2. A singles tennis court is 25 m long and 8 m wide. Find:

   (i) Its perimeter   (ii) Its area

3. The area of a rectangular room is 12 square metres. Its length is 4 m. Find:

   (i) Its width

   (ii) The length of a diagonal

4. The perimeter of a rectangular garden is 34 metres. Its length is 12 m. Calculate:

   (i) Its width

   (ii) The length of a diagonal

5. The length of a rectangular page is 10 cm greater than its width. The perimeter is 1 m. Find the area of one page in square centimetres.

6. There is a path 3 metres wide around a small park as shown.

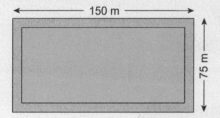

   Find:

   (i) The area of the park

   (ii) The area of the path

   (iii) The cost of replacing the path if each 2 m² of path cost €5.25

7. A wheel has a circumference of 308 cm.

   (i) Taking $\pi = \frac{22}{7}$, find the radius of the wheel.

   (ii) This wheel must be checked every 10,000 revolutions. How far would this be in km?

8. The area of a disc is 64π cm². Find its radius.

9. The area of a circle is 225π m². Find:

   (i) Its radius

   (ii) Its circumference (to one decimal place)

10. A circular swimming pool has a radius of 15 m. It is surrounded by a path of width 1.5 m. Taking $\pi = \frac{22}{7}$, find:

    (i) The area of the path

    (ii) The cost of paving the path if paving costs €5.50 per square metre

11. In a carnival a game is played where, if a dart hits the shaded region of a square board, a prize is given. Which board would you pick to have the best chance of winning?

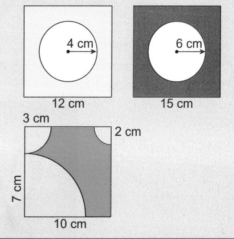

12. A landscaping firm charges €7.50 per m². Landscaping the garden shown costs €10,026. The owner decides to erect a fence to surround the garden. How many metres of fence will be needed? ($\pi = 3.14$)

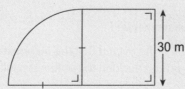

13. Two race tracks with semicircular ends have the same perimeter. Taking $\pi = \frac{22}{7}$, find:

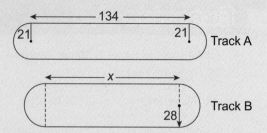

    (i) The perimeter of track A

    (ii) The length of the straight part of Track B

    [all dimensions are in metres]

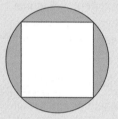

14. The width of a rectangle is x. Its length is y. The perimeter is 34 metres. The area is 30 square metres. Find the dimensions of the rectangle.

15. The radii of two circles are 4 cm and 16 cm respectively. Find the ratio of:

    (i) Their circumferences

    (ii) Their areas

16. A square is inscribed in a circle of radius 5 cm as shown. Find:

    (i) The area of the square

    (ii) The area of the shaded region to the nearest cm²

17. The diagram shows six circles with the same centre, each a distance x width apart. The diameter of the centre circle also measures x units.
    Which has the greater area: the inner shaded region or the outer shaded region?

18. The area of a circular swimming pool is 64π m². A protective tarpaulin to cover this pool needs to be bought.

    (i) The tarpaulin must have a radius of 50 cm greater than the radius of the pool in order to cover the pool correctly.

    Find the radius of the tarpaulin needed.

    (ii) After buying the tarpaulin, it is discovered that the incorrect size was bought. The diameter of this tarpaulin cover is 20 m. It is then decided to cut the tarpaulin so as to fit the pool correctly.

    Calculate the area of the cover that must be removed. ($\pi = 3.14$)

8.5 RECTANGULAR SOLIDS: CUBES AND CUBOIDS

In this section, we will deal with three-dimensional (3D) objects and their characteristics.

Volume

> **Volume (capacity)** is the amount of space an object occupies.

> When measuring volume, the units of measurement will always be units³, for example: mm^3, cm^3, m^3, etc.

One type of 3D object is the rectangular solid.
To find the volume of a rectangular solid (cuboid), we multiply out the three dimensions given.

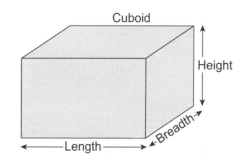

Cuboid

FORMULA

> **Volume of a cuboid** = length × breadth × height
> ∴ Volume = lbh

If all sides of the rectangular solid are equal, then it can be referred to as a **cube**.

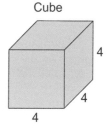

Cube

FORMULA

> **Volume of a cube** = length × length × length
> ∴ Volume = l^3

Surface Area and Nets

A cube or cuboid has six flat sides or faces.

> The line where two faces meet is called an **edge**.

> The corner where two edges meet is called a **vertex**.

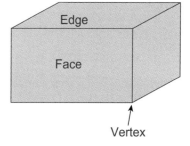

Edge

Face

Vertex

If we cut along the edges of a rectangular solid, we can create a **net** of that solid.

 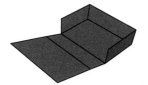 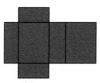

Net

> A **net** is a 2D (flat) shape that folds up along its edges to make a 3D shape.

There can be many different nets for one rectangular solid.

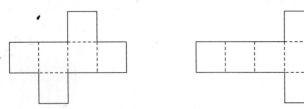

Nets can be used to help determine the **surface area** of a 3D shape.

> Surface area of a cuboid = the sum of the area of all six faces of its net.

ACTIVITY 8.4

Surface area = area of (top + base + front + back + side + side).

This can also be written as:

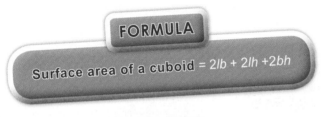
FORMULA
Surface area of a cuboid = 2*lb* + 2*lh* + 2*bh*

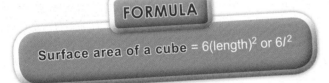
FORMULA
Surface area of a cube = 6(length)² or 6*l*²

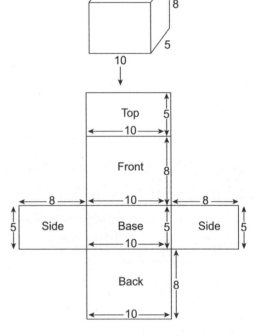

Worked Example 8.12

Find the volume (in litres) and the surface area of the following cuboid.

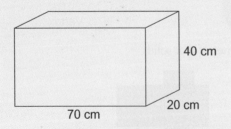

40 cm
20 cm
70 cm

Solution

Volume = *lbh* = length × breadth × height

$70 \times 20 \times 40 = 56{,}000$ cm³

= 56 litres

> 1 litre = 1,000 cm³

Surface area = 2*lb* + 2*lh* + 2*bh*

= 2(70)(20) + 2(70)(40) + 2(20)(40)

= 2,800 + 5,600 + 1,600

= 10,000 cm²

Remember: When working out the volume or surface area, make sure that the units are all the same.

Worked Example 8.13

The net of a rectangular solid is shown.
Find the volume and surface area of this solid.

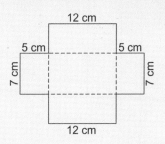

Solution

Volume

From the net drawing, we can work out the dimensions of the box.

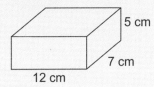

Length = 12 cm, breadth = 7 cm, height = 5 cm

Volume = lbh = 12 × 7 × 5 = 420 cm³

Surface area

Use the net of the shape.

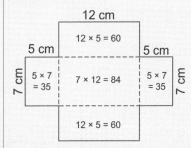

35 + 60 + 35 + 60 + 84 = 274 cm²

Exercise 8.5

1. Find the volume and surface area of each of the following rectangular solids:

(i)

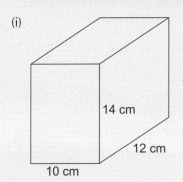

(ii)

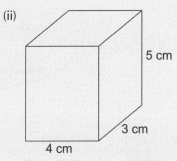

(iii)

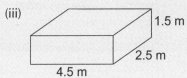

(iv)

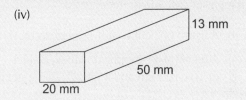

(v)

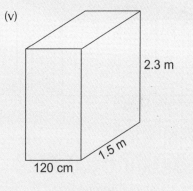

(vi)

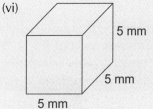

2. Use the nets of the following rectangular solids to find their volume and surface area:

(i)

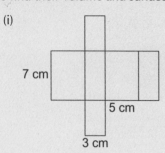

7 cm

5 cm

3 cm

(ii)

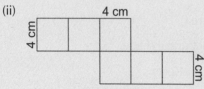

4 cm

4 cm

4 cm

(iii)

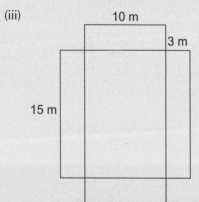

10 m

3 m

15 m

3. Draw nets of the following shapes (include dimensions of at least three faces).

(i) A figure of a cube with sides of 4 cm.

(ii) A figure of a cuboid with labelled sides of 10 cm, 7 cm and 4 cm.

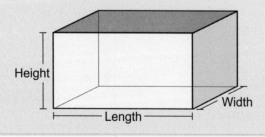

Height

Width

Length

4. (i) Which one of the following nets will not fold to make a cube?

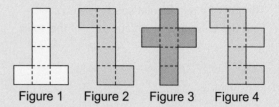

Figure 1   Figure 2   Figure 3   Figure 4

(ii) Draw two more different nets for a cube.

5. The net of a cardboard rectangular solid is shown.

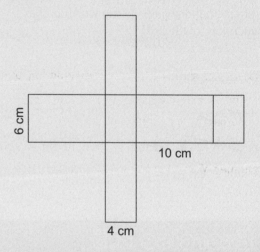

6 cm

10 cm

4 cm

(i) Find the area of this net.

(ii) How many cubes of side 2 cm can be formed from this solid?

6. A rectangular water tank is 55 cm long, 36 cm wide and 10 cm high. Find:

(i) The volume of water in the tank if the tank is half full.
Give your answer in litres.

(ii) The surface area in cm², if the tank has no lid

8.6 RIGHT PRISMS

A **prism** is a 3D shape that has the same cross-section (front face) along the whole length of its shape.

A **right prism** is a prism that has two bases, one directly above the other, and its side faces are rectangles.

The volume of a prism is simply the area of the cross-section multiplied by the length of the prism.

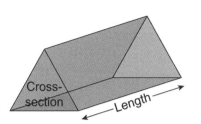
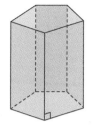

FORMULA

Volume of a prism = area of cross-section × length

ACTIVITY 8.5

The surface area of a prism can be found by using nets.

Worked Example 8.14

Find the volume and surface area of the following prism.

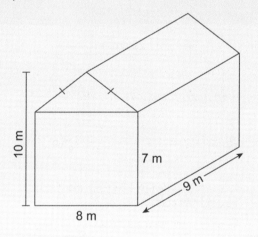

Solution

Volume

We work out the area of the cross-section (front face) of the shape.

A (rectangle) = (8)(7)
$= 56 \text{ m}^2$

B (triangle) = $\frac{1}{2}$(8)(3)
$= 12 \text{ m}^2$

$A + B = 68 \text{ m}^2$

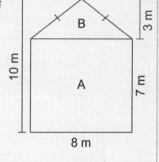

Volume = area of cross-section × length

$= (68)(9)$

$= 612 \text{ m}^3$

Surface area

We draw the net for the two shapes. Some faces are **not** included when calculating the surface area of the prism, as they are hidden. We shade these red.

$h^2 = 4^2 + 3^2$

$h^2 = 25$

$\therefore h = 5 \text{ m}$

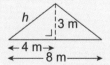

Top:

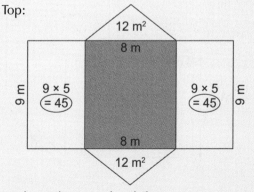

Work out the area of each face.

Surface area = 45 + 12 + 45 + 12 = 114 m²

LENGTH, AREA AND VOLUME

Bottom:

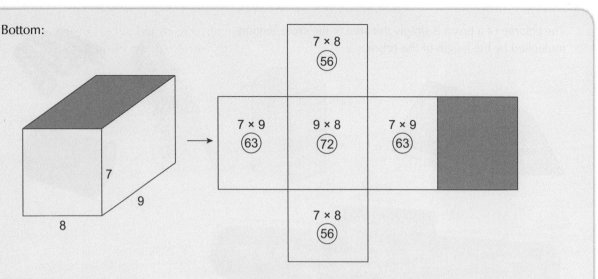

Work out the area of each face.

Surface area = 63 + 56 + 63 + 56 + 72 = 310 m²

∴ Total surface area = 114 + 310

= 424 m²

 Exercise 8.6

1. Find the volume and surface area of the following right prisms:

(i)

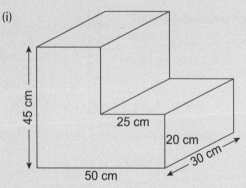

(ii)

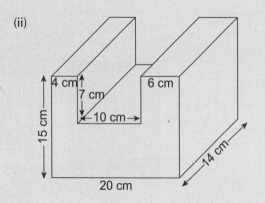

(iii)

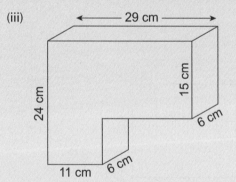

(iv)

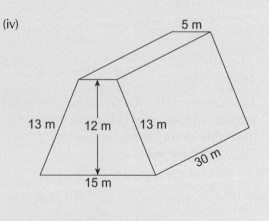

(v)

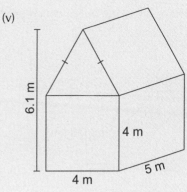

6.1 m
4 m
5 m
4 m

(vi)

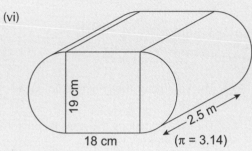

19 cm
18 cm
2.5 m
(π = 3.14)

2. Draw a net for each of the following right prisms

(i)

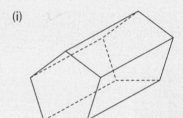

(ii)

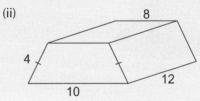

8
4
10
12

(iii)

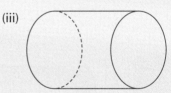

(iv)

(v)

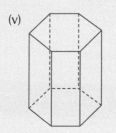

3. Find the volume and surface area of the right prisms whose nets are shown below.

(i)

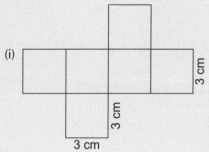

3 cm
3 cm
3 cm

(ii)

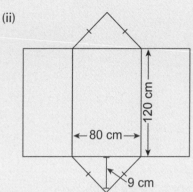

120 cm
80 cm
9 cm

(iii)

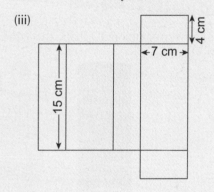

4 cm
7 cm
15 cm

4. The length of a Toblerone packet is 8 cm. The length of the base is 2 cm. The perpendicular height is 2 cm. Find its volume.

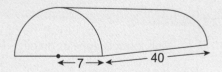

2
2
8

5. A straight tunnel has semi-circular ends as shown. The radius of the tunnel is 7 m; the length is 40 m.

7
40

Find:

(i) The area of each end, using $\pi = \frac{22}{7}$

(ii) The volume of the tunnel

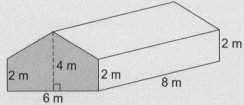

6.

(i) Find the area of the gable wall of the shed shown in the diagram.

(ii) Find the total volume of the interior of the shed.

7. A pair of steps are made out of concrete as shown.

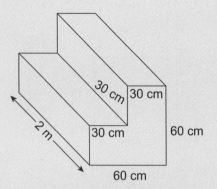

Find:

(i) The volume of the concrete (in cubic metres)

(ii) The cost of making the steps if concrete costs €88 per cubic metre

8.7 CYLINDERS

A cylinder is a very common 3D shape that can be used for a variety of different purposes.

Volume of a Cylinder

The volume of a cylinder is:

FORMULA

Volume of cylinder = $\pi \times$ (radius)$^2 \times$ height

$\therefore$ Volume = $\pi r^2 h$

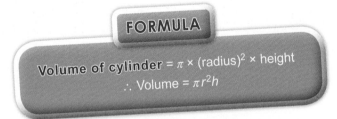

This formula appears on page 10 of *Formulae and Tables*.

Surface Area of a Cylinder

We can use a net to show how to calculate the two types of surface area of a cylinder.

ACTIVITY 8.6

Curved Surface Area (CSA) of a cylinder

This is the area of just the curved part of the cylinder.

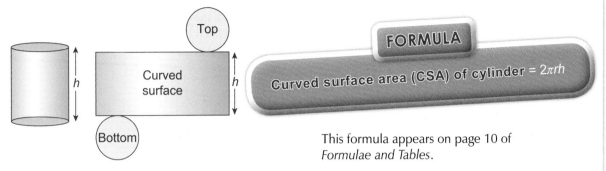

Top

Curved surface

h h

Bottom

FORMULA

Curved surface area (CSA) of cylinder $= 2\pi rh$

This formula appears on page 10 of *Formulae and Tables*.

Total Surface Area (TSA) of a solid cylinder

This is the area of the curved part of the cylinder **plus** the top and bottom circles.

[TSA $= 2\pi rh + \pi r^2$ if either no top or no bottom]

FORMULA

Total surface area (TSA) of a solid cylinder $= 2\pi rh + 2\pi r^2$

$\therefore$ TSA $=$ CSA $+ 2\pi r^2$ or $2\pi r(h + r)$

Worked Example 8.15

Find the volume of the following cylinders:

  (i) $r = 5$ cm, $h = 6$ cm ($\pi = 3.14$)

  (ii) $r = 10$ mm, $h = 2.5$ cm $\left(\pi = \dfrac{22}{7}\right)$

Solution

  (i)   Volume $= \pi r^2 h$

           $= 3.14 \times (5)^2 \times 6$

           $= 3.14 \times 25 \times 6$

           $= 471$ cm^3

  (ii) Volume $= \pi r^2 h$

            $= \dfrac{22}{7} \times (1)^2 \times 2.5$

> All dimensions should have the same units: 10 mm = 1 cm.

            $= \dfrac{22}{7} \times 1 \times 2.5$

            $= 7\dfrac{6}{7}$ cm^3

Worked Example 8.16

Find, in terms of π, the curved surface area and the total surface area of the solid cylinder shown below.

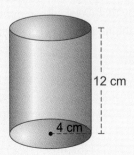

12 cm

4 cm

Solution

  (i)   CSA $= 2\pi rh$

            $= 2 \times \pi \times 4 \times 12$

            $= 96\pi$ cm^2

  (ii) TSA $= 2\pi rh + 2\pi r^2$

            $=$ CSA $+ 2\pi r^2$

            $= 96\pi + 2\pi(4)^2$

            $= 96\pi + 32\pi$

            $= 128\pi$ cm^2

Exercise 8.7

1. Find the volume of each of the following cylinders:

    (i) $r = 10$ cm, $h = 10$ cm ($\pi = 3.14$)

    (ii) $r = 12$ mm, $h = 4$ cm $\left(\pi = \dfrac{22}{7}\right)$

    (iii) $r = 9$ m, $h = 8$ m (in terms of π)

    (iv) $r = 25$ m, $h = 21$ m $\left(\pi = \dfrac{22}{7}\right)$

    (v) $r = 5$ mm, $h = 14$ mm ($\pi = 3.14$)

2. Find the curved surface area and the total surface area of each of the following cylinders:

    (i) $r = 0.25$ m, $h = 2$ m ($\pi = 3.14$)

    (ii) $r = 30$ mm, $h = 5$ cm (in terms of π)

    (iii) $r = 5$ cm, $h = 11$ cm ($\pi = 3.14$)

    (iv) $r = 22$ cm, $h = 44$ cm $\left(\pi = \dfrac{22}{7}\right)$

3. Find the volume and total surface area of each of the following cylinders:

    (i) $r = 14$ mm, $h = 2$ mm $\left(\pi = \dfrac{22}{7}\right)$

    (ii) $r = 2.25$ mm, $h = 0.5$ cm (in terms of π)

4. Using a ruler, measure the dimensions of each of the following cylinders and calculate their volume and curved surface area ($\pi = 3.14$):

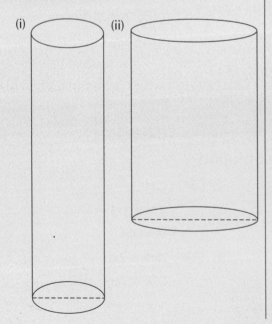

(i)   (ii)

5. Using a ruler and the appropriate scale, calculate the volume and total surface area of each of the following cylinders in terms of π:

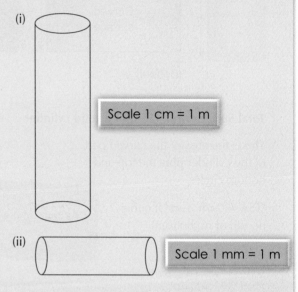

(i)

    Scale 1 cm = 1 m

(ii)   Scale 1 mm = 1 m

6. A cylindrical tin of paint has a radius of 14 cm and a height of 22 cm.
Taking π as 3.14, find:

    (i) The volume of paint in a full tin (Give answer in litres to 2 d.p.)

    (ii) The area of sheet metal needed to make the tin

7. Two cylinders have a height of 10 cm, but have radii of 16 and 8 cm, respectively. Find:

    (i) Their volumes in terms of π

    (ii) The ratio of their volumes

8. A cylindrical storage tank is filled with a liquid chemical to be used in food production. The tank has a height of 3 m and a diameter of 75 cm. One ml of this liquid weighs 1.035 g. The storage tank is made from a metal alloy that weighs 2.5 g per cm². (Assume the metal alloy is of negligible thickness.)

    Find the combined weight of the tank and the chemical. ($\pi = 3.14$)
(Give your answer in kg correct to 2 d.p.)

8.8 RIGHT CIRCULAR CONES

Another 3D shape that is commonly used is the cone.

If the top of the cone is directly over the centre of a circular base, its correct name is a **right circular cone**.

Volume of a Cone

This formula appears on page 10 of *Formulae and Tables*.

FORMULA

Volume of cone $= \frac{1}{3} \times \pi \times (\text{radius})^2 \times \text{height}$

$\therefore$ Volume $= \frac{1}{3}\pi r^2 h$

ACTIVITY 8.7

Surface Area of a Cone

There are two types of surface area of a cone.

Curved Surface Area (CSA) of a Cone

This is the area of just the curved part of the cone.
To calculate the CSA, we must have the slant height (l) of the cone.

FORMULA

$l^2 = h^2 + r^2$

FORMULA

Curved surface area (CSA) of cone $= \pi r l$

This formula appears on page 10 of *Formulae and Tables*.

Using Pythagoras' theorem, we can state that $l^2 = h^2 + r^2$.

Total Surface Area (TSA) of a Cone

This is the area of the curved part of the cone **plus** the circular base.

FORMULA

Total surface area (TSA) of cone $= \pi r l + \pi r^2$

$\therefore$ TSA $= \text{CSA} + \pi r^2$ or $\pi r(l + r)$

Worked Example 8.17

Find the volume of the following cones:

   (i) $r = 7.5$ m, $h = 11$ m ($\pi = 3.14$)

  (ii) $r = 4$ mm, $h = 15$ mm (in terms of π)

Solution

(i) Volume $= \frac{1}{3}\pi r^2 h$

$= \frac{1}{3} \times 3.14 \times (7.5)^2 \times 11$

$= 647.625$ m^3

(ii) Volume $= \frac{1}{3}\pi r^2 h$

$= \frac{1}{3} \times \pi \times (4)^2 \times 15$

$= 80\pi$ mm^3

Worked Example 8.18

Calculate the curved surface area and the total surface area of the cone shown. Give your answers in terms of π.

Solution

To find the surface area of a cone we must know the slant height and radius (r).

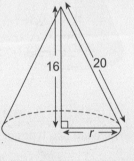

Step 1

$l^2 = h^2 + r^2$

$(20)^2 = (16)^2 + r^2$

$400 = 256 + r^2$

$400 - 256 = r^2$

$144 = r^2$

$12 = r$

Step 2

CSA $= \pi r l$

$= \pi \times 12 \times 20$

$\therefore$ CSA $= 240\pi$ units^2

Step 3

TSA $=$ CSA $+ \pi r^2$

$= 240\pi + \pi(12)^2$

$= 240\pi + 144\pi$

$= 384\pi$ units^2

Exercise 8.8

1. Find the volume of each of the following cones:

    (i) $r = 2$ cm, $h = 4$ cm (in terms of π)

   (ii) $r = 40$ mm, $h = 21$ mm ($\pi = \frac{22}{7}$)

  (iii) $r = 400$ mm, $h = 30$ mm ($\pi = 3.14$)

  (iv) $r = 1.5$ m, $h = 2.5$ mm ($\pi = 3.14$)

   (v) $r = 25$ cm, $h = 14$ cm ($\pi = \frac{22}{7}$)

  (vi) diameter $= 10$ cm, $h = 16$ cm ($\pi = 3.14$)

2. Find the curved surface area and the total surface area of each of the following cones:

    (i) $r = 6$ m, $h = 8$ m (in terms of π)

   (ii) $r = 11$ cm, $l = 61$ cm ($\pi = 3.14$)

  (iii) $l = 35$ mm, $h = 21$ mm ($\pi = \frac{22}{7}$)

  (iv) $r = 30$ cm, $l = 500$ mm (in terms of π)

3. Find the volume and total surface area of each of the following cones to two decimal places:

    (i) $r = 200$ mm, $h = 20$ cm

   (ii) $r = 1.8$ m, $h = 2.6$ m

4. Scaled diagrams of two conical storage silos are shown. Scale: 1 cm = 1 m.

A

12 cm

16 cm

B

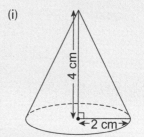

20 cm

4 cm

(i) Calculate the volume (in litres) of each silo.

(ii) Each silo is made up of sheets of corrugated iron panels. Each sheet measures 3 m by 1 m.
Find the total number of sheets needed to make each silo.

5. Using the given scale, calculate the volume and total surface area of each of the following cones $\left(\pi = \frac{22}{7}\right)$:
(Give answer correct to 2 d.p.)

(i)

Scale
1 cm = 200 m

4 cm

2 cm

(ii)

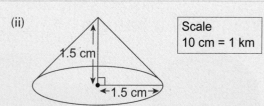

1.5 cm

1.5 cm

Scale
10 cm = 1 km

6. An ornament in the shape of a cone is to be **electroplated**.

> Electroplating is the process of coating metal onto an object's surface using electricity.

Find the cost of electroplating this ornament if it costs €5 per cm². (Take $\pi = 3.14$)

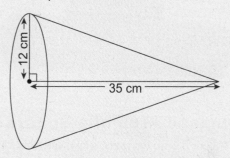

12 cm

35 cm

7. A space module consists of a cone on top of a cylinder. The radius of both is 4 m. The height of the cylindrical part is 8 m; the slant height of the conical part is 5 m.
Find, in terms of π, the total volume of the module.

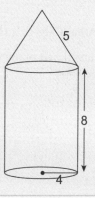

5

8

4

8.9 SPHERES AND HEMISPHERES

A ball or globe is an example of a **sphere**.

Volume of a Sphere

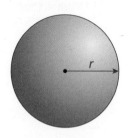

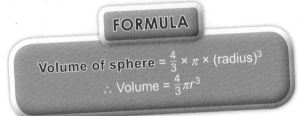

FORMULA

Volume of sphere $= \frac{4}{3} \times \pi \times (\text{radius})^3$

$\therefore$ Volume $= \frac{4}{3}\pi r^3$

This formula appears on page 10 of *Formulae and Tables*.

Volume of a Hemisphere

A hemisphere is **half** a sphere.

FORMULA

Volume of hemisphere $= \frac{2}{3}\pi r^3$

Surface Area of a Sphere

A sphere has no flat parts, so we can only have one type of surface area.

FORMULA

Surface area of sphere $= 4\pi r^2$

This formula appears on page 10 of *Formulae and Tables*.

Surface Area of a Hemisphere

A hemisphere has a flat circular part, so two types of surface area can be found.

Curved Surface Area (CSA) of a Hemisphere

The area of the curved part of the sphere is **half** that of the surface area of a sphere.

FORMULA

Curved surface area (CSA) of hemisphere $= 2\pi r^2$

Total Surface Area (TSA) of a Hemisphere

This is the area of the curved part of the hemisphere **plus** the circular top.

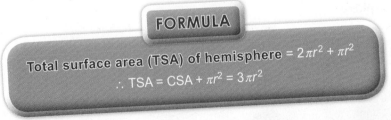

FORMULA

Total surface area (TSA) of hemisphere $= 2\pi r^2 + \pi r^2$

$\therefore$ TSA $= $ CSA $+ \pi r^2 = 3\pi r^2$

ACTIVITY 8.8

Worked Example 8.19

Find the volume of the following sphere, in terms of π:

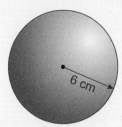

6 cm

Solution

Volume $= \frac{4}{3}\pi r^3$

$= \frac{4}{3} \times \pi \times (6)^3$

$= 288\pi$ cm^3

 Worked Example 8.20

Find the curved surface area and the total surface area of a hemisphere of radius 10 cm ($\pi = 3.14$).

Solution

CSA

$2\pi r^2$

$= 2 \times 3.14 \times (10)^2$

$= 628$ cm^2

TSA

CSA $+ \pi r^2$

$= 3\pi r^2$

$= 3 \times 3.14 \times (10)^2$

$= 942$ cm^2

 Exercise 8.9

1. Find the volume of each of the following spheres:

   (i) Radius = 9 cm (in terms of π)

   (ii) Radius = 12 cm $\left(\pi = \frac{22}{7}\right)$

   (iii) Radius = 5 mm ($\pi = 3.14$)

   (iv) Diameter = 21 cm $\left(\pi = \frac{22}{7}\right)$

   (v) Radius = 4 m (in terms of π)

2. Find the volume of each of the following hemispheres:

   (i) Radius = 13 cm $\left(\pi = \frac{22}{7}\right)$

   (ii) Diameter = 0.12 m (in terms of π)

   (iii) Radius = 1.5 m ($\pi = 3.14$)

   (iv) Radius = 20 mm (in terms of π)

   (v) Radius = 42 cm ($\pi = 3.14$)

3. Find the surface area of each of the following spheres:

   (i) $r = 9$ cm (in terms of π)

   (ii) $r = 12$ m $\left(\pi = \frac{22}{7}\right)$

4. Find the total surface area of each of the following hemispheres:

   (i) $r = 5$ mm ($\pi = 3.14$)

   (ii) $r = 100$ km $\left(\pi = \frac{22}{7}\right)$

5. Find the curved surface area and the total surface area (where applicable) of each of the following spheres or hemispheres:

   (i) Sphere: $r = 20$ mm (in terms of π)

   (ii) Hemisphere: $r = 15$ m ($\pi = 3.14$)

   (iii) Hemisphere: $r = 27$ cm ($\pi = 3.14$)

   (iv) Sphere: $r = 14\frac{1}{4}$ cm $\left(\pi = \frac{22}{7}\right)$

6. Find the volume and total surface area of each of the following (in terms of π):

   (i) Hemisphere: $r = 1.25$ m

   (ii) Sphere: $r = 500$ m

7. A spherical ball is made from a sheet of plastic. The diameter of the ball is 21.6 cm. Taking π as 3.14, find, to the nearest whole number:

   (i) The area of plastic material used to make the ball

   (ii) The volume of air inside the ball

8. A solid sphere of chocolate fits exactly into a cubic box. The radius of the sphere is 7 cm. Taking π as $\frac{22}{7}$, find:

   (i) The volume of the sphere

   (ii) The volume of the box

   (iii) The volume of the box not occupied by the sphere, written as a percentage (correct to one decimal place)

9. A cylindrical part of an engine has a height of 14 cm and a radius of 6 cm. A spherical ball bearing of radius 4.5 cm is placed in the cylinder and oil is then poured into the cylinder until it is full. Taking π as $\frac{22}{7}$, find:

   (i) The capacity of the cylinder

   (ii) The volume of the ball bearing

   (iii) The volume of the oil used

10. A tennis ball has a radius of 3.5 cm. Taking π as 3.14, find:

   (i) The volume of the tennis ball

Three tennis balls fit exactly into a cylindrical tube. Calculate:

   (ii) The height of the tube

   (iii) The radius of the tube

   (iv) The volume of the tube

   (v) The fraction of the volume of the tube taken up by the three tennis balls

11. A spinning top consists of a solid cone on a solid hemisphere. The radius of both is 3.5 cm and the height of the cone is 6 cm. Find the total volume of the spinning top to the nearest cubic centimetre.

Take $\pi = \frac{22}{7}$.

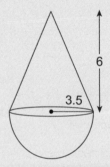

12. A golf-ball manufacturer produces golf balls with a diameter of 4 cm. It costs the manufacturer €0.12 to manufacture each cm³ of golf ball. Each ball is then painted with one coat of paint. Each cm² of golf ball painted costs 0.723 cents.
Find the costs to the manufacturer of producing an order of 10,000 golf balls.
(Take $\pi = 3.14$.)

8.10 FINDING DIMENSIONS WHEN GIVEN VOLUME OR SURFACE AREA

We may encounter problems where we must work backwards from the volume or surface area to find a length or radius.

Worked Example 8.21

The volume of a cuboid is 180 cm³. Find its breadth.

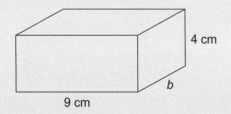

Solution

Write down what we are given	Volume = 180
Write down formula	$lbh = 180$
Fill in given dimensions	$(9)(b)(4) = 180$
	$36b = 180$
Solve	$b = 5$ cm

Worked Example 8.22

The volume of a cylinder is 847π cm³. If it has a radius of 11 cm, find its height.

Solution

Write down what we are given	Volume = 847π
Write down formula	$\pi r^2 h = 847\pi$
Fill in given dimensions	$\pi(11)^2(h) = 847\pi$
Solve	$121h = 847$ $h = 7$ cm

Worked Example 8.23

The volume of a sphere is $3{,}054\frac{6}{7}$ mm³. Taking $\pi = \frac{22}{7}$, find the radius of the sphere.

Solution

Write down what we are given	Volume = $3{,}054\frac{6}{7}$
Write down formula	$\frac{4}{3}\pi r^3 = 3{,}054\frac{6}{7}$
Fill in given dimensions	$\frac{4}{3}\left(\frac{22}{7}\right)(r^3) = 3{,}054\frac{6}{7}$ $\frac{88r^3}{21} = \frac{21{,}384}{7}$
Solve	$88r^3 = 64{,}152$ $r^3 = 729$ $r = \sqrt[3]{729}$ $r = 9$ mm

Worked Example 8.24

The total surface area of a cone is 373.66 cm². Find the slant height of the cone if its radius is 7 cm ($\pi = 3.14$).

Solution

Write down what we are given	TSA = 373.66
Write down formula	$\pi r l + \pi r^2 = 373.66$
Fill in given dimensions	$(3.14)(7)(l) + (3.14)(7)^2 = 373.66$ $21.98l + 153.86 = 373.66$
Solve	$21.98l = 373.66 - 153.86$ $21.98l = 219.8$ $l = \frac{219.8}{21.98}$ $l = 10$ cm

ACTIVITY 8.9

Exercise 8.10

Fill in the following tables. Make sure you show all your work.

(i) Rectangular solids

Length (cm)	Breadth (cm)	Height (cm)	Volume (cm³)	Surface area (cm²)
4	5		180	
2		3	6	
	7.5	2	210	
	$1\frac{1}{2}$	$3\frac{1}{3}$	5	
0.5		0.25		1

(ii) Cylinders

π	r (cm)	h (cm)	Volume (cm³)	CSA (cm²)	TSA (cm²)
π	5		100π		
3.14		11	2,797.74		
3.14	13			81.64	
$\frac{22}{7}$		14		616	
$\frac{22}{7}$	9				$1,046\frac{4}{7}$

(iii) Cones

π	r (cm)	h (cm)	l (cm)	Volume (cm³)	CSA (cm²)	TSA (cm²)
π	4			16π		
$\frac{22}{7}$	7			1,232		
3.14			41		1,158.66	
3.14		84			3,469.7	4,000.36
$\frac{22}{7}$		99		$41,485\frac{5}{7}$		

(iv) Spheres/hemispheres

(a) Spheres

π	r (cm)	Volume (cm³)	TSA (cm²)
π		$166\frac{2}{3}\pi$	
$\frac{22}{7}$			$50\frac{2}{7}$
3.14		3,052.08	
π			676π

(b) Hemispheres

π	r (cm)	Volume (cm³)	TSA (cm²)	CSA (cm²)
π		$83\frac{1}{3}\pi$		
$\frac{22}{7}$			$37\frac{5}{7}$	
3.140				508.68
π				338π

LENGTH, AREA AND VOLUME

8.11 PROBLEMS INVOLVING VOLUME AND SURFACE AREA

Worked Example 8.25

A cylinder of wax of radius 12 cm and height 21 cm is melted down into two candles, one in the shape of a sphere and the other in the shape of a cone with a radius of 7 cm and a height of 5 cm.
Assuming no wax is wasted in the melting, calculate the radius of the sphere to the nearest cm.

Solution

Volume of the cylinder $= \pi r^2 h$

$\qquad = \pi(12)^2(21)$

$\therefore$ Volume of cylinder $= 3{,}024\pi$ cm^3

Volume of the cylinder = volume of the sphere + volume of cone

$\therefore$ Volume of sphere + volume of cone $= 3{,}024\pi$ cm^3

$$\frac{4}{3}\pi r^3 + \frac{1}{3}\pi r^2 h = 3{,}024\pi$$

$$\frac{4}{3}r^3 + \frac{1}{3}(7)^2(5) = 3{,}024$$

$$\frac{4}{3}r^3 + 81\frac{2}{3} = 3{,}024$$

$$\frac{4}{3}r^3 = 3{,}024 - 81\frac{2}{3}$$

$$\frac{4}{3}r^3 = 2{,}942\frac{1}{3}$$

$$r^3 = \frac{2{,}942\frac{1}{3}}{\frac{4}{3}} = 2{,}206\frac{3}{4}$$

$$r = \sqrt[3]{2{,}206\frac{3}{4}}$$

$$r = 13.0192 \text{ cm}$$

$$\therefore r = 13 \text{ cm (nearest cm)}$$

Worked Example 8.26

An experiment to measure the volume of a metal spherical ball is conducted. The ball is dropped into a cylinder of water. The cylinder has a radius of 5 cm and a height of 9 cm and is half-full of water. When the ball is dropped in, the water level rises by 4 cm.

Find the radius of the metal spherical ball correct to one decimal place.

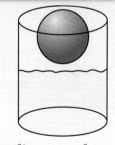

Solution

When the ball is dropped in, the water level rises by 4 cm.

The volume of the sphere is equal to the volume of the displaced water.

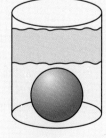

4 cm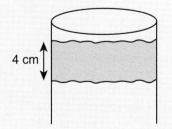

Volume of displaced water $= \pi r^2 h = \pi \times (5)^2 \times 4$

$\qquad = 100\pi$ cm^3

$\therefore$ Volume of sphere $= 100\pi$ cm^3

$$\frac{4}{3}\pi r^3 = 100\pi$$

$$\frac{4}{3}r^3 = 100$$

$$r^3 = 75$$

$$\Rightarrow r = \sqrt[3]{75}$$

$$\Rightarrow r = 4.2172 \text{ cm}$$

$$\therefore r \approx 4.2 \text{ cm}$$

1. A cuboid has a volume of 2,700 cm³. It is has a length of 10 cm and a width of 15 cm. Find its height.

2. A rectangular solid has a surface area of 5,900 cm².
   Find its width, if it has a length of 25 cm and a height of 40 cm.

3. A solid metal sphere of radius 6 cm is melted down and remoulded into a solid cone of radius 3 cm.

3 cm

Find:

(i) The volume of the sphere in terms of π

(ii) The height of the cone

4. A solid sphere of diameter 18 cm is made of plasticine. It is remoulded to form a cone of height 81 cm. Find the radius of the cone.

5. A toy in the shape of a hemisphere has a volume of 1,526.04 cm³.
   Find the radius of this toy ($\pi = 3.14$).

6. A cone of radius 10 cm has the same volume as a cylinder with height 8 cm and radius 4 cm. Find the height of the cone to the nearest millimetre.

7. A rectangular block of metal shown is melted down into two identical metal spheres.

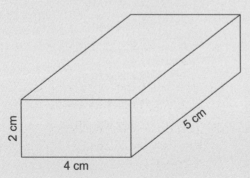

2 cm

5 cm

4 cm

10% of the volume was lost in the melting of the block of metal. Find the radius of these spheres correct to two decimal places. ($\pi = 3.14$)

8. A test-tube consists of a hollow cylinder and a hollow hemisphere. Find the height of the cylinder if the tube has a diameter of 3 cm and a volume of 29.25π cm³.

9. A buoy consists of a cone and a hemisphere. The diameter is 12 cm and the volume of the buoy is 264π cm³.

⊢———12———⊣

Find:

(i) The height of the conical part

(ii) The surface area of the buoy $\left(\pi = \dfrac{22}{7}\right)$ (Answer correct to 2 d.p.)

10. A toy consists of a solid hemisphere surmounted by a solid cone.

    The toy fits exactly into a cylindrical container, as shown.

(a) The radius of the cone is of length 6 cm. The volume of the cone is one third of the volume of the hemisphere. Find:

   (i) The volume of the hemisphere in terms of π

   (ii) The height of the cone

   (iii) The overall height of the toy

(b) Does the toy take up more than half of the capacity of the container? Show clearly how you arrived at your answer.

11. A candle is in the shape of a cone on top of a cylinder. The cylinder has radius 4 cm. The slant height of the cone is 5 cm.

Find:

(i) The height, h, of the cone

(ii) The volume of the cone in terms of π

(iii) The height of the cylinder, given that its volume is ten times the volume of the cone

12. A rectangular tank with no lid has a surface area of 486 cm². If its length is twice its height and its width is half its height, find the dimensions of the tank.

13. A cuboid has three dimensions in the ratio 1 : 2 : 3. Find all three lengths if its volume is 10,368 cm³.

14. A cylindrical tank of radius 12 cm is partly filled with water. A sphere of radius 6 cm is immersed in the water.
By how much will the water rise?

15. A cylindrical tank of radius 4 cm is partly filled with water. A cone of radius 2 cm and height 3 cm is immersed in the water.
By how much will the water rise?

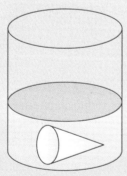

16. A closed plastic container is in the shape of a hollow cylinder on a hollow hemisphere, both of radius-length 3 cm. The container is partly filled with water, to a depth of 10 cm.

(i) Find the volume of the water, in terms of π.

(ii) If the container is turned upside down, what will the depth of the water be in the cylindrical part?

17. Water flows through a cylindrical pipe at a rate of 35 cm per second. The pipe has diameter 4 cm. How long would it take to pour out 22 litres of water?
$\left(\text{Take } \pi = \frac{22}{7}\right)$
(1 litre = 1,000 cm³)

18. Two cones have their radii in the ratio 3 : 2 and their heights in the ratio 5 : 12. Which has the greater volume?

19. Three cylinders (A, B and C) have radii in the ratio 5 : 3 : 2 and heights in the ratio 3 : 8 : 19.

Which has the greatest volume?

20. Water flows through a cylindrical pipe at a rate of 10 cm per second. The diameter of the pipe is 7 cm. The water is poured into an empty rectangular tank of length 55 cm and width 20 cm.

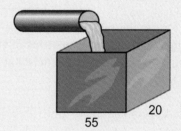

What is the depth of the water in the tank after one minute? ($\pi = 3.14$)
(Give answer correct to nearest cm.)

21. A ladle is in the shape of a hemisphere of diameter 3 cm. It is used to remove soup from a cylindrical container of radius 6 cm.

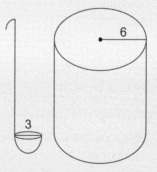

(i) Find the volume of one ladleful in terms of π.

(ii) How far will the depth of the soup drop if 24 ladlefuls of soup are removed?

(iii) If the depth of the soup is now $2\frac{1}{2}$ cm, how many more ladlefuls could still be removed?

8.12 TRAPEZOIDAL RULE

We have encountered many formulae in this chapter that cover finding the area or volume of defined shapes or objects.

In real life we meet many irregularly shaped objects.

When we try to measure the area of an irregular shape, we will only be able to get an approximate answer. We can use a rule that is based on trapeziums.

ACTIVITY 8.10

The **trapezoidal rule** is used to estimate the area under a curve.

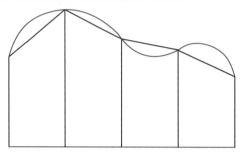

When we use this rule, the shape to be measured must be divided into **segments or strips of equal length**. We then need to measure the height at each interval.

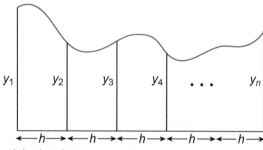

Area $\approx \dfrac{h}{2}$ [first height + last height + 2(the sum of the rest of the heights)]

When using the trapezoidal rule, the smaller the distance between each interval, the more accurate the approximation of area will be.

FORMULA

Area $\approx \dfrac{h}{2}[y_1 + y_n + 2(y_2 + y_3 + y_4 + \dots + y_{n-1})]$

This formula appears on page 12 of *Formulae and Tables*.

Worked Example 8.27

Estimate the area of the piece of land shown below. (units are in metres.)

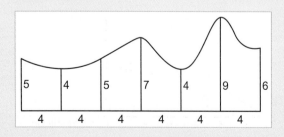

Solution

$h = 4$ m

First height = 5 m

Last height = 6 m

Area $\approx \dfrac{4}{2}[5 + 6 + 2(4 + 5 + 7 + 4 + 9)]$

$\qquad = 2[11 + 2(29)]$

$\qquad = 2[69]$

$\qquad = 138$ m^2

Worked Example 8.28

Estimate the area of the shape shown below.
(Units are in metres.)

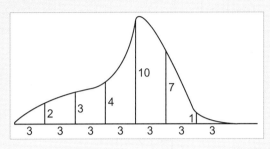

Solution

$h = 3$ m

First height = 0 m

Last height = 0 m

Area $\approx \dfrac{3}{2}[0 + 0 + 2(2 + 3 + 4 + 10 + 7 + 1)]$

$= \dfrac{3}{2}[0 + 2(27)]$

$= \dfrac{3}{2}[54]$

$= 81$ m^2

We may be given the area and asked to work backwards.

Worked Example 8.29

The area of the following shape was estimated to be 800 cm^2 using the trapezoidal rule. Find the width of each segment.

Solution

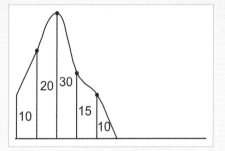

$h = ?$ cm   First height = 10 cm   Last height = 0 cm

Area = 800 cm^2

$\therefore \dfrac{h}{2}[10 + 0 + 2(20 + 30 + 15 + 10)] = 800$

$\dfrac{h}{2}[10 + 2(75)] = 800$

$\dfrac{h}{2}[160] = 800$

$80h = 800$

$\therefore h = 10$ cm

Exercise 8.12

Use the trapezoidal rule to estimate the area of each of the following:

1.

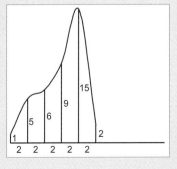

2.

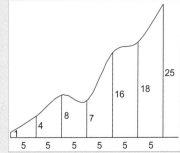

3.

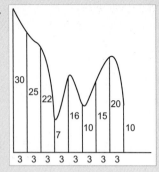

4.

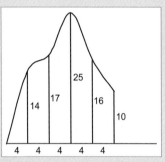

5.

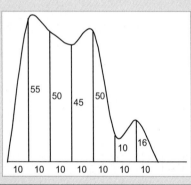

6.

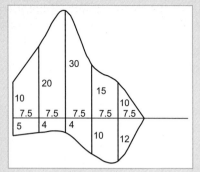

7.

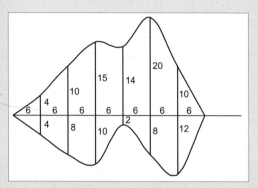

8. Estimate the area of these plots of land in hectares. (1 hectare = 10,000 m²)
Measurements are in metres.

(i)

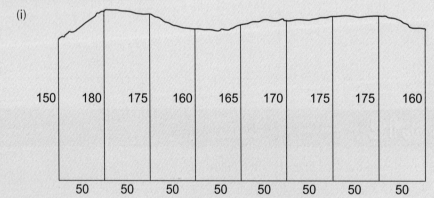

(ii)

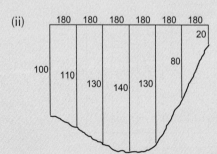

9. The area of this irregular shape is approximately 230 square units. Find the value of *x*.

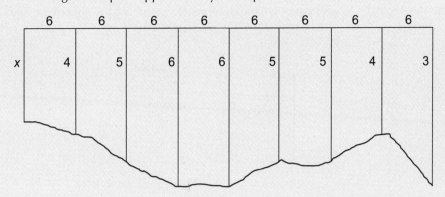

10. The area of this irregular shape is approximately 1,200 square units. Find the value of *y*.

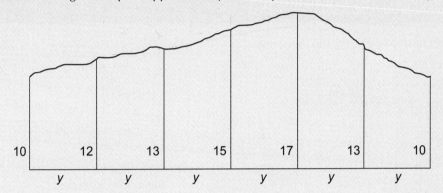

11. The area between the curve and the line was estimated to be 40 units² using the trapezoidal rule. Calculate the value of *x*.

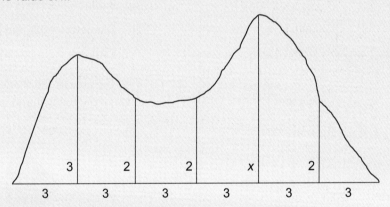

12. The area of this field is approximately 1.5 hectares. Find the value of *h*.
(1 hectare = 10,000 square metres) Measurements are in metres.

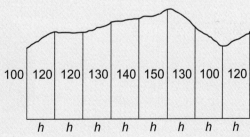

13. A map of a fields is shown, using a scale of 1 cm = 10 m.
Use the trapezoidal rule with your own measurements to estimate the area of the field.

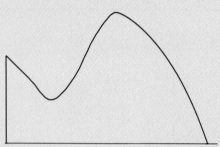

Revision Exercises

1. **(a)** Find the area of each of the following shapes:

(i)

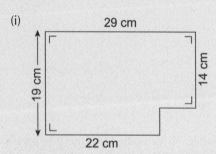

29 cm

19 cm

14 cm

22 cm

(ii)

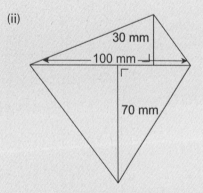

30 mm

100 mm

70 mm

(iii)

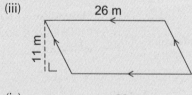

26 m

11 m

(iv)

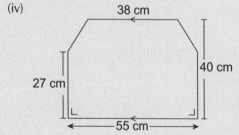

38 cm

27 cm

40 cm

55 cm

(v)

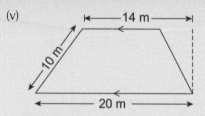

14 m

10 m

20 m

(b) Find the area and perimeter of each of the following circles:

(i)   Radius = 25 cm (in terms of π)

(ii) Radius = 18 cm (π = 3.14)

(iii) Diameter = 0.5 mm $\left(\pi = \frac{22}{7}\right)$

(iv) Radius = 12.5 cm (in terms of π)

2. **(a)** Find the area of the shaded region in each of the following shapes:

(i)

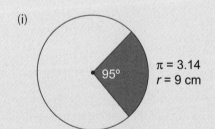

95°

π = 3.14
r = 9 cm

(ii)

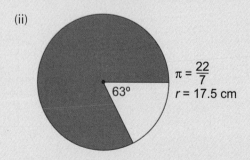

63°

$\pi = \frac{22}{7}$
r = 17.5 cm

(iii)

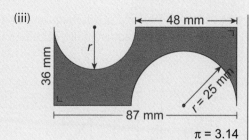

$\pi = 3.14$

(iv)

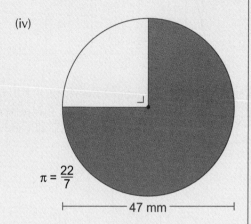

$\pi = \dfrac{22}{7}$

47 mm

(b) By using the information from each diagram below, find the value of x.

(i)

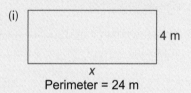

4 m

x

Perimeter = 24 m

(ii)

12 m

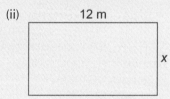

x

Area = 64 m²

(iii)

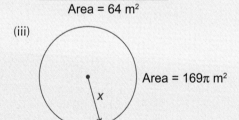

Area = 169π m²

x

(iv)

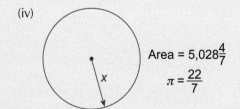

Area = $5{,}028\dfrac{4}{7}$

$\pi = \dfrac{22}{7}$

x

(v)

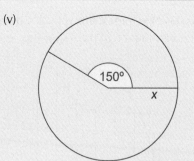

150°

x

Length of minor arc = 110 mm

$\pi = \dfrac{22}{7}$

(vi)

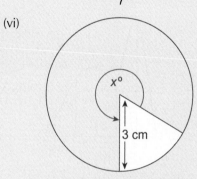

x°

3 cm

Area of shaded region = 5.495 cm²

$\pi = 3.14$

3. (a) The propellers of a wind turbine are shown.

On a certain day, the propellers complete 20 revolutions per minute and have a speed at their tip of 45 m/s.

Calculate the radius of a propeller to one decimal place. ($\pi = 3.14$)

(b) The slant height of a cone is 17 cm. The height is 15 cm.

Find:

(i) The radius length

(ii) The volume of the cone in terms of π

4. (a) Use the trapezoidal rule to estimate the area of each of the following:

(i)

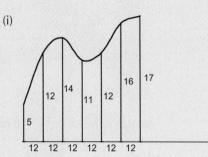

(ii)

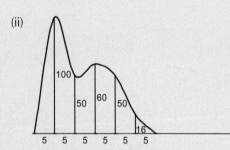

(iii)

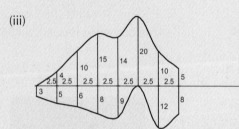

(iv)

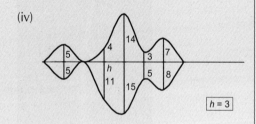

$h = 3$

(b) (i) The area of this irregular shape is 255 square units. Find the value of x.

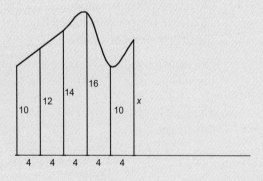

(ii) The area of this irregular shape is 3,395 square units. Find the value of x.

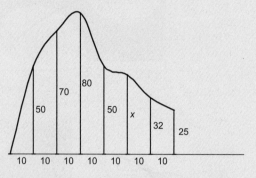

(iii) The area of this shape is estimated at 820 square units. Calculate the width of each strip, if all widths are of equal length.

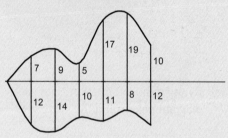

5. (a) Find the volume and surface area of the following right prisms (to 2 d.p.):

(i)

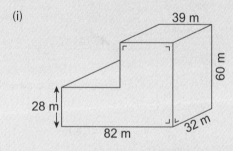

(ii)

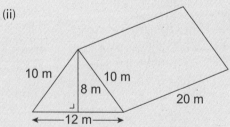

(iii)

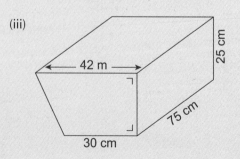

(b) Draw a net for the following right prisms and hence calculate their volume and surface area (to 2 d.p.).

(i)

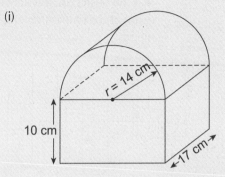

(ii)

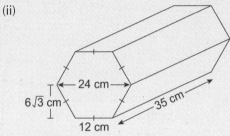

(c) An overflow water tank is shown.

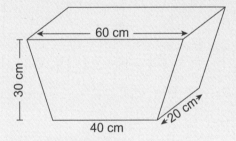

The tank is designed to fill up to 70% of its full capacity.

(i) How many litres of water is the tank designed to hold?

A water pipe connects to this tank and its takes 10 minutes to fill this tank to its designated volume.

(ii) Calculate the average rate of flow of this water pipe in cm³ per second.

6. (a) Find the area of this sector, using $\pi = 3.14$:

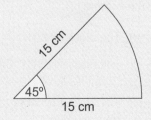

(b) A solid metal sphere of radius 4 cm is melted and recast into a cone of radius 8 cm. Find the height of the cone.

7. (a) A hollow cylindrical pipe has inner radius 3 cm and outer radius 4 cm. The height is 50 cm. Using $\pi = \frac{22}{7}$, find the volume of material needed to make this pipe.

(b) A rectangular box is 1 m by 150 cm by 80 cm. Another box is to be built that will hold 4 times as much as the first. The length, height and width of this box are all different.

Give one set of possible values for the dimensions of the box.

8. (a) Water is kept cool in a cylindrical container of diameter 28 cm and height 30 cm.

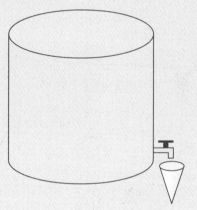

The water is poured into small conical cups, each of diameter 3 cm and height 3.5 cm.

When the cooler is full, how many cupfuls does it contain?

(b) Estimate the area of this irregular shape:

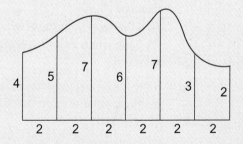

9. (a) A rectangular box with a lid is 63 cm long, 42 cm wide and 21 cm high. Using $\pi = \frac{22}{7}$:

    (i) Find the capacity of the box.

    (ii) Find the volume of the biggest sphere which will fit inside the box.

    (iii) Find the volume of the biggest cylinder which will fit inside the box.

(b) The area of this field is estimated as 500 square metres. Measurements are in metres.

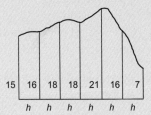

15   16   18   18   21   16   7

h   *h*   *h*   *h*   *h*   *h*

Find the value of *h*, the width of each strip.

10. (a) Find the area and perimeter of this sector, using $\pi = 3.14$:

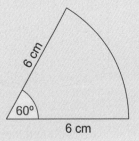

6 cm

60°

6 cm

(b) (i) A soup ladle is in the shape of a hemisphere of diameter 9 cm, with a handle attached. Find the volume of one ladleful in terms of π.

    (ii) This ladle is used to remove soup from a cylindrical container of diameter 36 cm. Find the drop in the level of the soup when 24 ladlefuls are removed.

    (iii) If the remaining soup has a depth of 6 cm, how many more ladlefuls can be removed?

Soup

11. (a) (i) The diagram shows the plan of a lake. Use the trapezoidal rule to estimate the area of the lake, given that the offsets are a distance 10 m apart, and all measurements are in metres.

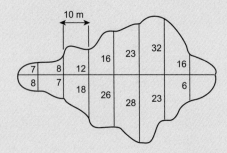

10 m

7   8   12   16   23   32   16
8   7   18   26   28   23   6

    (ii) If the average depth of the lake is 7 m, estimate the volume of water in the lake.

(b) A rectangular block has height 6 cm, length 11 cm and width 8 cm.

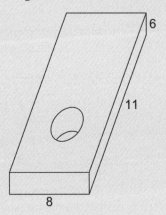

6

11

8

    (i) Find its volume.

    (ii) A vertical cylindrical hole of radius *r* centimetres is drilled in the block, as shown. The volume of the remaining piece is $87\frac{1}{2}$% of the original volume. Find *r*, correct to one decimal place. (Take $\pi = \frac{22}{7}$.)

12. (a) A solid rectangular block of wood measures 6 cm x 8 cm x 10 cm. Find (in terms of π, where necessary) the volume of:

    (i) The block

    (ii) The biggest sphere that can be cut from the block

    (iii) The biggest cylinder that can be cut from the block

(b) The perimeter of the shaded region consists of three semi-circles. Find, in terms of π:

   (i) The perimeter of the region

   (ii) The area of the region

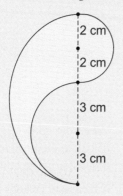

2 cm
2 cm
3 cm
3 cm

13. (a) Two spheres have radii in the ratio 3 : 1. What is the ratio of their volumes?

   (b) The ratio of the volumes of two spheres is 8 : 1. Find the ratio of the lengths of their radii.

14. (a) A 1.08 kg gold bar is shown below.

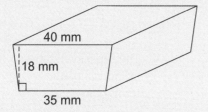

40 mm
18 mm
35 mm

If 1 cm³ of gold weighs approximately 20 g, find the length of the bar.

   (b) The sides of a square are each of length $2r$, as shown. Circles are drawn inside and outside the square.

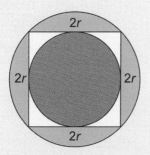

2r
2r
2r
2r

   (i) Find the radius of each circle in terms of r.

   (ii) Verify that the areas of the two circles are in the ratio 2 : 1.

15. (a) A cone has height 12 cm and radius 10 cm. It is cut half way up (as shown) so that a new cone of height 6 cm and radius 5 cm is formed. Find the ratio original cone's volume : new cone's volume.

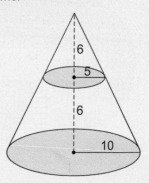

6
5
6
10

   (b) Water pours through a pipe of radius 3 cm at a rate of 15 cm per second. It flows into a conical tank of height 0.9 metres and radius 0.6 metres.

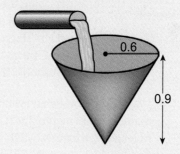

0.6
0.9

How long will it take to fill the tank?

16. (a) A cylindrical hole is bored through a trapezoidal block of metal as shown below. The volume of metal bored out was equal to $\frac{1}{3}$ of the total volume of the block. Find the diameter of the hole. ($\pi = 3.14$) (Give answer correct to 1 d.p.)

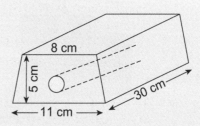

8 cm
5 cm
30 cm
11 cm

(b) Three athletes A, B and C run around a track, as shown. The track is rectangular with semicircular ends. Each athlete runs in a lane which is 1 metre wide. All measurement shown are in metres.

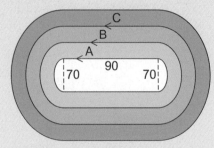

Answer these questions to the nearest metre:

(i) If A runs around the entire track once, how far does she travel?

(ii) If B travels around the entire track once in the next lane, how far does she travel?

(iii) The organisers want the three athletes to compete in a 400-metre race. How much 'stagger' must runners B and C be given (i.e. how far ahead of A should they start)?

17. (a) Water flows through a cylindrical pipe of diameter 3.5 cm into a rectangular tank of length 1.1 metres, width 1.4 metres and height 1.5 metres. The tank is filled in 40 minutes.
Find $\left(\text{using } \pi = \frac{22}{7}\right)$ the rate at which the water flows through the pipe (in cm/s).

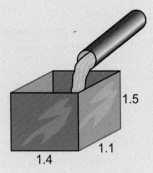

(b) A cone has radius 2 cm and height $\frac{27}{8}$ cm. It is totally immersed in water inside a cylindrical tank of radius 6 cm.

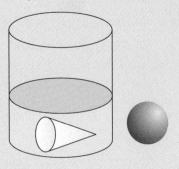

(i) When the cone is removed, calculate the drop in the depth of the water in the tank.

(ii) A sphere of radius r cm is then immersed in the water, which returns to its previous level. Find the value of r.

18. (a) A closed container consists of a cylinder joined to a cone. The height of the cylinder is 10 cm and its diameter is 7 cm.

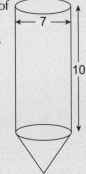

Calculate:

(i) The capacity of the cylindrical part in terms of π

(ii) The vertical height of the cone, given that its capacity is one-fifth of the capacity of the cylinder

(iii) The volume of the water (in terms of π) in the container when its depth is 13 cm

(iv) The height of the water in the cylinder if the container were inverted

(b) The area of this field is approximately 1.5 hectares. Find the value of h.
(1 hectare = 10,000 square metres)
Measurements are in metres.

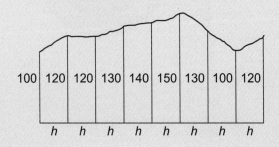

19. (a) A test-tube consists of a hollow cylinder on a hemisphere. Both have diameter 3 cm. The overall height of the test-tube is 8.5 cm.

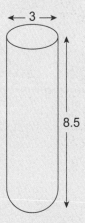

    (i) Find the volume of the liquid in the test-tube (when full) in terms of π.

    (ii) Find the depth of the liquid in the test-tube when it is half-full.

(b) Two cylinders have radii in the ratio 11 : 7 and heights in the ratio 2 : 5. Which has the greater volume?

20. (a) A sphere fits exactly into an open cylindrical container. Show that both have the same curved surface area.

(b) The radius of a solid metal hemisphere is 6 cm. Express its volume in terms of π.

The hemisphere is melted down and some of the molten metal is used to make a solid cone and a solid cylinder, both having base radius 3 cm and height 6 cm.
What percentage of the molten metal remains unused?

21. (a) Find the volume of a cylinder of radius 6 mm and height 20 mm.

Give your answer in two forms, as follows:

  (i) In terms of π

  (ii) Correct to two decimal places

(b) A solid rectangular block measures 60 mm × 35 mm × 20 mm.

Cylindrical holes of radius 6 mm are drilled, one at a time, through the block, in the direction shown.

After how many holes will more than half of the original block have been removed?

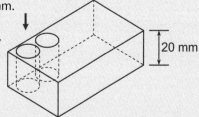

SEC Project Maths Paper 2,
Leaving Certificate Ordinary Level, 2011

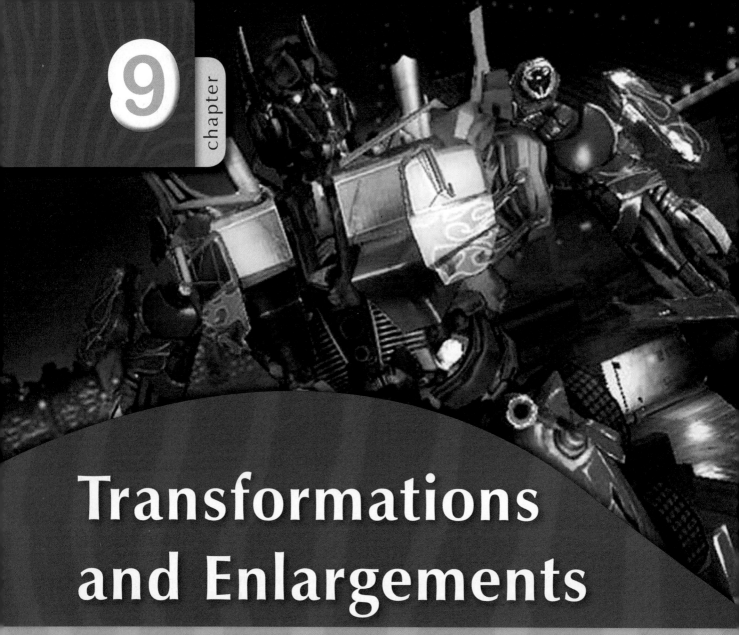

9 chapter

Transformations and Enlargements

Learning Outcomes

In this chapter you will learn to:

- Recognise points and objects under different transformations:
    - Translation
    - Central symmetry
    - Axial symmetry
- Locate the centre of symmetry
- Enlarge a rectilinear figure by the ray method, given the centre of enlargement and the scale factor k, where $0 < k < 1$, $k > 1$, $k \in Q$

- Investigate the length BC with respect to $B'C'$ when triangle ABC is enlarged by a scale factor k, centre of enlargement A
- Calculate the scale factor of an enlargement
- Find the centre of an enlargement
- Investigate the effect on area when a region is enlarged by a scale factor k

9.1 TRANSFORMATIONS

We see many examples of shapes being transformed in everyday life. In geometry, a transformation is when a shape's size or position is changed or **transformed**.

The point or shape we start with is called the **object**. The transformed shape is called the **image**.

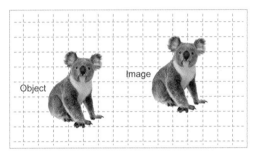

Object   Image

YOU SHOULD REMEMBER...

■ Geometry notation

■ Axial symmetry

■ Transformations

KEY WORDS

■ **Symmetry**

■ **Object**

■ **Image**

■ **Translation**

■ **Central symmetry**

■ **Enlargement**

■ **Centre of enlargement**

■ **Scale factor**

■ **Similar**

■ **Area**

Translation

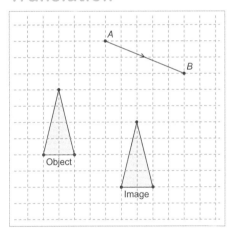

Object

Image

> A **translation** is when a point or shape is moved in a straight line. A translation moves every point the same distance and in the same direction without changing the orientation of the shape or rotating it.

Each point in the object shape has been moved the same distance as $|AB|$, parallel to AB and in the direction of A to B.

> In a translation, the image and the object are identical and face the same way.

We can move the triangle ABC under the translation $\overrightarrow{PQ}$.

> If $\triangle ABC$ is the object, then the image can be labelled as $\triangle A'B'C'$.

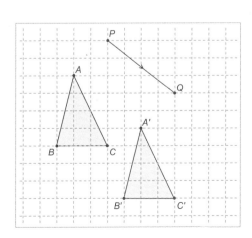

If the triangle *ABC* had been moved or mapped under the translation $\overrightarrow{QP}$, it would have moved in the opposite direction.

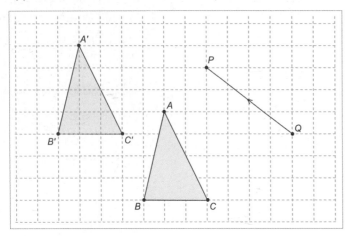

A translation may also be given by using one letter: for example, the translation $\vec{p}$.

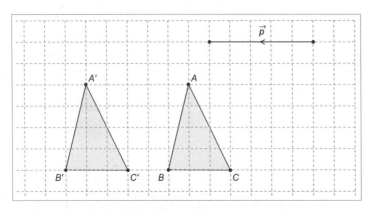

Central Symmetry (Through a Point)

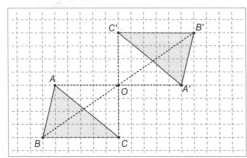

In a **central symmetry**, each point is mapped through the point *O* and reflected out the other side.

$|AO| = |OA'|$, $|BO| = |OB'|$ and $|CO| = |OC'|$

A central symmetry is a reflection through a point.

In a central symmetry, the image will be upside down and facing the object.

Centre of Symmetry

Certain shapes can be mapped onto themselves under a central symmetry in a point. This point is called the **centre of symmetry**.

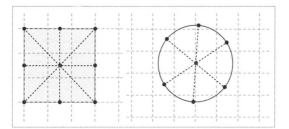

If a shape can be mapped onto itself under a central symmetry in a point, this point is called a **centre of symmetry**.

Not all shapes have a centre of symmetry.

Axial Symmetry (Through a Line)

In an **axial symmetry**, each point is mapped through a line (axis) at right angles and reflected the same distance out the other side.

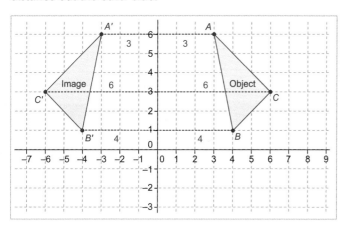

In an axial symmetry in the y-axis, each point is mapped through the y-axis and reflected out the same distance on the other side.

An **axial symmetry** is a reflection in a line or axis. The line acts as a mirror.

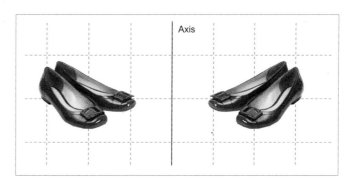

In an axial symmetry, the image and object are the same distance from the axis used, and one is a mirror image of the other.

TRANSFORMATIONS AND ENLARGEMENTS

Worked Example 9.1

The following images are produced by a translation, an axial symmetry in the x-axis and a central symmetry in the origin. Match each image with the correct transformation.

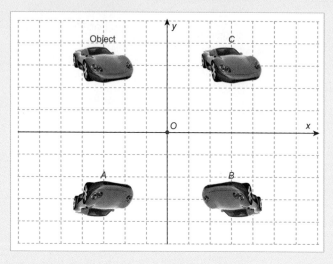

Solution

A: Axial symmetry in the x-axis (mirror image of the object)

B: Central symmetry (upside down and facing the object, each point mapped through the point O)

C: Translation (facing in the same direction as the object, all points moved in a straight line, for the same distance)

Exercise 9.1

1. Identify in each diagram the image of the object under the translation $\overrightarrow{AB}$.

(i)

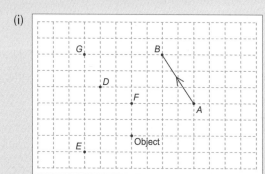

(ii)

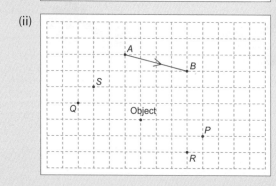

(iii)

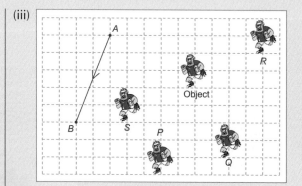

(iv)

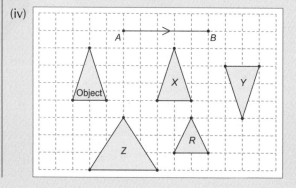

2. Identify in each diagram the image of the object under a central symmetry in the point O.

(i)

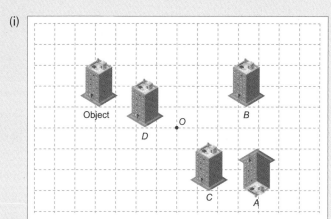

(ii)

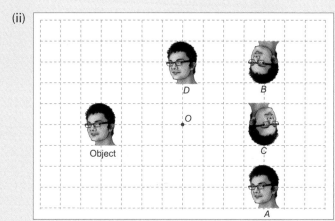

(iii)

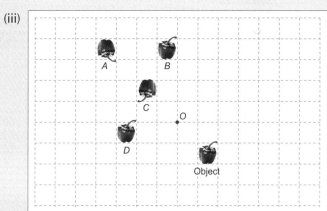

(iv)

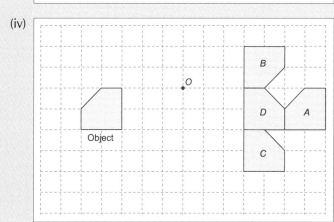

3. Show the centre of symmetry (if it exists) of each of these shapes, and label with the letter C.

(i)

(iii)

(ii)

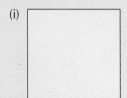

(iv)

4. Identify in each diagram the image of the object under an axial symmetry in the named axis.

(i) Axial symmetry in the x-axis

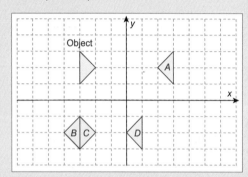

(iii) Axial symmetry in the y-axis

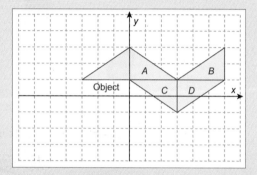

(ii) Axial symmetry in the x-axis

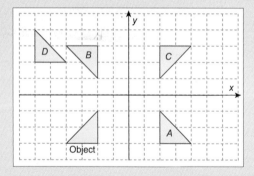

(iv) Axial symmetry in the y-axis

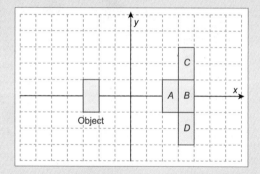

5. In each case, three images labelled A, B and C are the images of the object under a transformation. The transformations could be a translation, an axial symmetry or a central symmetry.

For each image, state which transformation is used.

(i)

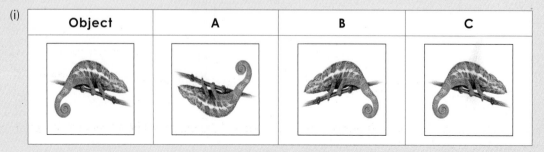

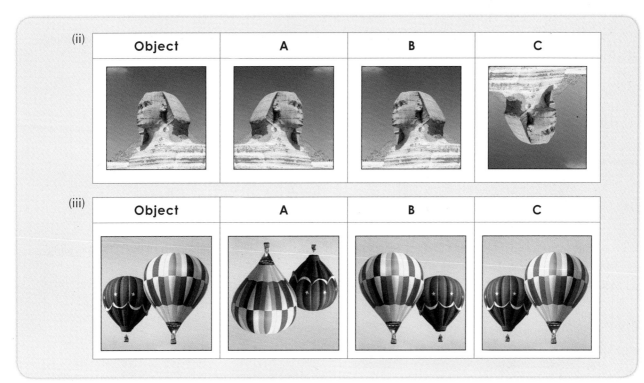

| (ii) | Object | A | B | C |

| (iii) | Object | A | B | C |

9.2 ENLARGEMENTS

We see many examples of **enlargements** in the modern world.

> An **enlargement** is a transformation in which both the size and the position of a shape changes.

In geometry, when we enlarge a figure we need to know two things:

- The **centre of enlargement**
- The **scale factor**, k

> The **centre of enlargement** is the point from which the enlargement is constructed.

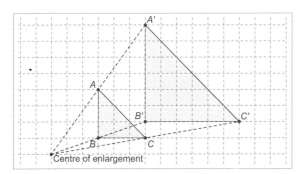

> The **scale factor**, k, is the number by which the object is enlarged.

If we enlarge a shape by a scale factor of k, then each side of the image will be k times the length of the corresponding side of the object.

A scale factor of 2 means that the length of each image side will be twice the length of the corresponding object side.

> Any scale factor *k* which is greater than 1 will result in the image being bigger than the object.

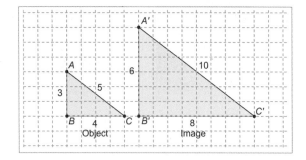

A scale factor of $\frac{1}{2}$ would mean that the length of each image side will be $\frac{1}{2}$ the length of the corresponding object side.

> Any scale factor that is greater than 0 and less than 1 will result in the image being smaller than the object.
> This is still described as an enlargement.

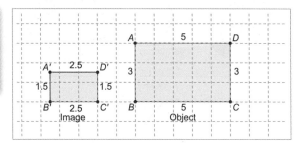

Worked Example 9.2

Enlarge the triangle *ABC* by a scale factor of 3, with a centre of enlargement *O*.

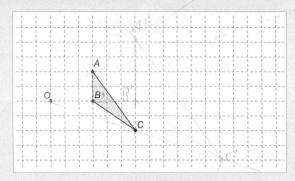

Solution

Draw rays from *O*, the centre of enlargement, though each of the vertices of the shape.

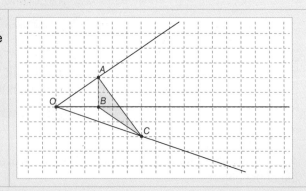

Using a compass or ruler, measure the distance |OA|. |OA| = 1.4 cm	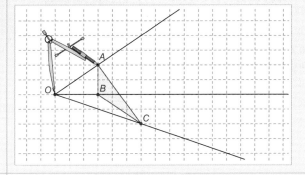
Mark off a new point A' such that |OA'| is three times the distance |OA|. |OA'| = 3 |OA| = 3 × 1.4 |OA'| = 4.2 cm	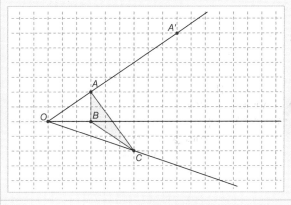
Measure |OB|. Mark off a new point B' such that |OB'| is three times the distance |OB|.	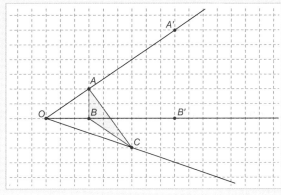
Measure |OC|. Mark off a new point C' such that |OC'| is three times the distance |OC|.	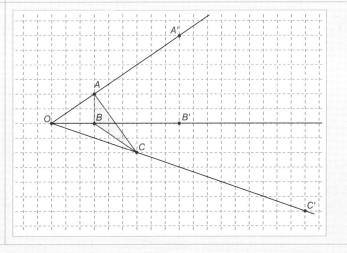

Draw the triangle $A'B'C'$.

The triangle $A'B'C'$ is the image of the triangle ABC under the required enlargement.

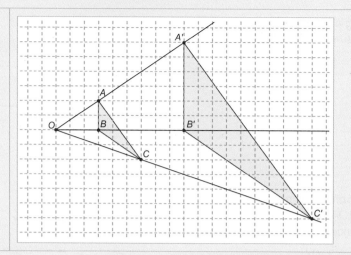

Worked Example 9.3

Enlarge the rectangle $PQRS$ by a scale factor of $\frac{1}{2}$ with a centre of enlargement O.

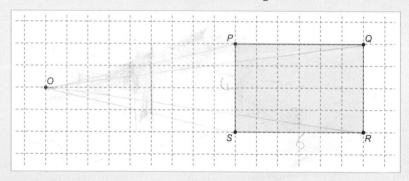

Solution

Draw rays from O though each of the vertices of the shape.	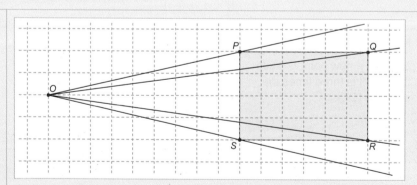
Using a compass or ruler, measure the distance $\lvert OP \rvert$.	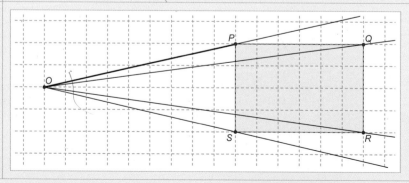

Mark off a new point P' such that $\|OP'\|$ is half $\|OP\|$.	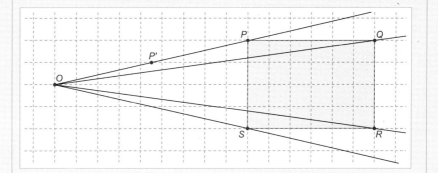
Repeat for the other vertices Q, R and S.	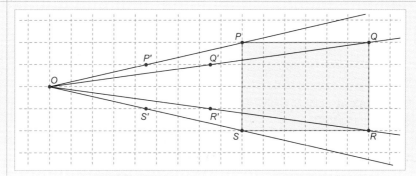
Draw the rectangle $P'Q'R'S'$. The rectangle $P'Q'R'S'$ is the image of the rectangle $PQRS$ under the required enlargement.	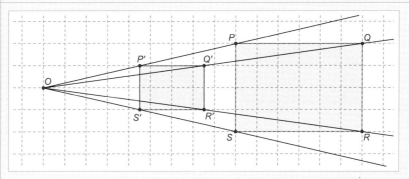

We sometimes encounter enlargements where the centre of enlargement is a point either on or inside the object.

Worked Example 9.4

Enlarge the triangle ABC by a scale factor of 2 with a centre of enlargement A.

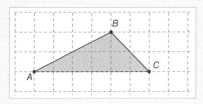

Draw rays from *A* through each of the remaining vertices.

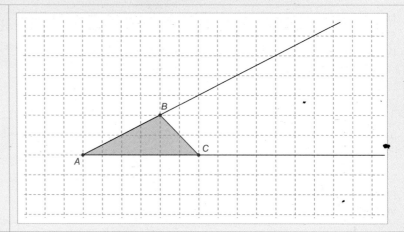

Using a compass or ruler, find |*AB*|.

Mark off a new point *B'* such that |*AB'*| = 2|*AB*|.

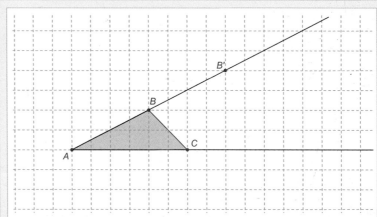

Find |*AC*|.

Mark off a new point *C'* such that |*AC'*| = 2|*AC*|.

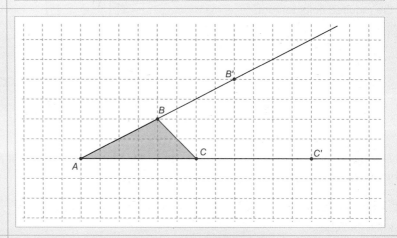

Draw the triangle *AB'C'*.

The triangle *AB'C'* is the image of the triangle *ABC* under the required enlargement.

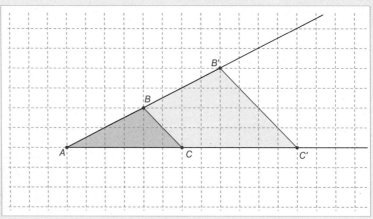

ACTIVITY 9.1

Exercise 9.2

1. Copy the following diagrams onto graph paper, and show the image of each of the shapes under an enlargement with a scale factor of 2 and centre O.

(i)

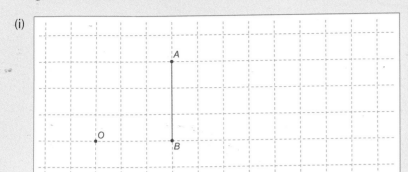

(ii)

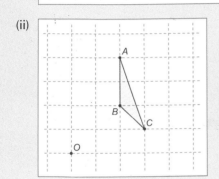

(iv)

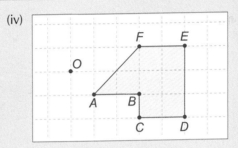

(iii)

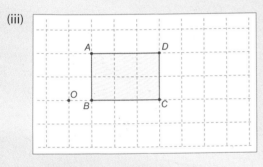

(v)

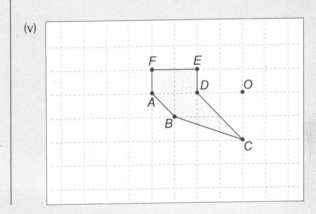

2. Copy the following diagrams onto graph paper, and show the image of each of the shapes under an enlargement with a scale factor of $\frac{1}{2}$ and centre P.

(i)

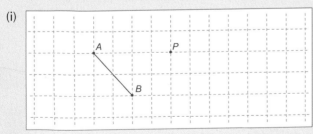

(ii)

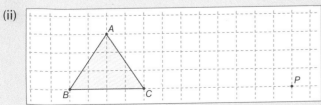

(iii)

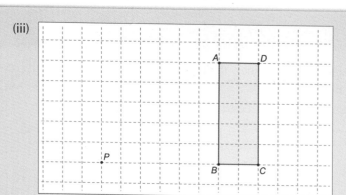

(iv)

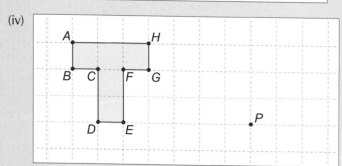

(v)

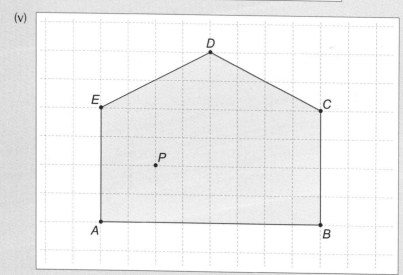

3. Copy the following diagrams onto graph paper, and show the image of each of the shapes under an enlargement with a scale factor of 1.5 and centre *A*.

(i)

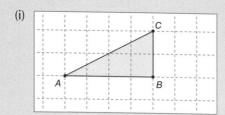

(ii)

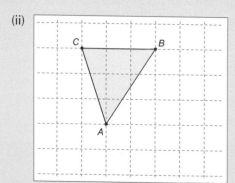

(iii)

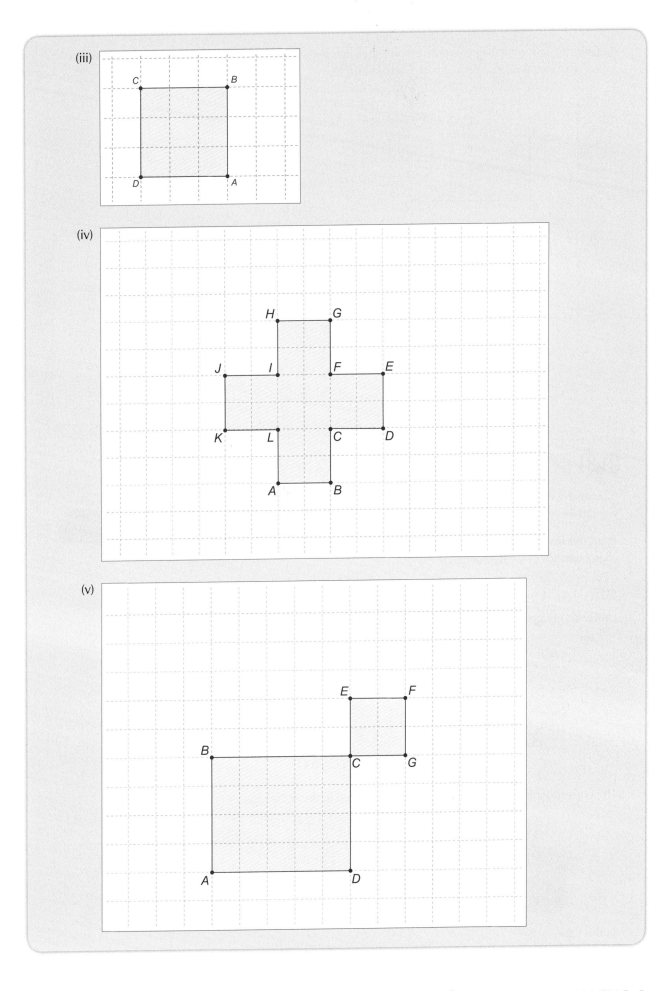

(iv)

(v)

4. Copy the following diagrams onto graph paper, and show the image of each of the shapes under an enlargement with a scale factor of $\frac{1}{3}$ and centre Q.

(i)

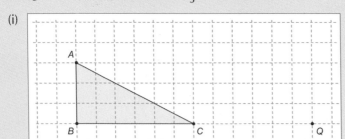

(ii)

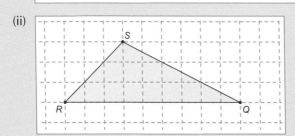

(iii)

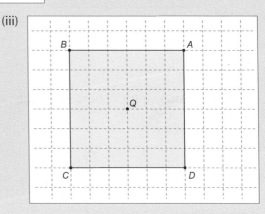

9.3 PROPERTIES OF ENLARGEMENTS

Now that we have explored how enlargements are constructed, we can investigate the various properties of enlargements.

ACTIVITIES 9.2, 9.3

From our investigations, we can determine the following characteristics of enlargements.

Similarity

Under an enlargement, **the object and image are similar to each other**.

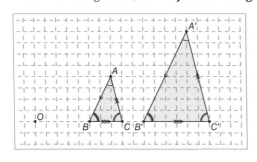

$|\angle ABC| = |\angle A'B'C'|$

$|\angle ACB| = |\angle A'C'B'|$

$|\angle BAC| = |\angle B'A'C'|$

$AB \parallel A'B'$

$AC \parallel A'C'$

$BC \parallel B'C'$

The corresponding sides of the object and image are in the same ratio:

FORMULA

$$\frac{|AB|}{|A'B'|} = \frac{|AC|}{|A'C'|} = \frac{|BC|}{|B'C'|}$$

In this case:

$$\frac{|AB|}{|A'B'|} = \frac{4.5}{9} = \frac{1}{2} \qquad \frac{|AC|}{|A'C'|} = \frac{4.1}{8.2} = \frac{1}{2} \qquad \frac{|BC|}{|B'C'|} = \frac{3}{6} = \frac{1}{2}$$

Find the Centre of Enlargement

To find the centre of enlargement, we draw lines through the corresponding vertices of the object and image.

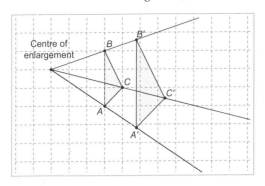 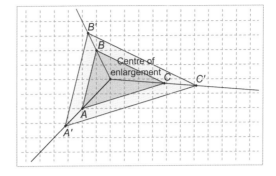

The point where these lines intersect is called the **centre of enlargement**.

> We usually only need to connect two pairs of corresponding vertices to find the centre of enlargement.

Find the Scale Factor

To find the scale factor, we measure the length of a side of the image and the length of the corresponding side in the object.

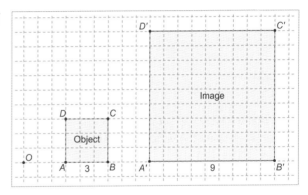

FORMULA

Scale factor $(k) = \dfrac{\text{Image length}}{\text{Object length}}$

In this example:

Scale factor $= \dfrac{9}{3} = 3 = k$

> It is important to remember that it is **Image length ÷ Object length** that will give us the scale factor.

Scale Factor and Area

If an object is enlarged by a scale factor of k, then the area of the image will be increased by a factor of k^2. This can be written as the following formula:

FORMULA

$$\dfrac{\text{Image area}}{\text{Object area}} = k^2$$

or

Image area $= k^2 \times$ Object area

TRANSFORMATIONS AND ENLARGEMENTS

For the example shown:

Image area = $(3)^2 \times$ Object area

$= 9 \times 9$

$= 81$ units

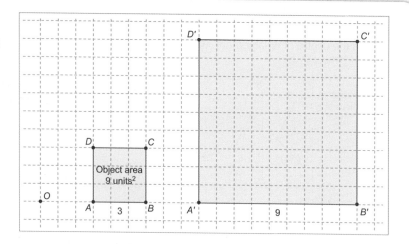

Worked Example 9.5

$\triangle ABC$ is the image of $\triangle PQR$ under an enlargement of scale factor k and centre O.

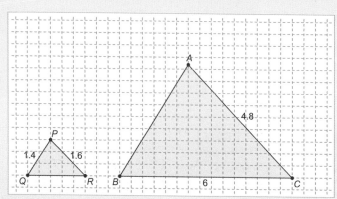

(i)   Find the value of k.

(ii) Find the length of $[AB]$.

(iii) Find the length of $[QR]$.

(iv) The area of $\triangle ABC$ is 10 square units; find, correct to one decimal place, the area of $\triangle PQR$.

Solution

(i) The value of k

$$k = \frac{\text{Image length}}{\text{Object length}} = \frac{4.8}{1.6} = 3$$

(ii) $|AB|$

$$k = 3$$

$$\therefore |AB| = 3 \times |PQ|$$

$$|AB| = 3 \times 1.4$$

$$|AB| = 4.2$$

We could also have used the properties of similar triangles to find $|AB|$:

$$\frac{|AB|}{|PQ|} = \frac{|AC|}{|PR|}$$

$$\frac{|AB|}{1.4} = \frac{4.8}{1.6} \Rightarrow \frac{|AB|}{1.4} = \frac{3}{1}$$

$$|AB| = 3 \times 1.4$$

$$|AB| = 4.2$$

(iii) $|QR|$

$$k = 3$$

$$\therefore |BC| = 3 \times |QR|$$

$$\Rightarrow |QR| = \frac{1}{3} \times |BC|$$

> We are going from image to object here, so the scale factor is reversed.

$$|QR| = \frac{1}{3} \times 6$$

$$|QR| = 2$$

Again, we could have used the properties of similar triangles to find $|QR|$:

$$\frac{|QR|}{6} = \frac{1.6}{4.8}$$

$$\frac{|QR|}{6} = \frac{1}{3}$$

$$3|QR| = 6$$

$$|QR| = 2$$

(iv) The area of $\triangle ABC$ is 10 square units; find, correct to one decimal place, the area of $\triangle PQR$.

We remember that $\dfrac{\text{Image area}}{\text{Object area}} = k^2$, and let the area of $\triangle PQR = x$.

$$\Rightarrow \frac{10}{x} = 3^2$$

$$\frac{10}{x} = 9$$

$$9x = 10$$

$$x = 1.1 \text{ square units (one decimal place)}$$

 Worked Example 9.6

The polygon $A'B'C'D'E'F'G'$ is the image of the polygon $ABCDEFG$ under an enlargement of scale factor k and centre O.

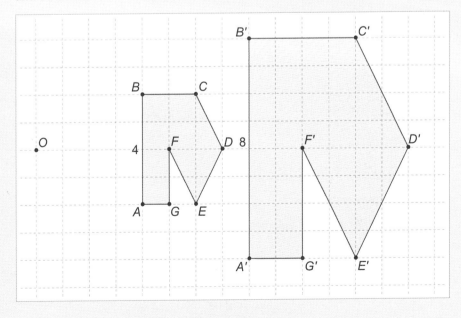

(i) Find the value of k (scale factor).

(ii) Find the area of the polygon $A'B'C'D'E'F'G'$ if the area of the polygon $ABCDEFG$ is 9 sq units.

Solution

(i) The value of k (scale factor).

$$k = \frac{\text{Image length}}{\text{Object length}} = \frac{8}{4} = 2$$

(ii) Find the area of the polygon $A'B'C'D'E'F'G'$, if the area of the polygon $ABCDEFG$ is 9 sq units.

> **Remember**
>
> $$\frac{\text{Image area}}{\text{Object area}} = k^2$$

Let image area $= x$, and $k = 2$

$$\frac{x}{9} = (2)^2$$

$$\frac{x}{9} = 4$$

$$x = 9 \times 4$$

$$x = 36 \text{ sq units} \implies \text{Image area} = 36 \text{ sq units}$$

Exercise 9.3

1. Copy the following diagram onto graph paper. $\triangle A'B'C'$ is an enlargement of $\triangle ABC$.

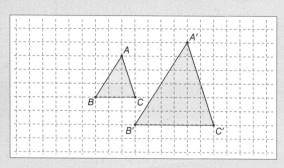

   (i) Find the centre of enlargement.

   (ii) Find the scale factor.

2. Copy this diagram of two rectangles onto graph paper. $A'B'C'D'$ is the image of the rectangle $ABCD$ under an enlargement.

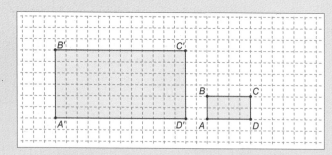

   (i) Find the centre of enlargement.

   (ii) Find the scale factor, k.

   (iii) Show that the ratio
   Area of $A'B'C'D'$: Area of $ABCD$
   $= k^2 : 1$.

3. The square $PQRS$ is the image of $ABCD$ under an enlargement.

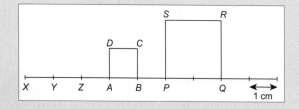

   (i) Find the centre of enlargement.

   (ii) Find the scale factor.

   (iii) Find the ratio
   Area of $PQRS$: Area of $ABCD$.

4. The rectangle *ABCD* is the image of *MNSO* under an enlargement.

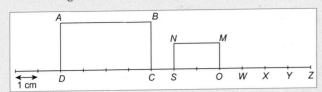

(i) Find the centre of enlargement.

(ii) Find the scale factor.

5. The regular pentagon *A'B'C'D'E'* is the image of the polygon *ABCDE* under an enlargement with a scale factor of 2.5 and with centre *F*.

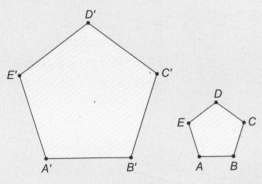

(i) If $|AB| = 2$ cm, find $|A'B'|$.

(ii) If the area of the pentagon *ABCDE* is 6.88 cm², find the area of the image *A'B'C'D'E'*.

6. The rectangle *D'E'F'G'* is the image of the rectangle *DEFG* under an enlargement with centre *O*.

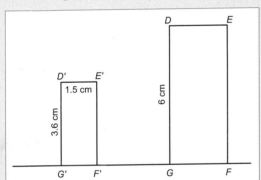

(i) Find the scale factor.

(ii) Find $|DE|$.

(iii) Write as a fraction in its simplest form:

$$\frac{\text{Area of rectangle } D'E'F'G'}{\text{Area of rectangle } DEFG}$$

7. The polygon *A'B'C'D'E'F'* is the image of the polygon *ABCDEF* under an enlargement with centre *O*. All measurements are in centimetres.

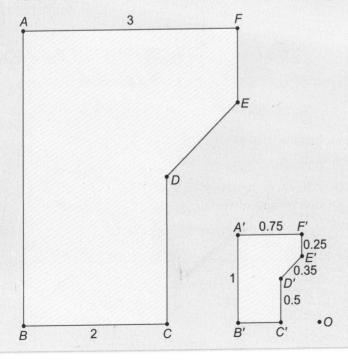

(i) Find the scale factor.

(ii) Find the lengths of all the missing sides.

(iii) If the area of the polygon *ABCDEF* is 9.5 cm², find the area of the polygon *A'B'C'D'E'F'*.

8. $O(0,0)$, $A(0,1)$, $B(2,0)$ are the vertices of $\triangle OAB$.

$P(-7,-1)$, $Q(-7,2)$, $R(-1,-1)$ are the vertices of $\triangle PQR$.

(i) Show these two triangles on the x–y co-ordinate plane.

(ii) If $\triangle PQR$ is the image of $\triangle OAB$ under an enlargement, with centre C and of scale factor k, find the co-ordinates of C and the value of k.

9. The trapezoid $A'B'C'D'$ is the image of the trapezoid $ABCD$ under an enlargement. The scale of the graph paper is 1 square has an area of 4 cm².

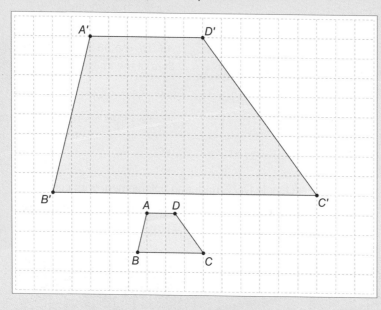

(i) Find the centre of enlargement.

(ii) Find the scale factor.

(iii) Find the ratio area $ABCD$: area $A'B'C'D'$.

10. The rectangle $P'Q'R'S$ is an enlargement of the rectangle $PQRS$.

$|RS| = 5$ cm, $|PS| = 8$ cm and $|Q'P'| = 15$ cm.

(i) Find the centre of enlargement.

(ii) Find the scale factor.

(iii) Find $|Q'R'|$.

(iv) Find $|PP'|$.

(v) Find the area of the region coloured yellow.

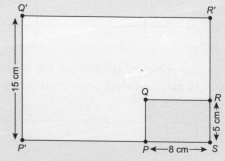

11. The triangle ADE is the image of the triangle ABC under an enlargement of scale factor k and centre A.

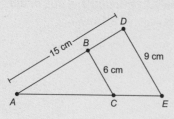

$|BC| = 6$ cm, $|AD| = 15$ cm and $|DE| = 9$ cm.

(i) Find the scale factor, k.

(ii) Find $|AB|$.

(iii) The area of the triangle ADE is 90 cm². Find the area of the triangle ABC.

(iv) Write down the area of the region $BCED$.

12. The cylinder shown is the image of a cylinder under an enlargement of scale factor 5.

If the surface area of the image is 50 cm², find the surface area of the object.

13. ΔPQR is an enlargement of ΔXYR. Both triangles are right-angled, as shown.

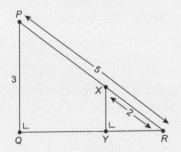

(i) Name the centre of enlargement.

(ii) Write down the value of k, the scale factor.

(iii) Find |QR|.

(iv) Find |XY| and |YR|.

(v) Calculate the ratio Area ΔPQR : Area ΔXYR.

14. ΔADE is the enlargement of ΔABC, with centre A and of scale factor k.

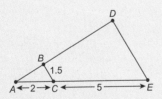

(i) Write down the value of k.

(ii) If |BC| = 1.5, find |DE|.

(iii) If |DB| = 3.5, find |AB|.

(iv) Write down the ratio Area ΔADE : Area ΔABC.

15. ABCD is a square of side 6 units. WXYZ, as shown, is a square of side 2 units.

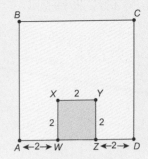

If ABCD is an enlargement of WXYZ, write down:

(i) The scale factor of the enlargement

(ii) The location of the centre of enlargement

(iii) The ratio |BD| : |XZ|

(iv) The ratio Area ABCD : Area WXYZ

(v) The ratio Perimeter ABCD : Perimeter WXYZ

16. A rectangular skyscraper is shown.

The skyscraper is 210 m tall, 30 m long and 45 m wide. A model of this skyscraper is to be built in the scale 1 : 2,000.

(i) What dimensions should the model be?

(ii) If the dimensions of the model were halved, what would be the scale of the model?

17. (i) Construct an equilateral triangle MNO of side 6 cm.

(ii) Construct the image of the triangle MNO under the enlargement of scale factor 1.75 and centre O.

(iii) Given that the area of the triangle MNO is $9\sqrt{3}$ cm², find the area of the image (of the triangle) to the nearest whole number.

18. The right-angled triangle *ABC* is the image of the triangle *DEC* under the enlargement of centre *C* and scale factor *k*.

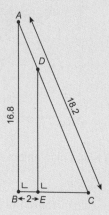

Find:

(i) |*EC*|

(ii) The scale factor, *k*

(iii) |*DE*|

(iv) The area of the triangle *DEC*

(v) The area of the figure *ADEB*

19. The triangle *PQ'R'* is the image of triangle *PQR* by an enlargement with centre *P*, as shown.

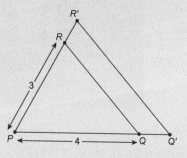

Given that |*PR'*| = 3.6, calculate:

(i) The scale factor

(ii) |*RR'*|

(iii) |*RQ*| : |*R'Q'*|, written in the form *m* : *n*, where *m, n* ∈ N

(iv) Area Δ*PQ'R'* : Area Δ*PQR*

20. A cardboard model of the container shown is built with dimensions 24 cm long, 10 cm high and 10 cm wide.

(i) Calculate the surface area (external) of the cardboard container.

(ii) Calculate the volume of the cardboard container.

The actual container is to be built using a scale of 1 : 25 and will be made of metal.

(iii) Calculate the surface area (external) of the metal container.

(iv) Calculate the volume of the metal container.

(v) Find as a ratio, the surface area of the model : surface area of the container. What do you notice?

(vi) Find as a ratio, the volume of the model : volume of the container. What do you notice?

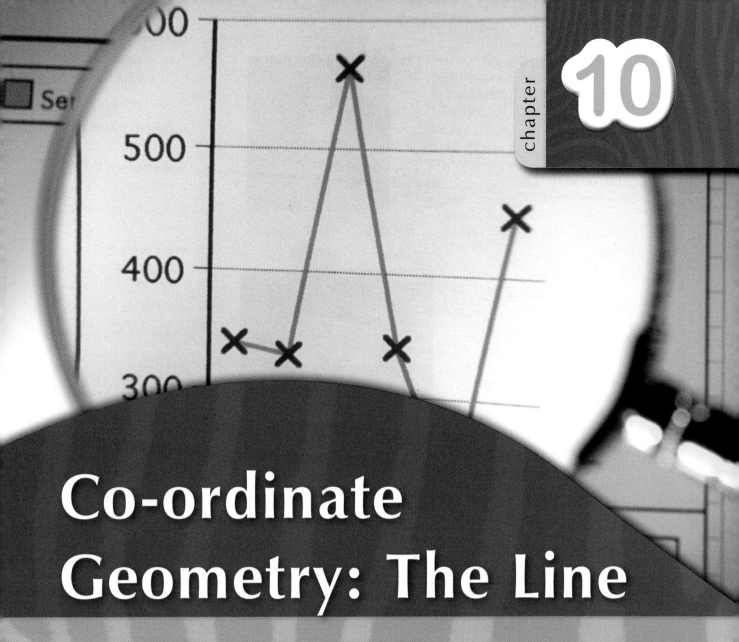

chapter 10

Co-ordinate Geometry: The Line

Learning Outcomes

In this chapter you will learn how to:

⮕ Find the distance between two points

⮕ Find the midpoint of two points

⮕ Find the slope of a line

⮕ Find the equation of a line

⮕ Find the point of intersection of two given lines

⮕ Find the equations of lines parallel to and perpendicular to a given line and through a given point

⮕ Solve real-life problems using co-ordinate geometry

⮕ Find the area of a triangle

Co-ordinate geometry was invented by the French mathematician René Descartes (1596–1650). His work on co-ordinate geometry first appeared in 1631 in a book entitled *Discourse on Method*. Descartes' co-ordinate system was much easier to work with than Euclid's geometry, and even today it is the foundation for many branches of modern mathematics. It is sometimes called Cartesian geometry in honour of Descartes.

René Descartes

Co-ordinate geometry has applications in such diverse areas as geography, astronomy, engineering and economics. For example, when you look up the location of a place on a map, it is usually given as a set of co-ordinates. The location of a ship at sea is determined by longitude and latitude, which is an application of the co-ordinate system to the curved surface of the earth. Astronomers can

The Crab Nebula viewed from the NASA Hubble Space Telescope

precisely locate even the most distant objects, such as stars or galaxies, by referring to their co-ordinates.

In co-ordinate geometry, we refer to the plane on which we work as the x–y plane, or the Cartesian plane.

YOU SHOULD REMEMBER...

- The theorem of Pythagoras
- How to find the area of a parallelogram
- How to find the area of a triangle
- How to find the area of a rectangle
- A circle is the set of all points that are a fixed distance from a given point
- Distance = Speed × Time

KEY WORDS

- **Distance**
- **Midpoint**
- **Slope of a line**
- **Equation of a line**

10.1 DISTANCE BETWEEN TWO POINTS

In this section, we will derive a very important formula for finding the distance between any two points on the x–y plane. Finding the distance between two points A and B is the equivalent of finding the length of the line segment [AB]. Therefore, the distance formula will also be used to find the length of a line segment.

ACTIVITY 10.1

In Activity 10.1, you will derive the formula for the distance between two points.

FORMULA

$$|AB| = \sqrt{(x_2 - x_1)^2 + (y_2 - y_1)^2}$$

This formula appears on page 18 of the *Formulae and Tables*.

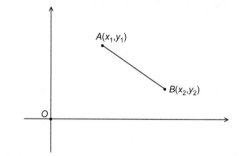

Worked Example 10.1

Plot the following co-ordinates and say in which quadrant each point lies:

$A(-2,1)$ $B(5,2)$ $C(-3,-4)$ $D(5,-2)$

Solution

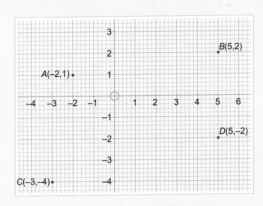

A lies in the second quadrant. C lies in the third quadrant.
B lies in the first quadrant. D lies in the fourth quadrant.

Worked Example 10.2

Find the distance between $A(-1,1)$ and $B(20,21)$.

Solution

$D = \sqrt{(x_2 - x_1)^2 + (y_2 - y_1)^2}$ $D = \sqrt{(20 + 1)^2 + (21 - 1)^2}$

$x_1 = -1$ $y_1 = 1$ $= \sqrt{(21)^2 + (20)^2}$

$x_2 = 20$ $y_2 = 21$ $= \sqrt{441 + 400}$

$= \sqrt{841}$

$= 29$ $\therefore |AB| = 29$

Exercise 10.1

1. Write down the co-ordinates of the points that are plotted on the x–y axis.

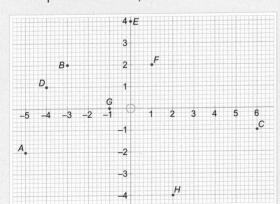

2. Name the quadrant in which each of the following points lies:

   (i) $(-4,2)$ (v) $(5,5)$ (ix) $(2,20)$

   (ii) $(3,-8)$ (vi) $(3,2)$ (x) $(-2,-8)$

   (iii) $(-3,6)$ (vii) $(3,-4)$

   (iv) $(-2,-5)$ (viii) $(-5,-15)$

3. On which axis do the following points lie:

   (i) $(-5,0)$ (iv) $(5,0)$ (vii) $(0,-100)$

   (ii) $(0,4)$ (v) $(100,0)$

   (iii) $(0,-2)$ (vi) $(-300,0)$

4. Find the value of x and the value of y for each of the following cases if A(x,y) are the co-ordinates of the point A on the x–y plane:

   (i) A lies on the positive x-axis a distance of 3 units from (0,0).

   (ii) A lies on the negative x-axis a distance of 4 units from (0,0).

   (iii) A lies on the positive y-axis a distance of 5 units from (0,–2).

   (iv) A lies on the negative y-axis a distance of 4 units from (0,2).

5. Find the distance between the following pairs of points:

   (i) (2,2) and (3,5)　　(iii) (3,8) and (5,8)

   (ii) (1,5) and (12,11)　　(iv) (5,2) and (5,6)

6. Find the distance between the following pairs of points:

   (i) (–1,3) and (5,6)

   (ii) (4,–1) and (2,1)

   (iii) (7,–4) and (0,0)

   (iv) (–2,–2) and (3,–6)

7. Find |AB| in each of the following:

   (i) A(5,2) and B(2,–4)

   (ii) A(–3,–2) and B(3,–2)

   (iii) A(6,2) and B(–2,1)

   (iv) A(9,7) and B(1,–5)

8. A(0,0), B(12,5), C(17,–7) and D(5,–12) are the vertices of the rhombus ABCD.

   (i) Plot the points A, B, C and D.

   (ii) Find the length of the side [AB].

   (iii) Find the length of the diagonal [AC].

   (iv) Investigate if |BD| = |AC|.

9. A(–2,–2), B(2,2), C(3,0) and D(–1,–4) are the vertices of a parallelogram ABCD.

   (i) Plot the points A, B, C and D.

   (ii) Show that |AB| = |DC|.

   (iii) Find the length of the side [BC].

   (iv) Find the length of the diagonal [AC].

   (v) Are the diagonals of ABCD equal in length? Explain your answer.

10. A(0,–2), B(3,2) and C(6,6) are the co-ordinates of three points.

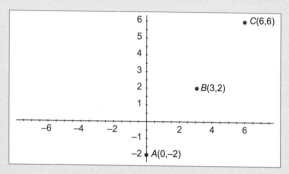

A, B and C will lie on a straight line if |AB| + |BC| = |AC|. Show that the points A, B and C lie on a straight line.

11. Show that the triangle with vertices A(1,3), B(2,5) and C(3,2) is an isosceles triangle.

12. Show that the triangle with vertices W(0,0), X(1,√3), Y(2,0) is an equilateral triangle.

13. If a circle is drawn with centre (0,0) and radius length 5, would (3,3) be inside or outside the circle? Explain your answer.

14. A circle has centre C(3,4), and the point A(–1,2) is on its circumference. Calculate |CA|, its radius length.

15. A(5,0), B(–4,3) and C(4,4) are the co-ordinates of three points.

   (i) Which of these points is furthest from the origin (0,0)?

   (ii) On graph paper, plot the points A, B and C.

   (iii) Explain why the points A(5,0) and B(–4,3) lie on the circle of radius length 5 and with its centre at the origin (0,0).

16. A(3,5) and B(7,k) are two points. If |AB| = 5, find two possible values for k.

17. The distance between the points X(5,k) and Y(–3,1) is √65. Find two possible values for k.

10.2 MIDPOINT OF A LINE SEGMENT

The point that bisects a line segment is called the midpoint of the line segment. If C is the midpoint of $[AB]$, then $|AC| = |CB|$.

In Activity 10.2, you will derive a formula for finding the midpoint of a line segment.

 **ACTIVITY 10.2**

FORMULA

$$\text{Midpoint} = \left(\frac{x_1 + x_2}{2}, \frac{y_1 + y_2}{2}\right)$$

This formula appears on page 18 of the *Formulae and Tables*.

 Worked Example 10.3

$A(11,-2)$ and $B(-3,14)$ are two points. Find the midpoint of $[AB]$.

Solution

$x_1 = 11 \qquad x_2 = -3 \qquad y_1 = -2 \qquad y_2 = 14$

$$\text{Midpoint} = \left(\frac{x_1 + x_2}{2}, \frac{y_1 + y_2}{2}\right)$$

$$\text{Midpoint of } [AB] = \left(\frac{11 + (-3)}{2}, \frac{-2 + 14}{2}\right)$$

$$= \left(\frac{8}{2}, \frac{12}{2}\right)$$

$$= (4,6)$$

 Worked Example 10.4

$A(11,-2)$ and $C(-3,14)$ are two points. Find the co-ordinates of B, if C is the midpoint of $[AB]$.

Solution

Method 1

If (x_2, y_2) are the co-ordinates of the point B, then:

$$\left(\frac{11 + x_2}{2}, \frac{(-2) + y_2}{2}\right) = (-3,14)$$

$$\therefore \frac{11 + x_2}{2} = -3 \quad \text{and} \quad \frac{-2 + y_2}{2} = 14$$

$$\therefore 11 + x_2 = -6 \quad \text{and} \quad -2 + y_2 = 28$$

$$\therefore x_2 = -6 - 11 \quad \text{and} \quad y_2 = 28 + 2$$

$$\therefore x_2 = -17 \quad \text{and} \quad y_2 = 30$$

The co-ordinates of the point B are $(-17,30)$.

Method 2

The second method uses the translation $\overrightarrow{AC}$ to translate C to B.

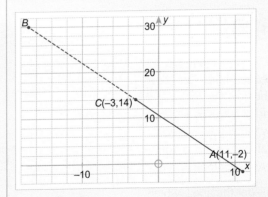

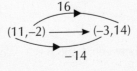

Rule
Subtract 14 from x
Add 16 to y

$(-3,14) \longrightarrow (-17,30)$

B has co-ordinates $(-17,30)$.

Exercise 10.2

1. Find the midpoints of the line segments joining the following pairs of points:

   (i) (4,2) and (6,4)   (iii) (3,7) and (9,9)

   (ii) (1,7) and (7,5)   (iv) (1,2) and (3,6)

2. Find the midpoints of the line segments joining the following pairs of points:

   (i) (−1,3) and (7,6)   (iii) (7,−4) and (0,0)

   (ii) (4,−1) and (2,1)   (iv) (−2,−2) and (3,−6)

3. Find the midpoint of [AB] in each of the following:

   (i) A(2,2) and B(3,−5)

   (ii) A(1,−6) and B(−3,−2)

   (iii) A(5,3) and B(2,1)

   (iv) A(6,−7) and B(−1,−5)

4. The line k bisects the line segment [AB].

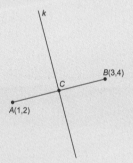

   Find the co-ordinates of the point C.

5. Show that the midpoint of P(3,−7) and Q(5,7) lies on the x-axis.

6. [AB] is a diameter of the circle shown below.

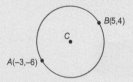

   (i) Find the co-ordinates of the centre of the circle.

   (ii) Find the radius length of the circle.

7. A(1,3) and B(5,−7) are the co-ordinates of two points.

   (i) Find M, the midpoint of [AB].

   (ii) Verify that |AM| = |MB|.

8. A(4,y) and B(x,7) are two points. If (3,5) is the midpoint of [AB], find the value of x and the value of y.

9. For each of the following, find the co-ordinates of B, if C is the midpoint of [AB].

   (i) A(2,2), C(3,−5)   (iii) A(6,3), C(2,2)

   (ii) A(−1,−2), C(4,−2)   (iv) A(6,7), C(−1,−4)

10. A(−2,y) and B(x,11) are two points. If (−1,3) is the midpoint of [AB], find the value of x and the value of y.

10.3 SLOPE OF A LINE

The slope of a line is a measure of the 'steepness' of the line. We measure the slope of a line by finding how much the line rises or falls as we move from left to right along it.

Consider the line l, which contains the points A(1,1) and B(4,3).

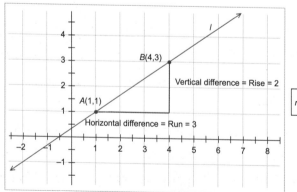

The horizontal difference between A and B is 3. We sometimes call this number the **run**.

The vertical difference between A and B is 2. This number is called the **rise**.

The slope of l is $\frac{rise}{run} = \frac{2}{3}$. We use the letter m to denote slope; therefore, $m = \frac{2}{3}$ for our line l.

Consider the line k, which contains the points $C(-2,3)$ and $D(2,1)$.

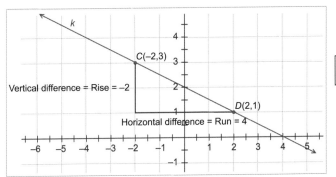

The horizontal difference (the run) between C and D is 4. The vertical difference (the rise) between C and D is -2. The rise is negative here, as we are dropping down from C to D.

The slope of k is: $m = \frac{\text{rise}}{\text{run}} = \frac{-2}{4} = -\frac{1}{2}$.

The slope is negative because the line goes down from left to right.

In Activity 10.3, you will derive the formula for finding the slope of a line:

FORMULA

$$\text{Slope} = m = \frac{y_2 - y_1}{x_2 - x_1}$$

This formula appears on page 18 of the *Formulae and Tables*.

ACTIVITY 10.3

Worked Example 10.5

Find the slope of the line containing the points $G(-3,-5)$ and $H(3,4)$.

Solution

$x_1 = -3 \qquad y_1 = -5$

$x_2 = 3 \qquad y_2 = 4$

$m = \frac{y_2 - y_1}{x_2 - x_1}$

$m = \frac{4 - (-5)}{3 - (-3)}$

$m = \frac{4 + 5}{3 + 3}$

$m = \frac{9}{6} = \frac{3}{2}$

Exercise 10.3

1. Find the slope of the line which passes through these pairs of points:

   (i) $(3,3)$ and $(4,6)$ (iii) $(5,8)$ and $(6,8)$

   (ii) $(2,6)$ and $(4,2)$ (iv) $(3,3)$ and $(4,7)$

2. Find the slope of the line which passes through these pairs of points:

   (i) $(0,6)$ and $(5,7)$ (iii) $(2,-4)$ and $(0,0)$

   (ii) $(4,-2)$ and $(1,0)$ (iv) $(-6,-3)$ and $(3,-5)$

3. Find the slope of the line which passes through these pairs of points:

   (i) $A(0,1)$ and $B(4,-3)$

   (ii) $A(-2,-3)$ and $B(4,-1)$

   (iii) $A(7,5)$ and $B(3,-2)$

   (iv) $A(5,8)$ and $B(-1,-3)$

4. Find the slope of each of these lines.

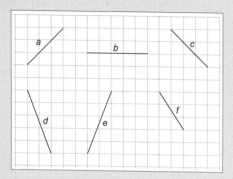

5. Match the correct line with the given slopes.

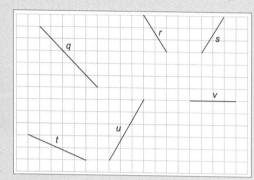

Slope	Line	Slope	Line
$\frac{5}{3}$		0	
$-\frac{2}{5}$		$\frac{3}{2}$	
-1		$-\frac{3}{2}$	

6.

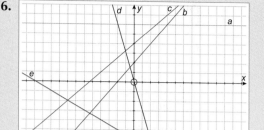

(i) Which line has a slope of $\frac{3}{4}$?

(ii) Find the slopes of the other lines on the diagram.

7. Using the same axes and scales, draw two lines with slope $\frac{5}{8}$.
What do you notice about the two lines?

8. Using the same axes and scales, draw two lines, one line with slope $-\frac{3}{5}$ and another line with slope $\frac{5}{3}$.
What do you notice about the two lines?

9. $W(-1,3)$, $X(5,4)$, $Y(4,-2)$ and $Z(-2,-3)$ are four points.

(i) Plot the quadrilateral $WXYZ$ on the x–y plane.

(ii) Prove that $WXYZ$ is a parallelogram by showing that opposite sides have the same slope.

10. You are given the following points: $P(1,3)$, $Q(5,3)$, $R(6,-4)$ and $S(2,-4)$.

(i) Verify that $PQRS$ is a parallelogram by showing that opposite sides in the quadrilateral have the same slope.

(ii) Show that $|PQ| = |RS|$ and $|PR| = |QS|$.

(iii) Find M, the midpoint of $[PR]$.

(iv) Verify that M is also the midpoint of $[QS]$.

10.4 THE EQUATION OF A LINE

The equation of a line tells us how the x co-ordinate and the y co-ordinate of every point on the line are related to each other.

For example, consider the equation $x + y = 5$. This equation tells us that, for every point on this line, the x co-ordinate added to the y co-ordinate equals 5. Therefore, points on this line would include (0,5), (5,0), (1,4), (4,1), (2,3), (3,2), (6,−1), (−1,6) and so on.

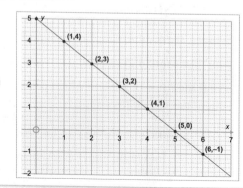

l is the line $2x + y = 8$.

(i) Find three points on l.

(ii) Draw the line.

(iii) Find the slope of l.

(iv) Investigate if $(58, -108)$ is on l.

Solution

(i) To find three points on l, we randomly select values for x and y. Substitute into the given equation to find the corresponding ordinate.

l: $2x + y = 8$

Let $x = 3$.

$2(3) + y = 8$

$6 + y = 8$

$y = 2$

$\therefore$ Point $(3,2)$

Let $y = 0$.

$2x + (0) = 8$

$2x = 8$

$x = 4$

$\therefore$ Point $(4,0)$

Let $x = 5$.

$2(5) + y = 8$

$10 + y = 8$

$y = -2$

$\therefore$ Point $(5,-2)$

(ii)

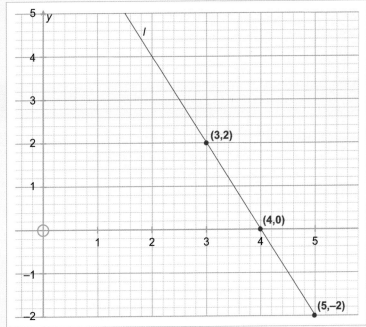

(iii) We can now use any two points on l to find the slope. Let's use $(4,0)$ and $(5,-2)$.

$x_1 = 4 \qquad y_1 = 0$

$x_2 = 5 \qquad y_2 = -2$

$m = \dfrac{y_2 - y_1}{x_2 - x_1}$

$m = \dfrac{-2 - 0}{5 - 4}$

$m = \dfrac{-2}{1} = -2$

(iv) Is $(58, -108)$ on l?

Substitute in for x and y into l:

l: $2x + y = 8$

$2(58) + (-108) = 8$

$116 - 108 = 8$

$8 = 8$

$\therefore$ $(58, -108)$ is on l.

Worked Example 10.7

Find the equation of the line parallel to the y-axis containing the point (3,2).

Solution

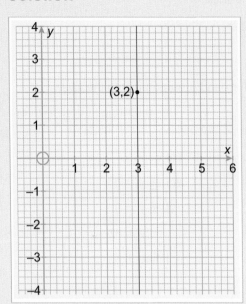

The slope of any line parallel to the y-axis is undefined. Therefore, our approach to finding the equation cannot include a formula containing the slope. Notice that the x-value of all points along the line is 3. We say that the equation of the line is $x = 3$.

Exercise 10.4

1. Which of these lines passes through the point (3,2)?

Line	Insert ✓ or ✗
$2x + y = 8$	
$x + y = 5$	
$2x - y = 4$	
$x - y + 1 = 0$	
$3x + y = 11$	

2. Which of these lines passes through the point (–2,6)?

Line	Insert ✓ or ✗
$x + y = 2$	
$3x + y = 0$	
$2x + y = 2$	
$6{,}000x + 2{,}000y = 0$	
$x - y = 4$	

3. In each case, write down four points on the line and then draw the line.

   (i) $x + y = 6$ (v) $x + 3y = 10$

   (ii) $x + y = 9$ (vi) $x + 2y = 6$

   (iii) $x - y = 4$ (vii) $2x + y = 9$

   (iv) $2x + y = 12$ (viii) $x - y = 4$

4. Investigate if (11,–14) is on the line $2x + y - 8 = 0$.

5. Only one of the points (3,1), (–7,–7), (–1,–2), (8,5) is **not** on the line $4x - 5y = 7$. Which one? Justify your answer.

6. Investigate if (–31,17) is on the line $x + 2y = 2$.

7. k is the line $x + 3y = 6$.

   (i)   Find three points on k.

   (ii) Draw the line.

   (iii) Find the slope of k.

   (iv) Investigate if (–54,20) is on k.

8. *l* is the line $2x - y = 8$.

   (i) Find three points on *l*.

   (ii) Draw the line.

   (iii) Find the slope of *l*.

   (iv) Investigate if (50,43) is on *l*.

9. (4,–1) is on the line $4x + 3y = k$. Find the value of *k*.

10. (–2,5) is on the line $2x - y + k = 0$. Find the value of *k*.

11. (2,–1) is on the line $5x + 3y = c$. Find the value of *c*.

12. The point (*k*,3) is on the line $3x + y = 15$. Find the value of *k*.

13. The point (*c*,–4) is on the line $2x + y = 10$. Find the value of *c*.

14. Find the equation of the line parallel to the *y*-axis and containing the point:

   (i) (5,6)   (iii) (–1,2)

   (ii) (–2,3)   (iv) (2,6)

15. Find the equation of the line parallel to the *x*-axis and containing the point:

   (i) (2,3)   (iii) (6,–3)

   (ii) (5,–2)   (iv) (7,5)

Equations of the Form $y = mx + c$

Many equations that model or represent real-life situations are of the form $y = mx + c$. So, it makes sense to study equations of the form $y = mx + c$.

When we use equations to solve everyday problems, we usually refer to the equation as a **model** of the problem.

Given the equation $y = mx + c$, *m* is the slope and (0,*c*) is the *y*-intercept, i.e. the point where the line crosses the *y*-axis.

For example, the equation that converts degrees Celsius (*x*) to degrees Fahrenheit (*y*) is:

$$y = \frac{5}{9}x - \frac{160}{9}$$

The slope is $\frac{5}{9}$ and $\left(0, -\frac{160}{9}\right)$ is the *y*-intercept.

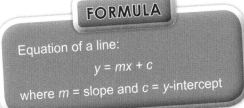

FORMULA

Equation of a line:
$$y = mx + c$$
where *m* = slope and *c* = *y*-intercept

This formula appears on page 18 of the *Formulae and Tables*.

 ACTIVITY 10.4

 Worked Example 10.8

l is the line $y = \frac{3}{4}x - 9$.

   (i) Write down the slope of *l*.

   (ii) Write down the co-ordinates of the *y*-intercept of *l*.

   (iii) Graph the line *l*.

   (iv) Find the *x*-intercept of *l*.

Solution

(i) $m = \frac{3}{4}$

(ii) (0,–9)

(iii) (0,–9) is a point on *l*.

$$m = \frac{3}{4} = \frac{\text{Rise}}{\text{Run}}$$

Start at (0,–9), rise 3 and run 4.

This gives us a second point on *l*, (4,–6).

Alternatively, we could find a second point on *l* and then graph it.

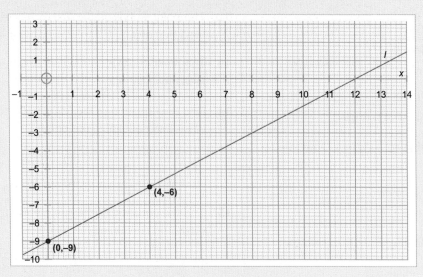

(iv) The y co-ordinate of any point on the x-axis is 0.
Let $y = 0$ in the equation of l and solve the equation to find x.

$$0 = \tfrac{3}{4}x - 9$$

$$0 = 3x - 36 \quad \text{(Multiplying both sides by 4)}$$

$$3x = 36$$

$$x = 12$$

(12,0) is the x-intercept.

Worked Example 10.9

k is the line $3x - 4y = 12$.

(i) Find the co-ordinates of the point where k cuts the x-axis.

(ii) Find the co-ordinates of the point where k cuts the y-axis.

(iii) Hence, draw the line k.

Solution

(i) The y co-ordinate of any point on the x-axis is 0. Let $y = 0$ in the equation of k and solve the equation to find x.

$$3x - 4(0) = 12$$

$$3x = 12$$

$$x = \frac{12}{3}$$

$$x = 4$$

(4,0) are the co-ordinates of the point where k cuts the x-axis.

(ii) The x co-ordinate of any point on the y-axis is 0. Let $x = 0$ in the equation of k and solve the equation to find y.

$$3(0) - 4y = 12$$

$$-4y = 12$$

$$y = \frac{-12}{4}$$

$$y = -3$$

(0,−3) are the co-ordinates of the point where k cuts the y-axis.

(iii)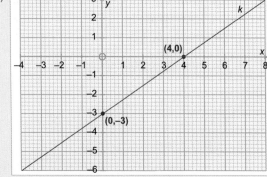

1. Write down the slopes of the following lines.

    (i) $y = 2x + 6$ (iii) $y = 7x + 8$

    (ii) $y = 3x - 5$ (iv) $y = \frac{1}{2}x - 3$

2. Write down the slopes of the following lines:

    (i) $y = 2x - 8$ (iii) $y = -2x + 12$

    (ii) $y = \frac{2}{3}x - 6$ (iv) $y = -\frac{6}{5}x + 20$

3. Find the co-ordinates of the y-intercept of the following lines (i.e. the point where the lines cross the y-axis):

    (i) $y = \frac{4}{5}x - 8$ (iii) $y = \frac{1}{2}x + 3$

    (ii) $y = 5x - 4$ (iv) $y = -5x - \frac{1}{3}$

4. Find the co-ordinates of the y-intercept of the following lines (i.e. where the lines cross the y-axis):

    (i) $y = \frac{2}{3}x - 2$ (iii) $y = \frac{5}{2}x - 5$

    (ii) $y = 3x - 8$ (iv) $y = 2x - \frac{2}{5}$

5. Using graph paper, graph the following lines:

    (i) $y = \frac{1}{3}x + 5$ (v) $y = \frac{2}{3}x - 10$

    (ii) $y = 2x - 7$ (vi) $y = 2x - 5$

    (iii) $y = \frac{1}{2}x - 4$ (vii) $y = \frac{3}{2}x - 1$

    (iv) $y = -x - \frac{1}{3}$ (viii) $y = 5x - \frac{2}{5}$

6. Using graph paper, graph the following lines:

    (i) $y = 3x + 1$ (ii) $y = 2x + 3$

Using your graph, find the co-ordinates of the point where the two lines meet.

7. Using graph paper, graph the following lines:

    (i) $y = \frac{1}{3}x + 3$ (ii) $y = \frac{1}{4}x + 2$

Using your graph, find the co-ordinates of the point where the two lines meet.

8. Using graph paper, graph the following lines:

    (i) $y = x + 3$ (ii) $y = 2x$

Using your graph, find the co-ordinates of the point where the two lines meet.

9. Find the co-ordinates of the y-intercept of the following lines:

    (i) $y = 2x - 6$ (iii) $y = 4x + 8$

    (ii) $y = x + 2$ (iv) $y = 3x - 12$

10. Find the co-ordinates of the x-intercept of the following lines:

    (i) $y = 2x + 8$ (iii) $y = 2x - 18$

    (ii) $y = 2x - 12$ (iv) $y = 7x - 14$

11. Find the co-ordinates of the x-intercept and the y-intercept for each of the following lines, and hence graph the lines:

    (i) $x + y = 3$ (iv) $5x - y = 15$

    (ii) $x + 2y = 6$ (v) $5x + 3y = 30$

    (iii) $2x + y = 8$

10.5 FINDING THE EQUATION OF A LINE

l is a line containing the point (x_1, y_1), and (x, y) is any other point on *l*.

Then, $\frac{y - y_1}{x - x_1} = m$, where *m* is the slope of the line *l*.

$\Rightarrow y - y_1 = m(x - x_1)$

This is the equation of the line. Therefore, to find the equation of a line, we need the slope of the line, *m*, and a point on the line, (x_1, y_1).

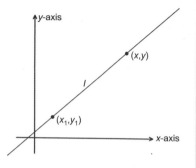

FORMULA

Equation of a line:

$$y - y_1 = m(x - x_1)$$

This formula appears on page 18 of the *Formulae and Tables*.

Worked Example 10.10

Find the equation of the line which passes through the points $(-1, 5)$ and $(2, 6)$.

Solution

$x_1 = -1 \quad y_1 = 5$

$x_2 = 2 \quad y_2 = 6$

$m = \frac{y_2 - y_1}{x_2 - x_1}$

$m = \frac{6 - 5}{2 - (-1)}$

$m = \frac{1}{2 + 1} = \frac{1}{3}$

$m = \frac{1}{3}$ Point = $(-1, 5)$

$y - y_1 = m(x - x_1)$

$y - 5 = \frac{1}{3}(x + 1)$ (Multiply across by 3)

$\therefore 3(y - 5) = 1(x + 1)$

$\therefore 3y - 15 = x + 1$

$\therefore x - 3y + 16 = 0$

Exercise 10.6

1. Find the equation of the line containing the point *A* and with slope *m*:

   (i) $A(1,1); m = 2$ (iv) $A(-5,-4); m = \frac{1}{2}$

   (ii) $A(-3,2); m = -1$ (v) $A(2,-8); m = -\frac{1}{3}$

   (iii) $A(-6,-2); m = -5$

2. Find the equations of the following lines containing the point *B* and with slope *m*:

   (i) $B(-3,2); m = \frac{3}{2}$ (iv) $B(-2,6); m = -\frac{1}{7}$

   (ii) $B(-1,5); m = -\frac{4}{3}$ (v) $B(4,-8); m = -\frac{3}{5}$

   (iii) $B(-2,6); m = \frac{2}{5}$

3. Find the equation of the line through the points *A* and *B*:

   (i) $A(2,1); B(3,2)$ (iv) $A(-3,6); B(5,-2)$

   (ii) $A(-1,3); B(2,4)$ (v) $A(1,-3); B(2,-10)$

   (iii) $A(-5,-1); B(-2,5)$

4. Find the equation of the line through the points *A* and *B*:

   (i) $A(-2,2); B(-5,3)$ (iv) $A(1,1); B(-2,-1)$

   (ii) $A(1,7); B(-2,4)$ (v) $A(-3,4); B(-2,-5)$

   (iii) $A(6,-5); B(-3,9)$

5. Find the equation of each line on this graph:

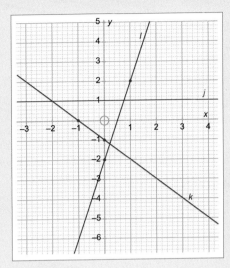

6. Find the equation of each line on this graph:

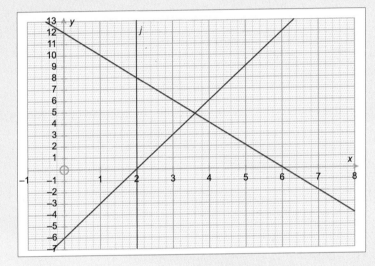

7. Plot the points A and B, and hence write down the equation of the line containing A and B.

(i) $A(1,1); B(1,2)$

(ii) $A(-1,3); B(-1,4)$

(iii) $A(-5,-6); B(-5,4)$

(iv) $A(-1,4); B(3,4)$

(v) $A(1,3); B(-2,3)$

8. Find the equation of the line through the points $A(3,1)$ and $B(-5,2)$. Show that the line contains $C(-13,3)$.

9. Find the equation of the line through the points $A(2,1)$ and $B(-1,-1)$. Show that the line contains $C(8,5)$.

10. Find the equation of the line through $C(3,1)$ that contains the midpoint of $A(3,1)$ and $B(-5,2)$.

10.6 INTERSECTING LINES

There are two methods for finding where two lines intersect.

1. Graph the two lines, and read the point of intersection from the graph.

2. Find the point that satisfies the equations of both lines. We do this by solving the equations simultaneously.

Worked Example 10.11

m is the line $x + 2y - 4 = 0$, and n is the line $x - y - 1 = 0$.

(i) Using the same axes and scales, draw the lines m and n.

(ii) Use your graph to find the point of intersection of m and n.

(iii) Check your answer by solving the equations simultaneously.

Solution

(i) We graph the lines by finding the co-ordinates of the x-intercept and y-intercept for both lines.

Intercepts for m ($x + 2y - 4 = 0$)

Let $y = 0$

$\therefore x - 4 = 0$

$x = 4$

(4,0) are the co-ordinates of the x-intercept.

Let $x = 0$

$\therefore 2y - 4 = 0$

$2y = 4$

$y = 2$

$\therefore$ (0,2) are the co-ordinates of the y-intercept.

Intercepts for n ($x - y - 1 = 0$)

Let $y = 0$

$\therefore x - 1 = 0$

$x = 1$

(1,0) are the co-ordinates of the x-intercept.

Let $x = 0$

$\therefore -y - 1 = 0$

$-y = 1$

$y = -1$

$\therefore$ (0,−1) are the co-ordinates of the y-intercept.

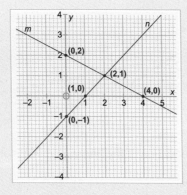

(ii) Reading from the graph, the point of intersection is (2,1).

(iii) We solve simultaneous equations by eliminating either x or y.

We do this by multiplying one or both equations to get equal numbers of one variable in both equations.

In this example, we have equal numbers of x's in both equations, so if we subtract one equation from the other, we will eliminate the x's.

$$x + 2y - 4 = 0$$
$$- \quad \underline{x - y - 1 = 0}$$
$$3y - 3 = 0$$
$$3y = 3$$
$$\therefore y = 1$$

Put $y = 1$ into either equation to find the x co-ordinate:

$$x + 2(1) - 4 = 0$$
$$x + 2 - 4 = 0$$
$$x - 2 = 0$$
$$\therefore x = 2$$

(2,1) are the co-ordinates of the point of intersection of m and n.

Exercise 10.7

1. *l* is the line $y - 3x = 9$, and *k* is the line $y = x - 3$.

   (i) Using the same axes and scales, draw the lines *l* and *k*.

   (ii) Use your graph to find the point of intersection of *l* and *k*.

   (iii) Check your answer by solving the equations simultaneously.

2. *m* is the line $x + 4y - 8 = 0$, and *n* is the line $x - y + 7 = 0$.

   (i) Using the same axes and scales, draw the lines *m* and *n*.

   (ii) Use your graph to find the point of intersection of *m* and *n*.

   (iii) Check your answer by solving the equations simultaneously.

3. *r* is the line $3x - y + 4 = 0$, and *s* is the line $5x + y - 10 = 0$.

   (i) Using the same axes and scales, draw the lines *r* and *s*.

   (ii) Use your graph to find the point of intersection of *r* and *s*.

   (iii) Check your answer by solving the equations simultaneously.

4. *l* is the line $x - y - 1 = 0$, and *k* is the line $x + 2y - 13 = 0$.

   (i) Using the same axes and scales, draw the lines *l* and *k*.

   (ii) Use your graph to find the point of intersection of *l* and *k*.

   (iii) Check your answer by solving the equations simultaneously.

5. *p* is the line $3x + 2y = 49$, and *q* is the line $y = 2x$.

   (i) Using the same axes and scales, draw the lines *p* and *q*.

   (ii) Use your graph to find the point of intersection of *p* and *q*.

   (iii) Check your answer by solving the equations simultaneously.

6. *a* is the line $x + y = 48$, and *b* is the line $y = 3x$.

   (i) Using the same axes and scales, draw the lines *a* and *b*.

   (ii) Use your graph to find the point of intersection of *a* and *b*.

   (iii) Check your answer by solving the equations simultaneously.

7. Two numbers, *x* and *y*, sum to 21 and have a difference of 13.

   (i) Set up a pair of simultaneous equations in *x* and *y*.

   (ii) Solve the equations to find *x* and *y*.

8. Two numbers, *x* and *y*, have a difference of 26. Twice the larger number minus the smaller number equals 94.

   (i) Set up a pair of simultaneous equations in *x* and *y*.

   (ii) Solve the equations to find *x* and *y*.

10.7 PARALLEL AND PERPENDICULAR LINES

In Activity 10.3, you showed that parallel lines have the same slope. In Activity 10.5, you will find the connection between the slopes of perpendicular lines.

Parallel lines: $m_1 = m_2$

Perpendicular lines: $m_1 \times m_2 = -1$

ACTIVITY 10.5

Also, if the slope of $l = \dfrac{a}{b}$ and $k \perp l$, $\Rightarrow$ the slope of $k = -\dfrac{b}{a}$.

For example, if the slope of $l = \dfrac{3}{5}$ and $k \perp l$, $\Rightarrow$ the slope of $k = -\dfrac{5}{3}$.

Worked Example 10.12

l is the line $3x - 2y = 6$. The line k contains the point $(1,1)$ and is perpendicular to l. Find the equation of k.

Solution

To find the equation of k, we need:

1. A point on k

2. The slope of k

We are told that k contains $(1,1)$.

As $k \perp l$, we will be able to figure out the slope of k from the slope of l.

Slope of l

Write the equation of l in the form $y = mx + c$:

$$3x - 2y = 6$$

$$-2y = -3x + 6$$

$$2y = 3x - 6$$

$$y = \tfrac{3}{2}x - 3$$

The slope of l is $\tfrac{3}{2}$, so therefore the slope of k is $-\tfrac{2}{3}$.

Equation of k

The point on k is $(1,1)$, and the slope of k is $-\tfrac{2}{3}$.

Using the formula $y - y_1 = m(x - x_1)$, we can now find the equation of k:

$$y - 1 = -\tfrac{2}{3}(x - 1) \text{ (Multiply across by 3)}$$

$$3(y - 1) = -2(x - 1)$$

$$3y - 3 = -2x + 2$$

$$k: 2x + 3y = 5$$

Worked Example 10.13

k is the line $y = 2x + 6$. Write down the equation of the line p that is perpendicular to k and has the same y-intercept as k.

Solution

The slope of k is 2, so the slope of p is $-\tfrac{1}{2}$.

Therefore, the equation of the line p is $y = -\tfrac{1}{2}x + 6$ (using $y = mx + c$).

Exercise 10.8

1. Copy and complete the table:

Slope	Slope of parallel line	Slope of perpendicular line
$\frac{3}{4}$	$\frac{3}{4}$	$-\frac{4}{3}$
$\frac{5}{2}$		
-3		
$\frac{1}{2}$		
-2		
$-\frac{1}{4}$		
$-\frac{8}{11}$		

2. The line t has a slope of $\frac{5}{8}$.
Find the slope of u, if $t \perp u$.

3. The line r has a slope of $\frac{1}{2}$.
Find the slope of s, if $r \parallel s$.

4. The line m has a slope of $-\frac{3}{4}$.
Find the slope of n, if $m \perp n$.

5. The line a has a slope of 4.
Find the slope of b, if $a \parallel b$.

6. The line k has a slope of $\frac{4}{5}$.
Find the slope of l, if $l \perp k$.

7. The line v has a slope of -5.
Find the slope of w, if $v \perp w$.

8. A is the point $(1,1)$ and B is the point $(2,3)$.

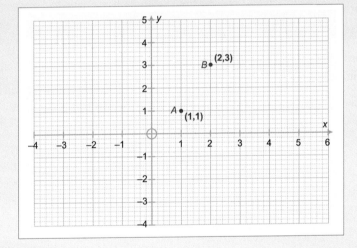

(i) Find the slope of the line AB.

(ii) Find the slope of a line perpendicular to AB.

9. Write down the equation of the line that is perpendicular to each of the following lines and that passes through the same point on the y-axis.

(i) $y = \frac{3}{5}x - 2$

(ii) $y = 4x - 5$

(iii) $y = \frac{9}{8}x + 2$

(iv) $y = -2x + \frac{1}{3}$

(v) $y = \frac{5}{9}x - 8$

(vi) $y = 5x - 3$

(vii) $y = \frac{3}{2}x + 11$

(viii) $y = -5x + \frac{2}{5}$

(ix) $y = \frac{3}{7}x + 2$

10. Write down the equation of the line that is perpendicular to each of the following lines and that passes through the same point on the y-axis.

(i) $y = 5x - 4$

(ii) $y = 3x + 2$

(iii) $y = 2x + 8$

(iv) $y = 5x - 12$

(v) $y = -9x + 10$

(vi) $y = \frac{5}{6}x - 3$

(vii) $y = -7x + 28$

(viii) $y = -\frac{3}{5}x - 12$

(ix) $y = -x + 6$

11. Find the slopes of the following lines by writing them in the form $y = mx + c$.

    (i) $2x - y = 7$ (iii) $5x - y = 4$ (v) $4x + 9y = 15$

    (ii) $x - 3y = 5$ (iv) $2x - y = 12$ (vi) $7x - 3y = -2$

12. l is the line $3x - 2y + 4 = 0$. The line k contains the point $(2, -3)$ and is parallel to l.
Find the equation of k.

13. m is the line $x - 6y + 12 = 0$. The line n contains the point $(-3, 2)$ and is perpendicular to l.
Find the equation of n.

14. p is the line $2x - y + 14 = 0$. The line q contains the point $(-1, 2)$ and is parallel to p.
Find the equation of k.

15. l is the line $x - y + 2 = 0$. The line k contains the point $(2, 2)$ and is perpendicular to l.
Find the equation of k.

10.8 REAL-LIFE PROBLEMS

Worked Example 10.14

The graph below shows that the cost for hiring a conference centre depends on the number of people attending the conference.

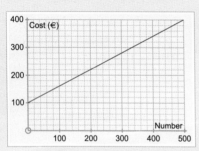

   (i) What is the basic fee for hiring the hall?

  (ii) If 200 people attend a conference, then from the graph estimate the cost of hiring the centre for this group.

 (iii) The organiser of a conference has just received a bill of €280 for hiring the centre. From the graph, estimate the number of people who attended the conference.

 (iv) Find the equation of the line in the form $y = mx + c$.

  (v) Use your equation to find the cost of hiring the centre for a group of 350 people.

Solution

   (i) When $x = 0$, $y = 100$. This means that there is a basic fee of €100 before any people attend the conference.

  (ii) Reading from the graph, we see that the cost of hiring the hall for 200 people is €220.

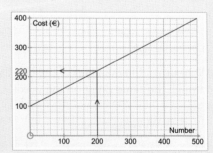

 (iii) If the bill was for €280, then 300 people attended the conference.

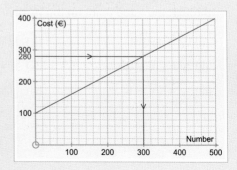

(iv) Two points on the graph are (0,100) and (500,400).

$$m = \frac{y_2 - y_1}{x_2 - x_1}$$

$$m = \frac{400 - 100}{500 - 0} = \frac{300}{500} = \frac{3}{5}$$

$y - y_1 = m(x - x_1)$ Point (0,100) $m = \frac{3}{5}$

$$y - 100 = \frac{3}{5}(x - 0)$$

$$\therefore y = \frac{3}{5}x + 100$$

(v) $y = \frac{3}{5}(350) + 100 = €310$

Exercise 10.9

1. The graph below shows the monthly wage of a salesperson. The wage consists of a basic wage plus a commission that depends on sales.

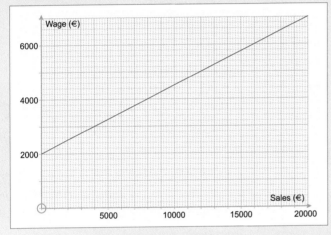

(i) What is the basic wage?

(ii) In a certain month, the salesperson sells €10,000 worth of goods. Using the graph, find her wages for that month.

(iii) Find, in the form $y = mx + c$, the equation of the line.

(iv) Using the equation, find the value of her sales in a month in which she earns €5,000.

2. A plumber charges €P for a repair. The charge is dependent on t, the time taken in minutes to do the repair. P is calculated according to the relationship $P = 0.8t + 60$.

   (i) Draw the graph of $P = 0.8t + 60$ for $0 \leqslant t \leqslant 120$.

   (ii) Use the graph to find how much the plumber charges for a repair lasting 40 minutes.

   (iii) From the graph, estimate how much the plumber charges for a repair lasting 1½ hours.

   (iv) A customer has been charged €80 for repair. How long did it take the plumber to complete the repair?

3. John has been negotiating his pocket money. He has been given two options:

   Option 1: €20 per week pocket money with 50c for every chore he does during the week

   Option 2: €25 per week pocket money with 30c for every chore he does during the week

   (i) Using the same axes and scales, graph both options. The units on the x-axis will be the number of chores done during the week. The units on the y-axis will be the money he receives.

   (ii) Which option do you think John will favour? Explain your answer.

   (iii) How many chores will he need to do to receive the same amount of money under both options?

4. The following equation converts degrees Celsius to degrees Fahrenheit:

$$y = \frac{9}{5}x + 32$$

Here, x represents degrees Celsius and y represents degrees Fahrenheit.

(i) Using graph paper, sketch the equation for x between 0 and 100.

(ii) Use your graph to convert 0°C to degrees Fahrenheit.

(iii) Use your graph to convert 51°F to degrees Celsius.

(iv) Use the equation to convert 100°C to degrees Fahrenheit.

5. A car passes a junction travelling at a speed of 30 km/h. Its speed is increasing at a rate of 2 km/h every second.

(i) What is the speed of the car 2 seconds after passing the junction?

(ii) What is the speed of the car 4 seconds after passing the junction?

(iii) Complete the following table. The first row in the table contains the times that have elapsed after passing the junction. The second row gives the speed of the car at those times.

Time (secs)	2	4	6	8	10
Speed (km/h)					50

(iv) Draw a graph that represents the speed of the car during the first 10 seconds after passing the junction.

(v) Use your graph to find the speed of the car after 9 seconds.

6. Rex goes on a short run. He carries a bag for the first part of the outward leg and runs at a speed of 4 m/s. For the second part of the outward leg, he drops the bag and now runs at a speed of 5 m/s. His total time for the outward leg is 29 s.

(i) If x represents the distance for the first part of the outward leg and y represents the distance for the second part, then show that $\frac{x}{4} + \frac{y}{5} = 29$.

For the return leg, Rex is facing into a strong breeze. He begins by running at a speed of 4 m/s. He then picks up the bag and has to reduce his speed to 3 m/s. He runs the return leg in 37.5 s.

(ii) Write an equation in x and y that describes the return leg.

(iii) At what distance from the start of the run did Rex drop the bag?

7. Electricity bills are issued every two months. At present, bills include a fixed charge of €22.12. The graph below shows the electricity charges for customers who use between 0 and 1,000 units of electricity every two months. Use the graph to answer the following questions.

(i) Estimate the bill for a customer who has used 700 units of electricity.

(ii) Estimate the bill for a customer who has used 920 units of electricity.

(iii) John has received an electricity bill for €170 for this period. How many units of electricity has John used in this period?

(iv) The equation of the straight line in the graph is
$y = 0.164x + 22.12$.

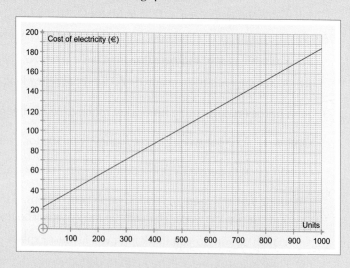

If y represents cost of electricity and x represents number of units used, use the equation to find the cost of 1,500 units of electricity.

10.9 AREA OF A TRIANGLE

Graphical Approach

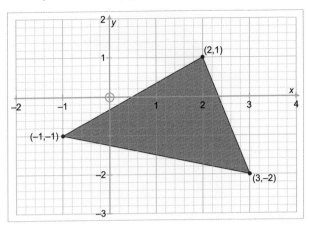

The diagram above shows a triangle with vertices (2,1), (3,−2), and (−1,−1).
The area of the triangle can be found using the following graphical approach.

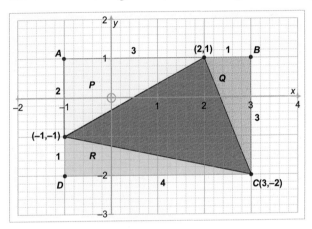

Step 1

Construct a rectangle *ABCD* around the triangle as shown, and find its area:

Area of rectangle = 4 × 3 = 12

Step 2

Find the area of each of the triangles labelled *P*, *Q* and *R*:

- Area of ΔP = ½(2)(3) = 3
- Area of ΔQ = ½(1)(3) = 1.5
- Area of ΔR = ½(4)(1) = 2
- Area of ΔP + Area of ΔQ + Area of ΔR = 3 + 1.5 + 2 = 6.5

Step 3

The area of the triangle is found by subtracting the areas of *P*, *Q* and *R* from the area of *ABCD*.

Area = 12 − 6.5 = 5.5 units^2

Formula Approach

The diagram below shows a triangle with vertices $(0,0)$, (x_1, y_1) and (x_2, y_2).

The area of this triangle is given by:

FORMULA

$$\frac{1}{2}|x_1 y_2 - x_2 y_1|$$

This formula appears on page 18 of the *Formulae and Tables*.

To use this formula, one vertex must be (0,0).

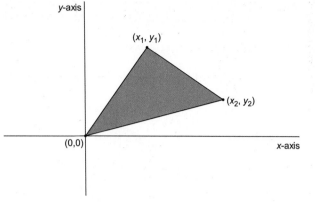

Worked Example 10.15

Find the area of the triangle whose vertices are $A(3,6)$, $B(7,2)$ and $C(4,1)$.

Solution: Method 1

Step 1

Construct a rectangle around triangle ABC.

Area of rectangle $= 5 \times 4 = 20$ units^2

Step 2

Area of ΔP + Area of ΔQ + Area of ΔR

$= \frac{1}{2}(1)(5) + \frac{1}{2}(4)(4) + \frac{1}{2}(3)(1) = 12$ units^2

Step 3

Area of $\Delta ABC = 20 - 12 = 8$ units^2

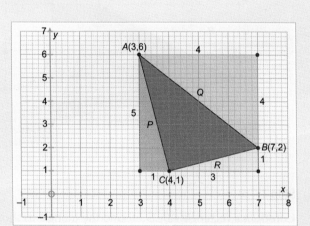

Solution: Method 2

We can also use the formula to find the area of the triangle. We need to move (translate) the triangle until one of the vertices is $(0,0)$.

$(4,1) \rightarrow (0,0)$
$(3,6) \rightarrow (-1,5)$
$(7,2) \rightarrow (3,1)$

Here we take 4 from each x-value and 1 from each y-value for each of the three points.

Area $= \frac{1}{2}|x_1 y_2 - x_2 y_1|$ $x_1 = -1$ $y_1 = 5$

$= \frac{1}{2}|(-1)(1) - (3)(5)|$ $x_2 = 3$ $y_2 = 1$

$= \frac{1}{2}|-1 - 15|$

$= \frac{1}{2}|-16|$

$= 8$ units^2

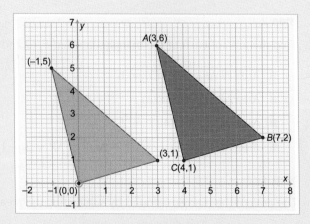

Worked Example 10.16

$A(2,1)$ and $B(4,3)$ are two points.

C is the midpoint of $[AB]$, and k is the line through C perpendicular to AB.

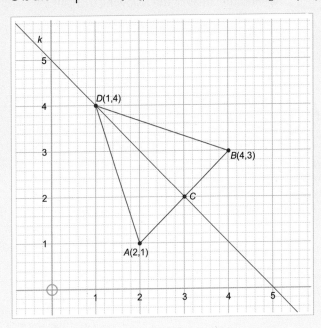

(i) Find the co-ordinates of C.

(ii) What is the slope of AB?

(iii) Using your answers to parts (i) and (ii), find the equation of k.

(iv) Verify that $D(1,4)$ lies on k.

(v) Find $|AB|$ and $|CD|$.

(vi) Hence, find the area of $\triangle ABD$.

Solution

(i) Midpoint $= \left(\dfrac{x_1 + x_2}{2}, \dfrac{y_1 + y_2}{2}\right)$ $\quad A(2,1) \quad B(4,3)$
$\qquad\qquad\qquad\qquad\qquad\qquad\quad x_1, y_1 \quad x_2, y_2$

$$C = \left(\frac{2 + 4}{2}, \frac{1 + 3}{2}\right) = \left(\frac{6}{2}, \frac{4}{2}\right) = (3,2)$$

(ii) $m = \dfrac{y_2 - y_1}{x_2 - x_1}$

$m = \dfrac{3 - 1}{4 - 2} = \dfrac{2}{2} = 1$

(iii) The slope of k is -1, as k is perpendicular to AB.

$C(3,2)$ is a point on k.

$y - y_1 = m(x - x_1)$

$y - 2 = -1(x - 3)$

$y - 2 = -x + 3$

$k: x + y = 5$

(iv) Substitute $D(1,4)$ into the equation of k:

$x + y = 5$

$\therefore 1 + 4 = 5$

$5 = 5$

$\therefore D(1,4)$ lies on k.

(v) $|PQ| = \sqrt{(x_2 - x_1)^2 + (y_2 - y_1)^2}$

$|AB| = \sqrt{(4 - 2)^2 + (3 - 1)^2} = \sqrt{4 + 4} = \sqrt{8}$

$|CD| = \sqrt{(3 - 1)^2 + (2 - 4)^2} = \sqrt{4 + 4} = \sqrt{8}$

(vi) As k is perpendicular to AB, we can use the fact that the area of a triangle is **half the base length by the perpendicular height** to find the area of $\triangle ABC$.

Area of $\triangle ABC = \dfrac{1}{2}\sqrt{8}\sqrt{8} = 4$ units^2

Exercise 10.10

1. Use the formula $\frac{1}{2}|x_1 y_2 - x_2 y_1|$ to find the areas of the triangles with these vertices:

   (i) $A(6,3)$, $B(0,0)$, $C(0,5)$

   (ii) $A(2,4)$, $B(3,8)$, $C(0,0)$

   (iii) $A(1,1)$, $B(0,2)$, $C(0,0)$

   (iv) $A(5,3)$, $B(2,2)$, $C(0,0)$

2. Use a graphical approach to find the areas of the triangles with these vertices:

   (i) $X(5,3)$, $Y(1,6)$, $Z(3,5)$

   (ii) $X(2,4)$, $Y(1,1)$, $Z(-5,6)$

   (iii) $X(-1,-1)$, $Y(3,2)$, $Z(-1,8)$

   (iv) $X(-1,3)$, $Y(2,2)$, $Z(6,-10)$

3. Find the areas of the triangles with these vertices:

   (i) $P(3,8)$, $Q(2,-1)$, $R(3,0)$

   (ii) $P(-1,3)$, $Q(1,2)$, $R(2,-7)$

   (iii) $P(-5,6)$, $Q(-1,1)$, $R(5,0)$

   (iv) $P(-1,-5)$, $Q(1,2)$, $R(-3,-2)$

4. If the area of a triangle is zero, then the vertices of the triangle are collinear, i.e. they lie on a straight line.

   Show that the following points are collinear. Use the formula $\frac{1}{2}|x_1 y_2 - x_2 y_1|$.

   (i) $T(5,4)$, $U(1,6)$, $V(3,5)$

   (ii) $T(-3,1)$, $U(1,1)$, $V(-1,1)$

   (iii) $T(-5,14)$, $U(3,2)$, $V(-1,8)$

   (iv) $T(-1,3)$, $U(2,2)$, $V(5,1)$

5. $P(-3,1)$, $Q(1,3)$, $R(3,0)$ and $S(-1,-2)$ are the vertices of a parallelogram.

   (i) Show $PQRS$ on a diagram.

   (ii) Find the area of $PQRS$ by dividing it into two triangles.

6. $A(0,-4)$, $B(-1,-1)$, $C(5,4)$ and $D(8,0)$ are the vertices of a quadrilateral.

   (i) Show $ABCD$ on a diagram.

   (ii) Find the area of $ABCD$ by dividing it into two triangles.

7. **The area of a triangle is half the base length by the perpendicular height**. Use this fact to find the areas of the following triangles:

   (i)
   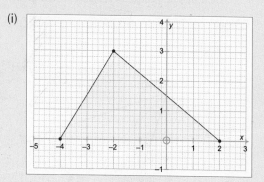

   (ii)
   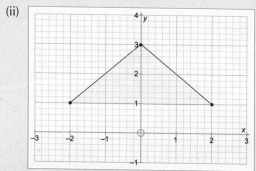

   (iii)
   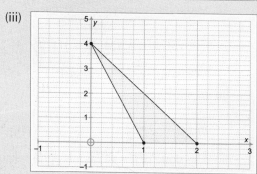

   (iv)
   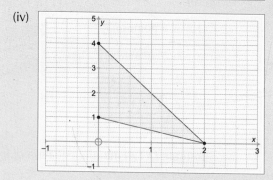

8. $A(-1,-6)$ and $B(3,-2)$ are two points. C is the midpoint of $[AB]$, and k is the line through C perpendicular to AB.

  (i) Find the co-ordinates of C.

  (ii) On graph paper, plot the points A, B and C.

  (iii) What is the slope of AB?

  (iv) Using your answers to parts (i) and (iii), find the equation of k.

  (v) Verify that $D(-4,1)$ lies on k.

  (vi) Show the line k on your graph.

  (vii) Find $|AB|$ and $|CD|$.

  (viii) Hence, find the area of $\triangle ABD$.

9. $W(0,-2)$ and $X(10,2)$ are two points. Y is the midpoint of $[WX]$, and l is the line through Y perpendicular to WX.

  (i) Find the co-ordinates of Y.

  (ii) On graph paper, plot the points W, X and Y.

  (iii) What is the slope of WX?

  (iv) Using your answers to parts (i) and (iii), find the equation of l.

  (v) Verify that $Z(3,5)$ lies on l.

  (vi) Show the line l on your graph.

  (vii) Find $|WX|$ and $|YZ|$.

  (viii) Hence, find the area of $\triangle WXZ$.

10. $O(0,0)$, $A(6t,t)$ and $B(2t,3t)$ are the vertices of a triangle. If the area of the triangle is 72 square units, find two possible values of t.

11. $O(0,0)$, $X(7k,k)$ and $B(k,3k)$ are the vertices of a triangle. If the area of the triangle is 40 square units, find two possible values of k.

12. The area of a triangle whose vertices are $P(0,0)$, $Q(x,6)$ and $R(1,3)$ is 7½ square units. Find two possible values for x.

13. $A(3,-2)$, $B(1,6)$ and $C(7,0)$ are the vertices of a triangle. Let M be the midpoint of $[BC]$.

  (i) Find the co-ordinates of M.

  (ii) Verify that area $\triangle ABM =$ area $\triangle ACM$.

 Revision Exercises

1. $A(-2,1)$ and $B(4,-5)$ are two points.

  (i) Plot the two points on graph paper.

  (ii) Find M, the midpoint of $[AB]$.

  (iii) Verify that $|AM| = |MB|$.

  (iv) Find the slope of AB.

  (v) Find the equation of AB.

  (vi) Find the co-ordinates of the point where AB cuts the x-axis.

2. Two points $A(0,-1)$ and $B(1,1)$ are shown on the diagram below.

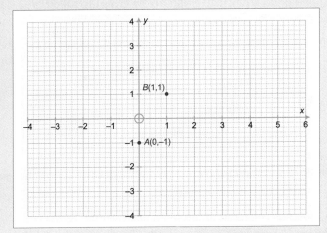

  (i) Plot two suitable points C and D such that $ABCD$ is a parallelogram.

  (ii) Write down the co-ordinates of C and D.

  (iii) By performing suitable calculations, verify that the points $ABCD$ do form a parallelogram.

  (iv) Show that the diagonal $[AC]$ bisects the area of the parallelogram.

3. $P(0,0)$, $Q(3,0)$ and $R(3,4)$ are three points.

 (i) Plot the three points.

 (ii) Find M, the midpoint of $[PQ]$.

 (iii) Find the slope of RM.

 (iv) Find the equation of RM.

 (v) Find the co-ordinates of the point where RM cuts the y-axis.

 (vi) Working from your graph, find the area of the triangle PQR.

4. $M(-5,1)$ and $N(2,6)$ are two points.

 (i) Plot the two points on graph paper.

 (ii) Find the slope of MN.

 (iii) Find the equation of MN.

 (iv) Find the co-ordinates of the point where MN cuts the y-axis.

 (v) Hence, write the equation of MN in the form $y = mx + c$.

5. l is the line $3x + y = 6$.

 (i) Verify that $(2,0)$ lies on l.

 (ii) If $(0,k)$ is a point on l, then find the value of k.

 (iii) Plot the line l.

 (iv) Find the slope of l using the slope formula.

 (v) Find the slope of l by writing the equation in the form $y = mx + c$.

6. Find the equation of the line l shown on the graph below.

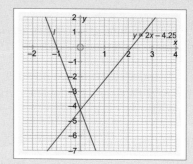

7. $P(1,3)$, $Q(2,0)$ and $R(4,4)$ are the vertices of the triangle PQR.

 (i) Plot the points P, Q and R.

 (ii) Show that $|PR| = |PQ|$.

 (iii) Find $|RQ|^2$.

 (iv) Verify that $|RQ|^2 = |PR|^2 + |PQ|^2$.

8. Two common units of measurement in cooking are the tablespoon and the cup. The table shown gives some conversions.

 (i) Using suitable axes and scales, draw a straight line graph of the conversion.

Tablespoon	4	8	12	16
Cup	$\frac{1}{4}$	$\frac{1}{2}$	$\frac{3}{4}$	1

 (ii) Using the graph, convert 6 tablespoons to cups.

 (iii) Find the slope of the line.

 (iv) Hence, write down the equation of the line in the form $y = mx$.

 (v) Use your equation to convert 50 tablespoons to cups.

9. A car passes a traffic light travelling at a speed of 30 km/h. The graph below gives the speed of the car during the 20-second period after passing the traffic light.

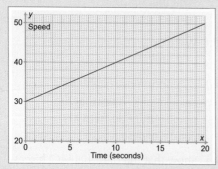

 (i) What is the speed of the car 10 seconds after passing the light?

 (ii) How many seconds does it take the driver to reach a speed of 48 km/h?

 (iii) Find the equation of the line.

 (iv) What is the y-intercept of this line? What value does it represent?

 (v) By how many kilometres per hour does the speed change in the 20-second period?

 (vi) If the driver continues to change his speed (accelerates) at the same rate over the next 10-second period, then what will the speed of the car be 25 seconds after passing the light?

10. The charge for repairing a washing machine is made up of a fixed charge and a fee that depends on the time taken to repair the machine.

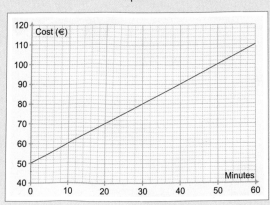

(i) What is the fixed charge for a repair?

(ii) What is the charge for a repair that takes 40 minutes?

(iii) Calculate the slope of the line.

(iv) What does the slope represent in the context of the question?

(v) Find the equation of the line.

(vi) Use your equation to find the cost of a repair that takes 2 hours.

11. The distance–time graph shows a train journey between two stations.

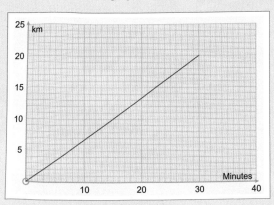

(i) What is the distance between the two stations?

(ii) How long does the journey last?

(iii) Find the distance travelled in the first 10 minutes of the journey.

(iv) Find the average speed of the train between the two stations.

12. The following equation gives the time (T) in minutes for cooking a turkey whose weight (w) is in kilograms:

$$T = 44w + 20$$

(i) Plot the graph for $0 \leqslant w \leqslant 10$.

(ii) Find the time needed to cook a turkey whose weight is 4.8 kg.

(iii) A turkey was cooked for 5 hours. Find an approximation for its weight in kilograms.

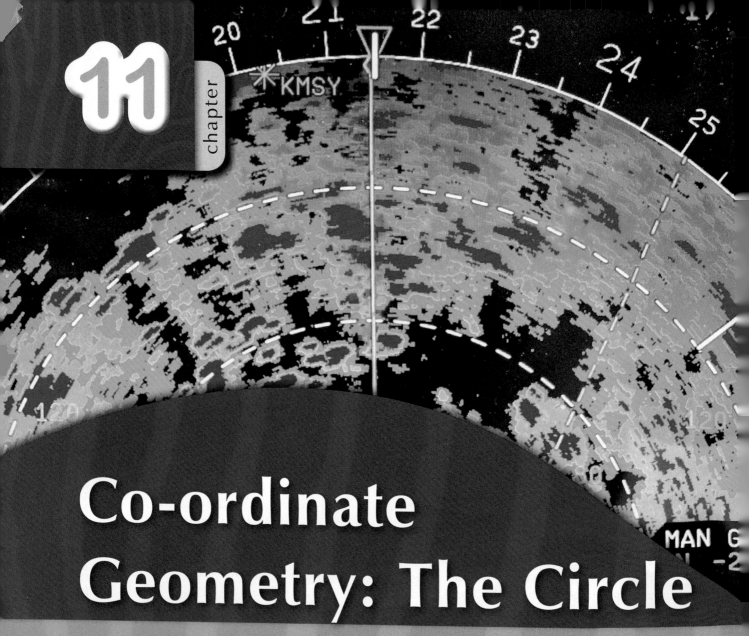

11

chapter

Co-ordinate Geometry: The Circle

Learning Outcomes

In this chapter you will learn how to:

⊃ Find the equation of a circle with centre (0,0) and radius length *r*

⊃ Find the points of intersection of a line and a circle

⊃ Prove that a line is a tangent to a circle

⊃ Find the equation of a circle with centre (*h,k*) and radius length *r*

⊃ Show whether a point is inside, outside or on a circle

Since the earliest human civilisations arose, people have been fascinated by the mathematics of the **circle**. The ancient Greeks believed that the circle was the perfect form, because circular forms occurred so frequently in nature. They also thought that the stars and planets travelled in circular paths around the universe.

YOU SHOULD REMEMBER...

■ How to find the distance between two points

■ How to find the midpoint of two points

■ How to solve quadratic equations

KEY WORDS

■ **Equation of a circle**

■ **Radius length**

■ **Tangent**

A **circle** is the set of all points in the plane that are equidistant from a fixed point, the centre. The distance from the centre to any point on the circle is called the **radius length** of the circle.

An interesting modern-day application of co-ordinate geometry of the circle is the mapping of 'great circle' routes. A great circle of a sphere is a circle that runs along the surface of the sphere so as to cut it into two equal halves. As the earth is almost spherical, we can draw imaginary great circles on the surface of the earth. The shortest route between any two points on the surface of a sphere will lie along a great circle. This is why intercontintental airlines fly along great circle routes – it minimises the distance they have to travel. On the map below, we can see examples of three great circle routes: New York to Moscow, Moscow to Tokyo and New York to Tokyo.

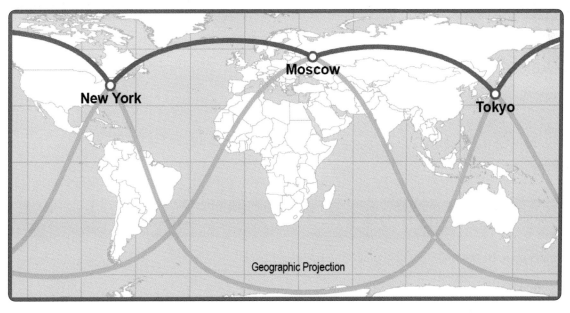

Geographic Projection

CO-ORDINATE GEOMETRY: THE CIRCLE

11.1 CIRCLES WITH CENTRE (0,0)

 **ACTIVITIES** 11.1, 11.2, 11.3

Consider the circle with centre $O(0,0)$ and radius length r.
Let $P(x,y)$ be the co-ordinates of any point on the circle.

$$|OP| = \sqrt{(x - 0)^2 + (y - 0)^2} = \sqrt{x^2 + y^2}$$

$$|OP| = \text{radius length} = r$$

Therefore,

$$\sqrt{x^2 + y^2} = r$$

and hence,

$$x^2 + y^2 = r^2$$

This last equation is the equation of a circle with centre (0,0) and radius length r.

> The equation of a circle with centre (0,0) and radius length r is:
>
> **FORMULA**
>
> $$x^2 + y^2 = r^2$$

Worked Example 11.1

Find the equation of the circle with centre (0,0) and radius length 7.

Solution

Equation: $x^2 + y^2 = r^2$ Given: $r = 7$

$\Rightarrow\ x^2 + y^2 = (7)^2$

$\therefore x^2 + y^2 = 49$

Worked Example 11.2

c is a circle with centre (0,0) and contains the point (5,12).

   (i) Draw the circle c.

   (ii) Find r, the radius length of c.

   (iii) Find the equation of c.

CO-ORDINATE GEOMETRY: THE CIRCLE

11

Solution

(i) ■ On graph paper, draw the x- and y-axes with a clearly marked common scale.

■ Plot the point (5,12).

■ With the compass point at (0,0) and pencil point at (5,12), draw the circle.

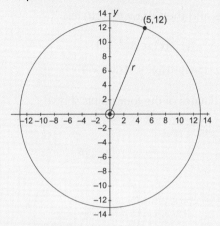

(ii) To find r, we get the distance from the centre, (0,0), to a point on the circle, (5,12).

$$r = \sqrt{(5-0)^2 + (12-0)^2}$$
$$= \sqrt{(5)^2 + (12)^2}$$
$$= \sqrt{25 + 144}$$
$$= \sqrt{169}$$
$$\therefore r = 13$$

(iii) $x^2 + y^2 = r^2$

$x^2 + y^2 = (13)^2$

$\therefore x^2 + y^2 = 169 \ ...$ (equation of c)

Worked Example 11.3

The equation of the circle s is $9x^2 + 9y^2 = 100$.

(i) Find the centre of s.

(ii) Find the radius length of s.

Solution

(i) Dividing both sides of the equation of s by 9 gives:

$$x^2 + y^2 = \frac{100}{9}$$

The equation is now in the familiar $x^2 + y^2 = r^2$ form.
The centre of s is (0,0).

(ii) The radius of s is:

$$r^2 = \frac{100}{9} \Rightarrow r = \sqrt{\frac{100}{9}}, \text{ as } r > 0$$

$$\Rightarrow r = \frac{10}{3}$$

Exercise 11.1

1. Write down the equation of each of the following circles with centre $O(0,0)$ and radius lengths of:

(i) 2   (ii) 3   (iii) 1   (iv) 12   (v) 5

(vi) $\sqrt{2}$ (vii) $\sqrt{5}$ (viii) $\frac{3}{4}$ (ix) $\frac{1}{2}$ (x) $2\frac{1}{3}$

2. Find the distance from $O(0,0)$ to $A(7,24)$.
   Now write down the equation of the circle that has the centre O and that contains the point A.

3. Find the distance from $O(0,0)$ to $B(-6,-8)$.
   Now write down the equation of the circle that has the centre O and that contains the point B.

4. Write down the equation of the circle that has the centre $O(0,0)$ and that contains the point $C(3,4)$.

5. Write down the centre and radius length of each of these circles:

(i) $x^2 + y^2 = 25$ (v) $x^2 + y^2 = 2^2$ (ix) $4x^2 + 4y^2 = 9$

(ii) $x^2 + y^2 = 100$ (vi) $x^2 + y^2 = 7^2$ (x) $9x^2 + 9y^2 = 100$

(iii) $x^2 + y^2 = 64$ (vii) $x^2 + y^2 = 3$ (xi) $25x^2 + 25y^2 = 49$

(iv) $x^2 + y^2 = 81$ (viii) $x^2 + y^2 = 5$ (xii) $36x^2 + 36y^2 = 121$

6. Write down the radius length of each of these circles and then draw the circles.

(i) $x^2 + y^2 = 49$ (iii) $x^2 + y^2 = 3^2$ (v) $4x^2 + 4y^2 = 1$

(ii) $x^2 + y^2 = 16$ (iv) $x^2 + y^2 = 5^2$ (vi) $16x^2 + 16y^2 = 1$

7. For each of the following circles, write down the co-ordinates of the four points shown:

(i)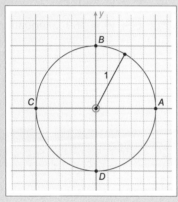

(iii)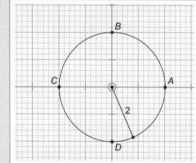

(ii)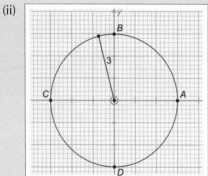

(iv)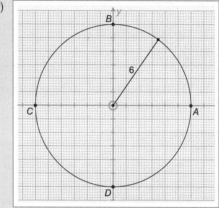

8. Find the equations of the following circles:

(i)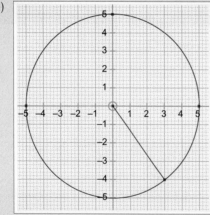

(ii)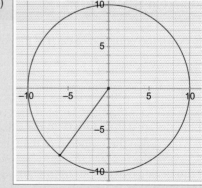

(iii)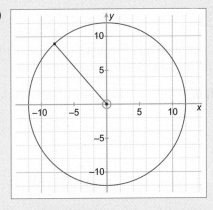

(iv)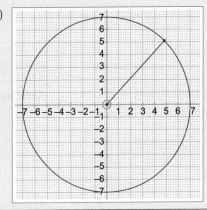

9. A circle has the equation $x^2 + y^2 = 4$.

  (i) Write down the co-ordinates of the centre of the circle.

  (ii) What is the radius length of the circle?

  (iii) Draw the circle.

  (iv) Using the formula $C = 2\pi r$, find the length of the circle.
  Give your answer correct to two decimal places.

10. A circle has the equation $x^2 + y^2 = 36$.

  (i) Write down the co-ordinates of the centre of the circle.

  (ii) What is the radius length of the circle?

  (iii) Draw the circle.

  (iv) Using the formula $C = 2\pi r$, find the length of the circle.
  Give your answer correct to two decimal places.

  (v) Is the length of the line segment joining $O(0,0)$ and $A(36,15)$ greater than the length of the circle? Explain your answer.

11. The line segment joining $A(-3,4)$ and $B(3,-4)$ is the diameter of a circle.

  (i) Find the centre of the circle.

  (ii) Draw the circle.

  (iii) Find the radius length of the circle.

  (iv) Write down the equation of the circle.

12. The line segment joining $A(-2,1)$ and $B(2,-1)$ is the diameter of a circle.

  (i) Find the centre of the circle.

  (ii) Draw the circle.

  (iii) Find the radius length of the circle.

  (iv) Write down the equation of the circle.

  (v) Using the formula $A = \pi r^2$, find the area of the circle. Give your answer correct to two decimal places.

13. The line segment joining $A(-5,1)$ and $B(5,-1)$ is the diameter of a circle.

  (i) Find the centre of the circle.

  (ii) Find the radius length of the circle.

  (iii) Write down the equation of the circle.

  (iv) Using the formula $A = \pi r^2$, find the area of the circle. Give your answer correct to two decimal places.

  (v) Is the area of the square with vertices $O(0,0)$, $A(9,0)$, $B(9,9)$ and $C(0,9)$ greater than the area of the circle? Explain your answer.

11.2 LINES AND CIRCLES

If a line and a circle are drawn on the plane, then the line and circle may meet at two points or at one point, or they may not meet at all. The diagrams below illustrate these three different situations.

Two points of intersection

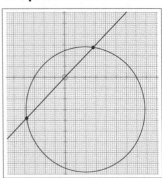

One point of intersection

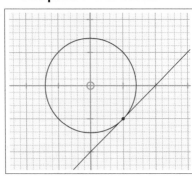

No points of intersection

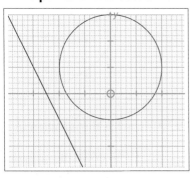

> If the line meets the circle at one point only, then we say the line is a tangent to the circle.

In this section, we will be finding the co-ordinates of the points where lines and circles meet. In our course, we will not concern ourselves with the situation where a line and a circle do not meet.

Worked Example 11.4

Find the points of intersection of the line l: $x + 2y = 7$ and the circle c: $x^2 + y^2 = 10$.

Solution

Step 1: Begin with the equation of the line and write x in terms of y or write y in terms of x, i.e. write the equation in the form $x = \ldots$ or $y = \ldots$, whichever is the easier.

$$x + 2y = 7$$

$$\therefore x = 7 - 2y$$

Step 2: Now take the equation of the circle and substitute $7 - 2y$ for x:

$$x^2 + y^2 = 10$$

$$(7 - 2y)^2 + y^2 = 10$$

$$49 - 28y + 4y^2 + y^2 = 10$$

$$5y^2 - 28y + 39 = 0$$

$$(5y - 13)(y - 3) = 0$$

$$\therefore 5y - 13 = 0 \quad \textbf{OR} \quad y - 3 = 0$$

$$5y = 13$$

$$\therefore y = \frac{13}{5} = 2.6 \quad \textbf{OR} \quad y = 3$$

Step 3: Now find the corresponding values of x, using the equation from Step 1.

$x = 7 - 2y$	
$y = 2.6$	$y = 3$
$x = 7 - 2(2.6)$	$x = 7 - 2(3)$
$x = 7 - 5.2$	$x = 7 - 6$
$x = 1.8$	$x = 1$

$\therefore$ Two points of intersection: $(1.8, 2.6)$ and $(1,3)$.

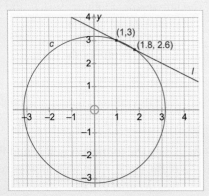

Prove that the line l: $x - 3y = 10$ is a tangent to the circle c: $x^2 + y^2 = 10$.

Solution

Step 1: $x - 3y = 10$

$\therefore x = 3y + 10$

Step 2: Now take the equation of the circle and substitute $3y + 10$ for x.

$$x^2 + y^2 = 10$$
$$(3y + 10)^2 + y^2 = 10$$
$$9y^2 + 60y + 100 + y^2 = 10$$
$$10y^2 + 60y + 90 = 0$$
$$y^2 + 6y + 9 = 0$$
$$(y + 3)(y + 3) = 0$$
$$\therefore y = -3$$

Step 3: Now find the corresponding value of x, using the equation from Step 1.

$$x = 3y + 10$$

If $y = -3$, then $x = 3(-3) + 10 = 1$.

Therefore, there is only one point of intersection, which is $(1, -3)$.

Hence, we can conclude that the line is a tangent to the circle.

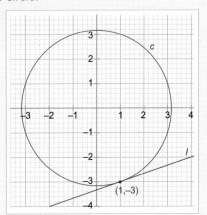

1. Reading from each of the following graphs, write down the co-ordinates of the point(s) of intersection of the line and the circle:

(i)

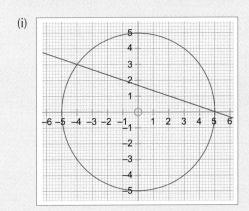

(ii)

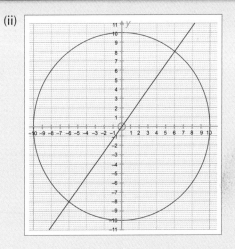

(iii)

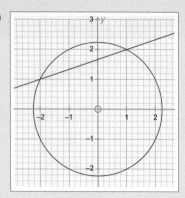

(iv)

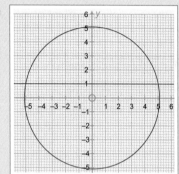

(v)

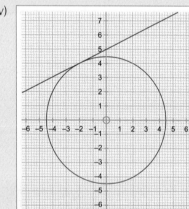

2.

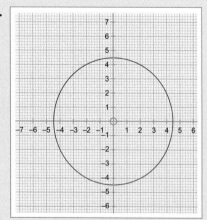

Using the graph, find the points of intersection of the above circle and the following lines:

(i) $x = 2$ (iii) $x = -2$

(ii) $y = 2$ (iv) $y = -2$

3.

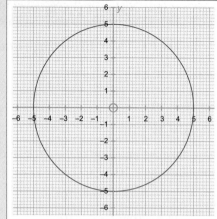

Using the graph, find the points of intersection of the above circle and the following lines:

(i) $x = 4$ (v) $x = 3$

(ii) $y = 4$ (vi) $y = 3$

(iii) $x = -4$ (vii) $x = -3$

(iv) $y = -4$ (viii) $y = -3$

4. Solve the following pairs of simultaneous equations.

(i) $x^2 + y^2 = 20$ (iii) $x^2 + y^2 = 20$
      $x = 10 - 3y$ $y = 2x$

(ii) $x^2 + y^2 = 25$ (iv) $x^2 + y^2 = 40$
      $x - 2y = 5$ $y = -2$

5. Find the points of intersection of the line $x + y = 4$ and the circle $x^2 + y^2 = 10$.

6. Find the points of intersection of the line $x - y = 1$ and the circle $x^2 + y^2 = 13$.

7. l is the line $2x + y - 3 = 0$, and s is the circle $x^2 + y^2 = 26$.
   Find the points of intersection of l and s.

8. m is the line $x + 7y - 4 = 0$, and n is the circle $x^2 + y^2 = 10$.
   Find the points of intersection of m and n.

9. The graph below shows a circle *s* with centre *A*(4,4). The circle touches the *x*-axis and the *y*-axis. *m* and *n* are tangents to the circle.

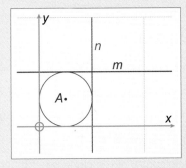

(i) Write down the radius length of *s*.

(ii) Write down the equation of *s*.

(iii) What is the equation of each of the tangents, *m* and *n*?

(iv) Find the point of intersection of *m* and *n*.

(v) Calculate the area of the square enclosed by *m*, *n*, the *x*-axis and the *y*-axis.

10. In each of the following, show that the line *l* is a tangent to the circle *s*:

(i) $s: x^2 + y^2 = 2$

$l: x = y + 2$

(ii) $s: x^2 + y^2 = 25$

$l: x = 5$

(iii) $s: x^2 + y^2 = 20$

$l: x = 2y - 10$

(iv) $s: 2x^2 + 2y^2 = 9$

$l: x + y = 3$

11. *l* is the line $y = x + 2$, and *s* is the circle $x^2 + y^2 = 10$.

(i) Write down the co-ordinates of *O*, the centre of *s*.

(ii) What is the radius length of *s*?

(iii) The co-ordinates of the point *A* are (3,1). Find $|OA|$.

(iv) Is *A* on the circle *s*? Explain.

(v) Draw the circle *s*.

(vi) Draw the line *l* and from your graph find the points of intersection of *s* and *l*.

(vii) Verify your answers to part (vi) by solving the simultaneous equations:

$$x^2 + y^2 = 10 \qquad y = x + 2$$

11.3 CIRCLES WITH CENTRE (*h,k*) AND RADIUS LENGTH *r*

We will now derive the equation of a circle centred outside of (0,0).

In Activity 11.6, you derived the equation of the circle with centre (*h,k*) and radius length *r*. Here, once again, is the derivation:

s is the circle with centre *O*(*h,k*).

Let *P*(*x,y*) be any point on *s*.

Let *r* be the length of the radius of *s*.

$|OP| = \sqrt{(x-h)^2 + (y-k)^2} = r$

$\therefore (x-h)^2 + (y-k)^2 = r^2$

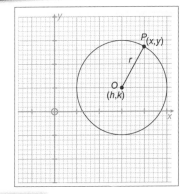

The equation of any circle with centre (*h,k*) and radius length *r* is:

FORMULA

$$(x-h)^2 + (y-k)^2 = r^2$$

This equation is on page 19 of the *Formulae and Tables*.

ACTIVITIES 11.4, 11.5, 11.6

Worked Example 11.6

Find the equation of the circle with centre $(1, -4)$ and radius length 5.

Solution

$(x - h)^2 + (y - k)^2 = r^2$

$h = 1, k = -4, r = 5$

$(x - 1)^2 + (y - (-4))^2 = (5)^2$

$(x - 1)^2 + (y + 4)^2 = (5)^2$

$\therefore (x - 1)^2 + (y + 4)^2 = 25$ is the equation of the circle.

Worked Example 11.7

Find the centre and radius length of the circle $(x + 2)^2 + (y - 8)^2 = 49$.

Solution

Given equation: $(x + 2)^2 + (y - 8)^2 = 49$

General equation: $(x - h)^2 + (y - k)^2 = r^2$

Comparing: $-h = 2, -k = -8, r^2 = 49$

$\therefore h = -2, k = 8, r = 7$

$\therefore$ The centre of the circle is $(-2, 8)$, and the radius length is 7.

Worked Example 11.8

The circle shown has a diameter with endpoints $(2, -3)$ and $(6, -8)$. Find:

(i) The centre of the circle

(ii) The radius length of the circle

(iii) The equation of the circle

Solution

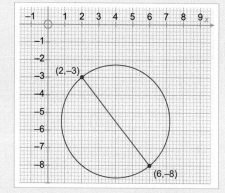

(i) The centre of the circle is the midpoint of the endpoints of the diameter:

$$\text{Midpoint} = \left(\frac{x_1 + x_2}{2}, \frac{y_1 + y_2}{2} \right)$$

$$\text{Centre} = \left(\frac{2 + 6}{2}, \frac{-3 - 8}{2} \right) = \left(\frac{8}{2}, -\frac{11}{2} \right) = \left(4, -\frac{11}{2} \right)$$

(ii) The radius of the circle is the distance from an endpoint of a diameter to the centre of the circle:

$$\text{Distance} = \sqrt{(x_2 - x_1)^2 + (y_2 - y_1)^2}$$

Points $(2, -3)$ and $\left(4, -\frac{11}{2} \right)$

$\therefore x_1 = 2, y_1 = -3$ and $x_2 = 4, y_2 = -\frac{11}{2}$

$$r = \sqrt{(4 - 2)^2 + \left(-\frac{11}{2} + 3 \right)^2}$$

$$r = \sqrt{4 + \frac{25}{4}} = \sqrt{\frac{41}{4}} \quad \text{(Leave in square root form.)}$$

(iii) Equation: $(x - h)^2 + (y - k)^2 = r^2$

Centre $\left(4, -\frac{11}{2} \right) \qquad r = \sqrt{\frac{41}{4}}$

$$(x - 4)^2 + \left(y + \frac{11}{2} \right)^2 = \frac{41}{4}$$

Exercise 11.3

1. Find the equations of the following circles:

    (i)   Centre = (1,4)   radius length = 5

    (ii) Centre = (–2,3)   radius length = 3

    (iii) Centre = (6,–5)   radius length = 1

    (iv) Centre = (0,7)   radius length = 4

    (v)   Centre = (–2,–1)   radius length = 2

    (vi) Centre = (0,0)   radius length = 8

    (vii) Centre = (8,1)   radius length = 6

    (viii) Centre = $(\frac{1}{2},-\frac{1}{4})$ radius length = 9

    (ix) Centre = (1,1.5)   radius length = 7

    (x)   Centre = (–3,–8)   radius length = $\frac{1}{2}$

2. A circle s that has centre (1,1) and that contains the point (5,6) is shown below:

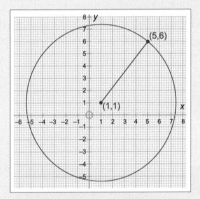

    (i) Find the radius length of s.

    (ii) Write down the equation of s.

3. A circle t that has centre (–2,–1) and that contains the point (2,–3) is shown below:

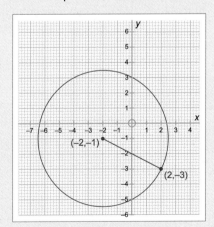

    (i) Find the radius length of t.

    (ii) Write down the equation of t.

4. A circle u with centre (2,4) is shown below. The x-axis is a tangent to the circle.

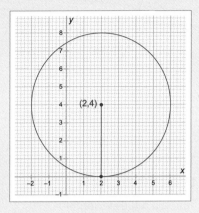

    (i) Find the radius length of u.

    (ii) Write down the equation of u.

5. A circle v with centre (3,–1) is shown below. The y-axis is a tangent to the circle.

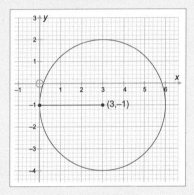

    (i) Find the radius length of v.

    (ii) Write down the equation of v.

6. The x-axis and the y-axis are both tangents to the circle w shown below.

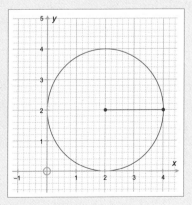

    (i) Find the radius length of w.

    (ii) Write down the equation of w.

7. The circle z shown in the diagram has a diameter with endpoints (−1,4) and (3,−2).

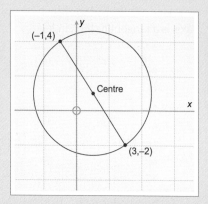

(i) Find the centre of z.

(ii) Find the radius length of z.

(iii) Write down the equation of z.

8. The circle h shown in the diagram has a diameter with endpoints (−2,−3) and (4,7).

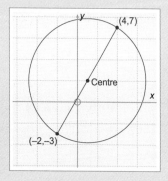

(i) Find the centre of h.

(ii) Find the radius length of h.

(iii) Write down the equation of h.

9. The centre of a circle is (1,2), and the circle contains the point (−2,3).

(i) Draw the circle.

(ii) Find the radius length of the circle.

(iii) Find the equation of the circle.

10. A circle has a diameter with endpoints $A(5,3)$ and $B(−1,3)$. Find the equation of the circle.

11. Find the centre and radius length of each of the following circles:

(i) $(x − 2)^2 + (y − 3)^2 = 25$

(ii) $(x + 2)^2 + (y − 5)^2 = 36$

(iii) $(x − 1)^2 + (y + 3)^2 = 49$

(iv) $(x + 5)^2 + (y + 8)^2 = 1$

(v) $(x − 3)^2 + (y − 4)^2 = 64$

12. Find the centre and radius length of each of the following circles:

(i) $x^2 + y^2 = 100$

(ii) $x^2 + (y − 8)^2 = 49$

(iii) $(x − 2)^2 + y^2 = 81$

(iv) $\left(x − \frac{1}{2}\right)^2 + \left(y − \frac{1}{3}\right)^2 = \frac{1}{9}$

(v) $(x − 2)^2 + (y − 3)^2 = 5$

13. The graph below shows two semicircles, h and k. Both have the same radius length. n is a horizontal tangent to both semicircles. m is a vertical tangent to k.

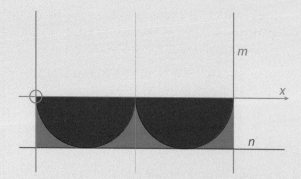

(i) $(x − 3)^2 + y^2 = 1$ is the equation of the circle containing k and the reflection of k in the x-axis. Write down the centre of k.

(ii) What is the radius length of k?

(iii) Write down the co-ordinates of the centre of h.

(iv) Find the area of the rectangle enclosed by m, n, the x-axis and the y-axis.

(v) Find, in terms of π, the area shaded blue.

14. The equation of the circle s is $(x - 2)^2 + y^2 = 1$.

    (i) Write down the equations of the other three circles in the diagram.

    (ii) Find, in terms of π, the sum of the areas of the three smaller circles.

    (iii) Find, in terms of π, the area of the large circle.

    (iv) Find, in terms of π, the area shaded blue.

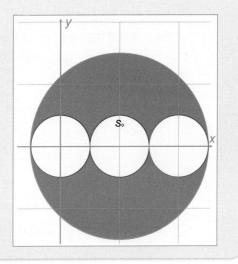

11.4 INTERCEPTS AND POINTS INSIDE, OUTSIDE OR ON A CIRCLE

Intercepts on the *x*-axis and *y*-axis

The points where a circle crosses the *x*-axis are called the *x*-intercepts of the circle and the points where a circle crosses the *y*-axis are called the *y*-intercepts of the circle.

The co-ordinates of points on the *x*-axis are always of the form $(a,0)$ and the co-ordinates of points on the *y*-axis are always of the form $(0,b)$. Hence:

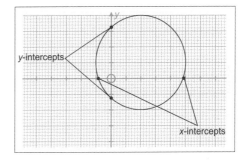

    ▇ We **let $y = 0$** in the equation of a circle and solve for x to find the co-ordinates of the **x-intercepts**.

    ▇ We **let $x = 0$** in the equation of a circle and solve for y to find the co-ordinates of the **y-intercepts**.

 ## Worked Example 11.9

Find the co-ordinates of the points at which:

    (i) The circle $x^2 + y^2 = 25$ intersects the *x*-axis

    (ii) The circle $(x + 1)^2 + (y - 9)^2 = 26$ intersects the *y*-axis

Hence, sketch each circle showing these intercepts clearly.

Solution

    (i) Intersects the *x*-axis:

        Let $y = 0$ in the equation of the circle.

$$x^2 + (0)^2 = 25$$
$$x^2 = 25$$
$$x = \pm 5$$

        Therefore, the co-ordinates of the *x*-intercepts are $(5,0)$ and $(-5,0)$.

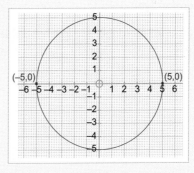

Centre $(0,0)$; points $(5,0)$ and $(-5,0)$

(ii) Intersects the y-axis:

Let $x = 0$ in the equation of the circle.

$$(0 + 1)^2 + (y - 9)^2 = 26$$

$$1 + (y - 9)^2 = 26$$

$$(y - 9)^2 = 26 - 1$$

$$(y - 9)^2 = 25$$

$$y - 9 = \pm 5$$

$$y - 9 = 5 \quad \textbf{or} \quad y - 9 = -5$$

$$y = 14 \quad \textbf{or} \quad y = 4$$

Therefore, the co-ordinates of the y-intercepts are (0,4) and (0,14).

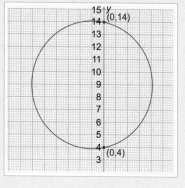

Centre (–1,9); points (0,14) and (0,4)

Points Inside, Outside or On a Circle

In a circle of the form $(x - h)^2 + (y - k)^2 = r^2$, a point (x_1, y_1) is:

(i)   Inside the circle, if $(x_1 - h)^2 + (y_1 - k)^2 < r^2$

(ii) Outside the circle, if $(x_1 - h)^2 + (y_1 - k)^2 > r^2$

(iii) On the circle, if $(x_1 - h)^2 + (y_1 - k)^2 = r^2$

ACTIVITY 11.7

Worked Example 11.10

Investigate if the points (7,–5) and (8,–6) are outside, inside or on the following circle:

$$(x - 4)^2 + (y + 1)^2 = 25$$

Solution

$(x - 4)^2 + (y + 1)^2 = 25$

Substitute (7,–5) into the left-hand side of the equation:

Is $(7 - 4)^2 + (-5 + 1)^2 = 25$?

$$(3)^2 + (-4)^2 = 25$$

$$9 + 16 = 25$$

$$25 = 25 \quad \text{True}$$

Therefore, the point (7,–5) is **on** the circle.

Substitute (8,–6) into the left-hand side of the equation:

Is $(8 - 4)^2 + (-6 + 1)^2 = 25$?

$$(4)^2 + (-5)^2 = 25$$

$$16 + 25 = 25$$

$$41 = 25 \quad \text{False}$$

$$41 > 25$$

Therefore, the point (8,–6) is **outside** the circle.

Exercise 11.4

1. The circle shown below has centre (0,0) and radius length 4.

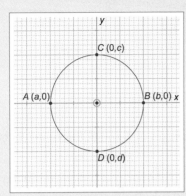

   (i) Find the values *a*, *b*, *c* and *d*.

   (ii) Write down the co-ordinates of *A* and *B*, the *x*-intercepts of the circle.

   (iii) Write down the co-ordinates of *C* and *D*, the *y*-intercepts of the circle.

2. The circle shown below has centre (0,0) and radius length 7.

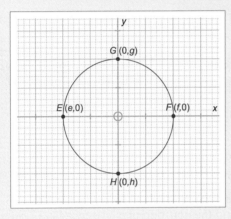

   (i) Find the values *e*, *f*, *g* and *h*.

   (ii) Write down the co-ordinates of *E* and *F*, the *x*-intercepts of the circle.

   (iii) Write down the co-ordinates of *G* and *H*, the *y*-intercepts of the circle.

3. For each of the circles shown below, write down the co-ordinates of the *x*- and *y*-intercepts of the circle.

   (i)
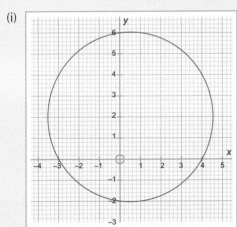

   (ii)
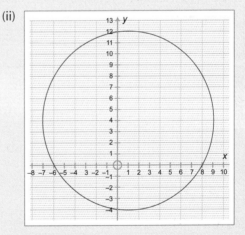

4. Find the *x*-intercepts and *y*-intercepts of each of the following circles:

   (i) $x^2 + y^2 = 4$

   (ii) $x^2 + y^2 = 9$

   (iii) $x^2 + y^2 = 16$

   (iv) $x^2 + y^2 = 36$

5. For each of the following circles, find the co-ordinates of the *x*-intercept:

   (i) $(x - 2)^2 + (y + 3)^2 = 34$

   (ii) $(x + 3)^2 + (y - 2)^2 = 40$

   (iii) $(x + 5)^2 + (y - 8)^2 = 164$

   (iv) $(x + 1)^2 + (y - 1)^2 = 50$

   (v) $(x - 4)^2 + (y - 3)^2 = 58$

   (vi) $(x - 10)^2 + (y - 11)^2 = 125$

6. For each of the following circles, find the co-ordinates of the y-intercept:

    (i) $(x - 3)^2 + (y - 4)^2 = 90$

    (ii) $(x + 2)^2 + (y - 5)^2 = 104$

    (iii) $(x - 6)^2 + (y + 1)^2 = 72$

    (iv) $(x - 1)^2 + (y + 1)^2 = 10$

    (v) $(x - 3)^2 + (y - 4)^2 = 58$

7. The equation of the circle c is $(x - 2)^2 + (y - 1)^2 = 13$.

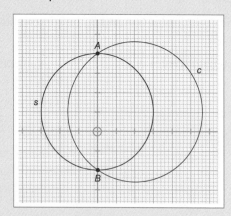

    (i) Find the co-ordinates of A and B, the y-intercepts of c.

    (ii) If A and B are the endpoints of a diameter of the circle s, then find the equation of s.

8. The equation of the circle m is $(x - 2)^2 + (y + 3)^2 = 34$.

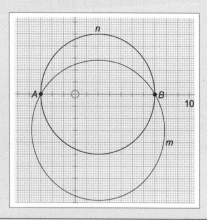

    (i) Find the co-ordinates of A and B, the x-intercepts of m.

    (ii) A and B are the endpoints of a diameter of the circle n. Find the equation of n.

9. For each of the circles c_1 to c_4, one and only one of the points A to D lie on the circle. Investigate which point is on which circle. Show all your workings.

Circle	Point
c_1: $x^2 + y^2 = 25$	A(−5,4)
c_2: $(x - 2)^2 + (y + 3)^2 = 5$	B(3,5)
c_3: $x^2 + (y - 2)^2 = 29$	C(3,−4)
c_4: $(x + 2)^2 + (y - 5)^2 = 58$	D(1,−2)

10. Show that the point A(−2,0) is inside the circle $(x + 4)^2 + (y - 1)^2 = 9$.

11. Show that the point B(7,3) lies outside the circle $(x - 1)^2 + (y - 2)^2 = 9$.

12. Complete the table by stating whether points W, X, Y and Z lie inside, outside or on the given circle. Show all your workings.

Circle	Point	Conclusion
c_1: $(x - 2)^2 + (y - 3)^2 = 9$	V(2,1)	Inside
c_2: $(x + 3)^2 + (y - 1)^2 = 25$	W(0,5)	
c_3: $x^2 + y^2 = 25$	X(4,4)	
c_4: $x^2 + y^2 = 26$	Y(5,1)	
c_5: $(x - 2)^2 + (y - 3)^2 = 49$	Z(0,0)	

Revision Exercises

1. (–7,0) and (1,0) are the endpoints of the diameter of the circle *c*.

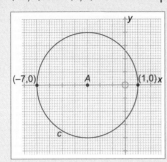

(i) What are the co-ordinates of *A*, the centre of *c*?

(ii) What is the radius length of *c*?

(iii) Write down the equation of *c*.

(iv) Find the co-ordinates of the *y*-intercepts of *c*.

2. *s* is a circle with equation $(x + 1)^2 + (y - 1)^2 = 25$.

  (i) Write down the co-ordinates of *R*, the centre of *s*.

 (ii) What is the radius length of *s*?

(iii) Using graph paper, draw *s*.

(iv) Show that the point $A(3, -2)$ is on the circle.

 (v) If [*AB*] is a diameter of *s*, find the co-ordinates of *B*.

3. *p*, *q* and *s* are three circles whose centres lie on the *x*-axis.

(3,0) are the co-ordinates of an endpoint of a diameter of *s*.

All circles touch each other at, at most, one point.

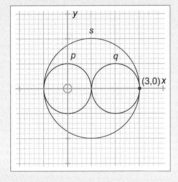

(i) From the graph, write down the co-ordinates of the centres of *p*, *q* and *s*.

(ii) Is the radius length of *s* equal to twice the radius length of *q*? Explain your answer.

(iii) Write down the equations of *p*, *q* and *s*.

4. The three circles *s*, *t* and *u* shown below have their centres along the *y*-axis.

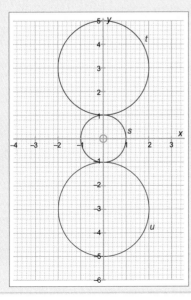

(i) Write down the co-ordinates of the centres and the radius lengths of each circle.

(ii) Write down the equation of each circle.

(iii) What is the length of the circumference of *s*? Leave your answer in terms of π.

(iv) What is the length of the circumference of *t*? Leave your answer in terms of π.

(v) If C_t is the length of the circumference of *t* and C_s is the length of the circumference of *s*, then write down the ratio $C_t : C_s$.

(vi) Is $C_t : C_s = r_t : r_s$, where r_t and r_s are the radii of *t* and *s*, respectively?

5. The diagram shows four circles of equal radius. The circles are touching as indicated.

The equation of s is $x^2 + y^2 = 16$.

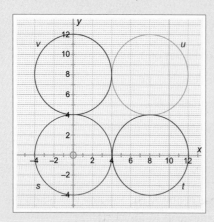

(i) Write down the radius length of s.

(ii) Write down the co-ordinates of the centre of u.

(iii) What is the radius length of u?

(iv) Write down the equation of u.

(v) What is the area of the square whose vertices are the centres of the four circles?

(vi) Is the area of the square greater than or less than the area of one of the circles? Show clearly how you arrived at your answer.

6. The circle s has the equation $x^2 + y^2 = 10$. The circle c has centre $(-2,2)$ and radius length $\sqrt{2}$.

The line l has the equation $x - y + 2 = 0$.

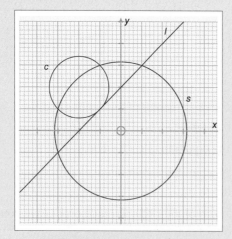

(i) Find the co-ordinates of the points of intersection of l and s.

(ii) Find the equation of the circle c.

(iii) Find the co-ordinates of the point where l meets c.

7. The triangle ABC has vertices $A(2,5)$, $B(-2,-1)$ and $C(5,3)$.

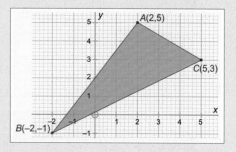

(i) Verify that $AB \perp AC$.

(ii) Find the midpoint of $[BC]$. Label this point as D.

(iii) Show the points A, B, C and D on graph paper.

(iv) On the same sheet of graph paper, draw the circle s, with centre D and containing A, B and C.

(v) Find the radius length of s.

(vi) Find the equation of s.

8. s is the circle $x^2 + y^2 = 25$ and m is the line $y = 4x - 8$. The line m intersects s at the points A and B.

The co-ordinates of B are $\left(\dfrac{13}{17}, -\dfrac{84}{17}\right)$.

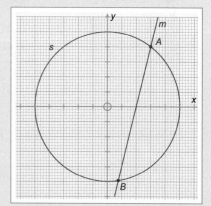

(i) Find the co-ordinates of the point A.

(ii) Find the co-ordinates of C, the midpoint of the chord $[AB]$.

(iii) Find the equation of n, the perpendicular bisector of $[AB]$.

(iv) Show that $O(0,0)$ lies on n.

9. k is the circle $x^2 + y^2 = 17$.

   (i) Write down the centre and radius length of k.

   (ii) Prove that the line $t: x + 4y = 17$ is a tangent to k.

   (iii) Draw a sketch of k and t.

   (iv) l is a second tangent to k, which is parallel to t. Find the equation of l.

10. The point $(1,-7)$ is on a circle k, which has its centre at $O(0,0)$.

   (i) Sketch the circle k.

   (ii) Find the equation of k.

   (iii) If (p,p) is a point on k, find two possible values of p.

   (iv) If the point $(3,n)$ is inside the circle k, find the greatest possible value of n, where $n \in N$.

11.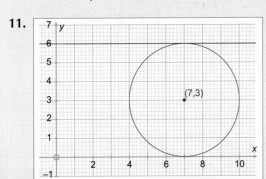

A circle has centre $(7,3)$. The line $y = 6$ and the x-axis are tangents to the circle.

   (i) Write down the radius length of the circle.

   (ii) Find the equation of the circle.

   (iii) Verify that the line $l: x - 2y - 1 = 0$ contains the centre of the circle.

   (iv) Find the point of intersection of l and the tangent $y = 6$.

12.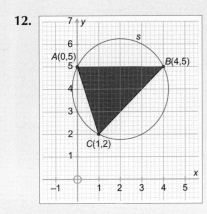

s is the circumcircle of the triangle ABC. The co-ordinates of the centre of s are $(2,4)$.

   (i) Find the radius length of s.

   (ii) Find the length of the chord $[AB]$, and hence, find the area of the triangle ABC.

   (iii) Find the area of s correct to two decimal places.

   (iv) Find, correct to two decimal places, the area of the triangle as a percentage of the area of the circle.

12 chapter

Trigonometry

Learning Outcomes

In this chapter you will learn how to:

➲ Solve right-angled triangles using the theorem of Pythagoras

➲ Use the trigonometric ratios sin, cos and tan to solve problems

➲ Define sin x and cos x for all values of x

➲ Define tan x

➲ Find trigonometric ratios in surd form for angles 30°, 45° and 60°

➲ Calculate the area of a triangle

➲ Use the Sine and Cosine Rules to solve problems

➲ Calculate the area of a sector of a circle

➲ Calculate the length of an arc of a circle

Trigonometry is the study of triangles, their angles, areas and lengths. It is not the work of any one mathematician or nation. Its history dates back thousands of years. Archaelogical evidence dating to 2150 BC suggests that the ancient Egyptians had a knowledge of trigonometry.

Much of the technology that we use in today's highly developed world would not have been possible without trigonometry. There are numerous applications of trigonometry. Astronomers use trigonometry to calculate distances to nearby stars. Engineers use trigonometry to construct bridges and build giant skyscrapers. Seismologists use trigonometry to study earthquakes. Here is a list of just some of the other areas to which trigonometry has been applied: navigation, medical imaging (MRI scans), computer graphics, electrical engineering, biology and economics.

12.1 RIGHT-ANGLED TRIANGLES AND PYTHAGORAS' THEOREM

Pythagoras, an ancient Greek mathematician, discovered a very famous feature of right-angled triangles. Today, this feature is known as **Pythagoras' theorem**.

> In a right-angled triangle, the area of the square on the hypotenuse is equal to the sum of the areas of the squares on the other two sides.

FORMULA

$c^2 = a^2 + b^2$

You can find this formula on page 16 of *Formulae and Tables*.

YOU SHOULD REMEMBER...

- The angles in a triangle sum to 180°.
- Angles at the base of an isosceles triangle are equal in measure.
- All angles in an equilateral triangle measure 60°.
- Distance = Speed × Time.

KEY WORDS

- **Right-angled triangle**
- **Pythagoras' theorem**
- **Opposite, adjacent, hypotenuse**
- **Sin, cos, tan**
- **Unit circle**
- **Reference angle**
- **Sine Rule**
- **Cosine Rule**

TRIGONOMETRY

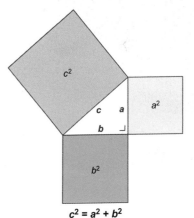

$c^2 = a^2 + b^2$

Worked Example 12.1

Use the theorem of Pythagoras to find the value of x.

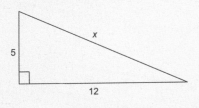

Solution

$x^2 = 12^2 + 5^2$ (theorem of Pythagoras)

$x^2 = 144 + 25$

$x^2 = 169$

$x = 13$

Worked Example 12.2

A flagpole is 15 m high. It is held firm by a wire of length 17 m fixed to its top and to a point on the ground. How far is it from the foot of the flagpole to the point on the ground where the wire is secured?

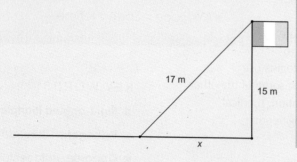

Solution

Let x be the distance from the foot of the flagpole to the point where the wire is secured.

$15^2 + x^2 = 17^2$ (theorem of Pythagoras)

$225 + x^2 = 289$

$x^2 = 289 - 225$

$x^2 = 64$

$x = 8$

$\therefore$ Distance = 8 m

Exercise 12.1

1. Find the value of x in each case:

   (i)
   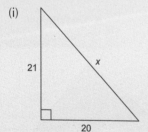

   (ii)
   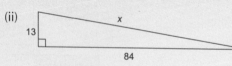

   (iii)
   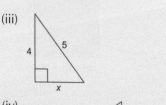

   (iv)
   (v)
   (vi)
   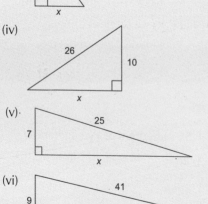

2. Find the value of x in each case (leave your answers in surd form):

   (i)

   (ii)
   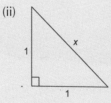

   (iii)
   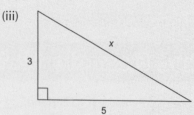

   (iv)
   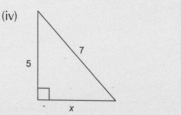

TRIGONOMETRY

3. A ladder is 6.5 m long and rests against a vertical wall. The top of the ladder reaches a point on the wall that is 6 m above the ground. Find the distance from the wall to the foot of the ladder.

4. Find the value of x and y in each case:

(i)

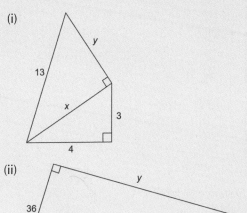

(iii)

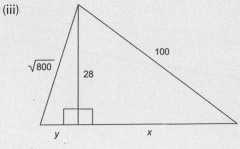

(ii)

(iv)

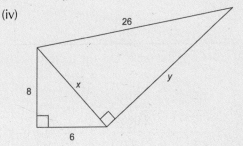

5. The perimeter of a rectangle is 280 cm. The length of the longest side is 80 cm. Find:

(i) The length of the shortest side

(ii) The length of a diagonal of the rectangle

(iii) The area of the rectangle

6. (a) Copy the table. Use the pattern to complete the table.

Side a	Side b	Hypotenuse c
3	4	5
6	8	10
9	12	15
12		
	20	
		30
21		

(b) Using your calculator, check if $a^2 + b^2 = c^2$ for each row in the above table.
Copy the table and show your results.

a^2	b^2	c^2	Tick if true
9	16	25	✓
36			

7. The width of a door frame is 84 cm and its height is 187 cm. What must x measure if the door frame must have interior angles of 90°?

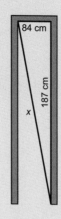

84 cm

187 cm

x

8. (a) Copy the table. Use the pattern to complete the table.

Side a	Side b	Hypotenuse c
2,000	2,100	2,900
200	210	290
20		
2	2.1	
	0.21	
0.02		
0.002		

(b) Using your calculator, check if $a^2 + b^2 = c^2$ for each row in the above table. Copy the table and show your results.

a^2	b^2	c^2	Tick if true
4,000,000	4,410,000	8,410,000	✓

9. The sides of a triangle are of lengths 85, 77 and 36.
By applying the theorem of Pythagoras, investigate if the triangle is right-angled.

10. The sides of a triangle are of lengths 7, 24 and 25.
By applying the theorem of Pythagoras, investigate if the triangle is right-angled.

11. The sides of a triangle are of lengths 11, 60 and 61.
By applying the theorem of Pythagoras, investigate if the triangle is right-angled.

12.2 RIGHT-ANGLED TRIANGLES AND THE TRIGONOMETRIC RATIOS

In a right-angled triangle, we have the following special ratios:

$$\sin A = \frac{\text{opposite}}{\text{hypotenuse}}$$

$$\cos A = \frac{\text{adjacent}}{\text{hypotenuse}}$$

$$\tan A = \frac{\text{opposite}}{\text{adjacent}}$$

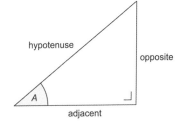

These ratios can be found on page 16 of the *Formulae and Tables*.

Worked Example 12.3

In the following right-angled triangle, write down the value of each of the following ratios:
sin A, cos A and tan A; also sin B, cos B and tan B.

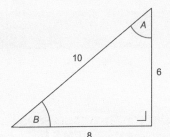

Solution

$$\sin A = \frac{8}{10} = \frac{4}{5} \qquad \sin B = \frac{6}{10} = \frac{3}{5}$$

$$\cos A = \frac{6}{10} = \frac{3}{5} \qquad \cos B = \frac{8}{10} = \frac{4}{5}$$

$$\tan A = \frac{8}{6} = \frac{4}{3} \qquad \tan B = \frac{6}{8} = \frac{3}{4}$$

Worked Example 12.4

Use your calculator to find the value of each of the following, correct to four decimal places:

(i) sin 32.4°

(ii) cos 45.6°

(iii) tan 22.5°

Solution

> Make sure your calculator is in degree mode.

(i) On the calculator, press:

The answer should be 0.5358 corrected to four decimal places.

(ii)

(iii)
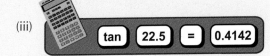

Finding Angles

How can we find the measure of the angle A?

From the diagram, we know that:

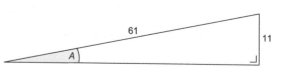

$$\sin A = \frac{11}{61} = 0.180328$$

We can now use the calculator to find A.

Key in the following:

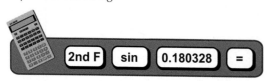

This gives an answer of 10.39° (to two decimal places).

This is written as:

$$\sin A = 0.180328$$
$$\therefore A = \sin^{-1} 0.180328$$
$$\Rightarrow A = 10.39°$$

Note: Individual calculators may differ from what is shown next.

Worked Example 12.5

Change 35.6° to degrees and minutes.

Solution

Note: On some calculators, D°M'S is replaced with ° ' ".

The answer 35° 36' 0" is displayed. Therefore, the answer is 35° 36'.

Worked Example 12.6

Change 64° 45' to degrees.

Solution

The answer 64.75 is displayed.

$$\Rightarrow 64° 45' = 64.75°$$

Worked Example 12.7

Use your calculator to find the measure of the angle X, if $\sin X = 0.5469$.

Give your answer to the nearest minute.

Solution

$\sin X = 0.5469$

$\Rightarrow X = \sin^{-1} 0.5469$

| 2nd F | sin | 0.5469 | = |

The answer 33.15459885 is displayed.
Now, convert this to the nearest minute:

| 2nd F | D°M'S |

The answer 33° 9' 16.556" is displayed.
This answer, corrected to the nearest minute, is 33° 9'.

Worked Example 12.8

If $\cos A = 0.2183$, then using your calculator, find:

  (i) The measure of the angle A to two decimal places

  (ii) The measure of the angle A to the nearest minute

Solution

  (i) Key in the following:

| 2nd F | cos | 0.2183 | = |

This gives an answer of 77.39° (to two decimal places).

  (ii) Key in the following:

| 2nd F | cos | 0.2183 | = | 2nd F | D°M'S |

This gives the answer 77° 23' (to the nearest minute).

Exercise 12.2

1. In each of the following triangles, write down the values of sin A, cos A, and tan A:

(i)
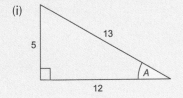

(ii)
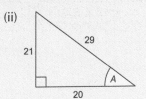

ACTIVE MATHS 2   **379**

TRIGONOMETRY

12

2. For each one of the following triangles, write down the values of sin A, cos A, tan A, sin B, cos B and tan B:

(i)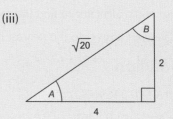

(ii)

(iii)

3. Use your calculator to find the value of each of the following, correct to four decimal places:

(i) sin 15°

(ii) cos 30°

(iii) tan 75°

(iv) sin 14°

(v) tan 42°

(vi) cos 85°

(vii) tan 12°

(viii) sin 30°

(ix) tan 80°

(x) tan 25.6°

(xi) cos 43.8°

(xii) sin 79.2°

(xiii) sin 31.4°

(xiv) tan 15.8°

(xv) cos 30.9°

(xvi) cos 56.7°

(xvii) sin 63.3°

(xviii) tan 82.4°

4. Use your calculator to find the measure of the angle A, 0° ≤ A ≤ 90°. Give your answers correct to two decimal places.

(i) sin A = 0.6192

(ii) cos A = 0.8694

(iii) tan A = 0.3592

(iv) sin A = 0.4375

(v) tan A = 0.3762

(vi) cos A = 0.1246

(vii) tan A = 1.6347

(viii) sin A = 0.7221

(ix) tan A = 2.1375

(x) cos A = 0.4523

5. Change each of the following to degrees and minutes. Give your answers to the nearest minute.

(i) 2.5°

(ii) 2.25°

(iii) 2.75°

(iv) 25.4°

(v) 1.2°

(vi) $\frac{1}{3}$ of a degree

6. Change the following to degrees. Give your answers correct to two decimal places.

(i) 2° 31′

(ii) 10° 40′

(iii) 25° 50′

(iv) 70° 22′

(v) 11° 37′

(vi) 33° 33′

7. Use your calculator to find the measure of the angle B, 0° ≤ B ≤ 90°. Give your answers to the nearest minute.

(i) sin B = 0.9701

(ii) cos B = 0.6661

(iii) tan B = 0.9628

(iv) sin B = 0.6635

(v) tan B = 0.3193

(vi) cos B = 0.8925

(vii) tan B = 3.4650

(viii) sin B = 0.2411

(ix) tan B = 0.4080

(x) cos B = 0.5297

8. Calculate to the nearest degree the value of the angle B.

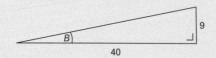

9. Calculate to the nearest minute the value of the angle C.

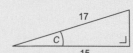

12.3 FINDING THE LENGTH OF A SIDE IN A RIGHT-ANGLED TRIANGLE

If we know the measure of just one angle in a right-angled triangle (other than the right angle) and the length of one side, then we can find the lengths of the remaining two sides.

Worked Example 12.9

Consider the triangle *ABC* shown below.
If $|AB| = 8$ cm and $|\angle BAC| = 35°$, then find $|BC|$, correct to one decimal place.

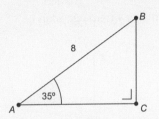

Solution

Let $|BC| = x$

$$\sin 35° = \frac{x}{8}$$

$8 \sin 35° = x$ (cross-multiplying)

$4.5886 = x$ (calculator)

$\therefore |BC| = 4.6$ cm (one decimal place)

Worked Example 12.10

Find the values for *x* and *y* in the diagram below, correct to two decimal places.

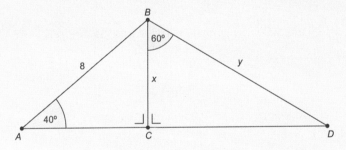

Solution

$$\sin 40° = \frac{x}{8}$$

$\Rightarrow x = 8 \sin 40°$ (cross-multiplying)

$x = 5.1423$ (calculator)

$x = 5.14$ (calculator)

$$\cos 60° = \frac{5.14}{y}$$

$y \cos 60° = 5.14$ (cross-multiplying)

$$y = \frac{5.14}{\cos 60°}$$

$y = 10.28$ (calculator)

Worked Example 12.11

Consider the triangle *ABC*. $|AB| = 16$ cm, $|BC| = 9.2$ cm.

Find to the nearest degree, the measure of $\angle BAC$.

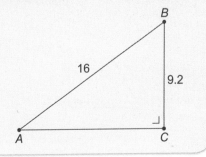

Solution

$\sin(\angle BAC) = \dfrac{9.2}{16}$

$\qquad\qquad = \dfrac{23}{40}$

$\therefore \ |\angle BAC| = \sin^{-1}\left(\dfrac{23}{40}\right)$

$\qquad\qquad = 35°$ (to the nearest degree)

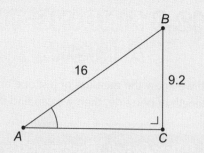

Exercise 12.3

1. Find the value of *x* in the following triangles (answer correct to two decimal places where necessary):

(i)

(ii)

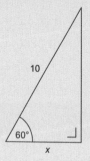

(iii)

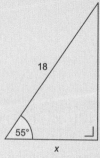

(iv)

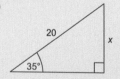

(v)

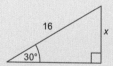

(vi)

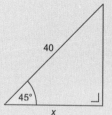

2. Find the value of *y* in the following triangles:

(i)

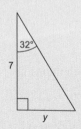

(ii)

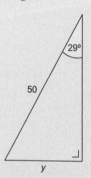

(iii)

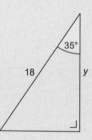

(iv)

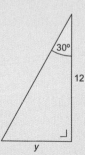

(v)

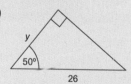

(vi)

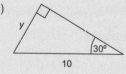

3. Solve for *x* and *y* to two decimal places.

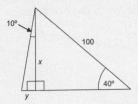

4. Solve for *x*, *y* and *z* to two significant figures.

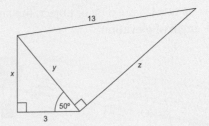

5. Find the measure of the angle *A* in each of the following (give your answer to the nearest degree).

(i)

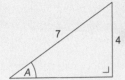

(ii)

(iii)

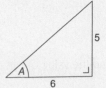

(iv)

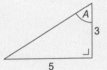

(v)

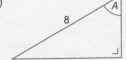

(vi)

12.4 USING TRIGONOMETRY TO SOLVE PRACTICAL PROBLEMS

Compass Directions

The diagram below shows the four main compass directions: North, South, East and West.

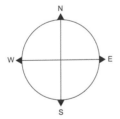

For all other compass directions, we can begin by looking North or South and then turning either East or West through the required number of degrees. This is shown in the diagrams below. One could also begin by looking East or West and then turning North or South through the required angle.

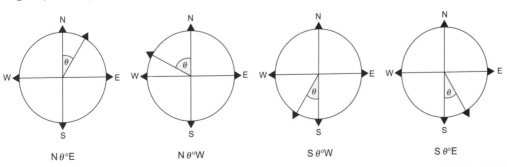

Angles of Elevation and Depression

If you look up at a tall building or object, the angle that your line of vision makes with the horizontal is called the **angle of elevation**.

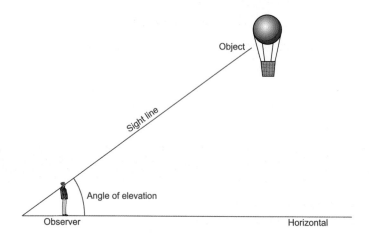

> The **angle of elevation** is the angle above the horizontal.

If you stand on top of a cliff and observe a swimmer out at sea, the angle that your line of vision makes with the horizontal is called the **angle of depression**.

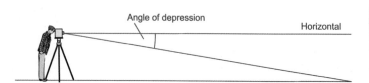

> The **angle of depression** is the angle below the horizontal.

Worked Example 12.12

A ship leaves a port A and sails a distance of 4 km in the direction N 30° E. The ship then changes direction and sails for a further 6 km in the direction S 60° E to a point C (see diagram).

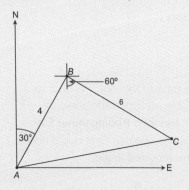

(i) Calculate the distance from the ship's present position at point C to port A. Give your answer to one decimal place.

(ii) Find $|\angle BCA|$, to the nearest degree.

(iii) Hence, find the direction of C **from** A.

Solution

(i)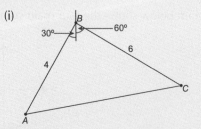

$$|\angle ABC| = 30° + 60° = 90°$$
$$|AC|^2 = 4^2 + 6^2 \text{ (theorem of Pythagoras)}$$
$$|AC|^2 = 52$$
$$|AC| = \sqrt{52}$$
$$|AC| = 7.2 \text{ km} \quad (1 \text{ d.p.})$$

(ii) Let $\angle BCA = \theta$.
$$\tan \theta = \frac{4}{6} = \frac{2}{3}$$
$$\theta = \tan^{-1}\left(\frac{2}{3}\right)$$
$$\theta = 33.69°$$
$$\therefore |\angle BCA| = 34° \text{ (to nearest degree)}$$

(iii)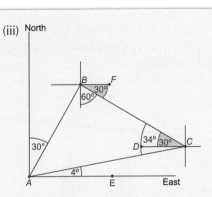

$|\angle FBC| = 90° - 60° = 30°$

$\therefore |\angle BCD| = 30°$ (alternate to $\angle FBC$)

$|\angle DCA| = 34° - 30° = 4°$

$\therefore |\angle CAE| = 4°$ (alternate to $\angle DCA$)

Hence, the direction of C from A is E 4° N.

 Exercise 12.4

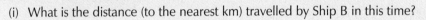

1. Two ships A and B leave the same harbour. Ship A travels due west and Ship B travels 67° south of west. After two hours, Ship A has travelled 46 km and is directly north of Ship B.

   (i)   What is the distance (to the nearest km) travelled by Ship B in this time?

   (ii) Find the speed (to the nearest km/h) of Ship A.

   (iii) Find the speed (to the nearest km/h) of Ship B.

2. The Empire State Building pictured below is one of New York's tallest buildings. Using the information given, calculate the height of the building.

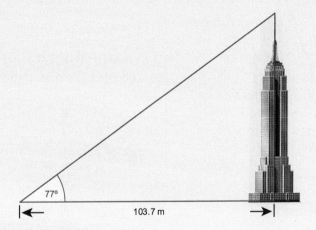

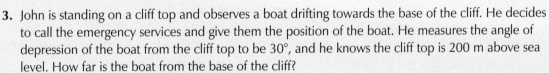

3. John is standing on a cliff top and observes a boat drifting towards the base of the cliff. He decides to call the emergency services and give them the position of the boat. He measures the angle of depression of the boat from the cliff top to be 30°, and he knows the cliff top is 200 m above sea level. How far is the boat from the base of the cliff?

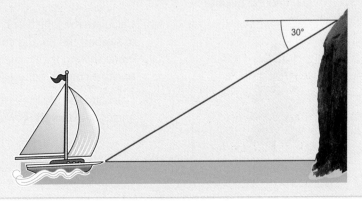

4. A vertical pole is tied to the horizontal ground by means of two wires. The longer wire is 22 m long and makes an angle of 47° with the ground. The shorter wire makes an angle of 63° with the ground.
Find to the nearest metre:

(i) The height of the pole

(ii) The length of the shorter wire

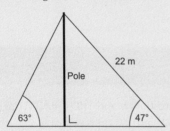

5. The Sears Tower in Chicago is one of the world's tallest structures. A tourist wishing to calculate the height of the tower makes the measurements shown in the diagram. Using these measurements, calculate the height of the tower.

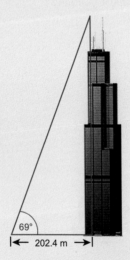

6. Liam wants to know the height of a tree in his back garden. Standing 5 m from the foot of the tree, and using a clinometer, he measures the angle of elevation of the top of the tree to be 33°. If Liam is 170 cm tall, find the height of the tree.

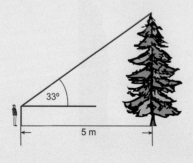

7. The Petronas Towers in Kuala Lumpur are among the world's tallest buildings. Using the information given in the diagram below, calculate the height, to the nearest metre, of the towers.

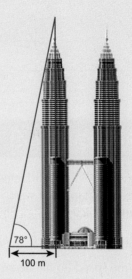

8. On a crane the structure between the point A and the point C is known as the jib of the crane. The structure between point B and point A is known as the counter jib. The cables connecting the jib and counter jib to the tower are known as jib ties.

$|AB| = 6$ m, $|AC| = 15$ m and the angle between counter jib and tie is $35°$.

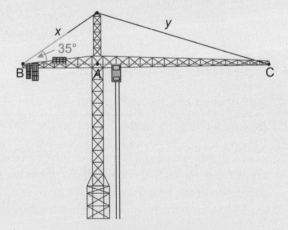

(a) Calculate the length of cable required to support the jib and counter jib on the crane shown. (Note: there are two strands of cable connected to each jib.)

(b) Calculate the measure of each of the angles between the tower and the jib ties.

9. The diagram below is a plan of a triangular shaped dormer window. All measurements are in feet. All line segments represent the frame of the window.

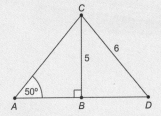

(a) Calculate $|BD|$ to the nearest inch.

(b) Calculate the measure of $\angle CDB$ to the nearest degree.

(c) Calculate the length of timber required to make this frame. Allow for 5% wastage.

10. The angle of elevation of the top of a pylon is measured from two points, A and B. The points A and B are 10 m apart on horizontal ground.

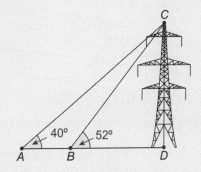

(a) Let $|CD| = h$ and $|BD| = x$. Write tan 52° and 40° in terms of h and x.

(b) Write h in terms of x and tan 52°.

(c) Write h in terms of x and tan 40°.

(d) Equate your expressions for h in parts (b) and (c).

(e) Solve for x.

(f) Find h.

12.5 SPECIAL ANGLES 30°, 45° AND 60°

Special Angles 30° and 60°

A 60° angle can be constructed as follows, with just a ruler and a compass:

(a) Construct an equilateral triangle with sides of length 2 units.

(b) Bisect one of the angles in the triangle.

(c) Let x be the distance from the vertex of the bisected angle to the opposite side.

(d) Use the theorem of Pythagoras to find x.

$$x^2 + 1^2 = 2^2$$
$$x^2 = 4 - 1$$
$$x^2 = 3$$
$$x = \sqrt{3}$$

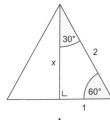

From the triangle, we have:

- $\sin 60° = \dfrac{\sqrt{3}}{2}$

- $\cos 60° = \dfrac{1}{2}$

- $\tan 60° = \sqrt{3}$

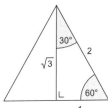

Also:

- $\sin 30° = \dfrac{1}{2}$

- $\cos 30° = \dfrac{\sqrt{3}}{2}$

- $\tan 30° = \dfrac{1}{\sqrt{3}}$

ACTIVITY 12.7

Special Angle 45°

A 45° angle can also be constructed with just a ruler and a compass.

(a) Construct a right-angled isosceles triangle with equal sides of 1 unit in length.

(b) Let x be the length of the hypotenuse.

(c) Use the theorem of Pythagoras to find x.

$$1^2 + 1^2 = x^2$$
$$2 = x^2$$
$$\sqrt{2} = x$$

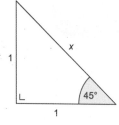

From the triangle, we have:

- $\sin 45° = \dfrac{1}{\sqrt{2}}$

- $\cos 45° = \dfrac{1}{\sqrt{2}}$

- $\tan 45° = 1$

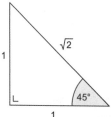

These ratios appear on page 13 of *Formulae and Tables*.

Exercise 12.5

1. Copy and complete the following table. Give your answers in surd form.

A	30°	45°	60°
sin A			
cos A			
tan A			

2.

(i) What is the measure of ∠BAC?

(ii) Find $|AB|$ in surd form.

(iii) Use the theorem of Pythagoras to find $|AC|$.

3.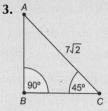

(i) Find the measure of ∠BAC.

(ii) Find $|BC|$.

4.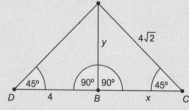

(i) Find the values of x and y.

(ii) What is the measure of ∠DAB?

5. Evaluate $\sin^2 45° + \cos^2 45°$.

[Note: $\sin^2 45° = (\sin 45°)^2$]

6. Evaluate $\sin^2 60° + \cos^2 60° + \tan^2 60°$.

7. Evaluate $\tan^2 30° + \sin^2 30° + \cos^2 30°$.

8. Show that $\dfrac{\sin 30°}{\cos 30°} = \tan 30°$.

12.6 AREA OF A TRIANGLE

In Activity 12.8 we derived a formula for the area of a triangle.

FORMULA

Area of a triangle $= \dfrac{1}{2} ab \sin C$

This formula is also given on page 16 of the *Formulae and Tables*.

To use this formula, we need to know the lengths of two sides of the triangle and the angle **between** these two sides.

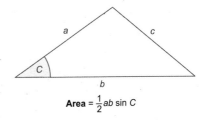

Area $= \dfrac{1}{2} ab \sin C$

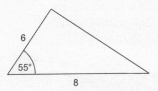

Worked Example 12.13

Find the area of the given triangle. Give your answer correct to two decimal places.

Solution

Area $= \dfrac{1}{2} ab \sin C$

$\quad = \dfrac{1}{2}(6)(8)(\sin 55°)$

$\quad = 19.6596$

$\quad = 19.66$ square units

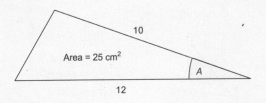

Worked Example 12.14

Find the measure of the angle A. Give your answer correct to the nearest degree.

Area $= 25$ cm^2

Solution

$\dfrac{1}{2} ab \sin C = \text{Area}$

$\dfrac{1}{2}(12)(10)(\sin A) = 25$

$(60)(\sin A) = 25$

$\sin A = \dfrac{25}{60}$

$\sin A = \dfrac{5}{12}$

$A = \sin^{-1}\left(\dfrac{5}{12}\right)$

$A = 25°$ (to the nearest degree)

Exercise 12.6

Find the area of each of the triangles in Questions 1 to 6 (answers correct to two decimal places).

1.

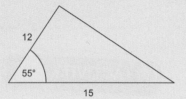

2.

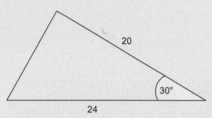

3.

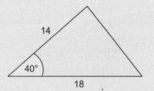

4.

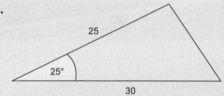

5.

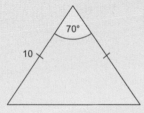

6.

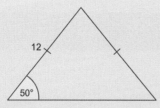

7. In a triangle ABC, $|AB| = 7$ cm, $|AC| = 8.4$ cm and $|\angle BAC| = 62°$.

Calculate, to the nearest square centimetre, the area of the triangle ABC.

8. In a triangle XYZ, $|XY| = 9$ cm, $|XZ| = 18.4$ cm and $|\angle YXZ| = 82°$.

Calculate, to the nearest square centimetre, the area of the triangle XYZ.

9. The area of each of the triangles shown is given. Find the measure of the angle A.

(i)

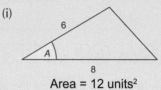

Area = 12 units²

(ii)

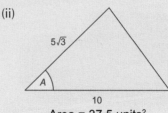

Area = 37.5 units²

10. The area of the triangle shown is 30 units². Find the length of the side marked x correct to the nearest whole number.

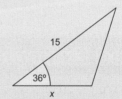

11. A tile is in the shape of a parallelogram. The area of the parallelogram is 50 units². Other dimensions are shown on the diagram.

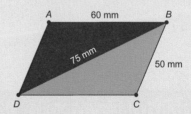

(a) Calculate $|\angle ABD|$ and $|\angle DBC|$.

(b) Hence, find $|\angle DAB|$.

12. In the triangle XYZ, $\cos \angle XYZ = \frac{3}{5}$.

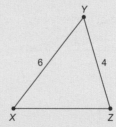

(i) By drawing a suitable triangle, find $\sin \angle XYZ$.

(ii) Hence calculate the area of $\triangle XYZ$.

TRIGONOMETRY

12.7 THE UNIT CIRCLE

The unit circle has its centre at (0,0) and has a radius length of 1 unit.

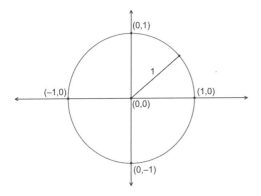

ACTIVITIES 12.9, 12.10

In Activities 12.9 and 12.10, using the unit circle, we defined the sine, cosine and tangent of an angle.

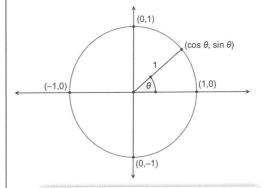

cos θ = x co-ordinate

sin θ = y co-ordinate

Also, $\tan \theta = \dfrac{\sin \theta}{\cos \theta}$

All of these definitions are on page 13 of *Formulae and Tables*.

Exercise 12.7

In Questions 1 to 13, use the unit circle to find the answer.

1. cos 270°
2. sin 270°
3. cos 90°
4. sin 90°

5. tan 180°
6. cos 180°
7. sin 180°

8. cos 0°
9. sin 0°
10. tan 0°

11. cos 360°
12. sin 360°
13. tan 360°

12.8 EVALUATING THE TRIGONOMETRIC RATIOS OF ALL ANGLES BETWEEN 0° AND 360°

Reference Angles

Consider an angle AOB, where |∠AOB| = 140°.

∠AOB will lie in the second quadrant of the unit circle.

| ∠AOB | = 140°

Reference angle
    = 180° − 140°
    = 40°

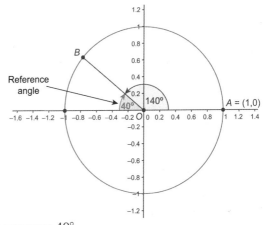

The acute angle formed by the terminal side of ∠AOB (i.e. where the angle ends) and the **x-axis** is called the reference angle of ∠AOB. In this case the reference angle measures 40°.

Here are similar examples for angles that lie in the third and fourth quadrants respectively.

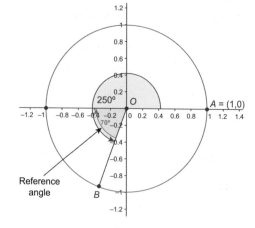

$|\angle AOB| = 250°$

Reference angle
$$= 250° - 180°$$
$$= 70°$$

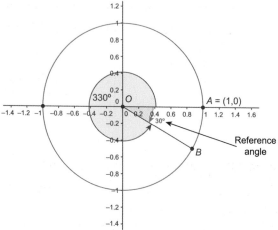

$|\angle AOB| = 330°$

Reference angle
$$= 360° - 330°$$
$$= 30°$$

The Sign of the Ratios in Each Quadrant

First Quadrant ($0° < \theta < 90°$)

In the first quadrant, all three ratios are positive.

- $\cos \theta$ is positive, as its value lies on the positive x-axis.

- $\sin \theta$ is positive, as its value lies on the positive y-axis.

- $\tan \theta = \dfrac{\sin \theta}{\cos \theta} = \dfrac{+}{+} = +$ Hence, $\tan \theta$ is positive.

Second Quadrant ($90° < \theta < 180°$)

In the second quadrant, sin is positive; cos and tan are negative.

- $\cos \theta$ is negative, as its value lies on the negative x-axis.

- $\sin \theta$ is positive, as its value lies on the positive y-axis.

- $\tan \theta = \dfrac{\sin \theta}{\cos \theta} = \dfrac{+}{=} = -$ Hence, $\tan \theta$ is negative.

Third Quadrant ($180° < \theta < 270°$)

In the third quadrant, tan is positive; sin and cos are negative.

- $\cos \theta$ is negative, as its value lies on the negative x-axis.

- $\sin \theta$ is negative, as its value lies on the negative y-axis.

- $\tan \theta = \dfrac{\sin \theta}{\cos \theta} = \dfrac{=}{=} = +$ Hence, $\tan \theta$ is positive.

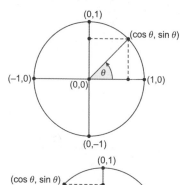

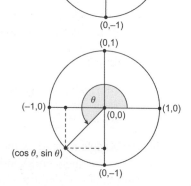

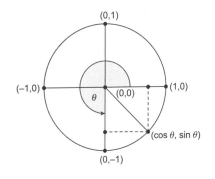

Fourth Quadrant (270° < θ < 360°)

In the fourth quadrant, cos is positive; sin and tan are negative.

- ■ cos θ is positive, as its value lies on the positive x-axis.
- ■ sin θ is negative, as its value lies on the negative y-axis.
- ■ $\tan \theta = \frac{\sin \theta}{\cos \theta} = \frac{-}{+} = -$ Hence, tan θ is negative.

CAST

The diagram on the left summarises this section.

S	A
T	C

(a) In the first quadrant, all (A) are positive.

(b) In the second quadrant, only sin (S) is positive.

(c) In the third quadrant, only tan (T) is positive.

(d) In the fourth quadrant, only cos (C) is positive.    **ACTIVITY 12.11**

Worked Example 12.15

Write in surd form:

    (i) cos 150°   (ii) sin 330°   (iii) tan 225°

Solution

(i) cos 150°

Step 1

Draw 150°.

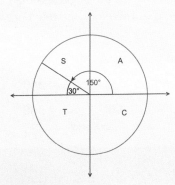

Step 2

The angle is in the second quadrant; therefore its cos is negative.

Step 3

The reference angle is 30° (180° – 150°).

$$\cos 30° = \frac{\sqrt{3}}{2}$$

Step 4

$$\therefore \cos 150° = -\frac{\sqrt{3}}{2}$$

(ii) sin 330°

Step 1

Draw 330°.

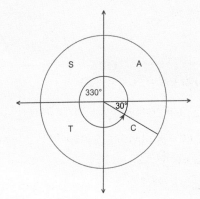

Step 2

The angle is in the fourth quadrant; therefore its sin is negative.

Step 3

The reference angle is 30° (360° – 330°).

$$\sin 30° = \frac{1}{2}$$

Step 4

$$\therefore \sin 330° = -\frac{1}{2}$$

(iii) tan 225°

Step 1

Draw 225°.

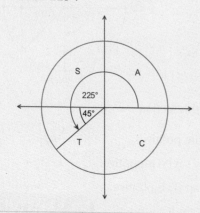

Step 2

The angle is in the third quadrant; therefore its tan is positive.

Step 3

The reference angle is 45° (225° − 180°).

tan 45° = 1

Step 4

∴ tan 225° = 1

Worked Example 12.16

Given $\cos A = -\frac{1}{2}$ and $0° \leqslant A \leqslant 360°$. Find two values of A that satisfy the equation.

Solution

Step 1 Locate the quadrants in which A Lies. As cos A is negative, then A lies in the S quadrant or in the T quadrant.

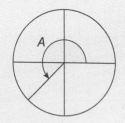   OR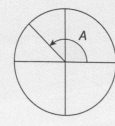

Step 2 Find A, the reference angle.

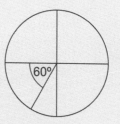   OR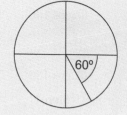

The reference angle is the angle less than 90°, whose cosine is $\frac{1}{2}$. Therefore, the reference angle is 60°.

Step 3 Find values for A.

$A = 180° + 60°$ $A = 360° - 60°$

$= 240°$ **OR** $= 300°$

Exercise 12.8

For Questions 1 to 10, write your answer in surd form.

For Questions 11 to 20, use your calculator and give your answer correct to two decimal places.

1. cos 135°   6. cos 315°   11. cos 145°   16. cos 325°

2. sin 150°   7. sin 120°   12. sin 160°   17. sin 140°

3. cos 240°   8. cos 210°   13. cos 230°   18. cos 230°

4. sin 330°   9. tan 300°   14. sin 355°   19. tan 350°

5. tan 210°   10. tan 60°   15. tan 220°   20. tan 160°

21. If $\sin A = \dfrac{1}{2}$, find two values for A, if $0° \leqslant A \leqslant 360°$.

22. If $\cos A = \dfrac{1}{\sqrt{2}}$, find two values for A, if $0° \leqslant A \leqslant 360°$.

23. If $\tan A = \sqrt{3}$, find two values for A, if $0° \leqslant A \leqslant 360°$.

24. If $\sin A = -\dfrac{1}{\sqrt{2}}$, find two values for A, if $0° \leqslant A \leqslant 360°$.

25. If $\tan A = -\dfrac{1}{\sqrt{3}}$, find two values for A, if $0° \leqslant A \leqslant 360°$.

26. If $\cos A = -\dfrac{\sqrt{3}}{2}$, find two values for A, if $0° \leqslant A \leqslant 360°$.

12.9 THE SINE RULE

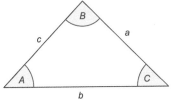

FORMULA

$$\frac{a}{\sin A} = \frac{b}{\sin B} = \frac{c}{\sin C}$$

or

FORMULA

$$\frac{\sin A}{a} = \frac{\sin B}{b} = \frac{\sin C}{c}$$

You can find this formula on page 16 of the *Formulae and Tables*.

Note: If you are solving a triangle and you know an angle and the opposite side, use the Sine Rule formula.

Worked Example 12.17

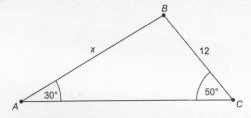

Find x, the distance from *A* to *B*.
Give your answer to two decimal places.

Solution

$$\frac{x}{\sin 50°} = \frac{12}{\sin 30°}$$

$$x(\sin 30°) = 12\sin 50°$$

$$x = \frac{12\sin 50°}{\sin 30°}$$

$$x \approx 18.39 \quad \text{(calculator)}$$

Worked Example 12.18

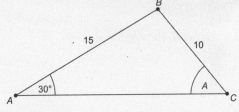

Find the value of *A*. Give your answer to the nearest degree.

Solution

$$\frac{\sin A}{15} = \frac{\sin 30°}{10}$$

$$10(\sin A) = 15(\sin 30°)$$

$$\sin A = \frac{15(\sin 30°)}{10} \qquad \sin A = 0.75$$

$$A = \sin^{-1} 0.75$$

$$\therefore A = 49° \text{ (to the nearest degree)}$$

Exercise 12.9

In Questions 1 to 5, use the Sine Rule to find the value of x. Write each answer correct to two decimal places.

1.

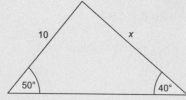

2.

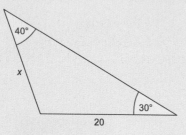

3.

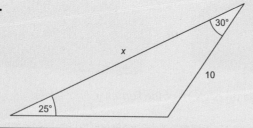

4.

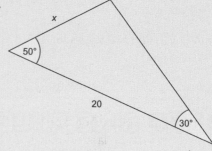

5.

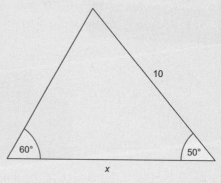

6. In the triangle shown, $a = 15$, $b = 25$ and $B = 50°$.

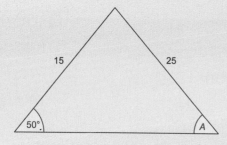

(i) Find A, correct to the nearest degree:

(ii) Find the measure of the angle C.

(iii) Hence, find the area of the triangle correct to one decimal place.

7. Find A correct to the nearest degree.

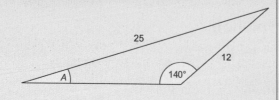

8. In the triangle shown, $B = 53°8'$, $b = 8$ and $a = 9.3$.

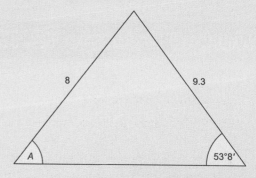

(i) Find A, correct to the nearest minute.

(ii) Find the measure of the angle C.

(iii) Hence, find the area of the triangle, correct to one decimal place.

(iv) Using the area of the triangle, find the length of side C.

9. Find A correct to the nearest degree.

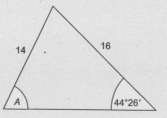

10. In the diagram $a = 7$, $b = 12$ and $B = 45°$

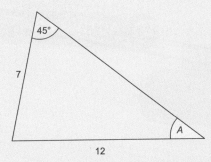

(i) Find A, correct to the nearest degree.

(ii) Find the area of the triangle, correct to one decimal place.

(iii) Hence find the length of side c.

11. John is standing at a point P on the southern bank of a river. He wants to swim across to the northern bank. There are just two landing points, Q and R, on the northern bank. R is 80 m downstream from Q. The path $[PQ]$ makes an angle of 50° with the bank, and the path $[PR]$ makes an angle of 60° with the bank. The situation is shown in the diagram below.

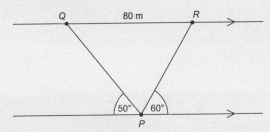

Using the Sine Rule, calculate $|PQ|$ and $|PR|$.

12. A farmer needs to fertilise one of his fields. He must know the area of the field, so that he can order the correct quantity of fertiliser. A diagram (including some measurements) of the field is shown below.

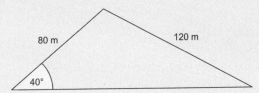

Calculate the area of the field.

(Hint: Find, using the Sine Rule, another angle in the triangle.)

13. John built the box shown below as part of a construction project. The lid has dimensions 100 cm by 50 cm and fits exactly on top of the box. The maximum angle to which the lid opens is 50°. The wood from which sides have been cut measures 1 cm in thickness.

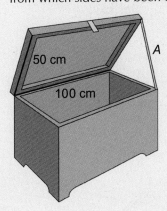

(a) Use the sine rule to find the length of support A, if the support keeps the lid open at the maximum angle.

(b) If the box has an internal height of 40 cm, find the capacity of the box in cubic metres.

(c) John has a thin metal bar of length 108 cm and he wishes to store the bar flat in the box. Will the bar fit in the box? Explain your reasoning.

(d) A bar of maximum length is stored in the box with the lid closed. Find the length of this bar.

12.10 THE COSINE RULE

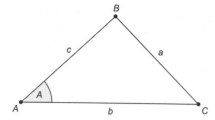

FORMULA

$$a^2 = b^2 + c^2 - 2bc \cos A$$

You can find this formula on page 16 of the *Formulae and Tables*.

Note: If the lengths of two sides of a triangle and the angle between these sides are known, then we can use the Cosine Rule to find the length of the third side in the triangle.

Note: If we know the lengths of all three sides in a triangle, then we can use the Cosine Rule to find the measure of any angle in the triangle.

Worked Example 12.19

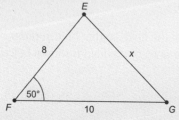

Find x, the distance from E to G. Give your answer to two decimal places.

Solution

$a^2 = b^2 + c^2 - 2bc \cos A$

$x^2 = 8^2 + 10^2 - 2(8)(10)\cos(50°)$

$x^2 = 61.15398$ (calculator)

$x = \sqrt{61.15398}$

$\therefore x = 7.82$

Worked Example 12.20

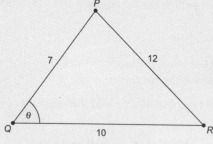

Find the measure of the angle θ. Give your answer to the nearest degree.

Solution

$a^2 = b^2 + c^2 - 2bc \cos \theta$

$12^2 = 7^2 + 10^2 - 2(7)(10) \cos \theta$

$144 = 49 + 100 - 140 \cos \theta$

$144 = 149 - 140 \cos \theta$

$140 \cos \theta = 149 - 144$

$140 \cos \theta = 5$

$\cos \theta = \dfrac{5}{140} = \dfrac{1}{28}$

$\theta = \cos^{-1}\left(\dfrac{1}{28}\right)$

$\theta \approx 88°$

Exercise 12.10

In Questions 1 to 5, use the Cosine Rule to find the value of *a*. Write each answer correct to two decimal places.

1.
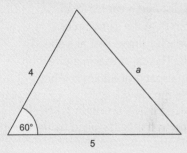

2.
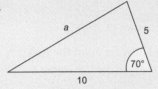

3.
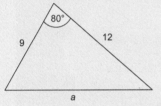

4.
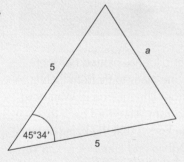

5.
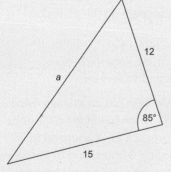

In Questions 6 to 10, use the Cosine Rule to find the value of *A*. Give your answers to the nearest degree.

6.
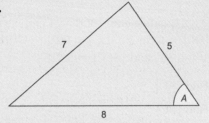

7.
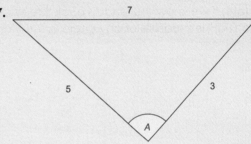

8.
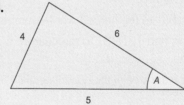

9.
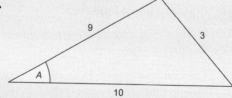

10.
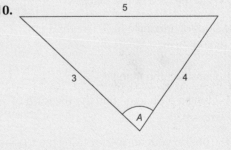

11.

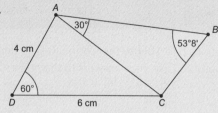

ABCD is a quadrilateral. $|AD| = 4$ cm, and $|DC| = 6$ cm. $|\angle ADC| = 60°$, $|\angle CAB| = 30°$, and $|\angle ABC| = 53° \, 8'$.

  (i)   Find $|AC|$.

  (ii)   Find $|BC|$.

  (iii)   Hence, find the area of the quadrilateral ABCD.

12. EFGH is a quadrilateral.

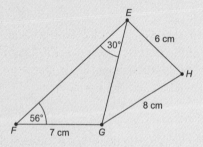

  (i)   Find $|EG|$ to the nearest whole number.

  (ii)   Hence, find $|\angle EHG|$ to the nearest degree.

  (iii)   What is the area of the quadrilateral EFGH?

13. The sides of a triangle have lengths 9 cm, 5 cm and 7 cm.

  (i)   Construct the triangle.

  (ii)   Using a protractor, find the measure of the largest angle.

  (iii)   Confirm your answer by using the Cosine Rule to find (to the nearest degree) the measure of the largest angle.

  (iv)   Find the area of the triangle.

14. The sides of a triangle have lengths 3 cm, 5 cm and 7 cm.

  (i)   Construct the triangle.

  (ii)   Using a protractor, find the measure of the smallest angle.

  (iii)   Confirm your answer by using the Cosine Rule to find (to the nearest degree) the measure of the smallest angle.

  (iv)   Find the area of the triangle.

15.

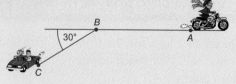

A motorcyclist and a car leave an intersection, B, at the same time. The motorcyclist drives east at a speed of 50 km/h. The car drives in a direction W 30° S at a speed of 60 km/h. After 15 minutes, the car stops.

  (i)   Find the distance travelled by the car in 15 minutes.

  (ii)   Find the distance travelled by the motorcyclist in 15 minutes.

  (iii)   Find the measure of $\angle ABC$.

  (iv)   Hence, find how far apart the two vehicles are when the car stops.

16.

A helicopter pilot has plotted her route on a map. She plans to fly from Dublin to Limerick, from Limerick on to Waterford and, finally, from Waterford back to Dublin. She knows that the flying distance between Dublin and Limerick is 176 km and that the distance between Waterford and Dublin is 135 km. She also has the measure of one angle on the triangular route.

  (i)   Find the flying distance between Limerick and Waterford.

  (ii)   If the helicopter has an average flying speed of 280 km/h and the pilot stops over in Limerick for 1 hour and in Waterford for 2 hours, find to the nearest minute the time taken for the pilot to complete the trip.

(iii) An Internet route planner gives the road distance between Limerick and Waterford as 127 km. As the helicopter takes off from Dublin, a driver begins his journey from Limerick to Waterford travelling at an average speed of 50 km/h. He has scheduled a meeting with the pilot. What is the maximum time the meeting can last if the pilot has to stick with the 2-hour stopover?

(iv) Suggest another method for finding the flying distance between Limerick and Waterford.

17.

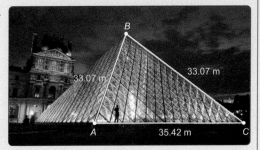

The Louvre Pyramid is a large glass pyramid in the main courtyard of the Louvre Palace in Paris. Some dimensions are given in the picture.

(i) Using the Cosine Rule, calculate to two decimal places the measure of $\angle ABC$.

(ii) Find the area of one face of the pyramid. Give your answer to two decimal places.

(iii) Hence, find the area of all four sides.

(iv) What is the area of the square base of the pyramid?

18.

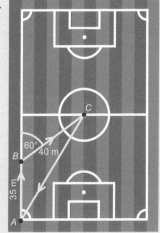

Rachel is training in her local soccer field. One of her training routines is a 10-lap run around the circuit shown in the diagram. $|AB| = 35$ m and $|BC| = 40$ m.

(i) Find $|AC|$.

(ii) What distance does Rachel cover in this routine?

(iii) What is the width of her local soccer field?

12.11 AREA OF A SECTOR AND LENGTH OF AN ARC

 ACTIVITY 12.14

Area of a sector of a circle $= (\pi r^2)\left|\dfrac{\theta}{360}\right|$, where θ is measured in degrees.

Length of an arc of a circle $= (2\pi r)\left|\dfrac{\theta}{360}\right|$, where θ is measured in degrees.

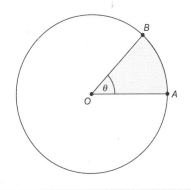

Worked Example 12.21

Find:

(i) The area of the sector *AOB*

(ii) The length of the minor arc *AB*

Give your answers in terms of π.

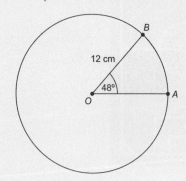

Solution

(i) Area of sector $= (\pi r^2)\left(\dfrac{\theta}{360}\right)$

$$\text{Area} = (\pi(12)^2)\left(\dfrac{48}{360}\right)$$

$$= (144\,\pi)\left(\dfrac{2}{15}\right)$$

$$= \dfrac{288\,\pi}{15}$$

$$= \dfrac{96\,\pi}{5}\ \text{cm}^2$$

(ii) Length of arc $= (2\pi r)\left(\dfrac{\theta}{360}\right)$

$$\text{Length} = (2\pi(12))\left(\dfrac{48}{360}\right)$$

$$= (24\pi)\left(\dfrac{2}{15}\right)$$

$$= \dfrac{48\pi}{15}$$

$$= \dfrac{16\pi}{5}\ \text{cm}$$

Exercise 12.11

1. Find the area of each of the following shaded sectors.

   Give your answers:

   (a) in terms of π

   (b) correct to two decimal places

   (i)

   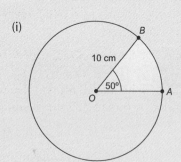

   (ii)

   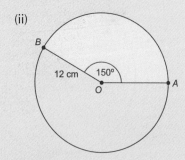

   (iii)

   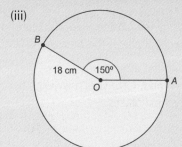

2. For each of the following find the length of the minor arc *AB*.

   Give your answers:

   (a) in terms of π

   (b) correct to two decimal places

   (i)

   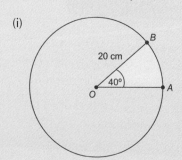

(ii)

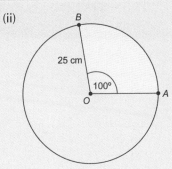

(iii)

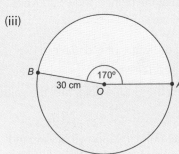

3. For each of the following, find the measure of the angle θ.

θ is measured in degrees.

(i)

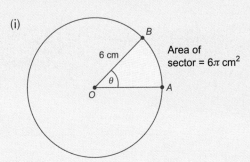

Area of sector = 6π cm²

(ii)

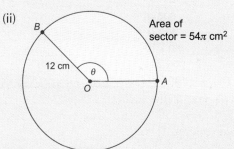

Area of sector = 54π cm²

(iii)

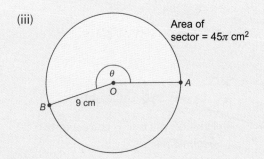

Area of sector = 45π cm²

4. For each of the following, find the measure of the angle θ.

θ is measured in degrees.

(i)

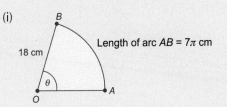

Length of arc AB = 7π cm

(ii)

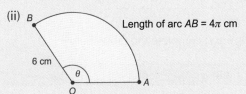

Length of arc AB = 4π cm

(iii)

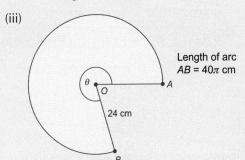

Length of arc AB = 40π cm

5.

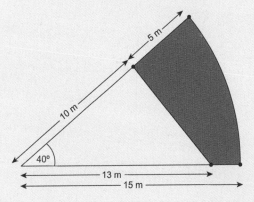

(i) Find the area of triangle ABC, correct to two decimal places.

(ii) Find the area of the sector ABC, correct to two decimal places.

(iii) Hence, find the area of the shaded region.

6. Find the area of the shaded region. Give your answer correct to three significant figures.

1. (a)

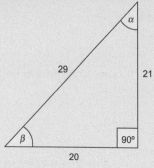

Copy and complete the tables below.

sin α	cos α	tan α

sin β	cos β	tan β

(b)

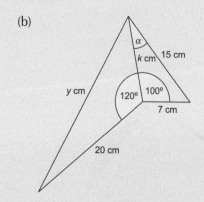

(i) Find the value of α. Give your answer to the nearest degree.

(ii) Find k, correct to two decimal places.

(iii) Using the Cosine Rule, evaluate y to two decimal places.

2. (a) Study the unit circle below. Then complete the table in terms of p and q.

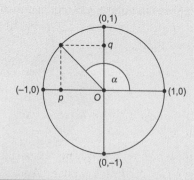

sin α	cos α	tan α

(b)

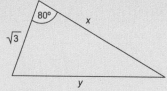

The area of the triangle shown above is 3 square units.

(i) Find the value of x, correct to two decimal places.

(ii) Using the Cosine Rule, find the value of y.

3. (a) Study the unit circle shown below, and then copy and complete the table. Give all answers in surd form.

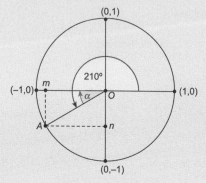

α	
sin α	
cos α	
tan α	
sin 210°	
cos 210°	
tan 210°	
m	
n	
A	(,)

(b)

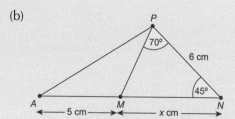

(i) Find the value of x, correct to two decimal places.

(ii) Now find the area of triangle *PAN*. Give your answer correct to two significant figures.

4. (a) Copy and complete the table below (entries in surd form, where necessary).

A	30°	45°	60°
sin A			
cos A			
tan A			

Using the given table, solve the following equations for A, B, C and D.

(i) $\sin A = \cos 60°$

(ii) $\tan B = 1$

(iii) $\sin C = \cos C$

(iv) $\sin D \cos 30° = \dfrac{3}{4}$

(b)

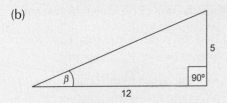

Evaluate the following:

(i) $\tan \beta$ (iii) $\sin \beta$

(ii) $\cos \beta$ (iv) $\sin 2\beta$

Hint: $\sin 2\beta = 2\sin\beta \cos\beta$

5. Two ships, A and B, leave a port O at the same time. Both ships sail for 2 hours.

Ship A sails in a direction E 20° N, at a speed of 12 km/h. Ship B sails in a direction E 70° S, at a speed of 16 km/h.

Find the distance between the ships after two hours sailing.

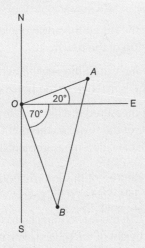

6. (a) Find the length of [PQ] and hence the length of [PR].

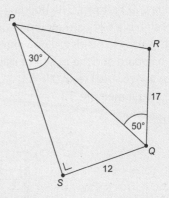

(b) A rectangular tile contains two right-angled triangles. Dimensions are shown in the diagram. Find the area of the tile.

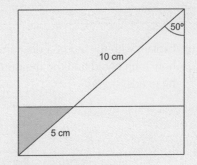

7.

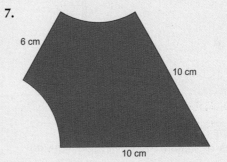

This is the new company logo for ABC Ltd. The logo is made by removing two equal sectors from an equilateral triangle. The sectors have their centres, respectively, on two vertices of the equilateral triangle. On the logo there are three straight edges, two measuring 10 cm and one measuring 6 cm.

(i) Find the radius length of one of the sectors that have been removed.

(ii) Find the area of the sectors that were removed.

(iii) Find the area of the equilateral triangle from which the logo has been taken.

(iv) Find the area of the logo.

8. John's construction studies teacher has asked him to construct a scaled model of any building in his town. The building John has chosen has a billboard mounted on one of its walls. He needs to know the height of the billboard and the height of its bottom edge above street level. He has a clinometer and a tape measure.

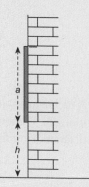

(i) Explain with the aid of a diagram, how John could find the measurements he needs.

(ii)

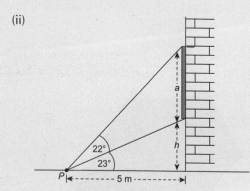

The diagram above shows the measurements John has taken with the help of the tape measure and clinometer. Calculate the value of *a* and the value of *h* to the nearest centimetre.

(iii) John, using the clinometer and tape measure, has estimated the height of the building to be 8 m. The height of his scaled model of the building has to be 1 m. What will be the height of the billboard in the scaled model? Give your answer to the nearest centimetre.

9. A Fifth Year maths class has been asked to find the width and height of a soccer goal. The students are equipped with just a clinometer. Any measurements have to be taken from the point *P*. The teacher has already given the class the distance from *P* to the foot of both uprights and also the measure of the angle at *P*, formed by the two uprights and the point *P*. The students decide to measure the angle of elevation from *P* to the top of one of the uprights. They find the angle of elevation to be 22°.

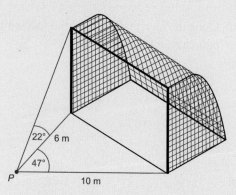

(i) Find the width of the goal. Give your answer to two decimal places.

(ii) Find the height of the goal. Give your answer to the nearest centimetre.

(iii) If the class had chosen to measure the angle of elevation of the other upright from *P*, then what measurement should they have found? Give your answer to the nearest degree.

10. To find the height of a tower standing on a small hill, Aoife made some measurements.

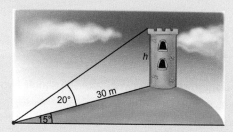

■ She measured the angle of elevation to the top of the tower: 20°.

■ She measured the angle at which the plane is inclined to the horizontal: 15°.

■ She measured the distance from the base of the tower to the point where she took elevation measurements: 30 m.

(i) Represent this information using two right-angled triangles.

(ii) Use these two triangles to find the height of the tower to the nearest metre.

11. (a) A stand is being used to prop up a portable solar panel. It consists of a support that is hinged to the panel near the top, and an adjustable strap joining the panel to the support near the bottom.

By adjusting the length of the strap, the angle between the panel and the ground can be changed.

The dimensions are as follows:

$|AB| = 30$ cm

$|AD| = |CB| = 5$ cm

$|CF| = 22$ cm

$|EF| = 4$ cm

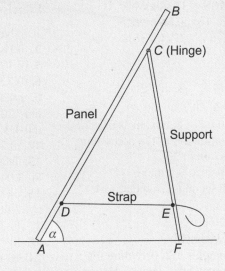

We want to find out how long the strap has to be in order to make the angle α between the panel and the ground equal to 60°.

(i) Two diagrams are given below – one showing triangle *CAF* and the other showing triangle *CDE*. Use the measurements given above to record on the two diagrams below the lengths of two of the sides in each triangle.

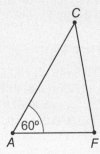

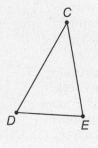

(ii) Taking $\alpha = 60°$ as shown, use the triangle *CAF* to find $|\angle CFA|$, correct to one decimal place.

(iii) Hence find $|\angle ACF|$, correct to one decimal place.

(iv) Use triangle *CDE* to find $|DE|$, the length of the strap correct to one decimal place.

SEC Project Maths Sample Paper, Leaving Certificate Ordinary Level, 2011

Answers

Chapter 1

Exercise 1.1

14. (ii) 10   (iii) 10   (iv) 10%   **15.** (ii) Walk
(iii) Rail   (iv) Categorical   **16.** (ii) Numerical
(iii) 35   (iv) 7   (v) 23   (vi) 7   **17.** (ii) 36%

Exercise 1.2

1. (ii) 80%   **2.** (ii) 25   (iii) $\frac{7}{25}$ **3.** (ii) 72
4. (ii) Tanya and Rachel   **5.** (ii) 27   (iii) 49
(iv) $33\frac{1}{3}$%   **6.** (ii) 85%   (iii) 2   **7.** No key is provided;
there are 11 pieces of data; data is not in ascending
order.   **8.** (i) 29   (ii) Bus   **9.** (i) 20
(ii) 1   **10.** (ii) The tallest person is a man.
11. (ii) 7 seconds   (iii) 38 seconds   (iv) Group 1

Exercise 1.3

1. (i) Symmetric   (ii) Skewed right
(iii) Skewed left   (iv) Symmetric   **2.** (i) Symmetric
(ii) Skewed right   (iii) Skewed left   (iv) Symmetric
3. (ii) Positively   **5.** (i) 13   (ii) 10   (iii) 15.38%
6. (ii) 35   (iii) 15   **7.** (ii) 20%   **9.** (i) Skewed right
(ii) Symmetric   (iii) Skewed left

Exercise 1.4

1. (i) W and Z   (ii) X   (iii) Y   **2.** (i) Z   (ii) Y   (iii) Z
3. (ii) Positive strong   **4.** (ii) Positive weak
5. (ii) Positive strong   **6.** (i) Positive weak
(ii) Negative strong   (iii) No correlation
(iv) Negative strong   (v) No correlation
(vi) Positive strong   **7.** (ii) Weak positive
8. (ii) Positive strong   **9.** (ii) Positive weak
10. (i) 8 litres/km   (ii) 1000 cc   (iii) Positive
11. (ii) Strong positive   **12.** (ii) Weak positive
13. (i) Positive   (ii) 3   (iii) 0   (iv) 6.8 cm
(v) 0.5; Positive.

Revision Exercises

1. (iii) 16.67%   **2.** (ii) −0.92   **3.** (vi) 80%
4. (iii) 4   (iv) 80%   **6.** (ii) Very weak positive 0.18
7. (i) 20 (iii) 65%   **8.** (i) 20   (iii) Skewed right
10. (ii) 0.98

Chapter 2

Exercise 2.1

1. {20, 21, 22, 23, 24, 25, 26, 27, 28, 29}
3. 12 possible   **7.** (i) 20   (ii) 12
8. {RR, RY, RO, YR, YY, YO, OR, OY, OO}
9. (ii) 3   **12.** (i) 1   (ii) 5   (iii) 18

Exercise 2.2

1. 20   **2.** 20   **3.** 75   **4.** 10   **5.** 120   **6.** 150
7. 260   **8.** 12   **9.** 624   **10.** 7,776   **11.** 1,024

12. 12   **13.** 336   **14.** 358,800   **15.** (i) 650,000
(ii) 486,720   (iii) 468,000

Exercise 2.3

1. (i) No   (ii) No   **2.** (ii) 4   (iii) 2
3. (i) List   (ii) 120   **4.** (i) 6   (ii) 2   (iii) 4
5. (i) 120   (ii) 24   (iii) 96   (iv) 24
6. (i) 720   (ii) 120   (iii) 360   **7.** 650
8. 9,000   **9.** 120   **10.** (i) 5,040   (ii) 720
(iii) 120   **11.** (i) 5,040   (ii) 720
(iii) 4,320   (iv) 2,160   (v) 2,880
12. (i) 24   (ii) 64   (iii) 12   (iv) 12
13. (i) (a) 24   (b) 256   (ii) 18   **14.** (i) 40,320
(ii) 5,040   (iii) 15,120   (iv) 720
15. (i) 362,880   (ii) 40,320   (iii) 201,600
(iv) 2,880   (v) 2,880   **16.** (i) 120   (ii) 12
17. (i) 39,916,800   (ii) 86,400   (iii) 172,800
18. (i) 720   (ii) 240   (iii) 48   (iv) 48   (v) 240
(vi) 480   **19.** (i) 5,040   (ii) 240   (iii) 1,440

Exercise 2.4

1. (i) 10   (ii) 56   (iii) 1,365   (iv) 435
2. (i) 184,756   (ii) 2,118,760   (iii) 3,921,225
(iv) 6   **3.** (i) 120   (ii) 120   (iii) 1,001
(iv) 12   **4.** (i) 120   (ii) 1   (iii) 19   (iv) 1
5. (i) 12   (ii) 17,640   (iii) 2.75   (iv) 1,230
8. (i) 8   (ii) 5   (iii) 12

Exercise 2.5

1. 170,544   **2.** 190   **3.** 455   **4.** 1,001
5. 8,145,060   **6.** (i) 155,177,520   (ii) 3,268,760
7. 78   **8.** (i) 536,878,650   (ii) 163,185
(iii) 450,978,066   **9.** 11,480   **10.** (i) 126   (ii) 21
(iii) 70   **11.** (i) 45   (ii) 9   (iii) 10   **12.** 136
13. (i) 35   (ii) 15   (iii) 20   (iv) 5   **14.** 462 games
15. (i) 45   (ii) 120   **16.** 101,745   **17.** 12,600
18. 155,040   **19.** 27   **20.** (i) 220   (ii) 10   (iii) 140

Revision Exercises

1. (ii) 6   **3.** 28   **4.** (iv) 2   (v) 1   **5.** (i) 210
(ii) 126   **6.** (i) 720   (ii) 240   (iii) 48   **7.** (i) 66
(ii) 35   (iii) 10   (iv) 45   **8.** (i) 120   (ii) 24
(iii) 48   (iv) 72   **9.** (i) 560   (ii) 270   (iii) 390
10. (i) 720   (ii) 240   (iii) 48   (iv) 48   (v) 240
11. (i) 210   (ii) 84   (iii) 126   **12.** (i) 120
(ii) 72   (iii) 36   (iv) 12   (v) 48   **13.** (i) 24   (ii) 6
(iii) 12   (iv) 6   (v) 2   **14.** (i) 210   (ii) 84   (iii) 7
(iv) 140   **15.** (i) 40,320   (ii) 5,040   (iii) 15,120
(iv) 720   (v) 4,320   **16.** (i) 362,880   (ii) 2,880
(iii) 2,880   **17.** (i) 120   (ii) 24   (iii) 72   (iv) 18
18. (i) 53,130   (ii) 12,600   (iii) 33,075
(iv) 1,771   **19.** (i) 270,725   (ii) 715   (iii) 1
(iv) 36   (v) 6,961   **20.** (i) 11   (ii) 11   (iii) 7

Chapter 3

Exercise 3.1

1. Evens 2. Unlikely (1 in 6 chance) 3. Certain
4. Evens 5. Evens 6. Likely 7. Evens
8. Unlikely 9. Likely (it could get stuck in a tree)
10. Unlikely 11. Likely 12. Evens
13. Evens 14. Unlikely 15. Impossible

Exercise 3.2

4. (i) E (ii) G (iii) I (iv) F (v) H
6. (i) Probability must lie between 0 and 1.
(ii) Probability should be between 0 and 1.
(iii) Incorrect – probability given should be $\frac{1}{6}$.

Exercise 3.3

1. $\frac{1}{4}$ 2. (i) $\frac{7}{20}$ (ii) $\frac{13}{20}$ 3. $\frac{13}{15}$ 4. $\frac{1}{550}$ 5. $\frac{2}{3}$
6. A $\frac{1}{10}$, B $\frac{1}{5}$, C $\frac{6}{25}$, D $\frac{1}{5}$, E $\frac{13}{50}$ 7. $\frac{2}{11}$ 8. (i) 120
(ii) $\frac{5}{12}$ (iii) $\frac{1}{6}$ 9. (i) 0.25 (ii) 1 (iii) 6
(iv) 36 10. (i) 46 (ii) $\frac{11}{46}$ (iii) $\frac{5}{23}$ (iv) $\frac{1}{2}$
11. (i) $\frac{49}{200}$ (ii) $\frac{43}{200}$ (iii) $\frac{103}{200}$
12. (i) Megan $\frac{1}{2}$, Alex $\frac{2}{7}$, Jack 0 (ii) Megan
13. (i) 7 (ii) 22 (iii) 32

Exercise 3.4

1. (i) $\frac{1}{2}$ (ii) $\frac{1}{2}$ (iii) 1 2. 0.25 3. (i) $\frac{8}{15}$ (ii) $\frac{7}{15}$
4. (i) $\frac{1}{20}$ (ii) $\frac{1}{20}$ (iii) $\frac{1}{20}$ (iv) $\frac{1}{2}$ (v) $\frac{1}{2}$ (vi) $\frac{2}{5}$
(vii) $\frac{11}{20}$ 5. (i) $\frac{1}{6}$ (ii) $\frac{1}{6}$ (iii) 0 (iv) 1 (v) $\frac{1}{2}$
(vi) $\frac{1}{2}$ (vii) $\frac{1}{2}$ 6. (i) $\frac{7}{10}$ (ii) $\frac{3}{10}$ 7. (i) $\frac{1}{2}$ (ii) $\frac{1}{2}$
(iii) $\frac{1}{52}$ (iv) $\frac{1}{26}$ (v) $\frac{1}{52}$ 8. (i) 60% (ii) 24%
(iii) 16% (iv) 84% (v) 60% 9. (i) $\frac{1}{9}$ (ii) $\frac{1}{9}$
(iii) $\frac{1}{3}$ (iv) $\frac{2}{3}$ 10. (i) $\frac{1}{5}$ (ii) $\frac{1}{5}$ (iii) $\frac{2}{5}$ (iv) $\frac{2}{5}$
11. (i) $\frac{1}{8}$ (ii) $\frac{1}{8}$ (iii) $\frac{1}{4}$ 12. (i) $\frac{3}{8}$ (ii) $\frac{1}{8}$ (iii) $\frac{3}{8}$
(iv) $\frac{5}{8}$ 13. (i) $\frac{3}{5}$ (ii) $\frac{1}{2}$ (iii) $\frac{3}{8}$ 14. (i) $\frac{1}{7}$ (ii) $\frac{6}{7}$
(iii) $\frac{2}{7}$ (iv) $\frac{5}{7}$ (v) $\frac{2}{7}$ 15. (i) $\frac{1}{4}$ (ii) $\frac{1}{2}$ (iii) $\frac{3}{4}$
16. (i) 0.06 (ii) ≈796 bowls 17. (i) 0.625
(ii) 207° 18. (i) $\frac{4}{13}$ (ii) $\frac{9}{13}$ (iii) 11 tokens

Exercise 3.5

1. 150 3. $\frac{1}{10}$ 4. (i) Yes (ii) 36 5. (i) 130
(ii) 60 (iii) 5 6. 11 7. 25 8. (i) 40 (ii) 80
9. 168 10. W = 1,000, C = 2,500, B = 1,500
11. (i) B = $\frac{1}{10}$, R = $\frac{11}{20}$, G = $\frac{1}{5}$, O = $\frac{3}{20}$ (ii) Red,
as the probability of winning is higher.
12. (ii) A = $\frac{5}{12}$, B = $\frac{1}{12}$, C = $\frac{2}{12}$, D = $\frac{4}{12}$

Exercise 3.6

1. (i) {1, 2, 3, 4} (ii) {5, 6, 7} (iii) $\frac{4}{7}$ (iv) $\frac{3}{7}$
2. (i) {a, e, i} (ii) {b, c} (iii) Mutually exclusive
events. (iv) $\frac{1}{2}$ (v) $\frac{1}{3}$ 3. (i) 3 (ii) 3 (iii) $\frac{3}{6}$ (iv) $\frac{5}{6}$
(v) $\frac{1}{6}$ 4. (i) $\frac{7}{20}$ (ii) $\frac{39}{40}$ (iii) $\frac{1}{10}$
5. (a) (i) $\frac{12}{13}$ (ii) $\frac{3}{13}$ (iii) $\frac{4}{13}$ (iv) $\frac{1}{13}$ (b) (i) $\frac{8}{13}$
(ii) 0 (iii) $\frac{1}{13}$ (iv) $\frac{5}{13}$ 6. (i) $\frac{3}{8}$ (ii) $\frac{5}{8}$ (iii) $\frac{9}{40}$
7. (i) $\frac{14}{25}$ (ii) $\frac{3}{50}$ (iii) $\frac{24}{25}$ (iv) $\frac{1}{25}$ 8. (ii) 0.25
(iii) 0.05 9. (ii) 0.45 10. (ii) $\frac{11}{30}$ (iii) $\frac{7}{10}$ or 0.7
11. (ii) $\frac{9}{20}$ (iii) $\frac{1}{20}$ 12. (i) $\frac{17}{70}$ (ii) $\frac{18}{70}$ (iii) $\frac{49}{70}$
13. (i) 2 (ii) 38 (iii) $\frac{3}{5}$ 14. (i) $\frac{3}{20}$ (ii) $\frac{2}{5}$ (iii) $\frac{17}{20}$
15. (i) $\frac{1}{3}$ (ii) 0 (iii) $\frac{5}{6}$

Exercise 3.7

1. (i) $\frac{1}{10}$ (ii) $\frac{2}{5}$ (iii) $\frac{1}{2}$ (iv) $\frac{1}{2}$ (v) $\frac{9}{10}$ (vi) $\frac{3}{5}$
2. (i) $\frac{3}{7}$ (ii) $\frac{1}{7}$ (iii) $\frac{4}{7}$ (iv) $\frac{3}{7}$ (v) $\frac{4}{7}$ 3. (i) $\frac{1}{9}$
(ii) $\frac{2}{9}$ (iii) $\frac{7}{9}$ (iv) $\frac{4}{9}$ (v) $\frac{7}{9}$ 4. (i) $\frac{1}{6}$ (ii) $\frac{1}{3}$ (iii) $\frac{1}{2}$
(iv) 1 (v) $\frac{1}{6}$ (vi) $\frac{2}{3}$ (vii) $\frac{1}{6}$ 5. (i) $\frac{1}{2}$ (ii) 1
(iii) $\frac{1}{26}$ (iv) $\frac{1}{26}$ (v) $\frac{4}{13}$ (vi) $\frac{10}{13}$ 6. (i) $\frac{1}{10}$ (ii) $\frac{11}{20}$
(iii) $\frac{3}{4}$ (iv) $\frac{1}{5}$ (v) $\frac{11}{20}$ (vi) $\frac{2}{20}$ (vii) $\frac{3}{20}$ 7. (i) $\frac{2}{25}$
(ii) $\frac{3}{25}$ (iii) $\frac{1}{5}$ (iv) $\frac{22}{25}$ (v) $\frac{3}{25}$ 8. (i) $\frac{1}{10}$ (ii) $\frac{3}{5}$
(iii) $\frac{2}{5}$ (iv) $\frac{3}{5}$

Exercise 3.8

1. (i) $\frac{1}{12}$ (ii) $\frac{1}{4}$ (iii) $\frac{1}{4}$ (iv) $\frac{3}{4}$ 2. (i) $\frac{1}{27}$ (ii) $\frac{1}{27}$
(iii) $\frac{2}{9}$ (iv) $\frac{8}{27}$ (v) $\frac{4}{9}$ 3. (i) $\frac{1}{4}$ (ii) $\frac{1}{4}$ (iii) $\frac{1}{6}$
(iv) $\frac{5}{6}$ 4. (i) $\frac{1}{9}$ (ii) $\frac{1}{2}$ (iii) $\frac{22}{36}$ (iv) $\frac{1}{18}$ 5. (i) $\frac{1}{4}$
(ii) $\frac{3}{4}$ 6. (i) $\frac{5}{36}$ (ii) $\frac{5}{12}$ (iii) 1 (iv) $\frac{5}{12}$ (v) 0
7. (b) (i) 0.33 (ii) 0.30 (iii) 0.35 (iv) 0.53
(v) $\frac{17}{67}$ (vi) $\frac{52}{67}$ 8. (i) $\frac{3}{4}$ (ii) $\frac{5}{24}$ (iii) $\frac{1}{8}$ (iv) $\frac{1}{12}$
(v) $\frac{1}{3}$ 9. (i) $\frac{1}{12}$ (ii) $\frac{2}{3}$ (iii) $\frac{1}{12}$ (iv) 0 (v) 1
10. (i) $\frac{1}{8}$ (ii) $\frac{3}{8}$ (iii) $\frac{1}{2}$ (iv) $\frac{1}{8}$ 11. (b) (i) $\frac{2}{15}$
(ii) $\frac{13}{15}$ (iii) $\frac{1}{6}$ (iv) $\frac{41}{150}$ (v) $\frac{1}{2}$ (vi) $\frac{41}{90}$
12. (ii) $\frac{1}{3}$ (iii) $\frac{2}{9}$ (iv) $\frac{1}{9}$ 13. (ii) 6 (iii) 2
(iv) $\frac{2}{9}$ (v) $\frac{1}{9}$ 14. (ii) $\frac{1}{16}$ (iii) $\frac{3}{4}$ (iv) $\frac{1}{4}$ (v) $\frac{1}{2}$
15. (b) (i) 0.344 (ii) 0.44 (iii) 0.064
(iv) 0.328 (c) 48

Exercise 3.9

1. $\frac{60}{289}$ 2. $\frac{1}{1,000}$ 3. (i) $\frac{25}{121}$ (ii) $\frac{30}{121}$ (iii) $\frac{60}{121}$
4. (i) $\frac{1}{36}$ (ii) $\frac{1}{6}$ (iii) $\frac{1}{4}$ 5. (i) $\frac{5}{18}$ (ii) $\frac{1}{6}$ (iii) $\frac{5}{6}$

6. (i) $\frac{16}{25}$ (ii) $\frac{1}{25}$ (iii) $\frac{24}{25}$ **7.** (i) $\frac{20}{81}$ (ii) $\frac{20}{81}$ (iii) $\frac{25}{81}$
(iv) $\frac{41}{81}$ **8.** (i) $\frac{400}{1,089}$ (ii) $\frac{169}{1,089}$ (iii) $\frac{569}{1,089}$ (iv) $\frac{520}{1,089}$
9. (i) 0.2625 (ii) 0.1625 (iii) 0.425 (iv) 0.5125
10. (i) $\frac{1}{16}$ (ii) $\frac{3}{16}$ (iii) $\frac{3}{8}$ **11.** (i) $\frac{1}{144}$ (ii) $\frac{1}{12}$ (iii) $\frac{11}{12}$
12. (i) $\frac{25}{102}$ (ii) $\frac{1}{17}$ (iii) $\frac{4}{663}$ (iv) $\frac{8}{663}$ **13.** (i) $\frac{5}{33}$
(ii) $\frac{7}{22}$ (iii) $\frac{35}{132}$ (iv) $\frac{35}{66}$ (v) $\frac{31}{66}$ (vi) $\frac{15}{22}$

Exercise 3.10

1. $\frac{1}{8}$ **2.** 0.096 **3.** (i) 0.25 (ii) 0.25 **4.** (i) 0.5
(ii) 0.25 (iii) 0.125; Probability of not
winning = 0.125. **5.** (i) $\frac{1}{6}$ (ii) $\frac{5}{36}$ (iii) $\frac{25}{216}$;
Probability of not winning = $\frac{125}{216}$. **6.** (i) 0.15
(ii) 0.1275 (iii) 0.108375 **7.** (i) $\frac{4}{52}$ (ii) $\frac{12}{169}$
(iii) $\frac{144}{2,197}$; Probability of not winning = $\frac{1,728}{2,197}$.
8. (i) 0.6 (ii) 0.24 (iii) 0.096 **9.** (i) 0.064
10. (i) $\frac{3}{16}$ (ii) $\frac{9}{64}$; Yes. The probability of winning is
now approximately 0.27 versus 0.25.

Exercise 3.11

1. 7 **2.** (i) −0.25 (ii) No **3.** No, on average
you lose 31 cents. **4.** 4; No **5.** (i) 1.33
(ii) −3.67 **6.** −1.50; No **7.** No **8.** (i) 21.25
(ii) 11.50 **9.** (i) 0.00030003 (ii) 13 cents
10. (i) Caroline (ii) Award John one sweet if he
rolls a 2. **11.** (i) −3.75 (ii) 24.375 (iii) 487.50

Revision Exercises

1. (a) (i) B (ii) A (c) (i) $\frac{1}{52}$ (ii) $\frac{1}{13}$ (iii) $\frac{1}{13}$ (iv) $\frac{4}{13}$
(v) $\frac{4}{13}$ (vi) $\frac{4}{13}$ **2.** (a) (i) $\frac{1}{10}$ (ii) $\frac{1}{5}$ (iii) $\frac{2}{5}$ (iv) $\frac{3}{5}$ (v) $\frac{2}{5}$
(vi) $\frac{3}{5}$ (vii) $\frac{2}{5}$ (viii) 0 (b) (ii) $\frac{1}{12}$ (iii) $\frac{1}{12}$ (iv) $\frac{1}{4}$ (v) $\frac{1}{4}$
4. (a) (ii) $\frac{1}{8}$ (iii) $\frac{1}{8}$ (iv) $\frac{3}{8}$ (v) $\frac{7}{8}$ (b) (i) $\frac{2}{21}$ (ii) $\frac{5}{21}$
(iii) $\frac{11}{21}$ (iv) $\frac{10}{21}$ **5.** (a) (ii) 0.15 (iii) 0.35
6. (a) (i) −0.30 (iii) −6 (b) (i) 0.375 (ii) 0.125
7. (a) (i) 0.5 (b) (i) $\frac{1}{6}$ (ii) $\frac{25}{216}$ (iii) $\frac{125}{216}$ (iv) $\frac{2}{27}$
8. (a) (i) $\frac{1}{16}$ (ii) $\frac{1}{16}$ (iii) $\frac{15}{16}$ (iv) $\frac{100}{169}$ (v) $\frac{25}{169}$
(b) (iii) 0.64 (iv) 0.04 (v) 0.32 **9.** (b) (ii) 0.05
(iii) 0.857375 (iv) 0.142625 (v) 500 **10.** (a) (ii) $\frac{5}{22}$
(iii) $\frac{4}{11}$ (b) (i) 0.25 (ii) 0.24375 (iii) 0.04375
(iv) 0.24375 226.875 times **11.** (a) (i) −0.08 (ii) No
(iii) $-\frac{1}{19}$; The game is not fair. (b) (i) 0.04 (ii) 0.64
(iii) 0.32 **12.** (a) (i) $\frac{1}{7}$ (ii) $\frac{6}{7}$ (iii) $\frac{1}{49}$ (iv) $\frac{12}{49}$ (v) $\frac{6}{7}$
(b) (i) 0.016 (ii) 0.144 (iii) 0.576 (iv) 0.224
(v) 0.984 **13.** (a) (i) $\frac{1}{2}$ (ii) $\frac{1}{2}$ (b) (i) $\frac{13}{20}$ (ii) $\frac{7}{20}$

(c) (ii) 0.125 (iii) 0.125 (iv) 0.375 (v) 0.375
(vi) 0.875 (vii) 0.125 **14.** (b) (ii) $\frac{41}{300}$ (iii) $\frac{122}{300}$
(iv) $\frac{35}{300}$ (c) $6\frac{2}{3}$ **15.** (a) (i) $\frac{1}{2}$ (ii) $\frac{1}{3}$ (b) (i) $\frac{1}{6}$
(ii) $\frac{1}{6}$; Expected value = 4 (c) (i) $36\frac{2}{3}$ cents
(ii) 27 games (iii) €19 **16.** (a) (i) 1,140
(ii) 210 (iii) 20 (iv) 230 (v) 0.18 (vi) 0.02
(vii) 0.2 (b) (i) 720 (ii) 120 (iii) 48 (iv) 240
(v) $\frac{1}{6}$ (vi) $\frac{1}{3}$ **17.** (a) 0.101 (b) 0.086 (c) €616.91
(d) €520.39 (e) €1,071.09; €503.61 (f) €448

Chapter 4

Exercise 4.1

1. (i) 6.6 (ii) 10 (iii) 8 (iv) −4.4 (v) 5
(vi) 0.5 **2.** (i) 6, 7 (ii) 5, 3 (iii) 2, 2 (iv) 7.5,
6, 7, 8 (v) 0, 0 **3.** (ii) 45 (iii) 25 (iv) 38
4. (i) 10.86 (ii) 10.38 **5.** (i) 43 (ii) 49
(iii) 10 (iv) In half **6.** (i) 12 (ii) 12, 12, 12,
12, 12, 13, 14, 14, 14, 15, 15, 15, 15, 16, 16, 16
(iii) 14 (iv) 13.9375 **7.** (i) 25 (ii) 20, 22, 22,
22, 23, 23, 24, 24, 24, 25, 25, 25, 25, 25, 25, 26
(iii) 24 (iv) 23.75 **8.** (i) 2000 (ii) 2009
(iii) 155,048.80 (iv) 155,696.50 **9.** (i) 2
(ii) 0, 0, 1, 1, 1, 1, 2, 2, 2, 2, 2, 2, 3, 4, 4, 5, 5, 5, 6
(iii) 2 (iv) 2.5 **10.** (i) 4.8 (ii) 5.45
(iii) 5.41 **11.** (i) B, C **12.** (i) 168 (ii) 240
(iii) 40.8 (iv) No **13.** (b) 2 and 10

Exercise 4.2

5. Mean = 32.8889; median = 18. The median is
used, as there is an extreme value in the data.

Exercise 4.3

1. (i) 4.7 (ii) 6 **2.** (i) 41.76 (ii) 26 **3.** (i) 7.83
(ii) $33\frac{1}{3}$% **4.** (i) 96 (ii) 33.90625 (iii) 25%
5. (i) 159.03 **6.** 58.18 **7.** (v) 1.85 (vi) 2.36
(vii) 2.38 (viii) 0.84% **8.** (v) 34.25 (vi) 34
(vii) 34.53 (viii) 1.5%

Exercise 4.4

1. (i) 2, 7, 5 (ii) 4, 7, 3 (iii) 2.5, 6.5, 4
(iv) 4, 7, 3 (v) −2, 2, 4 (vi) −3, 7, 10 **2.** (i) 30
(ii) 49 (iii) 19 **3.** (i) 3.2 (ii) 4.7 (iii) 1.5
4. (i) 17.5 (ii) 47.5 (iii) 30 **5.** Boys, Girls
(i) 56, 51 (ii) 43, 42 (iii) 69, 74 (iv) 26, 32
6. (ii) Symmetric (iii) 45 (iv) 114 (v) 103, 121, 18
7. (i) 40 (ii) 30, 50 (iii) 20 **8.** (i) Plot
(ii) Skewed right (iii) 5.8 (iv) 1.85 (v) 2.15
9. (ii) Symmetric (iii) 9 (iv) 11 (v) 3.5

Exercise 4.5

1. (i) 1.9 (ii) 2.6 (iii) 1.9 (iv) 3.7 (v) 0.1
2. (ii) 2.1, 3.9 **4.** 1.3 **5.** 1.1 **6.** (i) 7.95
(ii) 2.8 **7.** (i) 4.16 (ii) 2.4 **8.** (i) 70 (ii) 27
9. (i) 32 (ii) 18 **10.** (i) 1,000 (ii) 32 (iii) 17

Exercise 4.7

2. (i) 18.6   (ii) 4.2   (iii) 14.4, 22.8   **3.** (i) 175, 225
(ii) 80, 120   (iii) 18, 22   (iv) 22.5, 27.5
4. (i) 210, 350   (ii) 60, 180   (iii) 21, 29   (iv) 24, 46
5. (i) 75, 225   (ii) 255, 345   (iii) 14, 26   (iv) 85, 115
6. (i) 150, 250   (ii) 60, 140   (iii) 16, 24
(iv) 20, 30   **7.** (i) 25, 55   (ii) 55, 145   (iii) 4, 40
(iv) 24, 36   **9.** 193.5   **11.** 68%

Revision Exercises

1. (v) 65   (vi) 70.4   (vii) 69.47   (viii) 1.3%
(ix) 11.34   **2.** (ii) 26   (iv) Symmetric   (v) 55
(vi) 54.6923   (vii) 0.3077   **3.** (i) 37   (iv) 7.73
(v) 4.1   **4.** (i) 41   (ii) 18   (iii) 53.5   (iv) 35.5
(v) 58   (vi) 37.8   **5.** (i) 6.29   **6.** (iv) Mean 2541;
median 2577.50   (v) 2,580   (vi) 2,527.5; 2,635;
107.5   **7.** (ii) Symmetric   (iii) Mean 5.4035;
median 5.2   (iv) 5.295, 5.515, 0.22
9. (i) 140.25, 177.75   (ii) 152.75, 165.25
(iii) 146.5, 171.5   **10.** (a) (i) 0.75   (ii) –0.97
(b) (i) 13   (iii) 80; 80; 80   (iv) 80   **11.** (iii) 27.7
(iv) 11.3   (v) $\frac{74}{85}$ (vii) 29.4   (viii) 9.8

Chapter 5

Exercise 5.1

1. (iv) RP, FE (v) XZ, ZY (vi) A, C, Y, B
(vii) X **3.** (i) 70° – acute   (ii) 115° – obtuse
(iii) 45° – acute   (iv) 260° – reflexive
(v) 120° – obtuse   **5.** (iv) No   **6.** (i) 65°   (ii) 27°
(iii) 44°   (iv) 63.5°   (v) 120°   (vi) 335°   (vii) 65°
7. (i) 10   (ii) 20   (iii) 6   (iv) 12   **8.** (i) $x = 22.5$,
$y = 45$ (ii) $x = 15$, $y = 8$

Exercise 5.2

1. (i) 65°   (ii) 55°   (iii) 63°   (iv) 90°
2. (i) $B = 25°$, $C = 155°$ (ii) $B = 100°$,
$C = 100°$ (iii) $B = 35°$, $C = 110°$
(iv) $B = 90°$, $C = 30°$ **3.** (i) $x = 40$, $y = 55$
(ii) $x = 18$, $y = 12$

Exercise 5.3

1. (i) $1 = 145°$, $2 = 35°$ (ii) $1 = 148°$, $2 = 148°$
(iii) $1 = 73°$, $2 = 107°$ (iv) $1 = 84°$, $2 = 96°$
(v) $1 = 72°$, $2 = 108°$ **2.** (i) Yes   (ii) Yes
(iii) No   **3.** (i) $A = 150°$, $B = 30°$, $C = 210°$,
$D = 150°$ (ii) $A = 84°$, $B = 84°$, $C = 96°$,
$D = 96°$ (iii) $1 = 28°$, $2 = 137°$, $3 = 152°$,
$4 = 28°$ (iv) $A = 99°$, $B = 81°$, $C = 99°$, $D = 99°$
(v) $A = 75°$, $B = 75°$, $C = 105°$, $D = 75°$
(vi) $1 = 104°$, $2 = 117°$, $3 = 63°$, $4 = 117°$
4. (i) $x = 42$, $y = 138$ (ii) $x = 52$, $y = 34$

Exercise 5.4

1. (i) $A = 90°$, $B = 53°$ (ii) $A = 120°$, $B = 60°$
(iii) $A = 75°$, $B = 30°$ (iv) $A = 20°$, $B = 50°$
(v) $A = 90°$, $B = 40°$ **2.** (i) $X = 42°$, $Y = 42°$,

$Z = 54°$ (ii) $X = 49°$, $Y = 58°$, $Z = 73°$
(iii) $X = 60°$, $Y = 48°$, $Z = 84°$ (iv) $X = 28°$,
$Y = 32°$, $Z = 28°$ (v) $X = 145°$, $Y = 120°$,
$Z = 60°$ (vi) $X = 15°$, $Y = 104°$, $Z = 76°$
(vii) $W = 119°$, $X = 66°$, $Y = 61°$, $Z = 74°$
3. (i) $A = 40°$, $B = 120°$ (ii) $A = 34°$, $B = 112°$
4. (i) $x = 12$, $y = 15$ (ii) $x = 7$, $y = 9$

Exercise 5.5

1. (i) A (ii) 1   (iii) $\angle XZY$ (iv) $\angle ACB$ (v) 2
2. (i) C (ii) BC (iii) DE (iv) PQ (v) RT
3. (i) No   (ii) Yes   (iii) Yes   (iv) Yes   (v) No
(vi) No   (vii) Yes   (viii) No   (ix) Yes   (x) No
4. Yes   **5.** (i) 2   (ii) 13   **6.** (i) 6   (ii) 18   **7.** (i) Smallest
length = 2.01 m; Largest length = 17.99 m
(ii) Minimum cost = €100.05; Maximum cost = €179.95
8. B and D **9.** Two ways
10. Elle's answer is correct.   **11.** (i) 6   (ii) 22
(iii) $6 \leqslant b \leqslant 22$ **12.** (i) 7   (ii) 25   (iii) $7 \leqslant c \leqslant 25$

Exercise 5.6

1. (i) $A = 85°$, $B = 95°$, $C = 95°$ (ii) $A = 103°$,
$B = 77°$, $C = 103°$ (iii) $A = 42°$, $B = 77°$,
$C = 61°$ (iv) $A = 78°$, $B = 74°$, $C = 102°$
(v) $A = 32°$, $B = 62°$, $C = 78°$ **2.** (i) 60°
(ii) 8   (iii) 120°   **3.** (i) 16   (ii) 18   (iii) 16
(iv) 5.8   **4.** (i) $A = 106°$, $B = 74°$, $C = 74°$
(ii) $A = 14°$, $B = 14°$, $C = 83°$ (iii) $A = 64°$,
$B = 36°$, $C = 64°$ (iv) $A = 90°$, $B = 63°$,
$C = 27°$, $D = 27°$ **5.** (i) $x = 15$, $y = 55$
(ii) $x = 6$, $y = 5$ **6.** (i) Seán is correct.

Revision Exercises

1. (a) (i) $\angle ABC$ (ii) $\angle CBD$ (iii) $\angle EBD$
(iv) $\angle EBD$ (v) $[BE$ (vi) BD (vii) $\angle ABE$, $\angle EBD$
(b) (i) False   (ii) True   (iii) True   (iv) True
(v) True   **2.** (a) (i) 85°   (ii) 110°   (iii) 95°
(iv) 70°   (v) 85°   (vi) 95°   (vii) 95°
(viii) 110°   **3.** (a) (i) Corresponding angles
(ii) Corresponding angles   (iii) Vertically opposite
angles   (iv) Supplementary angles
(v) Alternate angles   (vi) Corresponding angles
(b) (i) No   (ii) Yes   (c) (i) Yes   (ii) No
4. (a) (i) $A = 43°$, $B = 56°$, $C = 28°$
(ii) $A = 58°$, $B = 148°$, $C = 58°$, $D = 32°$
(iii) $A = 92°$, $B = 150°$, $C = 30°$, $D = 60°$
(iv) $A = 67°$, $B = 67°$, $C = 87°$, $D = 113°$
(v) $A = 6°$, $B = 15°$, $C = 75°$ (b) (i) No
(ii) No   (iii) Yes   (iv) Yes   (v) No
5. (a) (i) $A = 100°$, $B = 100°$, $C = 80°$
(ii) $A = 90°$, $B = 58°$, $C = 32°$ (iii) $A = 75°$,
$B = 55°$, $C = 55°$ (iv) $A = 39°$, $B = 42°$,
$C = 60°$ (b) (i) False   (ii) False   (iii) True
(iv) True   (v) False   **6.** (a) (i) $x = 10$, $y = 5$
(ii) $x = 14$, $y = 12$ (iii) $y = 3$, $x = 7$
(b) (i) $x = -\frac{35}{4}$, $x = 5$ (ii) $A = 60$, $B = 80$, $C = 40$
7. (a) (i) $[AB]$, $[BC]$, $[AC]$ (ii) $[EF]$, $[DF]$, $[DE]$
(iii) $[QR]$, $[PQ]$, $[PR]$ (c) (ii) B, C **8.** (a) (i) Always true

lways true   (iii) Sometimes true
metimes true   (v) Never true
ays true   (vii) Always true   (b) (i) 26 km
24 km   (c) (i) Shortest distance = 25 km; Longest
distance = 175 km   (ii) 25 km < x < 175 km
9. (a) (i) 120°   (ii) 165°   (b) (i) 6   (ii) Hexagon   (iii) 720°
10. Lowest price is €70; Highest price is €130.

Chapter 6

Revision Exercises

9. (ii) 60°   **10.** (ii) $|RS| = 6.8$ $|ST| = 9.8$
11. (ii) $\angle BAC$ (iv) 90°, 10 cm   (v) They are opposite
each other.   **12.** (iii) 17.5 cm²   (iv) SAS
14. (ii) 10 cm   (iv) 8 cm   (v) 53°, 90°, 37°
(vi) Right-angled   **15.** (iii) 4   **17.** (ii) $A = 23°$;
$B = 67°$ **19.** (ii) 90°   (iii) 140°   (iv) 9.4 cm
(v) $[AO]$ $[OB]$ $[OC]$ **21.** (iv) O
23. (ii) $|\angle ABC| = |\angle CBA|$; $|\angle BAD| = |\angle BCD|$
(iv) Same length   (v) Same   **24.** (ii) 22.5 cm²
25. (ii) 5 m   (iii) Pythagoras' theorem
29. (ii) 125.5°, 65°   **30.** (ii) 68°   (iii) 1 cm : 1 m

Chapter 7

Exercise 7.1

1. (i) Yes   (ii) Yes   (iii) Yes   (iv) Yes   (v) No,
not enough information is given.   (vi) No, we cannot
assume the diagram is accurate.   (vii) Yes
(viii) Yes   (ix) Yes   (x) No   **2.** (i) $|\angle RST| = 47$,
$|\angle SUT| = 43$ (ii) Isosceles   (iii) Yes, SAS   **3.** (i) 5 cm
(ii) Isosceles   (iii) ASA

Exercise 7.2

1. (i) 15   (ii) 4.5   **2.** (i) $x = 3.5, y = 2.1$
(ii) $x = \frac{3}{2}, y = 1$ **3.** (i) $x = 4.2, y = 6$
(ii) $x = 12, y = 9$ **4.** $58\frac{7}{15}$ cm

Exercise 7.3

1. (i) 3 : 6, 5 : 2   (ii) 9 : 3, 7 : 5   (iii) 6 : 9,
2 : 7   **2.** (i) 8   (ii) 6   (iii) 9   (iv) 8   (v) 5
3. (i) 3.6   (ii) 10   (iii) 17.6   (iv) 25   (v) 5
4. (i) 21   (ii) 24   (iii) 7 : 8   **5.** (i) 5 : 2
(ii) 7 : 5   (iii) 7 : 5   (iv) Yes   **6.** (i) $\frac{4}{3}$ (ii) $\frac{4}{3}$ (iii) $\frac{7}{3}$
(iv) 6   (v) 5.25   (vi) 12.25   **7.** No   **8.** Yes
9. (i) 2.5   (ii) $\frac{7}{2}$

Exercise 7.4

2. (i) 14   (ii) 12   (iii) $5\frac{11}{23}$ (iv) 3.75   (v) 7.5
3. (i) $y = 8, x = 12$ (ii) $x = 14.4, y = 4.8$
(iii) $x = 19.8, y = 22$ (iv) $x = 17\frac{1}{3}, y = 10$
(v) $x = 13\frac{1}{2}, y = 28\frac{1}{3}$ **4.** (i) Similar   (ii) Not similar
5. (i) $x = 6, y = 6$ (ii) $x = 7, y = 21$
(iii) $x = 10\frac{2}{3}, Y = 23\frac{1}{3}$ (iv) $x = 19.5, y = 9.375$
6. (ii) 10   (iii) 8   (iv) 4   **7.** (i) 4   (ii) $2\frac{2}{3}$
8. (ii) 3 : 2   (iii) 3 : 2   (iv) 5 : 2   **9.** 8.75

10. 7.68 m   **11.** (i) Student B is taller.   (ii) 1.81 m
(iii) 2.13 m   **12.** (i) $h \approx 8.92$ m   (ii) $y \approx 10$ m
13. (ii) 2.05 m   **14.** (ii) 11 m

Exercise 7.5

1. (i) 85 cm   (ii) 75 cm   (iii) 25 cm
(iv) 72 cm   (v) 10 cm   (vi) 60 cm   (vii) 45 cm
(viii) 25 cm   (ix) 0.45 m   (x) 200 km
2. (i) 8.6 m   (ii) 7.55 cm   (iii) 18.76 cm
(iv) 11.31 cm   (v) 15.56 cm   **3.** (i) $4\sqrt{5}$ cm
(ii) $25\sqrt{3}$ (iii) 6   (iv) 5   (v) 1   **4.** (i) No
(ii) Yes   (iii) Yes   (iv) No   **5.** (i) $x = 36, y = 60$
(ii) $x = 90, y = 48$ (iii) $x = 36, y = 48$
6. (i) $x = 4$ (ii) $x = 5$ **7.** 5 cm   **8.** 5.02 m
9. 3.99 m   **10.** 6.27 m   **11.** 16 cm   **12.** 152 m²
13. Square blocks: 1.25 cm × 1.25 cm
Smaller rectangular blocks: 1.25 cm × 2.5 cm
Larger rectangular blocks: 1.25 cm × 3.75 cm

Exercise 7.6

1. (i) 45   (ii) 31.5   (iii) 10.5   (iv) 10   (v) 50
2. (i) 105 cm²   (ii) 41.8 cm²   (iii) 72 cm²
(iv) 52 cm²   **3.** $h = 4$; 28 cm²   **4.** (i) 75 cm²
(ii) 64 cm²   (iii) 30 m²   **5.** (i) 15 cm²   (ii) 2 cm²
(iii) 700 m²   (iv) 420 sq. units   (v) 31.5 sq. units
6. (i) $x = 8.75$ (ii) $x = 10$ (iii) $x = 12$ (iv) $x = 4$

Exercise 7.7

1. (i) $\angle BAC$, $[BC]$ (ii) $\angle GFE$, $[GE]$ (iii) $\angle TVS$, $[TS]$
2. (i) 1 = 90°, 2 = 50°   (ii) 1 = 45°, 2 = 45°
(iii) 1 = 116°, 2 = 64°   (iv) 1 = 45°, 2 = 45°
3. (i) $A = 55°, B = 70°$ (ii) $A = 64°, B = 32°$
(iii) $A = 27°, B = 59°$ (iv) $A = 40°, B = 60°$
(v) $A = 54°, B = 72°$ (vi) $A = 118°, B = 28°$
(vii) $A = 70°, B = 36°$ **4.** (i) 17   (ii) 37
5. (i) 90°   (ii) 60°   (iii) 30°   (iv) Isosceles triangle
6. (i) 113°   (ii) 33.5°   (iii) 56.5°   (iv) 65°

Exercise 7.8

1. (i) 90°   (ii) 90°   (iii) 44°   (iv) 46°
2. (i) 90°   (ii) 33°   (iii) 57°   **3.** (i) 15   (ii) $5\sqrt{13}$
4. (i) 5 cm   (ii) 8 cm   (iii) 2 cm   (iv) R80 cm
5. (i) 5 cm   (ii) 3 cm   (iii) 8 cm   **6.** (i) 5 cm
(ii) 8 cm   **7.** 8 cm   **8.** (i) 5 cm   (ii) 10 cm
(iii) 1 cm   (iv) 25 cm   (v) $5\sqrt{26}$ cm
9. (i) 24 cm   (ii) 32 cm   (iii) 96 cm²   (iv) 96 cm²
10. (i) 9 cm   (ii) 2 cm   (iii) $14\sqrt{2}$ cm²

Revision Exercises

1. (a) (i) Yes   (ii) Yes   (iii) No   (iv) No   (v) Yes
(b) (i) Parallelogram   (iii) Yes, SAS   (iv) 6 cm
(c) (i) Isosceles   (iii) SSS   (iv) All sides are equal.
2. (a) (i) 5   (ii) $\frac{8}{3}$ (iii) 1.5   (iv) 4   (v) 10.15
(vi) 7.2   (b) (i) 1.2   (ii) 3   (iii) 3.84   (iv) 3.8
3. (a) (i) $x = 13, y = 20$ (ii) $x = 14.25, y = 6.75$
(iii) $x = 15.75, y = 7.875$ (iv) $x = 25, y = 18$
(v) $x = 14, y = \frac{4}{7}$ (b) (iii) 4.5 cm   (iv) $8\frac{8}{9}$ cm

(v) $1\frac{1}{9}$ cm (c) (ii) 1.56 cm (iii) 7.69 cm (iv) 0.2 cm
4. (a) (i) $x = 48$, $y = 14$ (ii) $x = 15$, $y = 8$
(iii) $x = 6\sqrt{5}$, $y = 18$ (iv) $x = 5\sqrt{5}$, $y = 5$
(v) $x = 3$, $y = 4$ (b) (i) $2\sqrt{41}$ (ii) $\frac{5\sqrt{41}}{2}$ (iii) 20.5
(c) (i) Triangle *MBC* (ii) $\angle MBC$, $\angle BMA$, $\angle CMD$
(iii) 10 cm (iv) 48 cm² (v) 9.6 cm
5. (a) (i) 37.5 cm² (ii) 80 cm² (iii) 108 cm²
(iv) 102 cm² (v) 20 cm² (b) (i) $x = 20\sqrt{3}$ cm;
692.82 cm² (ii) $x = 15$ cm; 570 cm²
(iii) $x = 8.32$ cm; 124.8 cm² (iv) $x = 4$ cm;
28 cm² (c) 4 m **6.** (a) (i) $B = 90°$, $A = 58°$
(ii) $B = 48°$, $A = 96°$ (iii) $A = 117°$, $B = 27°$
(iv) $A = 55°$, $B = 55°$, (v) $A = 36°$; $B = 32°$
(b) (i) Right-angled (ii) SAS (iii) 45°
(iv) $15\sqrt{2}$ cm (c) (i) $AM = 12$ mm, $DM = 5$ mm
(ii) $\angle AMD$, $\angle AMB$, $\angle DMC$, $\angle BMC$ (iii) 13 mm
(iv) Yes (v) 120 mm² **7.** (a) (i) 15 (ii) 9
(iii) 10 (iv) 17.5 (b) (i) 18 (ii) 35 (iii) 40
(c) 14 cm **8.** (iv) 3.75 m (v) 3.875 m **9.** (i) 293 m
(ii) €5,860 (iii) 361 m (iv) €7,220
(v) The original layout is cheaper; €1,360.
11. (ii) 12 m (iii) 24 m (iv) 34 m (v) 104 m²

Chapter 8

Exercise 8.1

1. (i) 9 cm² (ii) 45.5 cm² (iii) 90 cm² (iv) 100 cm²
(v) 390 cm² (vi) 56 cm² (vii) 62.64 cm²
(viii) 3,192 cm² (ix) 12 cm² (x) 120 cm²
2. (i) Area = 210 cm², Perimeter = 100 cm
(ii) Area = 1064 cm², Perimeter = 150 cm
(iii) Area = 236.5 cm², Perimeter = 54 cm
(iv) Area = 256 m², Perimeter = 67 m
(v) Area = 36 cm², Perimeter = 74 cm
(vi) Area = 160 m², Perimeter = 67 m²
(vii) Area = 36.54 cm², Perimeter = 47.6 cm
3. (i) 60 cm² (ii) 1,667 tiles (iii) 100,000 cm² or 10 m²
4. (i) €56 (ii) 560 panels **5.** (i) 81.25%
6. (a) (i) 216 m² (ii) 225 m² (b) ≈€3,059

Exercise 8.2

1. (i) Area = 314 cm², Circumference = 62.8 cm
(ii) Area = 3.14 m², Circumference = 6.28 m
(iii) Area = 45,216 mm², Circumference = 753.6 mm
(iv) Area = 80,384 cm², Circumference = 1,004.8 cm
2. (i) Area = $28\frac{2}{7}$ cm², Circumference = $18\frac{6}{7}$ cm
(ii) Area = 61,600 cm², Circumference = 880 cm
(iii) Area = $24,894\frac{4}{7}$ cm², Circumference = $559\frac{3}{7}$ cm
(iv) Area = 98.56 cm², Circumference = 35.2 cm
3. (i) Area = 100π cm² Circumference = 20π cm,
(ii) Area = 16π mm², Circumference = 8π mm
(iii) Area = 144π m², Circumference = 24π m
(iv) Area = 0.0625π cm², Circumference = 0.5π cm
4. (i) Area = 31.4 cm², Arc Length = 6.28 cm,
Perimeter = 26.28 cm (ii) Area = 235.5 cm²,
Arc Length = 31.4 cm, Perimeter = 61.4 cm

(iii) Area = 79.86 cm², Arc Length = 24.2 cm,
Perimeter = 37.4 cm (iv) Area = $905\frac{1}{7}$ cm²,
Arc Length = $100\frac{4}{7}$ cm, Perimeter $136\frac{4}{7}$ cm
(v) Area = 1039.5 cm², Arc Length = 99 cm,
Perimeter = 141 cm **5.** (i) Area = 124.2325 cm²,
Perimeter = 47.99 cm (ii) Area = 2,582.3125 cm²,
Perimeter = 191.05 cm (iii) Area = 1,324.28 m²,
Perimeter = 131.96 m (iv) Area = 754.875 cm²,
Perimeter = 100.65 cm (v) Area = 383 cm²,
Perimeter ≈ 133.81 cm **6.** ≈54 minutes
7. (i) ≈7.0711 cm (ii) ≈7 minutes 4 seconds
8. (i) 433 complete parts (iii) 87.92 cm

Exercise 8.3

1. (i) 6 (ii) 10 (iii) $x = 10$ (iv) $x = 12$ (v) $x = 40$
(vi) 9 (vii) $x = 4.3$ **3.** (i) $r = 21$ cm (ii) $r = 60$ cm
(iii) $\theta° = 90°$ (iv) $\theta° = 142.8°$ (v) $\theta° = 167.5°$

Exercise 8.4

1. (i) 102 cm (ii) 630 cm² **2.** (i) 66 m (ii) 200 m²
3. (i) 3 m (ii) 5 m **4.** (i) 5 m (ii) 13 m **5.** (i) 600 cm²
6. (i) 9,936 m² (ii)1,314 m² (iii) €3,449.25
7. (i) $r = 49$ cm (ii) 30.8 km **8.** $r = 8$ cm
9. (i) $r = 15$ m (ii) 94.2 m **10.** (i) 148.5 m²
(ii) €816.75 **11.** Red has the largest shaded area.
Pick red. **12.** 149.12 m **13.** (i) 400 m (ii) 112 m
14. Width = 2 m, Length = 15 m **15.** (i) 1 : 4
(ii) 1 : 16 **16.** (i) 50 cm² (ii) ≈29 cm²
17. The inner shaded region has the greater area.
18. (i) 8.5 m (ii) 87.135 m²

Exercise 8.5

1. (i) Volume = 1,680 cm³, Surface Area = 856 cm²
(ii) Volume = 60 cm³, Surface Area = 94 cm²
(iii) Volume = 16.875 m³, Surface Area = 43.5 m²
(iv) Volume = 13,000 mm³, Surface Area = 3,820 mm²
(v) Volume = 4.14 m³, Surface Area = 16.02 m²
(vi) Volume = 125 mm³, Surface Area = 150 mm²
2. (i) Volume = 105 cm³, Surface Area = 142 cm²
(ii) Volume = 64 cm³, Surface Area = 96 cm²
(iii) Volume = 450 m³, Surface Area = 300 m²
5. (i) 248 cm² (ii) 30 cubes **6.** (i) 9.9 litres (ii) 3,800 cm²

Exercise 8.6

1. (i) Volume = 48,750 cm³, Surface Area = 8,950 cm²
(ii) Volume = 3,220 cm³, Surface Area = 1,636 cm²
(iii) Volume = 3,204 cm³, Surface Area = 1,704 cm²,
(iv) Volume = 3,600 m³, Surface Area = 1,620 m²
(v) Volume = 101 m³, Surface Area = 129.4 m²
(vi) Volume = 156,346.25 cm³,
Surface Area = 25,165.77 cm² **3.** (i) Volume = 27 cm³,
Surface Area = 54 cm² (ii) Volume = 43,200 cm³,
Surface Area = 20,160 cm² (iii) Volume = 420 cm³,
Surface Area = 386 cm² **4.** 16 cm³ **5.** (i) 77 m²
(ii) 3,080 m² **6.** (i) 18 m² (ii) 144 m³ **7.** (i) 0.54 m³
(ii) €47.52

,140 cm³   (ii) $18\frac{18}{175}$ cm³   (iii) 648π m³

(iv) 41,250 m³   (v) 1,099 mm³   **2.** (i) **CSA:** 3.14 m²
TSA: 3.5325 m²   (ii) **CSA:** 30π cm² **TSA:** 48π cm²
(iii) **CSA:** 345.4 cm² **TSA:** 502.4 cm²

(iv) **CSA:** $6,084\frac{4}{7}$ cm² **TSA:** $9,126\frac{6}{7}$ cm²

3. (i) **Vol:** 1,232 mm³ **TSA:** 1408 mm²
(ii) **Vol:** 25.3125 mm³ **TSA:** 36.625 mm²
4. (i) **Vol:** 21.98 cm³ **CSA:** 43.96 cm²
(ii) **Vol:** 48.08125 cm³ **CSA:** 54.95 cm²
5. (i) **Vol:** 2.8125π m³ **TSA:** 8.625π m²
(ii) **Vol:** 750π m³ **TSA:** 350π m²   **6.** (i) $\approx$13.54 l
(ii) 3,165.12 cm²   **7.** (i) $2,560\pi$ cm³, 640π cm³
(ii) 4 : 1 **8.** $\approx$1,569.75 kg

Exercise 8.8

1. (i) $\frac{16\pi}{3}$ cm³   (ii) 35,200 mm³   (iii) 5,024 cm³

(iv) $5,887\frac{1}{2}$ cm³   (v) $9,166\frac{2}{3}$ cm³   (vi) $418\frac{2}{3}$ cm³

2. (i) **CSA:** 60π m² **TSA:** 96π m²
(ii) **CSA:** 2,106.94 cm² **TSA:** 2,486.88 cm²
(iii) **CSA:** 3,080 mm² **TSA:** 5,544 mm²
(iv) **CSA:** $1,500\pi$ m² **TSA:** $2,400\pi$ m²
3. (i) **Vol:** 8,377.58 cm³ **TSA:** 3,033.79 cm²
(ii) **Vol:** 8.82 m³ **TSA:** 28.06 m²
4. (i) **A:** 3.21536 l **B:** 0.33493
(ii) **A:** 603 full panels **B:** 103 full panels
5. (i) **Vol:** 134,095,238.10 m³
TSA: $\approx$ 1,627,279.90 m²   (ii) **Vol:** $\approx$ 0.03 km³
TSA: $\approx$ 0.17 km²   **6.** €9,231.60   **7.** 144π m³

Exercise 8.9

1. (i) 972π cm³   (ii) $7,241\frac{1}{7}$ cm³   (iii) $523\frac{1}{3}$ mm³

(iv) 4851 cm³   (v) $\frac{256}{3}\pi$ m³   **2.** (i) $4,603\frac{5}{21}$ cm³

(ii) 144π m³   (iii) 7.065 m³   (iv) $\frac{16}{3}\pi$ cm³

(v) 155,090.88 cm³   **3.** (i) 324π cm²   (ii) $1,810\frac{2}{7}$ m²

4. (i) 235.5 mm²   (ii) $94,285\frac{5}{7}$ km²   **5.** (i) **TSA:** 16π cm²

(ii) **CSA:** 1,413 m² **TSA:** 2,119.5 m²
(iii) **CSA:** 4,578.12 cm² **TSA:** 6,867.18 cm²

(iv) $2,552\frac{11}{14}$ cm²   **6.** (i) **Vol:** $\frac{125}{96}\pi$ m³

TSA: 4.6875π m²   (ii) **Vol:** $\frac{1}{6}\pi$ km³ **TSA:** $\frac{3}{4}\pi$ km²

7. (i) $\approx$1,465 cm²   (ii) $\approx$5,274 cm³

8. (i) $1,437\frac{1}{3}$ cm³   (ii) 2,744 cm³ (iii) $\approx$47.6%

9. (i) 1,584 cm³   (ii) $381\frac{6}{7}$ cm³   (iii) $1,202\frac{1}{7}$ cm³

10. (i) 179.50 cm³   (ii) 21 cm   (iii) 3.5 cm

(iv) 807.765 cm³ (v) $\frac{2}{3}$ **11.** $\approx$167 cm³

12. $\approx$€43,824.35

Exercise 8.10

(i)

L (cm)	B (cm)	H (cm)	V (cm³)	SA (cm²)
4	5	9	180	202
2	1	3	6	22
14	7.5	2	210	296
1	$1\frac{1}{2}$	$3\frac{1}{3}$	5	$19\frac{2}{3}$
0.5	0.5	0.25	0.0625	1

(ii)

π	r (cm)	h (cm)	V (cm³)	CSA (cm²)	TSA (cm²)
π	5	4	100π	40π	90π
3.14	9	11	2,797.74	621.72	1,130.4
3.14	13	1	530.66	81.64	1,142.96
$\frac{22}{7}$	7	14	2,156	616	924
$\frac{22}{7}$	9	9.5	$2,418\frac{3}{7}$	$537\frac{3}{7}$	$1,046\frac{4}{7}$

(iii)

π	r (cm)	h (cm)	l (cm)	V (cm³)	CSA (cm²)	TSA (cm²)
π	4	3	5	16π	20π	36π
$\frac{22}{7}$	7	24	25	1,232	550	704
3.14	9	40	41	3,391.2	1,158.66	1,413
3.14	13	84	85	14,858.48	3,469.7	4,000.36
$\frac{22}{7}$	20	99	101	$41,485\frac{5}{7}$	$6,348\frac{4}{7}$	$7,605\frac{5}{17}$

(iv) (a)

π	r (cm)	V (cm³)	TSA (cm²)
π	5	$166\frac{2}{3}\pi$	100π
$\frac{22}{7}$	2	$33\frac{11}{21}$	$50\frac{2}{7}$
3.14	9	3,052.08	1,1017.36
π	13	$2,929\frac{1}{3}$	676π

(b)

π	r (cm)	V (cm³)	TSA (cm²)	CSA (cm²)
π	5	$83\frac{1}{3}\pi$	75π	50π
$\frac{22}{7}$	2	$16\frac{16}{21}$	$37\frac{5}{7}$	$25\frac{1}{7}$
3.14	9	1526.04	763.02	508.68
π	13	$1,464\frac{2}{3}$	507π	338π

Exercise 8.11

1. 18 cm   **2.** 30 cm   **3.** (i) 288π cm³   (ii) 96 cm
4. 6 cm   **5.** 9 cm   **6.** $\approx$38 mm   **7.** $\approx$1.63 cm
8. 12 cm   **9.** (i) 10 cm   (ii) $\approx$446.20 cm²
10. (a) (i) 144π cm³   (ii) 4 cm   (iii) 10 cm
(b) more than half   **11.** (i) 3 cm   (ii) 16π cm³
(iii) 10 cm   **12.** h = 9 cm, l = 18 cm, w = 4.5 cm
13. 12, 24, 36 cm   **14.** 2 cm   **15.** 0.25 cm
16. (i) 81π cm³   (ii) 9 cm   **17.** 50 sec
18. 2nd cone has greater volume.
19. C has greatest volume. **20.** $\approx$21 cm
21. (i) 2.25π cm³   (ii) 1.5 cm drop   (iii)   40 ladlefuls

Exercise 8.12

1. 73 units² **2.** 330 units² **3.** 405 units²
4. 308 units² **5.** 2,260 units² **6.** 843.75 units²
7. 702 units² **8.** (i) 6.775 hectares
(ii) 11.7 hectares **9.** $3\frac{2}{3}$ **10.** 15 **11.** $4\frac{1}{3}$ **12.** 15

Revision Exercises

1. (a) (i) 516 cm² (ii) 5,000 mm² (iii) 286 m²
(iv) 2,089.5 cm² (v) 136 m²
(b) **Area:** (i) 625π cm² (ii) 1,017.36 cm²
(iii) $\frac{11}{56}$ mm² (iv) 156.25π cm² **Perimeter:** (i) 50π cm
(ii) 113.04 cm (iii) $1\frac{4}{7}$ mm (iv) 25π cm

2. (a) (i) 67.1175 cm² (ii) $794\frac{1}{16}$ cm²
(iii) 1,553.7575 mm² (iv) $1,301\frac{41}{56}$ mm²
(b) (i) 8 (ii) $5\frac{1}{3}$ (iii) 13 (iv) 40 (v) 42 (vi) 290°
3. (a) $\approx$21.5 m (b) (i) 8 cm (ii) 320π cm³
4. (a) (i) 912 units² (ii) 1,380 units²
(iii) 302.5 units² (iv) 231 units² (b) (i) 13.5
(ii) 45 (iii) $6\frac{2}{3}$ **5.** (a) (i) **V:** 113,408 m³ **SA:** 16,176 m²
(ii) **V:** 960 m³ **SA:** 736 m² (iii) **V:** 67,500 cm³
SA: 11,154.81 cm² (b) (i) **V:** $\approx$ 9,993.89 cm³
SA: 2,739.45 cm² (ii) **V:** 13094.30 cm³
SA: 3,268.25 cm² (c) (i) 21 litre (ii) 35 cm³/sec
6. (a) 88.3125 cm² (b) 4 cm **7.** (a) 1,100 cm³
(b) Possible: 2 m × 2.4 m × 1 m **8.** (a) 2,240 cupfuls
(b) 62 units² **9.** (a) (i) 55,566 cm³
(ii) 4,851 cm³ (iii) 29,079.54 cm³ (b) 5 m
10. (a) **Area:** 18.84 cm² **Perimeter:** 18.28 cm
(b) (i) 60.75π cm³ (ii) 4.5 cm drop
(iii) 32 ladlefuls **11.** (a) (i) 2,300 m² (ii) 16,100 m³
(b) (i) 528 cm³ (ii) $\approx$1.9 cm **12.** (a) (i) 480 cm³
(ii) 36π cm³ (iii) 96π cm³ (b) (i) 10π cm
(ii) 10π cm² **13.** (a) 27 : 1 (b) 2 : 1 **14.** (a) 8 cm
(b) (i) $\sqrt{2}\ r$ **15.** (a) 8 : 1 (b) $13\frac{1}{3}$ minutes
16. (a) $\approx$4.5 cm (b) (i) $\approx$400 m (ii) $\approx$406 m
(iii) B = 6 m, C = 12 m **17.** (a) 100 cm/s
(b) $\frac{1}{8}$ cm (i) $\frac{1}{8}$ cm drop (ii) 1.5 cm
18. (a) (i) 122.5π cm³ (ii) 6 cm (iii) 110.25π cm³
(iv) 9 cm (b) 15 m **19.** (a) (i) 18π cm³
(ii) 4.5 cm (b) 2nd cylinder has greater volume.
20. (b) 50% **21.** (a) (i) 720π mm³ (ii) 2261.95 mm³
(b) 10 holes

Chapter 9

Exercise 9.1

1. (i) D (ii) P (iii) P (iv) X **2.** (i) A (ii) C
(iii) C (iv) B **4.** (i) C (ii) B (iii) A (iv) A
5. (i) A Central symmetry; B Axial; C Translation
(ii) A Axial; B Translation; C Central (iii) A Central
symmetry; B Axial; C Translation

Exercise 9.3

1. (ii) 2 **2.** (ii) $k = 3$ **3.** (i) X (ii) $k = 2$
(iii) 4 : 1 **4.** (i) Z (ii) 2 **5.** (i) 4 cm (ii) 43 cm²
6. (i) $\frac{3}{5}$ (ii) 2.5 (iii) $\frac{9}{25}$ **7.** (i) $\frac{1}{4}$ or 0.25
(ii) $|AB|$ = 4 cm; $|CD|$ = 2 cm; $|DE|$ = 1.4 cm;
$|EF|$ = 1 cm; $|B'C'|$ = 0.5 cm (iii) 0.59375 cm²
8. (ii) C = (3.4, 0.4), $k = 3$ **9.** (ii) 4 (iii) 1 : 16
10. (i) 5 (ii) 3 (iii) 24 cm (iv) 16 cm (v) 320 cm²
11. (i) 1.5 (ii) 10 cm (iii) 40 cm² (iv) 50 cm²
12. 2 cm² **13.** (i) R (ii) 2.5 (iii) 4
(iv) $|XY|$ = 1.2, $|YR|$ = 1.6 (v) 6.25 : 1 **14.** (i) 3.5
(ii) $|DE|$ = 5.25 (iii) $|AB|$ = 1.4 (iv) 12.25 : 1
15. (i) 3 (ii) Midpoint of $[WZ]$ (iii) 3 : 1 (iv) 9 : 1
(v) 3 : 1 **16.** (i) 10.5 cm × 1.5 cm × 2.25 cm
(ii) 1 : 4,000 **17.** (iii) 48 cm² **18.** (i) 5 (ii) 1.4
(iii) 12 (iv) 30 units² (v) 28.8 units² **19.** (i) 1.2
(ii) 0.6 (iii) 5 : 6 (iv) 1.44 : 1 **20.** (i) 1,160 cm²
(ii) 2,400 cm² (iii) 72.5 m² (iv) 37.5 m³ (v) 1 : k^2
(vi) 1 : k^2

Chapter 10

Exercise 10.1

1. $A(-5,-2)$, $B(-3,2)$, $C(6,-1)$, $D(-4,1)$, $E(0,4)$, $F(1,2)$,
$G(-1,0)$, $H(2,-4)$ **2.** (i)2nd (ii) 4th (iii) 2nd (iv) 3rd
(v) 1st (vi) 1st (vii) 4th (viii) 3rd (ix) 1st (x) 3rd
3. (i) x (ii) y (iii) y (iv) x (v) x
(vi) x (vii) y **4.** (i) (3,0) (ii) (–4,0) (iii) (0,3)
(iv) (0,–2) **5.** (i) $\sqrt{10}$ (ii) $\sqrt{157}$ (iii) 2 (iv) 4
6. (i) $\sqrt{45}$ (ii) $\sqrt{8}$ (iii)$\sqrt{65}$ (iv)$\sqrt{41}$ **7.** (i) $\sqrt{45}$
(ii)$\sqrt{6}$ (iii) $\sqrt{65}$ (iv) $\sqrt{208}$ **8.** (ii) 13 (iii) $\sqrt{338}$
(iv) Yes **9.** (ii) $\sqrt{32}$; $\sqrt{32}$ (iii) $\sqrt{5}$ (iv) $\sqrt{29}$ (v) $\sqrt{61}$
13. Inside **14.** $\sqrt{20}$ **15.** (i) (4,4) **16.** (i) $k = 2$ or 8
17. $k = 0$ or 2

Exercise 10.2

1. (i) (5,3) (ii) (4,6) (iii) (6,8) (iv) (2,4)
2. (i) (3,4.5) (ii) (3,0) (iii) (3.5,–2) (iv) (0.5,–4)
3. (i) (2.5,–1.5) (ii) (–1,–4) (iii) (3.5,2)
(iv) (2.5,–6) **4.** $C(2,3)$ **5.** (4,0) **6.** (i) (1,–1)
(ii) $\sqrt{41}$ **7.** (i) (3,–2) **8.** x = 2; y = 3
9. (i) (4,–12) (ii) (9,–2) (iii) (–2,1) (iv) (–8,–15)
10. x = 0; y = –5

Exercise 10.3

1. (i) 3 (ii) –2 (iii) 0 (iv) 4 **2.** (i) $\frac{1}{5}$ (ii) $\frac{2}{-3}$ (iii) –2
(iv) $-\frac{2}{9}$ **3.** (i) –1 (ii) $\frac{1}{3}$ (iii) $\frac{7}{4}$ (iv) $\frac{11}{6}$ **4.** $a = 1$,
$b = 0$; $c = -1$; $d = -3$; $e = 3$; $f = -\frac{3}{2}$ **5.** $q = -1$;
$r = -\frac{3}{2}$; $s = \frac{3}{2}$; $t = -\frac{2}{5}$; $u = \frac{5}{3}$; $v = 0$ **6.** (i) C
(ii) Slope b = 1, slope d = –3, slope e = $-\frac{1}{2}$
10. (iii) (3.5,–0.5)

Exercise 10.4

4. On line   **5.** Not on line   **6.** Not on line
7. (iii) $\frac{-1}{3}$ (iv) On line   **8.** (iii) 2   (iv) Not on line
9. 13   **10.** 9   **11.** 7   **12.** 4   **13.** 7   **14.** (i) $x = 5$
(ii) $x = -2$ (iii) $x = -1$ (iv) $x = 2$ **15.** (i) $y = 3$
(ii) $y = -2$ (iii) $y = -3$ (iv) $y = 5$

Exercise 10.5

1. (i) 2   (ii) 3   (iii) 7   (iv) $\frac{1}{2}$ **2.** (i) 2   (ii) $\frac{2}{3}$
(iii) -2 (iv) $\frac{-6}{5}$ **3.** (i) $(0,-8)$ (ii) $(0,-4)$ (iii) $(0,3)$
(iv) $(0,\frac{-1}{3})$ **4.** (i) $(0,-2)$ (ii) $(0,-8)$ (iii) $(0,-5)$
(iv) $(0,\frac{-2}{5})$ **9.** (i) $(0,-6)$ (ii) $(0,2)$ (iii) $(0,8)$
(iv) $(0,-12)$ **10.** (i) $(-4,0)$ (ii) $(6,0)$ (iii) $(9,0)$
(iv) $(2,0)$ **11.** (i) $x = (3,0)$; $y = (0,3)$
(ii) $x = (6,0)$; $y = (0,3)$ (iii) $x = (4,0)$; $y = (0,8)$
(iv) $x = (3,0)$; $y = (0,-15)$ (v) $x = (6,0)$; $y = (0,10)$

Exercise 10.6

1. (i) $2x - y - 1 = 0$ (ii) $x + y + 1 = 0$
(iii) $5x + y + 32 = 0$ (iv) $x - 2y - 3 = 0$
(v) $x + 3y + 22 = 0$ **2.** (i) $3x - 2y + 13 = 0$
(ii) $4x + 3y - 11 = 0$ (iii) $2x - 5y + 34 = 0$
(iv) $x + 7y - 40 = 0$ (v) $3x + 5y + 28 = 0$
3. (i) $y = x - 1$ (ii) $x - 3y + 10 = 0$
(iii) $2x - y + 9 = 0$ (iv) $x + y - 3 = 0$
(v) $7x + y - 4 = 0$ **4.** (i) $x + 3y - 4 = 0$
(ii) $x - y + 6 = 0$ (iii) $14x + 9y - 39 = 0$
(iv) $2x - 3y + 1 = 0$ (v) $9x + y + 23 = 0$
5. $l: 4x - y - 2 = 0$; $k: x + y + 1 = 0$; $j: y = 1$
6. $j: x = 2$; $k: 3x - y - 6 = 0$; $l: 2x + y - 12 = 0$
7. (i) $x = 1$ (ii) $x = -1$ (iii) $x = -5$ (iv) $y = 4$
(v) $y = 3$ **8.** $x + 8y - 11 = 0$ **9.** $2x - 3y - 1 = 0$
10. $x + 8y - 11 = 0$

Exercise 10.7

1. (iii) $(-6,-9)$ **2.** (iii) $(-4,3)$ **3.** (iii) $(\frac{3}{4},\frac{25}{4})$
4. (iii) $(5,4)$ **5.** (iii) $(7,14)$ **6.** (iii) $(12,36)$
7. (i) $x + y = 21$; $x - y = 13$ (ii) $x = 17$; $y = 4$
8. (i) $x - y = 26$; $2x - y = 94$ (ii) $x = 68$; $y = 42$

Exercise 10.8

2. $-\frac{8}{5}$ **3.** $\frac{1}{2}$ **4.** $\frac{4}{3}$ **5.** 4   **6.** $-\frac{5}{4}$ **7.** $\frac{1}{5}$ **8.** (i) 2   (ii) $-\frac{1}{2}$
9. (i) $y = -\frac{5}{3}x - 2$ (ii) $y = -\frac{1}{4}x - 5$ (iii) $y = -\frac{8}{9}x + 2$
(iv) $y = \frac{1}{2}x + \frac{1}{3}$ (v) $y = -\frac{9}{5}x - 8$ (vi) $y = -\frac{1}{5}x - 3$
(vii) $y = -\frac{2}{3}x + 11$ (viii) $y = \frac{1}{5}x + \frac{2}{5}$ (ix) $y = -\frac{7}{3}x + 2$
10. (i) $y = -\frac{1}{5}x - 4$ (ii) $y = -\frac{1}{3}x + 2$ (iii) $y = -\frac{1}{2}x + 8$
(iv) $y = -\frac{1}{5}x - 12$ (v) $y = \frac{1}{9}x + 10$ (vi) $y = -\frac{6}{5}x - 3$
(vii) $y = \frac{1}{7}x + 28$ (viii) $y = \frac{5}{3}x - 12$ (ix) $y = x + 6$
11. (i) 2   (ii) $\frac{1}{3}$ (iii) 5   (iv) 2   (v) $-\frac{4}{9}$ (vi) $\frac{7}{3}$
12. $3x - 2y - 12 = 0$ **13.** $6x + y + 16 = 0$
14. $2x - y + 4 = 0$ **15.** $x + y - 4 = 0$

Exercise 10.9

1. (i) 2,000   (ii) 4,500   (iii) $y = 0.25x + 2,000$
(iv) $x = 12,000$ **3.** (iii) $x = 25$ **4.** (iv) 212°F
5. (i) 34 km/h   (ii) 38 km/h   **6.** (ii) $\frac{x}{3} + \frac{y}{4} = 37.5$
(iii) 60 m   **7.** (i) €137   (ii) €171   (iii) 902
(iv) €268.12

Exercise 10.10

1. (i) 15 units²   (ii) 2 units²   (iii) 1 units²
(iv) 2 units²   **2.** (i) 1 units²   (ii) 11.5 units²
(iii) 18 units²   (iv) 16 units²   **3.** (i) 4 units²
(ii) 8.5 units²   (iii) 13 units²   (iv) 10 units²
5. (ii) 16 units²   **6.** (ii) 33.5 units²   **7.** (i) 9 units²
(ii) 4 units²   (iii) 2 units²   (iv) 3 units²   **8.** (i) $(1,-4)$
(iii) 1   (iv) $x + y + 3 = 0$ (v) On line   (vii) $\sqrt{32}$; $\sqrt{50}$
(viii) 20 units²   **9.** (i) $(5,0)$ (iii) $\frac{2}{5}$
(iv) $5x + 2y = 25$ (v) On line   (vii) $\sqrt{116}$; $\sqrt{29}$
(viii) 29 units²   **10.** 3 or -3 **11.** 2 or -2
12. $x = -3$ or $x = 7$ **13.** (i) $(4,3)$ (ii) 9 units²

Revision Exercises

1. (ii) $(1,-2)$ (iv) -1 (v) $x + y + 1 = 0$ (vi) $(-1,0)$
3. (ii) $(1.5,0)$ (iii) $\frac{8}{3}$ (iv) $8x - 3y - 12 = 0$
(v) $(0,-4)$ (vi) 6   **4.** (ii) $\frac{5}{7}$ (iii) $5x - 7y + 32 = 0$
(iv) $(0,\frac{32}{7})$ (v) $y = \frac{5}{7}x + \frac{32}{7}$ **5.** (i) On line   (ii) 6
(iv) -3 (v) -3 **6.** $4.25x + y + 4.25 = 0$
7. (ii) $\sqrt{10}$ (iii) 20   **8.** (iii) $\frac{1}{16}$ (iv) $y = \frac{1}{16}x$
(v) $y = 3.125$ **9.** (i) 40 km/h   (ii) 18 seconds
(iii) $x - y + 30 = 0$ (iv) 30   (v) 20 km/h
(vi) 55 km/h   **10.** (i) €50   (ii) €90   (iii) 1
(v) $x - y + 50 = 0$ (vi) €170   **11.** (i) 20 km
(ii) 30 mins   (iii) 6.5 km   (iv) 40 km/h
12. (ii) 231.2 min   (iii) 6.36 kg

Chapter 11

Exercise 11.1

1. (i) $x^2 + y^2 = 4$ (ii) $x^2 + y^2 = 625$ (iii) $x^2 + y^2 = 1$
(iv) $x^2 + y^2 = 144$ (v) $x^2 + y^2 = 25$
(vi) $x^2 + y^2 = 2$ (vii) $x^2 + y^2 = 5$ (viii) $x^2 + y^2 = \frac{9}{16}$
(ix) $x^2 + y^2 = \frac{1}{4}$ (x) $x^2 + y^2 = \frac{49}{9}$
2. $x^2 + y^2 = 625$ **3.** $x^2 + y^2 = 100$
4. $x^2 + y^2 = 25$ **5.** All centre points $(0,0)$;
Radii: (i) 5   (ii) 10   (iii) 8   (iv) 9   (v) 2   (vi) 7
(vii) $\sqrt{3}$ (viii) $\sqrt{5}$ (ix) $\frac{3}{2}$ (x) $\frac{10}{3}$ (xi) $\frac{7}{5}$
(xii) $\frac{11}{6}$ **7.** (i) $A(1,0)$, $B(0,1)$, $C(-1,0)$, $D(0,-1)$
(ii) $A(3,0)$, $B(0,3)$, $C(-3,0)$, $D(0,-3)$ (iii) $A(2,0)$, $B(0,2)$,
$C(-2,0)$, $D(0,-2)$ (iv) $A(6,0)$, $B(0,6)$, $(-6,0)$, $D(0,-6)$
8. $x^2 + y^2 = 25$ (ii) $x^2 + y^2 = 100$ (iii) $x^2 + y^2 = 144$
(iv) $x^2 + y^2 = 49$ **9.** (i) $(0,0)$ (ii) $r = 2$ (iv) 12.57
10. (i) $(0,0)$ (ii) $r = 6$ (iv) 37.70

(v) Yes, as length is 39.   **11.** (i) (0,0)   (iii) $r = 5$
(iv) $x^2 + y^2 = 25$ **12.** (i) (0,0)   (iii) $r = \sqrt{5}$
(iv) $x^2 + y^2 = 5$ (v) 15.71 units^2 **13.** (i) (0,0)
(ii) $r = \sqrt{26}$ (iii) $x^2 + y^2 = 26$ (iv) 81.68 units^2
(v) No, as area of square is 81 units^2.

Exercise 11.2

1. (i) (−4,3); (5,0)   (ii) (−6,−8); (6,8)
(iii) (−2,1); (1,2)   (iv) (−5,1); (5,1)   (v) (−2,4)
2. (i) $x = 2$; (2,4); (2,−4)   (ii) $y = 2$; (−4,2); (4,2)
(iii) $x = -2$; (−2,4); (−2,−4)   (iv) $y = -2$; (−4,−2);
(4,−2)   **3.** (i) $x=4$; (4,3); (4,−3)   (ii) $y = 4$; (−3,4); (3,4)
(iii) $x = -4$; (−4,3); (−4,−3)   (iv) $y = -4$; (−3,−4); (3,−4)
(v) $x = 3$; (3,4); (3,−4)   (vi) $y = 3$; (4,3); (−4,3)
(vii) $x = -3$; (−3,4); (−3,−4) (viii) $y = -3$; (4,−3); (−4,−3)
4. (i) $x = 4, y = 2$; $x = -2, y = 4$ (ii) $x = 5, y = 0$;
$x = -3, y = -4$ (iii) $x = 2, y = 4$; $x = -2, y = -4$
(iv) $x = 6, y = -2$; $x = -6, y = -2$ **5.** (2,2); (0,4)
6. (3,2); (−2,−3)   **7.** $\left(\frac{17}{5}, -\frac{19}{5}\right)$; (−1,5)   **8.** $\left(\frac{79}{25}, \frac{6}{50}\right)$; (−3,1)
9. (i) 4 units   (ii) $s = (x - 4)^2 + (y - 4)^2 = 16$
(iii) $m : y = x$; $n : x = 8$ (iv) (8,8)   (v) 64 units^2
11. (i) (0,0)   (ii) $\sqrt{10}$ (iii) $\sqrt{10}$ (iv) Yes
(vi) Points of intersection (1,3) and (−3,−1)

Exercise 11.3

1. (i) $(x - 1)^2 + (y - 4)^2 = 25$ (ii) $(x + 2)^2 + (y - 3)^2 = 9$
(iii) $(x - 6)^2 + (y + 5)^2 = 1$ (iv) $(x - 0)^2 + (y - 7)^2 = 16$
(v) $(x + 2)^2 + (y + 1)^2 = 4$ (vi) $x^2 + y^2 = 64$
(vii) $(x - 8)^2 + (y - 1)^2 = 36$ (viii) $\left(x - \frac{1}{2}\right)^2 + \left(y + \frac{1}{4}\right)^2 = 81$
(ix) $(x - 1)^2 + (y - 1.5)^2 = 49$ (x) $(x + 3)^2 + (y + 8)^2 = \frac{1}{4}$

2. (i) $\sqrt{41}$ (ii) $(x - 1)^2 + (y - 1)^2 = 41$ **3.** (i) $\sqrt{20}$
(ii) $(x + 2)^2 + (y + 1)^2 = 20$ **4.** (i) 4
(ii) $(x - 2)^2 + (y - 2)^2 = 16$ **5.** (i) 3
(ii) $(x - 3)^2 + (y + 1)^2 = 9$ **6.** (i) 2
(ii) $(x - 2)^2 + (y - 2)^2 = 4$ **7.** (i) (1,1)   (ii) $\sqrt{13}$
(iii) $(x - 1)^2 + (y - 1)^2 = 13$ **8.** (i) (1,2)   (ii) $\sqrt{34}$
(iii) $(x - 1)^2 + (y - 2)^2 = 34$ **9.** (ii) $r = \sqrt{10}$
(iii) $(x - 1)^2 + (y - 2)^2 = 10$ **10.** $(x - 2)^2 + (y - 3)^2 = 9$
11. (i) (2,3); $r = 5$ (ii) (−2,5); $r = 6$ (iii) (1,−3); $r = 7$
(iv) (−5,−8); $r = 1$ (v) (3,4); $r = 8$ **12.** (i) (0,0); $r = 10$
(ii) (0,8); $r = 7$ (iii) (2,0); $r = 9$ (iv) $\left(\frac{1}{2}, \frac{1}{3}\right)$; $r = \frac{1}{3}$
(v) (2,3); $r = \sqrt{5}$ **13.** (i) (3,0)   (ii) 1 unit   (iii) (1,0)
(iv) 4 units^2 (v) $(4 - \pi)$ units^2 **14.** (i) 9   (ii) 3π units^2
(iii) 9π units^2 (iv) 6π units^2

Exercise 11.4

1. (i) $a = -4, b = 4, c = 4, d = -4$ (ii) A(−4,0), B(4,0)
(iii) C(0,4), D(0,−4)   **2.** (i) $e = -7, f = 7, g = 7,$
$h = -7$ (ii) E(−7,0), F(7,0)   (iii) G(0,7), H(0,−7)
3. (i) x-intercepts (−3,0), (4,0); y-intercepts (0,−2), (0,6)
(ii) x-intercepts (−6,0), (8,0); y-intercepts (0,12), (0,−4)
4. (i) x-intercepts (−2,0), (2,0); y-intercepts (0,2), (0,−2)
(ii) x-intercepts (−3,0), (3,0); y-intercepts (0,−3), (0,3)

(iii) x-intercepts (−4,0), (4,0); y-intercepts (0,4), (0,−4)
(iv) x-intercepts (−6,0), (6,0); y-intercepts (0,6), (0,−6)
5. (i) (−3,0), (7,0)   (ii) (3,0), (−9,0)   (iii) (−15,0), (5,0)
(iv) (6,0), (−8,0)   (v) (−3,0), (11,0)   (vi) (12,0), (8,0)
6. (i) (0,−5), (0,13)   (ii) (0,−5), (0,15)   (iii) (0,−7), (0,5)
(iv) (0,2), (0,−4)   (v) (0,11), (0,−3)
7. (i) A(0,4), B(0,−2)   (ii) $x^2 + (y - 1)^2 = 9$
8. (i) A(−3,0), B(7,0)   (ii) $(x - 2)^2 + y^2 = 25$
9. D   **12.** V inside; W on; X outside; Y on; Z inside

Revision Exercises

1. (i) (−3,0)   (ii) 4   (iii) $(x + 3)^2 + (y - 0)^2 = 16$
(iv) $(0, \sqrt{7})$ $(0, -\sqrt{7})$ **2.** (i) (−1,1)   (ii) 5
(iv) ON circle   (v) B(−5,4)   **3.** (i) p centre = (0,0);
q centre = (2,0); s centre = (1,0)   (ii) Yes
(iii) $p: x^2 + y^2 = 1$; $q: (x - 2)^2 + y^2 = 1$;
$s: (x - 1)^2 + y^2 = 4$ **4.** (i) t centre = (0,3), $r = 2$;
s centre = (0,0), $r = 1$; u centre = (0,−3), $r = 2$
(ii) $t: x^2 + (y - 3)^2 = 4$; $s: x^2 + y^2 = 1$;
$u: x^2 + (y + 3)^2 = 4$ (iii) 2π (iv) 4π
(v) 2 : 1   (vi) Yes   **5.** (i) $r = 4$ (ii) (8,8)   (iii) 4
(iv) $(x - 8)^2 + (y - 8)^2 = 16$ (v) 64 units^2 (vi) Yes
6. (i) (−3,−1), (1,3)   (ii) $(x + 2)^2 + (y - 2)^2 = 2$

(iii) (−1,1)   **7.** (ii) $D(\frac{3}{2},1)$ (v) $\sqrt{\frac{65}{4}}$
(vi) $\left(x - \frac{3}{2}\right)^2 + (y - 1)^2 = \frac{65}{4}$ **8.** (i) A(3,4)   (ii) $(\frac{32}{17}, -\frac{8}{17})$
(iii) $17x + 21y = 0$ **9.** (i) $\sqrt{17}$ (iv) $x + 4y + 17 = 0$
10. (ii) $x^2 + y^2 = 50$ (iii) $p = +5$ or $p = -5$
(iv) $n = 6$ **11.** (i) 3   (ii) $(x - 7)^2 + (y - 3)^2 = 9$
(iv) (13,6)   **12.** (i) $\sqrt{5}$ (ii) 4, 6 units^2 (iii) 15.71 units^2
(iv) 38.19%

Chapter 12

Exercise 12.1

1. (i) 29   (ii) 85   (iii) 3   (iv) 24   (v) 24   (vi) 40
2. (i) $\sqrt{10}$ (ii) $\sqrt{2}$ (iii) $\sqrt{34}$ (iv) $\sqrt{24}$ **3.** 2.5 m
4. (i) $x = 5; y = 12$ (ii) $x = 85; y = 77$
(iii) $x = 96; y = 4$ (iv) $x = 10; y = 24$
5. (i) 60 cm   (ii) 100 cm   (iii) 4,800 cm^2 **7.** 205 cm
9. Yes   **10.** Yes   **11.** Yes

Exercise 12.2

1. (i) $\sin A = \frac{5}{13}$ $\cos A = \frac{12}{13}$ $\tan A = \frac{5}{12}$
(ii) $\sin A = \frac{21}{29}$ $\cos A = \frac{20}{29}$ $\tan A = \frac{21}{20}$
2. (i) $\sin A = \frac{40}{58}$ $\cos A = \frac{42}{58}$ $\tan A = \frac{40}{42}$
$\sin B = \frac{42}{58}$ $\cos B = \frac{40}{58}$ $\tan B = \frac{42}{40}$
(ii) $\sin A = \frac{3}{\sqrt{13}}$ $\cos A = \frac{2}{\sqrt{13}}$ $\tan A = \frac{3}{2}$
$\sin B = \frac{2}{\sqrt{13}}$ $\cos B = \frac{3}{\sqrt{13}}$ $\tan B = \frac{2}{3}$
(iii) $\sin A = \frac{2}{\sqrt{20}}$ $\cos A = \frac{4}{\sqrt{20}}$ $\tan A = \frac{2}{4}$
$\sin B = \frac{4}{\sqrt{20}}$ $\cos B = \frac{2}{\sqrt{20}}$ $\tan B = \frac{4}{2}$
3. (i) 0.2588   (ii) 0.8660   (iii) 3.7321

0.2419   (v) 0.9004   (vi) 0.0872
) 0.2126   (viii) 0.5   (ix) 5.6713   (x) 0.4791
(xi) 0.7218   (xii) 0.9823   (xiii) 0.5210
(xiv) 0.2830   (xv) 0.8581   (xvi) 0.5490
(xvii) 0.8934   (xviii) 7.4947   **4.** (i) 38.26
(ii) 29.61   (iii) 19.76   (iv) 25.94   (v) 20.62
(vi) 82.84   (vii) 58.54   (viii) 46.23   (ix) 64.93
(x) 63.11   **5.** (i) 2° 30′   (ii) 2° 15′   (iii) 2° 45′
(iv) 25° 24′   (v) 1° 12′   (vi) 0° 20′   **6.** (i) 2.52°
(ii) 10.67°   (iii) 25.83°   (iv) 70.37°   (v) 11.62°
(vi) 33.55°   **7.** (i) 75° 57′   (ii) 48° 14′   (iii) 43° 55′
(iv) 41° 34′   (v) 17° 42′   (vi) 26° 49′   (vii) 73° 54′
(viii) 13° 57′   (ix) 22° 12′   (x) 58° 01′   **8.** 13
9. 28° 04′

Exercise 12.3

1. (i) 8.66   (ii) 5   (iii) 10.32   (iv) 11.47   (v) 8
(vi) 28.28   **2.** (i) 4.37   (ii) 24.24   (iii) 14.74
(iv) 6.93   (v) 16.71   (vi) 5   **3.** $x = 64.28$; $y = 11.33$
4. $x = 3.6$; $y = 4.7$; $z = 12$ **5.** (i) 35°   (ii) 71°
(iii) 40°   (iv) 59°   (v) 61°   (vi) 45°

Exercise 12.4

1. (i) 42 km   (ii) 23 km/h   (iii) 21 km/h
2. 449.2 m   **3.** 346 m   **4.** (i) 16 m   (ii) 18 m
5. 527.3 m   **6.** 4.95 m   **7.** 471 m   **8.** (a) 45.8 m
(b) 74.36°   **9.** (a) 3 feet 14 inches   (b) 56°
(c) 21.03 feet   **10.** (a) $\tan 52° = \frac{h}{x}$; $\tan 40° = \frac{h}{x + 10}$
(b) $x \tan 52°$ (c) $(x + 10) \tan 40°$
(d) $x \tan 52° = (x + 10) \tan 40°$ (e) 19.03 m
(f) 24.36 m

Exercise 12.5

2. (i) 30°   (ii) $\sqrt{3}$ (iii) 2   **3.** (i) 45°   (ii) 7
4. (i) $x = 4$; $y = 4$ (ii) 90°   **5.** 1   **6.** 4   **7.** $\frac{4}{3}$

Exercise 12.6

1. 73.72 units²   **2.** 120 units²   **3.** 80.99 units²
4. 158.48 units²   **5.** 46.98 units²   **6.** 70.91 units²
7. 25.96 cm²   **8.** 82.8 cm²   **9.** (i) 30°   (ii) 60°
10. 7   **11.** (a) $|\angle ABD| = 41.65°$
(b) $|\angle DBC| = 52.89°$ **12.** (i) $\sin \angle XYZ = \frac{4}{5}$
(ii) 96 units²

Exercise 12.7

1. 0   **2.** −1   **3.** 0   **4.** 1   **5.** 0   **6.** −1   **7.** 0
8. 1   **9.** 0   **10.** 0   **11.** 1   **12.** 0   **13.** 0

Exercise 12.8

1. $-\frac{1}{\sqrt{2}}$ **2.** $\frac{1}{2}$ **3.** $-\frac{1}{2}$ **4.** $-\frac{1}{2}$ **5.** $\frac{1}{\sqrt{3}}$ **6.** $\frac{1}{\sqrt{2}}$
7. $\frac{\sqrt{3}}{2}$ **8.** $-\frac{\sqrt{3}}{2}$ **9.** $-\sqrt{3}$ **10.** $\sqrt{3}$ **11.** −0.82
12. 0.34   **13.** −0.64   **14.** −0.09   **15.** 0.84
16. 0.82   **17.** 0.64   **18.** −0.64   **19.** −0.18
20. −0.36   **21.** 30° or 150°   **22.** 45° or 315°
23. 60° or 240°   **24.** 225° or 315°   **25.** 15° or 315°
26. 240° or 300°

Exercise 12.9

1. 12.92   **2.** 15.56   **3.** 19.38   **4.** 10.15
5. 10.85   **6.** (i) 27.36°   (ii) 102.64°
(iii) 180.0 units²   **7.** 18°   **8.** (i) 68° 26′
(ii) 164.69°   (iii) 9.65 units²   (iv) 2.59 units
9. 53°   **10.** (i) 24°   (ii) 39.21 units²   (iii) 16.07 units
11. 74 m; 65 m   **12.** 4,350.28 m²   **13.** (a) 42.26 cm
(b) 0.18816 m³   (c) 109.12 cm   (d) 116.22 cm

Exercise 12.10

1. 4.58   **2.** 9.53   **3.** 13.69   **4.** 3.87
5. 18.37   **6.** 60°   **7.** 120°   **8.** 41°
9. 17°   **10.** 90°   **11.** (i) 5.29   (ii) 3.31
(iii) 19.0845 cm²   **12.** (i) 12 cm   (ii) 117°
(iii) 63.2819 cm²   **13.** (iii) 96°   (iv) 17.4041 cm²
14. (iii) 22°   (iv) 6.5556 cm²   **15.** (i) 15 km
(ii) 12.5 km   (iii) 150°   (iv) 26.57 km   **16.** (i) 110 km
(ii) 4.5 hours   (iii) 1 hour 29 min   **17.** (i) 64.76°
(ii) 494.61 m²   (iii) 1,978.44 m²   (iv) 1,254.5764 m²
18. (i) 65 m   (ii) 140 m   (iii) 34.64 m

Exercise 12.11

1. (i) 13.89π   (ii) 60π   (iii) 189π   **2.** (i) 4.44π
(ii) 13.89π   (iii) 28.33π   **3.** (i) 60°   (ii) 135°
(iii) 200°   **4.** (i) 70°   (ii) 120°   (iii) 300°   **5.** (i) 23.02 cm²
(ii) 29.93 cm²   (iii) 6.91 cm²   **6.** 36.8 m²

Revision Exercises

1. (b) (i) 27°   (ii) 12.16 cm   (iii) 28.13 cm
2. (b) (i) 3.52   (ii) 3.64   **3.** (b) (i) 6.22 cm
(ii) 24 cm²   **4.** (a) (i) 30°   (ii) 45°   (iii) 45°
(iv) 60°   (b) (i) $\frac{5}{12}$ (ii) $\frac{12}{13}$ (iii) $\frac{5}{13}$ (iv) $\frac{120}{169}$
5. 40 km   **6.** (a) 24, 25   (b) 111 cm²   **7.** (i) 2 cm
(ii) 2.09 cm²   (iii) 43.30 cm²   (iv) 39.12 cm²
8. (ii) $a = 300$ cm, $h = 200$ cm   (iii) 38 cm
9. (i) 7.36 m   (ii) 2.42 m   (iii) 14°   **10.** (ii) 12.53 m
11. (ii) 79.8°   (iii) 40.2°   (iv) 13.4 cm